RIVERS of IRELAND

A Flyfisher's Guide

7TH EDITION

Peter O'Reilly

MERLIN UNWIN BOOKS

First published in Great Britain by Merlin Unwin Books in 1991
Reprinted 1991
Second edition 1993
Third edition 1995
Fourth edition 1998, reprinted 2000, 2001
Fifth edition 2002
Sixth edition 2004
Seventh edition 2009

Merlin Unwin Books Ltd
Palmers House
7 Corve Street
Ludlow, Shropshire SY8 1DB
U.K.

www.merlinunwin.co.uk
email: books@merlinunwin.co.uk

The author asserts his moral right to be identified as the author of this work.
A CIP catalogue record for this book is available from the British Library.

ISBN 978-1-906122-10-2 (7th edition)

Designed by Merlin Unwin Books
Printed and bound in the UK by Cromwell Press Group

To Niall Greene
and the
STOP SALMON DRIFT NETS NOW
campaign

Contents

List of Maps

Introduction

It is nearly 20 years since I researched the first edition of *Rivers of Ireland*. This is the seventh edition and there have been a number of reprints in-between. I have fished for nearly 60 years and was privileged to work in the fishery service for 27 years. This is an experience-based guide.

The previous edition of *Rivers of Ireland* was published five years ago. How things change! My aim was always to be objective and to provide my fellow anglers with hard, factual information. Now that the research has been completed, the last statistic checked, and the last chapter proof read, I can honestly say that there are literally thousands of changes and a great deal of updated information in this new edition. It has been a labour of love – love of the fish, love of the natural environment and a deep sense of gratitude for all the lovely, gentle, helpful people I met along the way.

We have seen more changes happen to the natural environment in the last sixty years than in the thousand years that preceded them. Even the 20-year span of this book has witnessed enormous changes for our game fisheries. It is easy, even understandable, to be negative and see only the dark side. When I began this latest edition in 2008, I feared that I would have little, if anything, positive to say about our rivers. Now that the project is completed, I am glad to report that the picture is much brighter than I imagined. I have discovered that there are still a lot of good things to report and a lot of good fishing to be enjoyed. Water quality has improved in many of our rivers according to the reports of the Environmental Agency and I have been reminded of dozens of little trout streams that I would love to fish. Drift netting for salmon off the coast has been banned (2007) and already an improvement can be noticed in the rod catch statistics for many of the fisheries.

But there have been disasters too. These losses are not just in monetary terms – although I regard the natural environment as part of the nation's wealth and rivers and the fish that swim in them are part of that environment – I refer rather to things that, once destroyed, cannot be replicated. Not in our lifetime anyway. Top of that sad list is arterial drainage and the 'maintenance' work that follows it; fish farming and the sea lice they generate; and the annihilation of salmon runs by hydro dams on some of our finest rivers. When I was a child, hundreds of salmon spawned in the rivers and streams close by our farm. One of my earliest memories is of watching their grey shadows in the river by my father's corn mill. Today there is not one pair of salmon left. Even the eels are disappearing!

Our life span is short and we pass on. But it is not natural for a fishery or a river to die. We should not have to write an obituary for any fishery. Sad to relate, where trout and salmon are concerned, man is their greatest enemy. The fragile balance of plants, animals and fish that share the Earth took millions of years to develop. Some life forms have survived episodes of mass destruction. Others like ourselves, the salmon, and the trout, are relative newcomers. Those that have perished will not return. Much of the habitat destruction has been caused by human influence. The web of life connects the smallest insect to the salmon and the trout, the whale and even the giant redwood. If we continue reducing the earth's biodiversity at the present rate, the consequences for the fish, and ultimately man, will be profound. For the angler it is the diversity of a natural river, with its insects and wildlife, its riffles, streams and pools, that holds the greatest attraction. Uniformity is becoming all too common.

The central and most urgent question we, as anglers, must ask ourselves is: how do we give the lead and get through the next fifty years without losing forever the genetic wealth of biodiversity?

Man has an insatiable appetite and, nowadays, he has the technology to satisfy it. But we must remember that when the last tree is cut down and the last river is poisoned and the last river is dead, we cannot eat money.

The ethical behaviour of anglers is a key component of the angling experience. Consideration for the wellbeing of the fish and of fellow anglers is important, as is the need to respect private property. Always ask permission and observe the laws, regulations, local customs and practices associated with a fishery. There is no public right of fishing on fresh water in Ireland.

Anglers should endeavour to conserve stocks by understanding the importance of limiting their catch. Catch-and-release is an important aspect of conserving fisheries that are heavily fished.

We are now in the twenty-first season since seatrout and wild salmon numbers began to decline in some of the north, west and south-west fisheries due to salmon fish farming in the estuaries. The situation continues to fluctuate as fish farms close and reopen again. The Government cannot be allowed to sit back and preside over such environmental disasters. The value of a wild salmon and seatrout fishery in terms of related tourism income and recreational angling far outweighs the unviable, fundamentally flawed industry that is salmon farming.

Licences and Permits

For rod licences in the Loughs Agency Area and the DCAL Area of Northern Ireland, please see the introduction to the respective chapters on those areas (Chapters 1 and 2).

In the rest of the country (under the regulations of the seven Regional Fisheries Boards) a state licence is required for salmon and seatrout fishing only. For the purpose of a licence, the country is divided into fishery districts and a range of licences are available depending on the areas an angler wants to fish, the duration of the visit and the age of the angler.

Seasons

Salmon, seatrout and brown trout fisheries open and close at various dates throughout the country, the earliest being January 1 and the latest date for closing is October 31. The exact dates are listed for the rivers throughout this guide.

Regulations

With the banning of drift net fishing off the coast controlled by the Regional Fisheries Boards in 2007, new controls came into effect following the enactment of various regulations and bye-laws. Some salmon fisheries are closed completely because stocks do not reach the conservation limit, others are open on a catch-and-release basis only using barbless hooks, and still others are subject to regulations restricting the fishing season and angling methods.

Because of the temporary nature of some regulations and the enactment of new bye-laws, anglers are advised to check the up-to-date situation on the various websites listed in this guide, e.g., Central Fisheries Board, www.cfb.ie

Guides and Instructors

A list of qualified guides and instructors can be accessed at: www.apgai-ireland.ie and www.pagin.net or by contacting the local tackle shop or licence distributor.

Acknowledgements

I received help from a lot of people in the course of compiling the information in this book. I would very much like to acknowledge their assistance and I can never adequately repay the kindness, courtesy and advice I received from so many of them. Without that kind of wholehearted co-operation this work could never have been completed. I acknowledge their huge contribution and thank them all from the bottom of my heart. I have listed some of these people on the following two pages.

I would like to express my sincere thanks to Mr. Ciaran Byrne, CEO, Central Fisheries Board for his advice and encouragement.

The staffs at the Loughs Agency, DCAL and the various Regional Fisheries Boards could not have been more helpful.

The Secretaries of the Trout Anglers Federation of Ireland (TAFI), the National Anglers Representative Association (NARA) and the Irish Trout Fly Fishers Association (ITFFA) gave me access to their lists of club secretaries and to them I am deeply indebted, as I am to all the fishery owners and fishery managers who completed and returned questionnaires.

A number of people have kindly supplied photographs and for these I thank them and especially James Carney, Navan, for the cover picture.

Bridie Fleming and Sandra Doyle typed their way diligently and efficiently through some 150,000 words of mostly hand-written manuscript and I especially thank them for their hard work and unfailing courtesy.

Thanks to Merlin Unwin of Merlin Unwin Books for asking me to undertake this Seventh Edition of *Rivers of Ireland* and to Karen, Joanne and Gillian at the office in Ludlow.

I am especially grateful to my wife, Rose, for her support and all the help with the proof reading.

To anyone else, inadvertently omitted, I say a big THANK YOU!

Peter O'Reilly, Ballybatter House
Boyne Hill, Navan, Co. Meath, Ireland

27 March, 2009

ACKNOWLEDGEMENTS

Dr. Milton Matthews, Northern Regional Board, Ballyshannon, Co. Donegal.
Lindsey Clarke, Northern Regional Fisheries Board, Ballyshannon, Co. Donegal.
Peter Kelly, Northern Regional Fisheries Board, Ballyshannon, Co. Donegal.
Michael Fitzpatrick, Sheegora, Boyle, Co. Roscommon.
Declan Ryan, Secretary, Buncrana AA, Buncrana, Co. Donegal.
Brendan McLoughlin, 27 Lr. Main Street, Buncrana, Co. Donegal.
Frank O'Donnell, Carrick Upper, Carrick, Co. Donegal.
Noel Carr, Teelin Road, Carrick, Co. Donegal.
Seamus Hartigan, Manager, Galway Fishery, Nun's Island, Galway.
Leslie Lyons, Tullaboy, Maam Cross, Co. Galway.
Frank Costello, Ashford, Cong, Co. Mayo.
Kathleen Dolly, Waterfall Lodge, Oughterard, Co. Galway.
Brian Curran, Aille, Inverin, Co. Galway.
Terry Gallagher, Bridge Cottage, Costello, Co. Galway.
Simon Ashe, Ballynahinch Castle, Co. Galway.
Nigel Rush, Moyard, Connemara, Co. Galway.
James Stafford, Aasleagh Lodge, Leenane, Co. Galway.
Peter Mantle, Delphi Lodge, Leenane, Co. Galway.
Lal Faherty, Lakeland, Portacarron, Oughterard, Co. Galway.
Gramville Nesbitt, Fortland, Easkey, Co. Sligo.
Declan Cooke, Moy River Manager, Ardnaree House, Ballina, Co. Mayo.
Markus Müller, Ardnaree House, Ballina, Co. Mayo.
Mrs. Mary Carlisle, Belgarriff, Foxford, Co. Mayo.
George Armstrong, Ballina Road, Foxford, Co. Mayo.
Jim Wilson, Mount Falcon Castle, Ballina, Co. Mayo.
Seamus Hughes, Ardglashin, Lisboduff, P.O., Co. Cavan.
Michael Callaghan, Virginia Road, Ballyjamesduff, Co. Cavan.
Lionel Knobbs, Loughs Agency, 22 Victoria Road, Derry.
Andrew Sides, Loughs Agency, 22 Victoria Road, Derry.
Marcus Carey, Screebe House, Rosmill, Co. Galway.
Mrs. Maire O'Connor, Lough Inagh Lodge Hotel, Recess, Co. Galway.
Tom Woods, 190 Aghafad Road, Clogher, Co. Tyrone.
Eamon Ross, Ardlougher, Ballyconnell, Co. Cavan.
Ms. Josie Mahon, Eastern Regional Board, 15a Main Street, Blackrock, Co. Dublin.
Michael Hennessy, Killaha East, Kenmare, Co. Kerry.
Ronnie Miley, 4 Dodder Park Road, Dublin 14.
John Higgins, Newbridge, Co. Kildare.
Thomas Deegan, River Grove, Broadleas, Ballymore Eustace, Co. Kildare.
David Lamb, Kilcoleman Park, Enniskeane, Co. Cork.
Michael J. O'Regan, Oliver Plunkett Street, Bandon, Co. Cork.
Tim Moore, Manager, Kerry Blackwater, Kenmare, Co. Kerry.
Michael J. Gass, Kylemore Lodge, Waterville, Co. Kerry.
Paddy Greene, Nobber, Co. Meath.

Mark Corps, 22 Hallcraig Road, Springfield, Co. Fermanagh.

Simon Hirsch, Ballyhooley Castle, Ballyhooley, Co. Cork.

Peter Lynch, DCAL, Forest Park, Castlewellan, Co. Down BT31 9BU.

David Wright, DCAL, Causeway Exchange, 1-7 Bedford Street, Belfast BT1 TFB.

Fiona Lowry, 1 Mahon Road, Portadown, Co. Armagh BT62 3EE.

Alan Keys, Cookstown, Co. Tyrone.

Mark Horton, Ballinderry Fish Hatchery, Cookstown, Co. Tyrone.

Gabriel Davey, 34 Boon Road, Belfast.

Brian Busby, Doagh, Ballyclare, Co. Antrim.

Dr. Paddy Sleeman, Department of Zoology, University College, Cork.

Ms. Mary O'Meara, ESB Fisheries Admin., Ardnacrusha, Co. Clare.

Dermot Broughan, Tudenham Lodge, Mullingar, Co. Westmeath.

Matthew Nolan, Tudenham Lodge, Mullingar, Co. Westmeath.

Fergus Lynch, Drumsna, Carrick-on-Shannon, Co. Leitrim.

Michael Cleary, Corofin, Co. Clare.

Sean Gurhy, Kinnypottle, Cavan.

John Devaney, Cloonmore, Ballymurray, Co. Roscommon.

John Ryan, Coolnafarna, Ballinlough, Co. Roscommon.

Richard Keays, Millbank House, Kenmare, Co. Limerick.

Shane O'Neill, Shane's Castle, Antrim, Co. Antrim.

Brian Finn, F.C.B., 1 Mahon Road, Portadown, Co. Armagh.

Andrew Ryan, Clonanav, Ballynacarbry, Co. Waterford.

Ms. Esta McCarthy, Elgin Cottage, Ballyduff Upr., Co. Waterford.

Justine Green, Ballyvolane House, Castlelyons, Fermoy, Co. Cork.

William O'Callaghan, Longueville House, Mallow, Co. Cork.

Eamon Holohan, Mount Juliet, Thomastown, Co. Kilkenny.

Stephen Glaves, Ballymaquirk Lodge, Banteer, Co. Cork.

Peter Bielski, Careysville, Fermoy, Co. Cork.

Dan O'Donovan, Craigside, Blackrock, Co. Cork.

John Murphy, Glenbeg, Caherdaniel, Co. Kerry.

Fergus Moore, Sheen Fall Lodge, Kenmare, Co. Kerry.

Mike O'Shea, Lynanes Lower, Glencar, Co. Kerry.

Dr. Martin O'Farrell, 4 The Nurseries, Killiney, Co. Dublin.

Barry McCarthy, Hon. Sec., TAFI, Lismore, Co. Waterford.

Aidan Barry, CEO, South Western Regional Fisheries Board, Macroom, Co. Cork.

Dr. Patrick Buck, Asst. CEO, South Western Regional Fisheries Board, Macroom, Co. Cork.

David Byrne, Central Fisheries Board, Swords Business Campus, Dublin

Myles Kelly, Central Fisheries Board, Swords Business Campus, Dublin

TOURIST INFORMATION DETAILS:

REPUBLIC OF IRELAND

Dublin Tourism
Suffolk Street, Dublin 2. Tel: 01 605 7700
www.discoverireland.ie/dublin

East & Midlands (Kildare, Laois, Longford, Louth, Meath, North Offaly, Westmeath, Wicklow)
Fáilte Ireland East & Midlands, Dublin Road, Mullingar, Co. Westmeath Tel: 044 9348761
www.discoverireland.ie/eastcoast

South East (Carlow, Kilkenny, South Tipperary, Waterford, Wexford)
Fáilte Ireland South East, 41 The Quay, Waterford. Tel: 051 875823
www.discoverireland.ie/southwest

South West (Cork, Kerry)
Fáilte Ireland South West, Áras Fáilte, Grand Parade, Cork. Tel: 021 4255100
www.discoverireland.ie/southwest

Shannon Development (Clare, Limerick, South Offaly, North Tipperary)
Shannon Development-Heritage & Tourism, Shannon Town Centre, Co. Clare. Tel: 061 361555
www.discoverireland.ie/shannon

Ireland West (Galway, Mayo, Roscommon)
Fáilte Ireland Western, Forster Street, Galway. Tel: 091 537700
www.discoverireland.ie/west

North West (Cavan, Donegal, Leitrim, Monaghan, Sligo)
Fáilte Ireland, North West, Temple Street, Sligo. Tel: 071 9160360
www.discoverireland.ie/northwest

NORTHERN IRELAND

Causeway Coast and Glens
11 Lodge Road, Coleraine, Co. Londonderry BT52 1LU. Tel: 02870 327720
www.causewaycoastandglens.com

Belfast Visitor and Conventions Bureau
47 Donegal Place, Belfast, BT1 5AD. Tel: 02890 246609
www.gotobelfast.com

Derry Visitor and Convention Bureau
44 Foyle Street, Londonderry, BT48 6AT. Tel: 02871 267284
www.derryvisitor.com

Armagh Down Tourism Partnership
40 West Street, Newtownards, Co. Down, BT23 4EN. Tel: 02891 822881
www.armaghanddown.com

Fermanagh Lakeland Tourism
Wellington Road, Enniskillen, Co. Fermanagh, BT74 7EF. Tel: 02866 323110
www.fermanaghlakelands.com

IMPORTANT NOTE

While every care has been taken to ensure the accuracy of the contents of this guide book, responsibility for errors or omissions cannot be accepted by the Publisher, the author or any of their agents. This book is a guide only and readers should contact the individuals or companies concerned for further information. Fishing, like many outdoor activities, can be hazardous and it is recommended that anyone fishing in Ireland should take our third party insurance and personal accident insurance.

The fishery regions of Ireland and the principal airports and ferry ports

1. The Loughs Agency

The Loughs Agency is one of the cross-border bodies set up under the British-Irish Agreement in 1999 with offices in Derry, Omagh and Carlingford. It operates across both jurisdictions (Northern Ireland and the Republic of Ireland) and is a key body in the management and conservation of inland fisheries in the Foyle and Carlingford catchments. It took over the functions of the Foyle Fisheries Commission (a cross-border body established in 1952 to conserve, manage and protect the fisheries of the Foyle area) and was given both an additional cross-border operational area in Carlingford and the additional functions of developing aquaculture and marine tourism. The Loughs Agency headquarters is at:

The Loughs Agency, 22 Victoria Road, Londonderry/Derry BT47 2AB
Tel: 02871 342100 (from ROI 04871 342100), fax: 02871 342720
Email: general@loughs-agency.org, web: www.loughs-agency.org

The Foyle area includes the Foyle catchment, Lough Foyle itself and the area seaward of Lough Foyle. The Foyle catchment covers over 3,600 sq. km (1,400 sq. miles) straddling the border in the counties of Donegal, Tyrone and Londonderry/Derry. It includes the River Foyle itself, and its tributaries, primarily the Rivers Deele and Finn in Donegal and the Rivers Faughan and Burn Dennet, plus the River Mourne and its tributaries.

The Foyle System is one of the most productive and stable fisheries in the whole of Ireland. It is also one of the healthiest seatrout systems and a number of rivers provide excellent angling. The brown trout of the Foyle System are small where seatrout dominate but of a good size in other areas.

The Carlingford area includes Carlingford Lough and the rivers flowing into it from counties Louth, Down and Armagh, primarily the Whitewater and Clanrye.

The principal game angling resource of the Carlingford area is its seatrout both in the rivers and along the coast.

Licences

A rod licence is required to fish on rivers and canals in the Loughs Agency area. These are available as a season licence £16, 14-day licence £8, 3-day licence £3.50 and juvenile licence £2 (prices correct at 2009).

Holders of fishing licences issued in other parts of Ireland (north and south) can obtain an endorsement from the Loughs Agency that authorises them to fish in Agency waters (£1 in 2009).

In addition to a rod licence, it is a requirement to hold a permit to fish on many stretches of river in the Foyle and Carlingford systems. Guidance is provided for each river described in this guide.

The Loughs Agency encourages anglers to release their quarry! Certainly, fish that are less than the permitted size must be returned and no more fish should be retained than the bag limit in force – annual limit, other limits generally or limits particular to a stretch of water.

The following *Game Angling Licences* are currently available from the Loughs Agency:
Season game fishing rod licence
14-day game fishing rod licence
Three-day game fishing rod licence
Juvenile (under 16 years) game fishing rod licence
Endorsement to FCB and Regional Board season game fishing rod licence

Permits
There are a number of private owners, angling clubs and organisations (including the Loughs Agency) that issue permits for their stretches of water.

Regulations
Prohibited Methods
- No use of a float with bait is permitted for game fishing on any waters in the Foyle area – other than in conjunction with a single artificial fly.
- Use of shrimp or prawn is strictly prohibited.
- No angling is permitted within 5 meters upstream and downstream of any weir – in certain cases the prohibited area is extended (check locally).

Angling information
The Loughs Agency, 22 Victoria Road, Londonderry/Derry BT47 2AB
Tel: 02871 342100 (from ROI 04871 342100), fax: 02871 342720 (from ROI 04871 342720), email: general@loughs-agency.org, web: www.loughs-agency.org

Angling guides
A guide can be arranged for almost all of the rivers by enquiring from the local licence/permit distributors or the Professional Angling Guides and Instructors Network (web: www.pagin.net) or the Association of Professional Game Angling Instructors (web: www.apgai-ireland.ie).

Accommodation
There are many hotels, bed and breakfast establishments, self-catering accommodation, camp sites and caravan parks in the area. These can be contacted through the local Tourist Information Centre or Tourist Information Office.

The Lough Agency website provides links to these offices and there is a handy map there which may help in planning where the best base will be for a visit.

Weblink to accommodation:
www.loughs-agency.org/tourism/content.asp?catid=161

Londonderry or Derry (the city and surrounding countryside)
Tourist Information Centre, 44 Foyle Street, Derry, Co. Londonderry/Derry
BT48 6AT. Tel: 02871 267284, fax: 02871 377992, email: info@derryvisitor.com
web: www.derryvisitor.com

Strabane area (north-west of Co. Tyrone)
Tourist Information Centre, The Alley Arts & Conference Centre, 1A Railway Street,
Strabane, Co. Tyrone BT82 8EF. Tel: 02871 381335, Alt: 02871 381335 (Text phone)
Email: tic@strabanedc.com, web: www.strabanedc.com

Omagh area (south west of Co. Tyrone)
Tourist Information Centre, Strule Arts Centre, Townhall Square, Omagh, Co. Tyrone
BT78 1BL. Tel: 02882 247831, email: info@omagh.gov.uk, web: www.omagh.gov.uk

Limavady area (north and west of Co. Londonderry or Derry)
Tourist Information Centre, Limavady Borough Council, 7 Connell Street, Limavady,
Co. Londonderry/Derry BT49 0HA. Tel: 02877 760307
Email: tourism@limavady.gov.uk, web: www.limavady.gov.uk

Donegal county (including the western shore of the Foyle)
Letterkenny Tourist Office, Letterkenny, Co. Donegal. Tel: 074 9121160
Email: info@donegaldirect.ie, web: www.donegaldirect.com

CULDAFF, RIVER   C 51 48

The Culdaff River is 10½ miles long and drains a catchment of 25 sq. miles of north-east Inishowen, in Co. Donegal, into Culdaff Bay near Malin Head, Ireland's most northerly point. It is a deep, sluggish river and flows partly through bogland which gives the water a dark brown stain. It is overgrown in places and access can be difficult. Local knowledge is essential.

It can hold a very good stock of seatrout in July and especially in August. The salmon come with the first flood in August, but numbers are small. The river holds fair numbers of brown trout to a pound. The seatrout draft net fishery at the mouth has been extinguished.

The best seatrout fishing is in the tidal water at Culdaff and – later in the season – up at Gleneely.

Permission
The fishing is with the landowners' permission. For information on the local angling club permits, contact:
The Post Office, Culdaff, Co. Donegal
Inishowen Tourism, The Diamond, Carndonagh, Co. Donegal. Tel: 074 9374933

THE RIVER FOYLE & TRIBUTARIES   H 34 99

The Foyle, with its extensive system of tributaries, drains a scenic mountainous catchment of some 1,130 sq. miles (3,670 sq. km) in the counties of Derry, Donegal and Tyrone, into Lough Foyle. It is primarily regarded as a salmon and seatrout system. In fact, it is probably one of salmon fishing's best-kept secrets and wild brown trout and seatrout are also abundant. The system has an exceptionally long season, stretching from March to October, due to the number and variety of rivers that go to make it up. The vast variety of waters available to the angler means that there is nearly always an opportunity to fish, whether the water is low or high. This is one of the most prolific Atlantic salmon-producing river systems in the country and of world significance for the species.

Season
Rivers Foyle and Finn: 1 March–15 September

The Foyle itself is tidal along its entire length, from the confluence of the Finn and Mourne to Culmore Point where it spills into the vast sea lough of the same name. It is joined by the Dennet and the Deele along its length and it is upstream of the Dennet that the best angling can be had. This stretch is known as The Islands. Below Lifford the river splits to flow either side of a 500 hectare island, forming a pool and riffle sequence along both channels. It is a very wide river (30-500m) with some remarkably shallow stretches at various points – be careful if using a boat! With a tide of 4-5 knots, angling tends to be restricted to periods of low flow between tides. There is access to the west bank south of Porthall and on the east bank at Cloghcor and opposite the Donemana-Artigarvan road junction on the A5. Thousands of salmon move along the Foyle, a conduit for the Finn, Mourne, Derg and other famous salmon rivers.

Salmon flies
Shrimp flies with red/orange/gold colouring, eg. Cascade or Curry's Gold

Rod licence
The Loughs Agency, 22 Victoria Road, Londonderry/Derry BT47 2AB
Tel: 02871 342100 (from ROI 04871 342100). Or from local licence/permit distributors.

Permit required
A Foyle permit is required and it is available from:
The Loughs Agency, 22 Victoria Road, Londonderry/Derry BT47 2AB.
Tel: 02871 342100 (from ROI 04871 342100), email: general@loughs-agency.org
David Campbell, Angler's Rest, 12 Killymore Road, Newtownstewart, Co. Tyrone BT78 4DT. Tel: 02881 661543
Rod & Line, 1 Clarendon Street, Londonderry/Derry BT48 7EP
Various tackle shops

Local tackle shops
Rod & Line, 1 Clarendon Street, Londonderry/Derry BT48 7EP. Tel: 02871 262877
North West Country Sports, 19 Butcher Street, Strabane, Co. Tyrone BT82 8BJ
Tel: 02871 883021

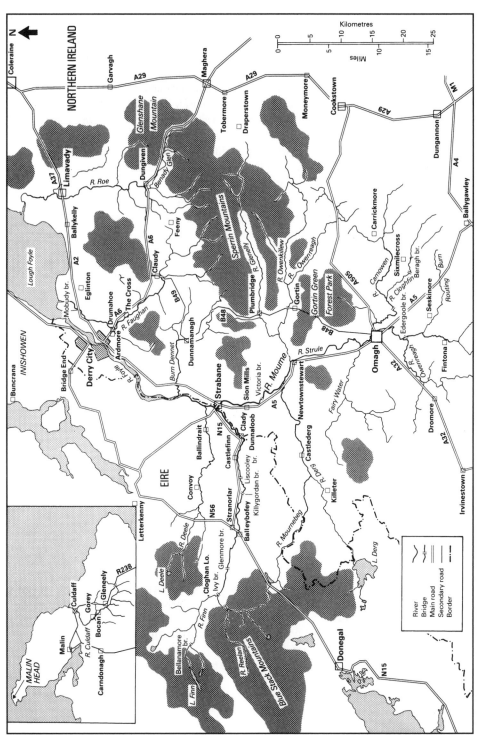

The rivers of the Foyle area and the river Culdaff (inset)

MOURNE, RIVER   H 35 96

The River Mourne extends from Strabane to its confluence with the River Derg. It is a big, wide, fast-flowing river. The salmon fishing can be very good from the end of May onwards and it gets an average run of seatrout from the end of June.

The Mourne is part of the Foyle System and, while it fishes best after a good spate, it is not a spate river in the sense that it only fishes for a short time as the water fines down. If there is a good two-foot flood, the river should fish well for the next week or so. Grilse, in particular, will sneak up-river even in very low water. The main tributaries of the Mourne are the Strule and Derg, both of which have substantial runs of fish. The Derg can rise very quickly and is less likely to colour up. The Strule holds its water better, but is inclined to be more coloured in high water.

Strabane and Lifford Angling Association has extensive double bank fishing on the River Mourne. This is a well developed fishery, with some excellent fly water. It holds spring salmon from the start of the season and grilse from late May. It will get fresh fish right up to the closing day on 20 October. The bottom of the Mourne is tidal and the river fishes best in low water. Access is good and so is the wading.

Season
Mourne: 1 April –20 October

Permit required
There are several private stretches, club waters and syndicates on this river. Day permits are available. For more information contact:

N & M Tackle, 131 Melmount Road, Sion Mills, Co. Tyrone BT82 9PY.
Tel: 02881 659501
North West Country Sports, 19 Butcher Street, Strabane, Co. Tyrone BT82 8BJ.
Tel: 02871 883021
Sion Mills Angling Club, 151 Melmount Road, Sion Mills, Co. Tyrone BT82 9PY.
Tel: 02881 658027

Local tackle shops
N & M Tackle (see above)
North West Country Sports (see above)

Local flytyer
John Murray, Birdstown, Lifford, Co. Donegal. Tel: 074 9142958

Fishing accommodation
There are many hotels, bed and breakfast establishments, self-catering accommodation, camp sites and caravan parks in the area. These can be contacted through the local Tourist Information Centre in Strabane (see page x for full details).

Abercorn Estates Fishery

This is classic fly water – both single and double bank – which provides excellent fishing for salmon and seatrout. It is also fly fishing only. This beat is at its best from mid-June. The wading can be tricky and visiting anglers are advised to take a gillie/guide. It is usually let by the week and is in four beats which are rotated daily and are not crowded.

Season

1 April–20 October

Permits

Abercorn Estates, Baronscourt, Newtownstewart, Co. Tyrone.
Tel: 02881 661683, (Monday to Friday: 09.00–17.00), email: info@barons-court.com

Accommodation

Four star self-catering accommodation in the Governors Lodge and the Clock Tower on the estate.

Brookeborough Fishery

The Brookeborough Fishery consists of approximately 1¾ miles of the River Mourne just above Victoria Bridge near Sion Mills in Co. Tyrone. The fishing is all from the left bank as you look downstream and is fly-only. This is fast flowing classic fly fishing water and requires some wading to get the best out of it, especially at the upper end of the beat. Chest waders and a wading stick are recommended. Generally, a 14 or 15 foot rod is best, but in low water conditions, a 10 foot single-handed rod will prove adequate for much of the water. The river flows through a scenic wooded valley over rock and shingle and has salmon, grilse and seatrout as well as small brown trout.

The fishing is let to a small number of syndicate rods and to two-day permit rods. The cost may be reduced if a whole week is taken. The management insists on visitors taking a gillie on their first day. This is to ensure that the visitor knows where and where not to wade, as well as being shown some of the best lies for fish.

The season opens on 1 April and although there is the occasional spring fish around, numbers increase in late April and May and it is really June before the fishing is at its best. Mid-June to late July and then again in September and October are often the best times, although a cool wet August can also be good. The bulk of the salmon are grilse and they start showing in the last week of May. They are in the 3–7lb bracket (the size goes up as the season progresses), with some summer salmon proper in the 13–18lb class. Seatrout fishing is best through June and July, with most of the fish being around the pound but with a fair number up to 3lb. Shrimp flies (sizes 6–12) are popular hereabouts and are available in the local tackle shops.

Permits

Viscount Brookeborough, Colebrooke Park, Brookeborough, Enniskillen
Co. Fermanagh BT94 4DW. Tel: 02889 531402, email: ahb@colebrooke.info
Web: www.colebrooke.info

Sion Mills Angling Club

Sion Mills Angling Club manages the fishing rights for the Department of Culture, Arts and Leisure (DCAL) on an eight-mile stretch of the Mourne, from Strabane to a point upstream of Victoria Bridge.

There is great fly water on this stretch, but spinning and worming are also popular. This part of the river does not necessarily require a spate and will, in fact, generally fish better in low water conditions. A gillie service is available with prior notice.

Day permits

There are 20 day permits available. Full DCAL permit holders pay less than others.

Day permits can be pre-booked.

Permits

Sion Mills Angling Club, 51 Melmount Road, Sion Mills, Co. Tyrone BT82 9PY
Tel: 02881 658027
N & M Tackle, 131 Melmount Road, Sion Mills, Co. Tyrone BT82 9PY
Tel: 02881 659501

GLENELLY RIVER   H 48 91

The Glenelly River is a tributary of the Owenkillew that rises in The Sperrins and flows past Plumbridge It is a spate river noted for late-running seatrout and occasional salmon.

Season

1 April–20 October

Permission

For the Gaff Angling Club water, or a number of private stretches from:

David Campbell, Angler's Rest, 12 Killymore Road, Newtownstewart
Co. Tyrone BT78 4DT. Tel: 02881 661543
Gabriel Treanor, 56 Main Street, Gortin, Co. Tyrone. Tel: 02881 648543

FAIRY WATER   H 40 75

The Fairy Water is a medium sized (5–20m width) river that rises in the hills above Drumquin. Some stretches are quite slow flowing – in fact, there is reasonable coarse fishing just above its confluence with the Strule, outside Omagh. There is a good pike population at various points, mainly in the mid-sections around Priests' Bridge. The river holds a good population of brown trout and occasional salmon.

Season

1 April–20 October

Permits
Omagh Anglers' Association hold some of this water and day permits are available from:

C. A. Anderson & Co, 64 Market Street, Omagh, Co. Tyrone BT78 1EF
Tel: 02882 242311, email: fishing.shooting@btconnect.com
David Campbell, Angler's Rest, 12 Killymore Road, Newtownstewart
Co. Tyrone BT78 4DT. Tel: 02881 661543

Local flytyers
Joe McDonald, 28 Orangefield Park, Omagh, Co. Tyrone. Tel: 02882 247192
Peter Canning, Rod & Line, Clarendon Street, Londonderry/Derry
John Murray, Birdstown, Lifford, Co. Donegal. Tel: 07491 42958
David Campbell (see above)

Popular salmon flies
Gold Shrimp, Murwee Shrimp, Red Shrimp, Curry's Red Shrimp, Apache Shrimp, Wilkinson Shrimp, Willie Gunn, Yellow Dog, Bann Special, Garry Dog, Cascade, Wye Bug.

Popular seatrout flies
Black Pennell, Peter Ross, Blue & Silver, Wickham's Fancy, Heckham & Red, Teal Blue & Silver, Butcher, Bloody Butcher, Watson's Fancy.

DERG, RIVER   H 28 84

The River Derg is a big spate river that flows out of Lough Derg, in south east Donegal, and flows eastwards for over 20 miles, through Killeter and Castlederg to join the Strule River, downstream of Newtownstewart. The gradient is steep and the river is fast flowing upstream of Castlederg, while most of the water from there to the confluence is deeper and slower flowing. Overall, it is a river with a lot of excellent fly water.

Salmon can be fished up as far as Killeter and further up where there is some very good salmon fishing. The Derg does not get a spring run but gets a good run of grilse on every spate from early July to the end of the season. The seatrout fishing is only fair, beginning at the end of June.

There are two angling clubs on the river.

Castlederg Anglers' Club has 17 miles of fishing.

Day permits
Eric Robinson, Variety Shop, Main Street, Castlederg, Co. Tyrone BT81 7AN
Tel: 02881 670689
Herbert Irwin, 4 Ceden Park, Castlederg, Co. Tyrone. Tel: 02881 671494

Ardstraw Community Angling Club has 3 miles of double bank fishing. Part of it (Crew Bridge to Ardstraw Bridge) is natural channel and the rest, down to New Bridge, is artificially drained channel.

Season
1 April–20 October

Permits
Daniel McHugh, 30 Aghalunny Road, Killeter, Co. Tyrone BT81 7EZ
Tel: 02881 671983
Taggart Jack, Hardware Store, Ardstraw, Co. Tyrone. Tel: 02881 661271

Regulations
Fly fishing, spinning and worm only

Tackle shop/flytyer
David Campbell (see below)

Fishing lodge/accommodation
David Campbell, Angler's Rest, 12 Killymore Road, Newtownstewart, Co. Tyrone
BT78 4DT. Tel: 02881 661543

Accommodation
Mrs May Magee, 18 Brocklis Road, Ardstraw, Newtownstewart, Co. Tyrone
BT18 4LS. Tel: 02881 658531, email: maymagee@thebarnardstraw.freeserve.co.uk

Self-catering and B & B
Mrs Rachel Craig, Derg View House, 5 Urbalreagh Road, Ardstraw, Newtownstewart,
Co. Tyrone BT78 4LR. Tel: 02881 662076, email: rachelcraig696@hotmail.com

Pettigo and District Angling Club has about three miles of fishing high up on the
River Derg. It requires water, but when conditions are right, it can provide excellent
sport from July onwards.

Day permit
Pettigo & District Anglers' Association, Tullyhommon, Kesh, Co. Fermanagh BT93
8BD. Tel: 02868 632391
The Post Office, Main Street, Pettigo, Co. Donegal

Further information
David Stinson, Drumgranaghan, Kesh, Co. Fermanagh BT93 8BD.
Tel: 02868 632391

BURN DENNET   C 40 04

The River Dennet, locally known as the Burn Dennet, rises in the Sperrin Mountains
and flows west through Dunnamanagh to the Foyle, downstream of Ballymagorry.
Downstream of Dunnamanagh, the river flows through rich agricultural land, while
above it, the countryside changes from rough pasture native woodland to mountain.
The river has a good stock of wild brown trout and fair-to-good seatrout fishing from
mid-July onwards. A few salmon move upstream in August and September but is
mainly regarded as a seatrout fishery.

Season
20 April–20 October

Club Secretary/permits
William O'Neill, 2 Carrickatane Road, Dunnamanagh, Co. Tyrone
Tel: 02871 398512
The Loughs Agency, 22 Victoria Road, Londonderry/Derry BT47 2AB
Tel: 02871 342100 (from ROI 04871 342100), fax: 02871 342720
Email: general@loughs-agency.org, web: www.loughs-agency.org
Tom's Tackle Shop, 31 Ardlough Road, Londonderry/Derry BT47 5SP
Tel: 02871 346265
North Western Country Sports, 19 Butcher Street, Strabane, Co. Tyrone BT82 8BJ
Tel: 02871 883021

Lodge/accommodation
Coach Inn, 366 Victoria Road, Strabane, Co. Tyrone. Tel: 02871 841362

Disabled anglers' facility
Limited. Downstream of Tullyard Bridge.

Local flytyer
Roy McBrien, Lisnaragh Road, Dunnamanagh, Co. Tyrone. Tel: 02871 398024

DEELE, RIVER   H 30 99

The River Deele flows through the village of Convoy to reach the Foyle below Lifford, a good brown trout river and traditionally known as an excellent seatrout river from June onwards. The River Deele has a late run of salmon running form mid-August to early September. Most popular stretch of water is from the townland of Gobnascale downstream to Convoy.

Season
1 April–20 October

Day and season permits
Billy Vance, Milltown, Convoy, Co. Donegal. Tel: 074 9147290

FINN, RIVER   H 26 95

The Finn and its main tributary, the Reelan, are probably the most prolific salmon and grilse rivers in Donegal. Rising high in the Blue Stack mountains, it forms Lough Finn in its upper reaches before dropping over a fifty kilometer length to form the River Foyle at its confluence with the River Mourne at Lifford. Well-known as a great spate river for spring fish but it also maintains a good head of salmon throughout the season. Obviously, these are rivers that are well worth a visit as the following totally unsolicited comment would appear to indicate: '45 salmon and 1 seatrout in 14 days fishing on the Finn and Reelan in August 2008 .... my only regret is that I am so far away and can't spend a lot more time on these wonderful rivers' (Larry Swire, Walsall, England). Seatrout run July to mid-August. The lower sections of this river are tidal with tides of up to three meters.

Permits
There are a number of private owners, angling clubs and organisations (including the Loughs Agency) that issue permits for their stretches of water.

Enquiries
Donnelly's Supermarket, Main Street, Stranorlar, Co. Donegal. Mobile: 087 9268389
Rod & Line, 1 Clarenden Street, Londonderry/Derry BT48 7EP. Tel: 02871 262877, fax: 032871 262877

Finn Angling Club Water (River Finn)
Glebe Angling Club Water (River Finn)
Finn Angling Club has approximately 15 miles of fragmented fishing on both banks between Liscooley Bridge and Stranorlar. Glebe Angling Club has 9 or 10 miles on both banks in the same area.

This stretch of river is mainly slow deep water, with the occasional stream. The banks are reasonably good and there are stiles and footbridges. This is primarily a spring salmon fishery and it is very good in the months of March, April and May. Club members probably take in excess of 300 salmon annually. It is fairly heavily fished but not crowded. The grilse fishing can be good in June and July and is not as heavily fished as the spring run.

Permits
N & M Tackle, 31 Melmount Road, Sion Mills, Co. Tyrone BT82 9PY
Tel: 02881 659501
North West Country Sports, 19 Butcher Street, Strabane, Co Tyrone BT82 8BJ
Tel: 02871 883021

The Killygordon Fishery (River Finn)
The Killygordon Fishery consists of 1¾ miles of single bank fishing. It holds spring salmon from 1 March, grilse from late May and seatrout from mid-June. Access is good – a two minute walk from the car park – and the banks are well provided with stiles and bridges. Waders are needed to fish the good fly pools, but some of it can be fished from the bank. This fishery gives its best on a falling flood. Killygordan is but a ten-minute drive from the Foyle if the Finn is running too low and only about 20 minutes from Cloghan and the upper river, should the water be too high.

Fishery Manager
James McNulty, The Curragh, Killygordan, Co. Donegal. Tel: 074 9149231

Ballybofey, Stranorlar and District Angling Club (River Finn)
This club has about 8 linear miles of double bank fishing (some single bank too) stretching from a short distance below Stranorlar up to a point about a mile downstream of Glenmore Bridge. The character of the river begins to change here and it becomes more streamy, with glides and pools. The spring salmon fishing is good, though not

perhaps as good as the downstream fisheries (best from mid-April to mid-June). The grilse tend to run through to the upper reaches and the seatrout fishing is quite good from the end of June, through July and August. The banks are well developed and the fishing not crowded.

Permits and information
John McCauley, Mr G Discount Store, Main Street, Ballybofey, Co. Donegal
J. McGavigan, Donegal Street, Ballybofey, Co. Donegal. Tel: 074 9132550

Cloghan Lodge and The Glenmore Fishery
The top of the River Finn and its tributary, the Reelan River, are controlled by Cloghan Lodge Hotel and the Glenmore Estate. Part of the fishery is in joint ownership for about 75 per cent of the river.

This is true spate water set against a background of exceedingly beautiful mountainous Donegal countryside. The Finn rises in Lough Finn and the Reelan originates deep in the Blue Stack Mountains. Both have steep gradients which – when they are in spate – provide the perfect characteristics for good fly fishing. The upper Finn has its share of spring fish from Glenmore to the Ivy Bridge from March to May, but it is as a grilse fishery that it really shines. The grilse run peaks in mid-June – depending on water – and there are fish up to Bellanamore Bridge and beyond and in the Reelan, by July. It can also get a very good run of autumn salmon from mid-August. The season closes on 15 September. The seatrout run is also very good, but they are usually taken as a by-product of the salmon fishing rather than fished for specifically. Under good conditions, the Reelan can provide quite exceptional grilse fishing to the fly.

Glenmore is fly fishing and spinning only. It has its own lodge and offers accommodation with full board or bed and breakfast.

Season
1 March–15 September

Permits/accommocation
Cloghan Lodge, Cloghan, Co. Donegal. Tel: 074 9133003
Glenmore Rivers, Glenmore Lodge, Welchtown, Ballybofey, Co. Donegal
Tel: 086 813869, email: info@glenmore-rivers.com

Salmon flies for The Foyle, Mourne and Finn
Primrose Shrimp, Gold Shrimp, Curry's Red Shrimp, Murwee Shrimp, Apacha Shrimp, Bann Special, Cascade, Willie Gunn, Wilkinson Shrimp, Garry Dog (sizes 6–10).

Seatrout flies
Donegal Blue, Black Pennell, Peter Ross, Butcher, Bloody Butcher, Teal Blue & Silver, Watson's Fancy, Sizes 12–4 (daytime) and 8–10 (night)

Brown trout flies
The usual patterns to represent Olives, Sedges (Caddis), Gnats, etc., plus Klinkhamers and Gold Heads.

FAUGHAN, RIVER   C 50 10

The Faughan rises on the northern slopes of the Sperrin Mountains and meanders for some 31 miles north westwards, towards Derry City, through a pretty valley of pasture and woodland, past Claudy, Ballyarton and Ardmore. At Drumahoe, the environment changes from rural to urban and the river swings north. About two miles downstream, it passes briefly through a rural setting once more before discharging through an industrial estate into Lough Foyle three miles north of Derry City. The Faughan is one of Ireland's most prolific seatrout rivers, is renowned for its salmon fishing and has provided a rich source of angling recreation for generations of anglers.

The season opens officially on 1 April (20 May angling club regulation and this date can vary) and closes 20 October.

The first salmon appear in the tidal water around the end of June and the first flood takes them over Campsie Dam and up to Ardmore. The salmon fishing is usually at its best from mid-June. While the Faughan is a spate river, its lower reaches (below the Pumping Station just upstream of Campsie Bridge) are tidal and will always hold fish. In this section, there is little flow and the flyfisher is helped greatly if there is a good wind ruffling the surface. One also needs to retrieve the fly or otherwise give it some movement. Bait fishing and spinning are also popular in this area.

Moving upstream as far as Killycor Bridge – some 12 miles (19km) – there are more than 50 named pools or lies offering the angler a succession of attractive streams, runs and pools, all well suited to the fly.

Shrimp flies are the most popular patterns on the Faughan. Curry's Red, Bann Special and the Faughan Shrimp (all in small sizes: 14–8) are proven killing patterns. The latter was developed by E. C. Heaney, author of *Fly Fishing for Trout & Salmon on The Faughan* (1947)

Catch returns
River Faughan Angling Ltd shows a ten year average of over 420 salmon per season. However, since less than 20% of rods submit catch returns, this figure is likely to be conservative.

Seatrout
The Faughan is arguably one of the best seatrout rivers on the Foyle System, consistently producing over 1,000 fish a year (again, based on low rod returns). The fish are of a good average size from 1–2½lb and there is always the possibility of fish up to 6lb (2.75kg).

The best of the seatrout fishing is from June to early August, with the usual patterns being effective especially in small sizes (14–12) during the day. One is likely to see small Black Pennells, Black Spiders, Connemara Blacks or a Peter Ross on the local angler's cast. At night, the same patterns are used but in bigger sizes (10–8).

Season
1 April (20 May local regulations)–20 October

Permits, guides and licences
River Faughan Angling Ltd, 26A Carlisle Road, Londonderry/Derry BT48 6JW
Tel: 02871 267781 or contact Sharon on 07790 018956
(Monday–Saturday: 09.00–21.00)

Local tackle shops/permits
Day and weekly permits available from:

River Faughan Angling Ltd, 26A Carlisle Road, Londonderry/Derry BT48 6JW
Tel: 02871 267781
Rod & Line, 1 Clarendon Street, Londonderry/Derry BT48 7EP. Tel: 02871 262877
Tom's Tackle Shop, 31 Ardlough Road, Londonderry/Derry BT47 5SP
Tel: 02871 346265
Ballyarton Fishing Tackle, 5 Ballyarton Road, Claudy, Londonderry/Derry BT47 3TA
Tel: 02871 338531
The Loughs Agency, 22 Victoria Road, Londonderry/Derry BT47 2AB
Tel: 02871 342100

ROE, RIVER   C 67 23

The River Roe's tributaries rise on the north-eastern slopes of the Sperrin Mountains
and on Glenshane Mountain and the river flows north through Dungiven and Limavady
into Lough Foyle. The river offers some fine salmon and seatrout fishing in the beautiful
surroundings of the Roe valley. It is a spate river, characterized by nice streams and
pools with some deeper, slow flowing water in the middle reaches.

Depending on water, salmon and seatrout can be taken up as far as the Benady Glen
upstream of Dungiven. The river gets a good run of grilse in July and a very good run
of salmon in late September and early October. This 'back end' run can be so good that
anglers reserve their holidays specially in order to fish it.

The originator of the Shrimp Fly, Pat Curry, fished the Roe with his brother, James,
as does the well-known present day flytyer, Robert McHaffie. The Red Shrimp and the
Gold Shrimp are still firm favourites, used mostly in sizes 8 and 6, but up to size 2 at
the back end.

The seatrout fishing is fair-to-good from early July onwards. Silver flies, such as the
Teal, Blue & Silver, are best early on, while later in the season, more sombre patterns
are used, such as the Blue Zulu. Fly, spinner or worm may be used during the day, but
the rule is fly-only, at night.

Season
1 April–20 October on DCAL water.
The angling clubs suspend fishing until 20 May and this can vary.

Permission
The Roe Anglers' Association now controls the greater part of the fishing.
There is a short private stretch at Carrickmore.

The DCAL has a mile-and-a-quarter stretch in the Roe Valley County Park, near
Limavady, and this may be fished with one of the local game fishing permits.

Permits
Mitchell & Co, 29 Main Street, Limavady, Londonderry/Derry BT49 0EP
Tel: 02877 722128

DCAL permits

The Loughs Agency, 22 Victoria Road, Londonderry/Derry BT47 2AB
Tel: 02871 342100 (from ROI 04871 342100)
Tom's Tackle Shop, 31 Ardlough Road, Londonderry/Derry BT47 5SP
Tel: 02871 346265
Claudy Tackle & Sport, The Diamond Centre, Baranilt Road, Claudy, Londonderry/
Derry BT47 4EA. Tel: 02871 337323

N.B. No day permits are issued during October.

Tackle shop

Richard Douglas, Rod and Gun, 6 Irish Street, Limavady, Londonderry/ Derry
Tel: 02877 763244

Flytyer

Robert McHaffie, Limavady, Londonderry/Derry

Regulations

Fly fishing only at night
Fishing is prohibited for 45.8m (or 50 yards) downstream of O'Cahan's Rock Weir and
Given's Weir
Bag limit: two fish per day

STRULE, RIVER   H 40 85

Omagh Anglers' Association/River Strule

The River Strule is an extension of the River Mourne, from the confluence of the River
Derg upstream to the town of Omagh. The Omagh Anglers' Association fishing extends
downstream from Omagh to a point a short distance downstream of Newtownstewart.
It holds salmon from June to September and occasional seatrout. The wild brown trout
fishing can be recommended on all of the Association's waters with trout to 2lb.

The salmon fishing can be quite good, depending on water conditions. The grilse
run up from the end of June or early July and it gets a run of summer salmon up to
17lb. The Strule and Mourne have a reputation for good quality, big, well-proportioned
fish.

The Drumragh River flows north to join the Strule at Omagh. Omagh Anglers'
Association has the greater part of the fishing up to Edergole Bridge. It has excellent
trout fishing and good fly hatches over its entire length and good salmon fishing from
July to October.

The Camowen River flows westwards from Carrickmore to Omagh. The Association
has the fishing on the majority of the river up to Drumduff Bridge. Good trout fishing.
Depending on a sufficiency of water, the salmon fishing can be good from mid-August
to the end of the season. Its tributary, the Cloughfin has excellent brown trout fishing.
Both flow through lush pastureland for most of their length.

The Owenkillew River flows westwards through Gortin, to join the Strule at
Newtownstewart and holds brown trout. It is a spate river and can give prime salmon
fishing from mid-July to the end of the season – 20 October. Omagh Anglers'
Association has some fishing on the lower reaches.

Season
1 April–20 October

Daily/weekly permits
Gabriel Treanor, 56 Main Street, Gortin, Co. Tyrone. Tel: 02881 648543
David Campbell, Angler's Rest, 12 Killymore Road, Newtownstewart, Co. Tyrone BT78 4DT. Tel: 02881 661543
C. A. Anderson & Co, 64 Market Street, Omagh, Co. Tyrone BT78 1EF.
Tel: 02882 242311, email: fishing.shooting@btconnect.com

There are also private stretches of water on the Owenkillew, eg. the Glen-Owen Fishery and the Blackiston-Houston Estate Fishery.

Glen-Owen Fishery
The Glen-Owen fishery is a private beat consisting of 1½ miles of prime salmon and seatrout fly-only water on the Owenkillew River. It is primarily fished for its salmon. Access is good, with car parking. There are good stiles, the pools are marked and the wading is easy – mostly over shingle. It takes two rods.

Enquiries
David Campbell, Angler's Rest, 12 Killymore Road, Newtownstewart, Co. Tyrone BT78 4DT. Tel: 02881 661543

Blakiston-Houston Estate Fishery
The Blackiston-Houston Estate lets day permits on a stretch of 1½ miles of the Owenkillew downstream of Trinamadan Bridge near Gortin. This is spate river fishing for salmon and seatrout in lovely countryside and can be quite good with a flood from July to October.

Day permits
Gabriel Treanor, 56 Main Street, Gortin, Co. Tyrone. Tel: 02881 648543

CLANRYE, RIVER   J 11 27

The Clanrye River meanders and winds its way through valleys and the scenic Mourne countryside from Rathfriland, by Sheepbridge, to the town of Newry. It is primarily regarded as a brown trout river, but it also gets a run of seatrout from June and efforts are being made to reintroduce salmon. It has hatches of olives, sedges, midges and stoneflies. The best of the brown trout fishing is from early in the season until June. The lower reaches, in the vicinity of the Crown Bridges, is deep and sluggish and considered mostly as pike water. In all, Newry & District Angling Association has about 12½ miles of fishing.

Season
1 March–31 October

Club Secretary
Ronald Peter McCamley, Hon. Secretary, Newry & District Angling Association, 28 High Street, Newry, Co. Down. Tel: 028 30268768, email: ronnie-p@tinternet.com

Day permits
Ronald Peter McCamley (see above)
Pat Hughes, 8 Toal Park, Belfast Road, Newry, Co. Down. Tel: 02830 266197

Tackle shop
Jack Smyth, Kildare Street, Newry, Co. Down. Tel: 02830 265303

WHITEWATER RIVER   J 31 04

This small spate river, near the village of Kilkeel in Co. Down, is primarily a seatrout fishery. It gets a good run of bigger-than-average seatrout that run on a spate in September and October.

Season
1 June–31 October

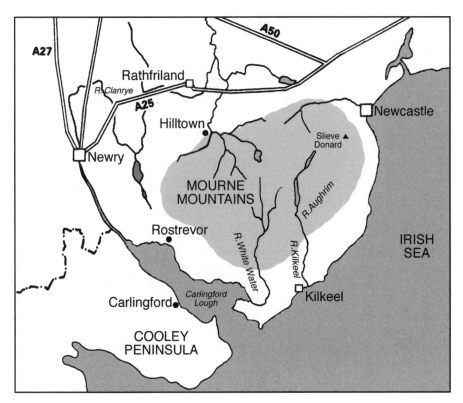

The Loughs Agency – Carlingford area

Day permits
Kilmorey Arms Hotel, The Harbour Stone, Kilkeel Post Office, Kilkeel, Co. Down
A-Blue Hardware Store, Kilkeel, Co. Down

Disabled anglers' facility
Available on the White Water River

Permits
Kilkeel Sub Post Office, The Square, Kilkeel, Co. Down. Tel: 02841 762225
Kilmorey Arms Hotel, 41 Greencastle Street, Kilkeel, Co. Down. Tel: 02841 762220

Regulations
No Sunday fishing.
All legal methods allowed.

Further information
The Secretary, Kilkeel Angling Club, c/o Kilmorey Arms Hotel, 41 Greencastle Street, Kilkeel, Co. Down. Tel: 02876 2220

2. Northern Ireland – DCAL Area

This chapter deals with the rivers in the north-east, west of the Foyle area. The Department of Culture, Arts and Leisure (DCAL) has responsibility under the Fisheries Act (NI) 1966, for the acquisition and development of public angling waters. The Public Angling Estate provides salmon, seatrout and wild brown trout angling in rivers and loughs and stocked brown and rainbow trout angling in reservoirs and loughs, as well as coarse angling at various locations.

Angling Clubs and Associations lease stretches of rivers and some make day permits available. There are also a number of privately-owned fisheries, some of which let rods on a day or week basis.

There is a wide range of game fishing available in Northern Ireland, which enjoys the longest season of anywhere in Ireland. Many of Northern Ireland's fisheries do not close till 31 October. The River Bann gets one of the best runs of Atlantic salmon in the country and there are others that can be equally good on the day.

Many rivers have superlative brown trout and dollaghan fishing, due to the efforts of the Inland Fisheries division of DCAL, as well as private enterprise and the extensive voluntary work carried out by angling clubs. Most rivers have good fly hatches and the northern rivers were especially noted for their early season olive hatches and good dry-fly fishing.

Excellent seatrout fishing can be found on a number of rivers and estuaries and the Irish record rod-caught seatrout from fresh water (16lb 6oz) was caught in this area in the River Shimna.

Regulations

It is forbidden to kill a salmon before 1 June. A carcass-tagging system requires that every rod caught salmon be tagged as soon as it is landed and killed.

There is a daily bag-limit of two salmon per rod. Half-day permit holders or anglers sharing a rod may take only one fish a day.

Copies of statutory regulations are available from:

The Stationary Office Bookshop, 16 Arthur Street, Belfast, BT1 4GD
Fisheries Conservancy Board, 1 Mahon Road, Portadown, Craigavon, Co. Armagh BT62 3EE. Tel: 02838 334666

Licences and permits

Anglers are sometimes confused as to the difference between a licence and a permit. A rod licence is required by law for each fishing rod used by anyone over 19 years of age to fish in freshwater anywhere in Northern Ireland (except for sea angling). A rod licence is also required by anglers under 18 years of age, when game fishing in the Foyle area. Licences are issued by either the Fisheries Conservancy Board (FCB) or the Loughs' Agency – a division of the Foyle, Carlingford and Irish Lights Commission (FCICL), depending on which area you are fishing.

The FCB and FCICL are conservation bodies responsible for protecting fish stocks generally in Northern Ireland. Both bodies issue angling licences in their respective jurisdictions. Payment of a supplementary charge allows the holder of a licence for one jurisdiction to fish in the other.

A permit is a separate document issued by the owner of a fishery, which confers the right to fish in that fishery. The owner may be a private individual, a company, an angling club or a Government department.

The following Game Fish Rod Licences are currently available from the FCB to game anglers:

Licence type

Game Season
Game 14-day
Game 3-day
*Game Season (Disabled)
(Available through Fisheries Board Headquarters only)
Game Season (OAP) (60 or over)
Game Season (Juvenile) (12–19 years)
Joint Game 14-day
Joint Game 3-day
Foyle Endorsement

The following Permits (game angling) are currently available, conferring the right to fish on DCAL waters:

Permit type

General game season
Juvenile season (Coarse/Game) (0–19 years)
General Game 14-Day
General Game 3-Day
Local Game Season
Coarse Season
Coarse 14-Day (2 rods)
Coarse 3-Day (2 rods)
Concessionary OAP Permit
*Concessionary Disabled Permit
(Available through Fisheries Board Headquarters only)

All licences available throughout Northern Ireland in various Tackle Shops etc, with the exception of the concessionary licences marked*

Distributors of rod licences and DCAL permits have been appointed throughout Northern Ireland. A list of local distributors is available from:

The Department of Culture, Arts & Leisure (DCAL), Inland Fisheries, Causeway Exchange, 107 Bedford Street, Belfast BT1 7FG. Tel: 02890 258873
Fisheries Conservancy Board (FCB), 1 Mahon Road, Portadown, Craigavon, Co. Armagh BT62 3EE. Tel: 02838 334666

Accommodation/tourist information
Causeway Coast and Glens, 11 Lodge Road, Coleraine, Co. Londonderry BT52 1LU. Tel: 02870 327720, fax: 02870 327719, email: mail@causeqaycoastandglens.com Web: www.causewaycoastandglens.com
Belfast Visitor and Convention Board, 47 Donegal Place, Belfast BT1 5AD Tel: 02890 246609, fax: 02890 312424, email: info@belfastvisitor.com Web: www.gotobelfast.com
Derry Visitor and Convention Bureau, 44 Foyle Street, Londonderry BT48 6AT Tel: 02871 267284, fax: 02871 377992, email: info@derryvisitor.com Web: www.derryvisitor.com
Armagh Down Tourism Partnership, 40 West Street, Newtownards, Co. Down BT23 4EN. Tel: 02891 822881, fax: 02891 822202, email: info@armaghanddown.com Web: www.armaghanddown.com
Fermanagh Lakeland Tourism, Wellington Road, Enniskillen, Co. Fermanagh BT74 7EF. Tel: 02866 323110, fax: 02866 325511
Email: info@fermanaghlakelands.com, web: www.fermanaghlakelands.com

Find an instructor
Lawrence Finney, APGAI-IRL, F/D, 8 Claremont Park, Moira, Co. Armagh BT67 OSF. Mobile: 07764 533823
Arthur Greenwood, APGAI-IRL, F/D, 17 Loughbeg Park, Carryduff, Belfast BT8 8PE
Pat Hughes, APGAI-IRL, S/H, 18 Toll House Park, Newry, Co. Down Tel: 02830 266197
Sean Melody, APGAI-IRL, S/H, 58A Ashgrove Road, Newry, Co. Down Mobile: 07970 971755
Pat Mulholland, APGAI-IRL, F/D, S/H, D/H, 74 Riverdale Park South, Belfast BT11 9DD. Tel: 02890 628919
Stevie Munn, APGAI-IRL, F/D, 109 Church Road, Newtownabbey, Co. Antrim BT36 6HG. Mobile: 07717 460131
Tommy McCutcheon, APGAI-IRL, S/H, D/H, 28a Spearstown Road, Moorfields, Ballymena, Co. Antrim BT42 3DD
Joe Statt, APGAI-IRL, S/H, F/O, FFF Master, 74 North Road, Carrickfergus, Co. Antrim. Mob: 07979 485279
Patrick Trotter, APGAI-IRL, S/H, FFF Master, 7 Tahinderry Estate, Maguiresbridge, Co. Fermanagh. Tel: 07821 538548

Sam Andrews, APGAI-IRL, S/H, 25a Drill Rd, Antrim, Co. Antrim. Tel: 078 89 423965

Marc Corps, APGAI-IRL, S/H 22 Hallcraig Road, Springfield, Co. Fermanagh
Tel: 08767 27194

Frankie McPhillips, APGAI-IRL, F/D, No. 5, The Butter Market, Enniskillen,
Co. Fermanagh,Tel: 02866 323047

Tom Woods, APGAI-IRL, S/H, FFF Master, 190 Aghafad Road, Clogher, Co. Tyrone
BT76 OXE. Tel: 07743 550804

Colin Charters, APGAI-IRL, S/H, FFF Master, 88 Colebrook Road, Fivemiletown,
Co. Tyrone. Tel: 07884 472121

Gary Bell, APGAI-IRL, S/H, 10 Arthur Street, Hillsborough, Co. Down BT26 6AP
Tel: 07828 976548

Guides/ghillies

Sam Andrews, 25a Oriel Road, Antrim BT41 4HP
Mobile: 07889 423965, email: samandrews100@hotmail.com

Arthur Greenwood, 17 Lough Beg Park, Carryduff, Belfast BT8 8PE.
Tel: 02890 813463, email: a.greenwood589@btinternet.com

Brian Connolly, 3 Great Georges Avenue, Warrenpoint Avenue, Newry BT34 3HY
Mobile 07752 975703, email: info@orielandling.com

Brian Crothers, 22 Ballyalton Park, Newtownabbey BT37 OET.
Mobile: 07745 423574, email: briancrothers47@hotmail.com

Bryan Ward, Lackin House, Cortiscashel Road, Gortin BT79 8NX.
Tel: 02881 648771, mobile: 07736 374105

Chris McAloon, Alta Walk, Rosslea, Fermanagh BT92 7AA.
Tel: 02867 751420, mobile: 07739 817445

Ciaran Bradley, 5 Oaklands, The Folley, Antrim BT41 1LS. Tel: 02894 487917
Mobile: 07790 202621, email: scullion_michelle@hotmail.com

Colin Chartres, Corcreevy, Fivemiletown BT75 OSA. Tel: 07884 72121
Email: colin@erneangling.com

Donal Lynch, Carrickmore, St. Johnston, Donegal. Tel: 07409 148280
Mobile: 07736 374129

Fred Lockhart, 40 Hammond Road, Lisburn BT28 2RY. Tel: 02892 613530
Mobile: 07843 62197

John Kelly, 3 Palmerston Park, Bayswater, Londonderry. Mobile: 087 123885
Email: johnj@matrix.ire.com

Leslie Holmes, Altikeeragh Road, Castle Rock, Londonderry. Tel: 02870 848380
Mobile: 07921 463396, email: info@stonefalls.co.uk

Mark Patterson, 78 Bryansburn Road, Bangor BT20 3SB. Tel: 02891 458866
Mobile: 07771 892506, rmail: markpattersonflyfishing@hotmail.com

Michael Shortt, Flatfield, Sydare, Ballinamallard BT94 2DU. Tel: 02866 388184
Mobile: 07808 204401, email: fish.teach@virgin.net

Patrick Trotter, 7 Tattlinderry, Maguires Bridge BT94 4SP. Tel: 02877 21877
Mobile: 07921 538548, email: Patrick_trotter@hotmail.com

Stephen Kennedy, Pikestone Cottage, 40 Scaddy Road, Downpatrick BT30 9BP
Tel: 02844 828346, mobile: 07740 609669, email: strangfordguidingco@btinternet.com

Steven Martin, 29 Edinburgh Park, Omagh BT70 ODN. Mobile: 07752 60908

Steven Moats, 9 Scaddy Road, Killyleagh Road, Downpatrick BT30 9BW
Tel: 02844 616969, mobile: 07863 863358

Stevie Munn, 109 Church Road, Newtownabbey BT36 6HQ. Tel: 02890 931293
Mobile: 07717 460131, email: anglingclassics@aol.com
Terry Jackson, 20 Cooks Brae, Kirkby, Down BT22 2SQ. Tel: 02842 738120
Mobile: 07725 338859, email: terry.jackson6@btopenworld.com
Tom Woods, 190 Aughnafad Road, Cougher BT75 OXE. Tel: 02885 548659
Mobile: 07743 550804, email: angling@yahoo.com
Willie Holmes,Moorbrook Lodge, 46 Glebe Road, Castle Rock. Tel: 02870 849408
Mobile: 07710 403199, email: Stephanie@moorbrooklodge.freeserve.co.uk
Nigel Crothers, Apt. 12 Ava House, 224 Clandeboye Road, Bangor BT19 1Q.
Mobile: 07775 557340, email: nigelcrothers25@hotmail.com
Freddie Boyd, Drumcrow, West Roscor, Bellek. Mobile: 07711 074625
Email: jfboyd900@hotmail.com
Ian Gamble, 10 Broomhill Avenue, Waterside, Derry. Mobile: 07754 030009
Email: info@anglingadventuresireland.com, web: www.anglingadventuresireland.com
Stephen Gamble, The Oaks Fishery, Judges Road, Londonderry BT47 1LN
Tel: 02971 860916, mobile: 07784 464983

BANN, RIVER   J 13 46

The River Bann rises in the Mourne Mountains, south east of Hilltown in Co. Down. It flows north to Lough Neagh, the biggest lough in these islands and thence to the sea at Coleraine. It is 86 miles long and, together with its own tributaries and the other rivers that run into Lough Neagh, it discharges into the North Channel the waters from a vast catchment of 2,243 sq. miles.

Salmon are taken in large numbers on the Lower Bann and in lesser numbers on the Upper Bann and many of the tributaries. The river gets only very occasional spring fish. The fishing picks up from early May. **Seatrout** run in big numbers to the weir at Carnroe and above to some tributaries.

Brown trout are dispersed throughout the system and runs of Lough Neagh trout, locally referred to as dollaghan add a special dimension to the late-season fishing. These trout attain weights of 6–7lb and better. They run up the inflowing rivers after a flood and are fished in the tributaries by using tactics similar to seatrout fishing.

For daytime fishing, the three most popular flies are Connemara Black, Fiery Brown and Mallard & Claret (size 10). At night they are fished for in the deep pools using a sinking line.

Bann System Ltd

The fishery rights on the Lower Bann and its tributaries belong to The Honourable Irish Society, a 400-year-old organisation which uses the income from its assets for charitable purposes locally. Bann Systems Ltd. is a wholly-owned subsidiary of the Society and has a lease over all the society's fisheries including the bed of the Lower Bann itself.

Bann System Ltd. operates angling beats on the Lower Bann River and it has sub-let all of the tributary rivers to local angling clubs.

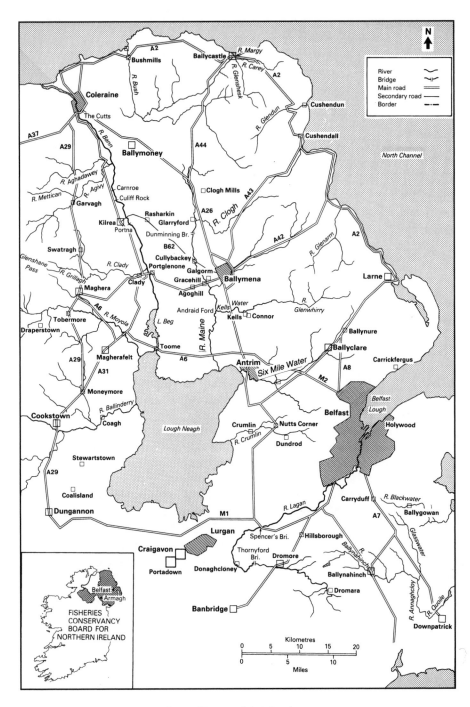

Lower Bann and Antrim rivers

LOWER BANN C97 05

An important feature of the Lower Bann is that it is a controlled river, to the extent that it contains five sets of locks and three sets of sluice gates along its length. These are part of a scheme started 160 years ago, which also included blasting out rock outcrops, to control flows coming out of Lough Neagh, both to help remove excess water levels as quickly as possible in flood conditions, and to maintain navigable flows during drier times. As a result, a large proportion of the river is deep with slow flows and hence is ideal for coarse fish and pike. However, the tributaries and the parts of the main channel circumvented by canals and locks still have ideal game fishing stretches, with fast flows and a good mixture of pools and riffles.

This is one of the best salmon rivers in Ireland. The river is the access route for thousands of returning salmon ascending into the rivers in the Lough Neagh catchment. The river is 38 miles long and drains 42% of the land area of Northern Ireland. Prime beats are Carnroe, Portna, Culiff Rock, The Cutts at Coleraine and Movanagher. Kilrea Bridge, Agivey Bridge, Portglenone Bridge and below the sluice gates at Toome (west bank) also provide good sport. Even with strict bag limits in place, it still produces between 2–3,000 fish to the rod each year.

The season opens in April and the quality of the salmon fishing can be excellent. The run can be huge as the river carried fish that spawn in 15 other rivers that flow into Lough Neagh. A feature of Bann grilse is their large average size: 6–7lb.

Season
Last Monday in April–13 October

Permission
Mr. Edward Montgomery, Director, Bann System Ltd, Cutts House, 54 Castleroe Road, Coleraine, Co. Londonderry BT51 3RL. Tel: 02870 344796, fax: 02870 356527, email: ed@irishsoc.freeseine.co.uk, web: www.bannsystem.com

BANN (LOWER), ESTUARY

The estuary of the Lower Bann is an excellent seatrout fishery. This is something of a well-kept secret, and for this reason only local anglers have enjoyed the full potential of this fantastic resource.

Seatrout move in and out of the estuary with each tide, but particularly between June and September. The angler at this time is likely to enjoy good sport, with fish around the 1lb mark being considered average, and those of 2–3lbs being frequently taken. Due to the need for light tackle in the clear water, the capture of such fish can become highly exciting, (with the possibility of line breaks being ever-present).

Due to the size of the area, local knowledge is essential in order to fish the estuary successfully. To achieve this, the use of a Bann System Ltd ghillie is recommended. Call Dessie Quinn. Tel: 02870 344796, mobile: 07703 208564.

The Cutts
The Cutts beat is located close to Coleraine and to the historic Mountsandel Fort, site of one of the very earliest human settlements in Ireland.

At the Cutts the Lower Bann tumbles into the brackish water of the estuary over a rock sill, on which are situated the famous Bann fish traps. Until 1995 these caught on average 2,500 fish annually, although it is reputed that, in 1963, 62 tons of salmon were caught in just one day! However, since the closure of these traps salmon are now free to progress upstream to spawn unhindered.

The river here is tidal and, to date, has only been fished on an experimental basis. However, the results of this have been most encouraging, with a number of salmon being caught. As a result plans are now afoot to create a specially-designed beat for up to eight rods.

The beat is usually let to Coleraine Angling Association. The Association positively welcomes non-member anglers to fish the beat.

Day permits
The Great Outdoors, Tackle Shop, Society Street, Coleraine, Co. Londonderry. Tel: 02870 320701
Smyth's Tackle, 17 Enagh Road, Ballymoney. Tel: 02827 664259

Guides
Mr. Edward Montgomery, Director, Bann System Ltd, Cutts House,54 Castleroe Road, Coleraine, Co. Londonderry BT51 3RL. Tel: 02870 344796, fax: 02870 356527, email: ed@irishsoc.freeseine.co.uk, web: www.bannsystem.com

Local tackle shops
The Great Outdoors

Carnroe
Carnroe is the premier angling beat on the river. Here, the shallow gravel ford lies below a weir constructed as part of the Lower Bann navigation system. Although there are two fish passes on the weir, fish will congregate in the low summer water and provide a superb angling opportunity. The average catch for the past 10 years is 1,300 fish p.a. but bag limits have now been introduced and catch-and-release is encouraged. Resident ghillies employed by the fishery owner are available at all times. There is intense competition for rods at Carnroe and Bann Systems Ltd. allocates the fishing through its office. It is advisable to apply in writing by the end of the previous year. The fishery is less than 1 hour from all the major air and ferry ports in Northern Ireland. Fishing is by wading, boat and bank and all legal methods are used, subject to water levels. The peak season is June and July, although September can also yield good bags.

All legal methods of angling are allowed at Carnroe, except trolling and use of maggots. However, there are some exceptions to this, as follows:

• If the water level on the gauge is above 16½ft, all methods, including spinning from bank or boat are allowed on the whole beat between the weir and the bottom of Risk.
• If the water level is below 16ft, only flyfishing is permitted on the Throw, between the weir and the white markers on both banks downstream. Spinning from boat or bank is permitted on the rest of the beat except on the upstream end of The Slope between the white and blue markers and on the Shingle Bank between the bottom blue post and the upstream red post. Maps on the permits will clarify this.

• The daily bag limit per ticket holder (including guest, if any) is two fish. The limit is one fish per half-day ticket holder (including guest, if any). If an angler reaches this limit, which is non-transferable, he must report this to the gillie and may then continue to fish, using single barbless hooks, releasing all further fish caught. Only flyfishing or shrimping methods may be used for this catch-and-release.

• A record of all catches must be made in the book provided in the fishing hut. Since the introduction of bag limits and catch-and-release in 1998, the average number of fish killed at Carnroe has dropped from an average of 1,882 per year in 1995–97, to an average of 897 per year in the 1998-2001 seasons. In 2001, 1,200 fish were landed, but only 790 were killed.

Betts' Beat

Betts' is a spinning and bait angling beat just downstream of Carnroe. The fishing is from boats provided by Bann Systems Ltd.

Day permits are available for 4 rods, on all days of the week from 29 April–13 October, from 08.00–21.00.

Two boats are available from the Carnroe ghillie

Permits are not issued on the beat and anglers should book through the office

Bag limit – two fish per day

Culiff Rock

Situated north of the Movanagher Angling Club beat, and opposite the Movanagher fish farm, Culiff Rock is a beautiful fast-flowing stretch of the Lower Bann. It is ideally suited to flyfishing, with large numbers of salmon being caught using this method each year. Although salmon are most plentiful between June and September, this beat is also renowned for its season-long brown trout fishing, with specimens of 6–7lbs being caught regularly.

Depending on weather conditions, spinning and bait fishing, which are also allowed, can prove successful. Boats, permits and ghillies are available through Bann Systems Ltd.

Movanagher Angling Club Beat

This is a ½ mile beat lying between Movanagher weir and Culiff Rock, just north of Kilrea. It is under the control of the Movanagher Angling Club and is currently only available to non-Club members through a private arrangement between the Club and Bann Systems Ltd. The water is primarily a trout fishery, with some salmon taken. Single-handed rods must be used. Wading is required and conditions can be difficult for the inexperienced. Flyfishing July.

A special day ticket is available through Bann System Ltd.

Portneal Lodge

This short beat is located downstream of the Bann Bridge, Kilrea. It offers excellent game fishing from June–October. There is a boat and ghillie service available, by contacting Portneal Lodge, 75 Bann Road, Kilrea BT51 5RX. Tel: 02829 541444.

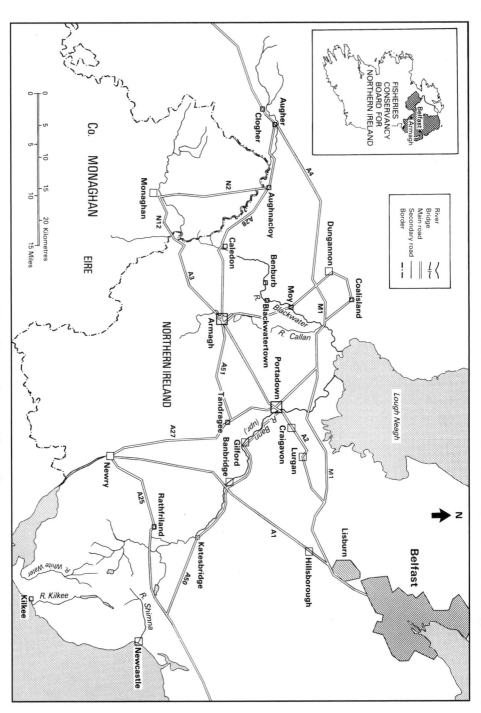

The Blackwater, Upper Bann and rivers of County Down

Portna

Portna is situated south-east of Kilrea town and has earned a reputation throughout as a top salmon beat.

The beat is in two parts, divided by Kilrea and District Angling Club's trout stretch. The upper half is directly below sluice gates used to control water to aid navigation. These have resulted in the formation of some excellent flyfishing water, with swift flows of a reasonable depth. Flyfishing is the most popular method here although a number of fish are caught by spinning or worming during heavy flows. Wading is possible in this section of the beat although great care should be taken due to the very rocky bottom of the river in this area.

The lower part of the beat has slightly slower water but still offers excellent flyfishing. In addition to salmon there are also good-sized brown trout to be had in both halves of the beat.

Enquiries to Bann System Ltd.

Ballymoney Burn

This small river is renowned locally for its trout fishing. It flows through the town of Ballymoney. There is no club operating on the river and the services of a ghillie is advised.

Ghillies/guides Moyola Catchment

Tom Maguire. Tel: 02879 642993, email:tom.maguire@lineone.net
Sean Henry. Tel: 02879 628624

Ghillies/guides on Lower Bann Catchment

Dessie Quinn. Tel: 02803 44796, mobile: 07703 208564
Hugh McIntyre. Tel: 02870 344796, mobile: 07703 560329
Ray Corr. Tel: 02870 344796
Harry Patton. Tel: 02870 344796, mobile: 07703 604838
Robbie Moffett. Tel: 02870 344796, mobile: 07801 185588
Peter Simpson. Tel: 02827 664311

Guide

Mike Shortt, Flatfield Flyfishing. Tel: 02866 388184

Licence and permit outlets

Albert Atkins, 67 Coleraine Road, Garvagh BT51 5HR. Tel 02829 558555
(Agivey Anglers' Association permits)
Maura's Shop, Main Street, Portglenone, Co. Antrim. Tel: 02825 822197
(Clady & District Angling Club permits)
Donaghy Brothers, Maghera Street, Kilrea, Co, Londonderry. Tel: 02829 540001
(Kilrea & District Angling Club permits)
Smyths Country Sports, 1 Park Street, Coleraine BT52 1BD. Tel: 02870 343970
(Coleraine Anglers' Association permits)
The Great Outdoors, 58 Society Street, Coleraine BT52 1LA. Tel: 02870 320701
(Coleraine Anglers' Association permits)

Tackle shops
Albert Atkins (see previous page)
Maura's Shop (see previous page)
Heustons, 55 Main Street, Castledawson BT45 8AA. Tel:02879 468282
Gerry Ewing, 41 Main Street, Castledawson. Tel: 02879 468282
Crawfords Sports Shop, Lower Main Street, Maghera BT46 5AE.
Tel: 02879 642672
Donaghy Brothers (see previous page)
Smyths Country Sports (see previous page)
The Great Outdoors (see previous page)
Richard McKnight, 18 Main Street, Portglenone BT44 8AB. Tel: 02825 822269
P. McGroggan, 34 Broughshane Street, Ballymena BT 43 6EB. Tel: 02825 646370
Smyth's Tackle, 17 Enagh Road, Ballymoney BT53 7PN. Tel: 02827 664259
The Great Outdoors, 28 Greenvale Street, Ballymena BT43 6AR. Tel: 04825 653433
Mid Antrim Angling Centre, 14 William Street, Ballymena, Co. Antrim BT43 6AW

Kilrea and District Angling Club

The Club has a quarter of a mile of fishing for brown trout, salmon and occasional dollaghan on the Lower Bann. The brown trout are a good average size and there are good hatches of sedges and some olives. Water clarity can be poor in summer. There are two day-permits available.

Club Secretary
Mr. David Laughlin, Culmore House, Bann Road, Kilrea, Co. Londonderry BT51 5R7. Tel: 02829 540272, email: dlaughlin@btconnect.com

Day permits
Donaghy Bros., Maghera Street, Kilrea, Co. Londonderry. Tel: 02829 540001/40429

Regulations
Fly-only
Bag limit: two fish per day

Local guide and flytyer
Mr. Albert Atkins (see previous page)

MACOSQUIN, RIVER   C 85 25

The river rises near the village of Macosquin and flows under the A29 and A54 before entering the Lower Bann west of Ballymoney. The Macosquin is a small river, seldom more than 10–15 feet wide. It has, however, a good reputation as a trout stream, especially from April to August. The fishing is fly-only. The river also produces a few salmon and seatrout late in the season. Access is mostly at the bridges and it has good hatches of large dark olives, BWOs and sedges.

Coleraine Anglers' Association

Club Secretary, Dr. Mark Henderson, 23 Ballyleague Road, Limavady, Co. Derry
Tel: 02877 766535

A superb Lough Neagh dolloghan of about 11lb caught (and released) by Mr R. Semple on the River Maine at Shane's Castle Estate in the summer of 2008.

Season
1 March–20 October

Regulations
Flyfishing only
Minimum size: 10 inches (trout)
Bag limit: two salmon per day
No Sunday fishing
Flyfishing only

Permits
Coleraine Anglers Association makes ten day permits available, from:
Smyth's Country Sports, Park Street, Coleraine, Co. Londonderry. Tel: 02870 343970
The Great Outdoors, 58 Society Street, Coleraine, Co. Londonderry BT52 1LA
Tel: 02870 320701

AGIVEY, RIVER   C 89 23

The River Agivey runs in an easterly direction from the Sperrin Mountains, passing through Garvagh and Aghadowey before entering the River Bann. The Agivey is a major tributary of the Lower Bann, which it joins about 10 miles from the sea. The

Agivey is therefore one of the first rivers in the Bann system to offer prime salmon fishing from the end of June through to the end of season. The river also abounds with wild brown trout, which offer good sport to both wet- and dry-fly.

Season
1 March–20 October

Permits
Agivey Angling Association makes available 12 day-permits, plus eight 'tourist' week-permits per week, from:
Albert Atkins, 69 Coleraine Road, Garvagh, Co. Londonderry. Tel: 02829 557691

Regulations
All legal methods, but no maggot, shrimp or prawn fishing permitted
Minimum size: 10 inches (trout)
Bag limit: two salmon per day

Local guide, tackle shop, flytyer
Mr. Albert Atkins (see page 31)

CLADY, RIVER   C 97 04

The River Clady rises near Glenshane Pass in the Sperrin Mountains and flows east past Swatragh and Clady to join the Bann near Portglenone. It is a lovely little salmon river, but the main run is quite late. Clady and District Angling Club leases all of the river and its tributary, the Grillagh River. Certain stretches are restricted to flyfishing-only and no shrimp, float or maggot fishing is allowed. It is almost exclusively bank fishing and wading is not necessary

Season
1 March–31 October

Clady & District Angling Club
Miss Margaret Dillon, Hon. Secretary, Clady and District Angling Club, 33 Mayogall Road, Magherafelt, Co. Londonderry BT45 8PD. Tel: 02879 643331
Email: mdillon@btinternet.com

Further information
Mr. William Evans. Tel: 02879 468464

Day permits
Maura's, 60 Main Street, Portglenone, Co. Antrim

Disabled anglers' facility
There are some facilities for disabled anglers.
Telephone in advance to arrange access.

Tackle shop
Crawfords Sports, Main Street, Maghera, Co. Londonderry
Richard Mulholland, Bellaghy, Co. Londonderry

Lodge
Portneal Lodge, 57 Bann Road, Kilrea, Co. Londonderry BT51 5RX.
Tel: 02829 541444

MOYOLA, RIVER   H 94 93

The Moyola River rises deep in the Sperrin Mountains and flows east for 31 miles, past Draperstown, Tobermore and Castledawson, to Lough Neagh. Like many of the Lough Neagh Rivers, it depends on water late in the season to get fish upstream which can provide some of the best sport of the season. The Moyola is a good salmon and dollaghan river and also holds some nice resident brown trout.

The river is characterised by winding, gravelly pools flowing from high mountain through agricultural land and woodland. Its chief attractions are free-rising brown trout, dollaghan from the first flood after June and salmon from May, water permitting. Access to the river is good and wading is necessary in places.

The Moyola Angling Association is one of the most active and hard-working I have encountered. It has its own state-of-the-art hatchery, where salmon, dollaghan and brown trout are reared and planted out in the river. This is undoubtedly a major contribution to the fine stocks of fish in the river.

The main fly hatches are iron blue duns, BWOs, hawthorn, black gnat and plenty of sedges.

Popular salmon flies are Curry's Red Shrimp, Bann Special, Wilkinson Shrimp and Ally's Shrimp.

Favourite dollaghan flies include Black Pennell, various Muddlers, Peter Ross, Kate McLaren and Connemara Black.

Season
1 March–31 October

Enquiries and local guides
Tom Maguire, 3 Craigmore Road, Maghera, Co. Londonderry BT46 5AL
Tel: 02879 642793, email: tom.maguire@lineone.net
Gerry Ewing, 41 Main Street, Castledawson, Co. Londonderry. Tel: 02879 6468517
Crawfords, 41 Main Street, Maghera, Co. Londonderry. Tel: 02879 642369
Seamus Donnelly, 33 Highfield Road, Magherafelt, Co. Derry BT45 5BN
Tel: 02879 631658
Sean Henry, 2 Brackesleigh Road, Draperstown, Co. Derry. Tel: 02879 628624

Day permits
Heuston's, 55 Main Street, Castledawson, Co. Londonderry. Tel: 02879 6468282

Regulations
Bag limit: two salmon per day
Minimum size: 9 inches (trout)
No maggot fishing

Flytyers
Mr. Albert Atkins, 69 Coleraine Road, Garvagh, Co. Londonderry. Tel: 02829 557691

Accommodation
The Rural College, Derrynoid Road, Draperstown, Co. Derry. Tel: 02879 629100
Portneal Lodge, 57 Bann Road, Kilrea, Co. Londonderry BT51 5RX.
Tel: 02829 541444

Local tackle shop
Hueston's (see previous page)

BALLINDERRY, RIVER   H 89 78

The Ballinderry River flows east from the Sperrin Mountains to Lough Neagh, through the towns of Cookstown and Coagh. It holds a good stock of resident brown trout with plenty of fish up to a pound. It is also noted for a very good run of dollaghan and a fair run of late summer and autumn salmon.

There are seven angling clubs on the water and details are listed below.

Season
1 March–31 October

Tullylagan Angling Club
Day permits and further information:
Tullylagan Country House Hotel, 40B Tullylagan Road, Cookstown, Co. Tyrone.
Tel: 02886 765100
Tullylagan Filling Station. Tel: 028 86765021

Unipark and Coagh Angling Club has about two miles of fishing.

Day permits
Mace Shop, 3 Main Street, Coagh, Co. Tyrone. Tel: 02886 736559
Alec Bradley, Coagh, Co. Tyrone. Tel: 02886 737085

Guides
David Hagan. Tel: 02886 737055
Leo Cassidy. Tel: 02879 48779

Mid Ulster Angling Club
The club has about three miles of fishing near Drapersfield, downstream of Cookstown.

There are 37 day-permits available from:

Information on the river
George Gourley. Tel: 028 86765920
The Lough Fea Bar, 140 Loughfea Road, Cookstown, Co. Tyrone. Tel: 028 86763517

The Royal Hotel, Coagh Street, ookstown, Co. Tyrone. Tel: 028 6762224
Outdoor World, 69 Chapel Street, Cookstown, Co. Tyrone. Tel: 028 86763682

Ballinderry Bridge Angling Club
The Ballinderry Bridge AC has approximately three miles of fishing on the river upstream of Cookstown.

For day permits and further information contact
Leo Cassidy. Tel: 028 794 18779

Kildress Angling Club
The Kildress Angling Club has about one mile of fishing. Day and season permits are available from:

Mr. Robin Black, Hon. Secretary, Kildress Angling Club, 24 Chestnutt Grove, Lower Kildress Road, Cookstown, Co. Tyrone BT80 9RN. Tel: 028 86763809

Kingsbridge Angling Club
Kingsbridge Angling Club has about two miles of fishing downstream of Kingsbridge, near Cookstown. For day permits and further information, contact:

Mr. Stanley Aspinall, 3 Rathbeg, Cookstown, Co. Tyrone. Tel: 02886 765905

TORRENT, RIVER   C 81 68

The Torrent River flows past Newmills and Coalisland, to join the Blackwater near Lough Neagh. There is about 1½ miles of fishing for brown trout with occasional dollaghan and salmon late in the season.

Further Information from:
Mr. Tony Kerr, Hon. Secretary, Coalisland & District Angling Club, 9 Torrent Drive, Coalisland, Co. Tyrone. Tel: 02887 748447
Alan Abraham. Tel: 02887 747808

CRUMLIN, RIVER   J 15 85

The Crumlin River is about 12 miles long and is situated off the A26 and A52, near Belfast International Airport. The Crumlin River is a beautiful medium-sized river which is part of the Lough Neagh system. The river has a good population of wild brown trout which will give the flyfisherman excellent sport throughout the summer. In mid-autumn, angling is enhanced with the arrival of dollaghan and salmon. Spinning in the lower reaches can produce good catches in September and October. Two new fish passes have been installed and they have greatly helped the run of salmon and dollaghan.

Season
1 March–31 October

Regulations
All legal methods
Minimum size: 10 inches (trout)
Bag limit: two salmon per day
No Sunday fishing
The use of maggots is banned

Permits
Crumlin & District Angling Association, Main Street, Crumlin, Co. Antrim. Tel: 028 9442356
Gabriel Davey, Hon. Secretary, Crumlin & District Angling Association, 34 Boon Road, Belfast BT11 96U. Tel: 028 90594479
Tourist Office, Antrim Town

SIX MILE WATER　　　　　　　　　　　　　　　　　　　　　　J 20 85

The Six Mile Water comes down from Ballynure and Ballyclare, then past Doagh, Templepatrick and Dunadry, before entering Lough Neagh west of Antrim town. It is one of the finest brown trout rivers in Northern Ireland from early April to the end of June. The river is perhaps most farmous for its dollaghan fishing, which is best from August to the end of the season. Salmon are also caught at this time of year.

The river gets a good hatch of early olives, blue-winged olives, cinnamon sedges and other small dark sedges.

There are two angling clubs on the river and the season for both is 1 March–31 October.

The river suffered a bad fish kill in 2008 and at the time of writing, the trout fishing is catch-and-release.

Ballynure Angling Club has about 5½ miles of fishing.

Day permits
Twelfth Milestone Filling Station, Templepatrick Road, Ballyclare, Co. Antrim

Ballynure Angling Club
Mr. John Arneil, Hon. Secretary, Ballynure Angling Club, 17 Collinview Drive, Ballyclare, Co. Antrim BT39 9PG. Tel: 02893 324716 (after 18.00)

Antrim and District Angling Association has about 10 miles of fishing.

Day permits
V. Harkness, Country Sports & Tackle, 9 Rough Lane, Antrim, Co. Antrim

Railway Spar, Railway Street, Antrim, Co. Antrim
The Twelfth Milestone Filling Station, Belfast Road, Templepatrick, Co. Antrim
Island Stores, Belfast Road, Muckamore, Antrim, Co. Antrim
J. S. Braddell & Sons, Tackle Shop, North Street, Belfast. Tel: 02890 320525

Further information on the Antrim & District Angling Club
Alan Fleming, 58 Cedar Court Road, Crumlin, Co. Antrim. Tel: 02894 453662

DOAGH, RIVER   J 26 90

The Doagh River flows for 4½ miles from the Five Corners, past the village of Doagh
(pronounced Doke) to the Six Mile Water. It holds brown trout of about half-a-pound
and gets good runs of dollaghan and salmon from August onwards. The fishing is
controlled by Doagh Angling Club, who take good care of it, and it is flyfishing only.

Season
1 March–31 October

Regulations
Flyfishing only
Barbless hooks
Minimum size: 10 inches (trout)
Bag limits: 4 trout per day, 2 salmon per season
No Sunday fishing

Permits
John McCullough, Chairman, Doagh Angling Club, 1 Mill Row, Doagh, Ballyclare,
Co. Antrim BT39 0PN. Day permits: £5 per day

Further information
Brian Busby. Tel: 028 93340960

MAINE, RIVER (AND TRIBUTARIES)   J 08 09

The River Maine (34 miles long) flows south from Clogh Mills, in north Antrim, past
Cullybackey, Ballymena and through the town of Randalstown to Lough Neagh. The
Kells Water and its headwaters, the Glenwhirry River, are its most important tribu-
taries.

   The River Maine holds a good stock of brown trout averaging half-a-pound and
gets a run of dollaghan and occasional salmon from July. There is a lot of nice fishing
on the entire system and the best approach to gaining fishing is through one of the
clubs, or on the private water.

Flies

Useful trout flies on the River Maine and tributaries include Hare's Ear, Wickham's Fancy, Ginger Quill, Grey Duster, Greenwell's Glory, Mallard & Claret, Fiery Brown, Connemara Black and Ballinderry Black, Ballinderry Olive and Ballinderry Brown. For salmon: Black Doctor, Silver Doctor, Curry's Shrimps, Thunder & Lightning, Wye Bug and cascade.

Shane's Castle Demesne Fishery

This unique fishery holds brown trout, dollaghan and salmon in season. Day and weekly permits are available for two rods.

Grilse arrive around the second week of July and the dollaghan (up to 8lb) come at the same time.

Shane's Castle Demesne Fishery rod catch 2004–2008

Year	2004	2005	2006	2007	2008
Salmon	28	24	11	85	54
Brown Trout	251	446	281	101	123
Dollaghan	19	19	24	71	24

Favourite flies

For salmon: Bann Special, Wilkinson and Apache Shrimps.
For brown trout: Klinkhamers and F-flies.

Permits

The Estate Office, Shane's Castle, Antrim BT41 4NE. Tel: 02894 428216
Email: shanescastle@nireland.com
Tackle Shop, Country Sports & Tackle, 9 Rough Lane, Antrim. Tel: 02894 467378

Guide/instructor

Sam Andrew, 25a Oriel Road, Antrim BT41 4HP. Mobile: 07889 423965
Email: samandrews100@hotmail.com

Randalstown Angling Club

The Club has about 5 miles of fishing on the river. Access points are limited but the banks are easily walked and there are good stiles.

Day permits

Slaght Post Office, Slaght Road, Ballymena, Co. Antrim
The Tackle Box, Newstreet, Randalstown, Co. Antrim
New Street Filling Station, 40 New Street, Randalstown, Co. Armagh
Tel: 02894 473979

Further information

Mr. John Ellis, 92 Ahoghill Road, Randalstown, Co. Antrim BT41 3DG
Tel: 02894 479475
Mr. Bill McWhinney, Whinney Hill, Randalstown, Co. Antrim. Tel: 02894 472409

Email: randalstownac@btinternet.com

Maine Angling Club

Maine Angling Club has about 3½ miles of fishing up at Cullybackey. This is mainly brown trout fishing with the chance of dollaghan on high water from June onwards. It can also give very good grilse fishing from July.

Day permits

Hayes Bridge Garage, Cullybackey, Co. Antrim. Tel: 028 25880278

Guides and further information

The Great Outdoors, 8 Dromona Road, Cullybackey, Ballymena, Co. Antrim B42 1NT. Tel: 02825 880752

Mid Antrim Angling Centre, 14 William Street, Ballymena Street, Ballymena, Co. Antrim BT43 6AW. Tel: 0282564 8159

Local tackle shop

Mr. E. Kennedy, 28 Green Vale Street, Ballymena BT43 6AR. Tel: 02825 653433

Gracehill, Galgorm and District Angling Club

Gracehill, Galgorm and District Angling Club has about four miles of fishing on the River Maine and three miles on the River Clogh, which flows into the Maine from the east just south of the village of Clogh. The River Clogh is small and mainly a brown trout stream with dollaghan later in the season. The River Maine is a much bigger river that holds brown trout and dollaghan and occasional salmon from July to the end of the season.

Day permits

Galgorm Post Office, 5 Fenaghy Road, Galgorm, Co. Antrim

Clogh Post Office, 17 Main Street, Clogh, Co. Antrim

Slatt Post Office, Slatt, Co. Antrim

Information

Mr. S. Tuff, 122 Toome Road, Ballymena, Co. Antrim. Tel: 02825 645202

Glenravel and Clogh Angling Club

Glenravel and Clogh Angling Club has about 4 ½ miles of fishing on the River Clogh (also known as the Clogh Water).

Information

Robin Russell, 2 Riverlea, Rathkenny, Ballymena BT43 6QG. Tel: 02821 758496

Stephen Coulter, 50 The Knockans, Broughshane, Co. Antrim. Tel: 02825 861616

Braid Angling Club

This club has approximately 9 miles of fishing on the River Braid, which flows into the Maine just west of Ballymena. It holds a good stock of brown trout and the fishing extends upstream from the M2 bridge to Braid Chapel. No Sunday fishing. The best of the fishing is from August to October and it is sometimes be over-fished.

Day permits
Spar Supermarket, 77 Glenravel Road, Martinstown, Co. Antrim. Tel: 02821 758396

Local guide
Stephen Coulter, 50 The Knockans, Broughshane, Co. Antrim. Tel: 02825 861616

Club Secretary
Mr. Robin Russell, Hon. Secretary, Braid Angling Club, 2 Riverlea, Rathkenny, Ballymena, Co. Antrim BT43 6QG. Tel: 02821 758496

Kells Water
The Kells Water joins the River Maine south of Ballymena and has approximately 12 miles of fishing. It is a spate river but with many holding pools for the large numbers of salmon and dollaghan which ascend the system every year. Wild brown trout are abundant, too, providing good sport throughout the season. The salmon and dollaghan enter the system on or about the first flood in July and continue to run the river right to the end of the season. Good night fishing can be had with the dollaghan once the water clarity improves after a flood. The river enjoys a good autumn run of large salmon and grilse.

Season
1 March–31 October

Regulations
No Sunday fishing
No maggots
Fly-only until 31 July
Minimum size: 10 inches (trout)

Permits
Kells, Connor and Glenwherry Angling Club, Mr. Trevor Duncan, Fernisky Road, Kells, Co. Antrim. Tel: 02825 891577
Gary Cooper, Secretary, 8 Fernisky Park, Kells, Co. Antrim. Tel: 02825 891812
Email: garycooper8@btinernet.com

Information
Mr. Philip Marley. Tel: 028 94473619

Flycasting instruction
Tommy McCutcheon, APGAI-IRL, 28A Spearstown Road, Moorfields, Ballymena, Co. Antrim BT42 3DD. Tel: 02890 249509 or 02825 892919

BUSH, RIVER   **C 94 41**

The River Bush is a spate river that flows north through Bushmills and into the sea at Portballintrae. The River Bush fishery is run primarily as an experimental salmon river for the study of the biology and management of salmon. The spring run of salmon is almost extinct and the grilse run, which begins in late June/early July is fair-to-good. The fishing is in three parts

Dundarave Stretch

The Department has four rods on the 'Private Stretch' which extends from the river mouth for about two miles upstream towards Bushmills. Flyfishing-only is permitted unless, in the opinion of the manager, conditions warrant spinning or worming. No shrimp or prawn fishing is allowed. A lot of this water is slow and deep and it fishes best with a wind on it to ripple the surface. At Portballintrae, there is the fabulous sea pool on the beach where the river joins the tide. This pool is a 'must' when fish are running and is best fished as the tide recedes.

The Day Ticket Stretch

This stretch is in three beats: the New Beat (three rods per day), the Town Beat (three rods per day) and the Leap Beat (six rods per day). The New Beat is only two miles from the sea and can fish well in medium-to-low water. The Doctor's Pool is regarded as being the best fly water on the Town Beat. The Leap Beat has five fast-flowing deep pools and fishes very well on a dropping spate. It is lovely water which takes six rods.

The Unrestricted Stretch

The unrestricted stretch extends upstream from Walkmills past the villages of Dervock, Stranocum and Ardmoy. It has a good variety of water, with slow-moving, deep pools interspersed with faster flowing water over gravel from Stroan Bridge to Magherahoney. The river extends into beautiful countryside near Armoy and Ballymoney. The river here has a good stock of native brown trout and some stocking takes place as well. There is some really nice trout fishing water above and below the village of Stranocum.

Season
1 March–20 October

Permits
The Fishery Office, River Bush Salmon Station, 2 Church Street, Bushmills,
Co. Antrim BT57 8ST. Tel: 028 20731435, web: www.deal-fishing.gov.uk.
N.B. May also be booked on the web

Disabled anglers' facility
Town Beat: day ticket stretch

MARGY, CAREY AND GLENSHESK (GLEN) RIVERS   D 12 40

The Margy (½ mile) and its tributaries, the Carey (2½ miles) and Glenshesk (1½ miles) flow into Ballycastle Bay. This is a noted seatrout system in September and October and it also gets a small run of salmon late in the season.

The Margy is fly-only between Bonamargy Bridge and the confluence of the Carey River. The remainder of the Margy is fly, spinning and worm, as are the Carey and Glenshesk Rivers.

The fishing on the Margy is almost entirely from the right bank by agreement with the riparian owner, Ballycastle Golf Club. Anglers should be alert to the golfer's cry of 'fore'. On certain golf competition days, fishing is restricted and notices are posted.

Season
1 March–31 October

Permits
At present there is no limit on the number of day-permits available. The first 12 full DANI permit holders on any day are entitled to a free permit: six of these are for the Margy only and six for the Carey and Glenshesk. The other day-permits are available to non-DANI permit holders, on payment of a fee, which allows fishing on all three rivers.

Day-permits are available from the following tackle shops:

Moyle Outdoor Angling & Leisure, 17 Castle Street, Ballycastle, Co. Antrim
Mr. R. Bell, 40 Ann Street, Ballycastle, Co. Antrim

Club Secretary
Bill Williamson, Hon. Secretary, Ballycastle & District Angling Club, 26 Cushendall Road, Ballycastle, Co. Antrim, BT54 6QR. Tel: 02820 762693

Regulations
Flyfishing, spinning and worm. No shrimp or prawn. No spinning or worm before 1 July

Local tackle shop
Moyle Outdoor Angling & Leisure (see above)
Mr. R. Bell (see above)

DUN, GLENARRIFF AND DALL, RIVERS   D 20 30

The Glens Rivers are all spate rivers located in the beautiful surroundings of the Glens of Antrim.

The Dun River is the largest of the Glens Rivers and winds its way down through the beautiful Glendunn to the sea at Cushendun. The Dun is largely a spate river, although in the bottom reaches there are a number of good holding pools. Seatrout fishing is excellent in the town stretch and indeed throughout the river. The river at the town is tidal and therefore produces good fishing especially on an evening tide. The Dun has a good population of wild brown trout. The river also boasts a good run of large salmon from late August through to the end of October. The Glenariff and Dall, although small rivers, have a number of good holding pools and can provide excellent seatrout fishing. Local methods are worming, spinning and flyfishing.

Season
1 June–31 October

Permits
The Glens Angling Club issues permits through:

O'Neill's Country Sports, 25 Mill Street, Cushendall, Co. Antrim. Tel: 02821 772009
The Mace Shop, 5 Main Street, Cushendun, Co. Antrim. Tel: 028 2176 1355

GLENARM, RIVER   D 30 16

The Glenarm is a medium-sized spate river. June sees the arrival of seatrout which continue to run the river right to the end of the season. While there will be a few salmon in June and July, the best of this fishing is from August to October. The fishing is usually fly-only though spinning and worming may be allowed in high water. I have heard great praise for this river, with some very big (16lb) back-end salmon always a possibility. This is a syndicate water and there is a club on it as well.

Season
1 March–31 October

Permits
There are two day-permits, which may be pre-booked from:
Cherry Robinson, Antrim Estates Office, Glenarm, Co. Antrim. Tel: 02828 841203

INVER, RIVER   D 36 02

The Inver River is a small spate river, which flows into Larne Lough and gets impressive runs of seatrout from late July and a few salmon. The fishing extends upstream for two miles from the river mouth and the bottom two sea pools are fly-only.

Season
1 March–31 October

Permits
Larne & District Game Angling Association make six day-permits available from Highways Hotel, Ballyloran, Larne, Co. Antrim. Tel: 02828 272272

Guides
Frank Quigley, 124 Low Road, Islandmagee, Larne, Co. Antrim. Tel: 02828 382610

DCAL permit outlets (tackle shops) in Belfast area
Belfast Welcome Centre, 47 Donegall Place, Belfast BT1 5AD. Tel: 02890 246609
Get Hooked, 4 Woodburn Crescent, Belfast BT11 9PH. Tel: 02890 623431
J. Braddell & Sons Ltd, 11 North Street, Belfast BT1 1NA. Tel: 02890 320525
T. McCutcheon, 100 Sandy Row, Belfast BT12 5EX. Tel: 02890 249509
Tight Lines, 198-200 Albertbridge Road, Belfast BT5 4GU. Tel: 02890 457357
Village Tackle Shop, 55a Newtownbreda Road, Belfast BT8 7BS. Tel: 02890 491916
East Belfast Coarse Angling Club, 7 Knockvale Grove, Belfast BT5 6HL
Tel: 02890 525794

LAGAN, RIVER   J 12 55

The Lagan rises on Slieve Croob, south of Dromara in Co. Down, and flows in a crescent-like course through Dromore, Donaghcloney, past Lurgan and Lisburn, to the tide at Belfast Lough.

Under an agreement with the Department of Agriculture, Iveagh Angling Club exercises the fishing rights on all stretches (14 miles) of the River Lagan between Thorneyford Bridge, outside Dromore, to Spencer's Bridge, at Flatfield, Co. Down.

This is a well-stocked, well-maintained and beautiful river to fish. It offers some of the nicest brown trout fishing in Northern Ireland and the stretches at Donaghcloney and Blackscull can be especially recommended.

Notices are posted at access points on all stretches indicating permitted methods and restrictions, where applicable. Day permits issued for Sunday fishing do not permit holders to fish those stretches signposted 'No Sunday Fishing'.

The river here is well-known for the quality of its fly hatches and brown trout fishing, particularly in late April, May and June.

Season
1 March–31 October

Permits
New Forge House, Magheralin, Co. Armagh
McIlduff Fishing and Field Sports, Unit 2 B, Gilpinstown Road, Lurgan, Co. Armagh BT66 8RL. Tel 02838 349709

Dromore Angling Club
Dromore Angling Club has approximately nine miles of fishing from one mile downstream of Dromore and extending upstream to Dromara. This water holds an excellent stock of mostly small trout with occasional fish of 12 or 13 inches. It fishes best from March to May.

Permits
Jackie McCracken, Gallow Street, Dromore, Co. Down. Tel: 02892 693247

Guides and further information
Donald McClearn, 23 Jubilee Park, Dromore, Co. Down. Tel: 02892 692820

Guide, flytyer and flytying instructor
Arthur Greenwood, APGAI, 17 Loughbeg Park, Carryduff, Belfast BT8 8PE
Tel: 02890 813463
Pat Mulholland, APGAI, 74 Riverdale Park, South Belfast, BT11 9DD
Tel: 02890 628919

Lawrence Finney, 8 Claremont Park, Moira, Co. Armagh. Mobile: 07764 533823

Flyfishing instructors
Pat Mulholland, APGAI, 74 Riverdale Park, South Belfast BT11 9DD
Tel: 02890 628919 Tommy McCutcheon (Tackle Shop), 100 Sandy Row, Belfast BT12 5EX. Tel: 02890 249509

INLER, RIVER

This small river flows north of the town of Comber into the north-west corner of Strangford Lough. The Inler Angling Club stocks the river and it is primarily a brown trout water that fishes best from April to June. There is a chance of a seatrout after a flood in September and October.

Season
1 March–31 October

Day permits
The Texaco Garage, Killinchy Road, Comber, Co. Down

Regulations
Flyfishing-only upstream of the school bridge. All legal methods are allowed in the tidal water.

Further information
Mr. Ian Kittle, 52 Dermott Road, Comber, Co. Down   BT23 5QP. Tel: 02891 872297
Mr. John Rowan, 75 Belfast Road, Comber, Co. Down BT23 5QP. Tel: 02890 813463

QUOILE, RIVER   J 46 46

The Ballynahinch River and the Glasswater River join to become the Annaghcloy River. It becomes known as the Quoile River just west of Downpatrick. The Quoile basin, at the bottom of the river, has brown trout.

Blackhead Angling Club has an access agreement on approximately two miles of fishing, predominantly brown trout. The river is a designated game fish river and flyfishing is encouraged. The fishing is best early in the season with good hatches of large dark olives, medium olives, blue-winged olives, sedges, black gnats and hawthorn flies.

Upstream of Kilmore Bridge, housing development makes for difficult access.

Season
1 March–31 October

Club Secretary
Mr. George Meharg, Hon. Secretary, Blackhead Angling Club, 26 Kingsway Park, Belfast, BT5 7EW. Tel: 028 90483175

Guide/flydresser
Arthur Greenwood, 17 Loughbeg Park, Carryduff, Belfast BT8 9PE. Tel: 02890 813463
email: geomeharg@hotmail.com.

Day permits
Available from the Secretary, only to guests of club members.

SHIMNA, RIVER   J 37 32

The Shimna is a small spate river with good deep holding pools. It drains the northern slopes of the Mourne Mountains into the sea at Newcastle, Co. Down. It gets a good run of seatrout from July and a late run of salmon. The seatrout are above average in size and the river holds the Irish freshwater rod-caught seatrout record of 16lb 6oz, which was caught in 1983 by Tom McManus of Newcastle.

Two and a half miles are under the control of the Department and can be fished with a Department of Agriculture game-fishing permit.

The remaining six miles of the river is controlled by Shimna Angling Club. Access is good, waders are not really necessary, but they are useful if fishing for seatrout at night. Popular seatrout patterns are: Teal Blue & Silver, Butcher, Bloody Butcher, Kingfisher Butcher, Medicine, Dunkeld and Squirrel Blue & Silver.

Season
1 March–31 October

Club Secretary
Mr. Ian Watts, Hon. Secretary, Shimna Angling Club, 7 Tullybrannigan Road, Newcastle, Co. Down BT33 DDX. Tel: 028 437 22454
Email: sac-secretary@hotmail.com.

Day permits (DCAL stretch and Club stretch)
Four Seasons Pet & Sports Shop, Main Street, Newcastle, Co. Down.
Tel: 028 43725078

Regulations
All legal methods
Bag limit: four fish (salmon or seatrout) per day
No hen fish of 45cm or over to be killed
Only one cock fish of 45cm or over to be killed, per angler, per day

Disabled anglers' facility
There is a wheelchair access point upstream of Shimna Road Bridge.

Local tackle shop
Four Seasons Pet & Sports Shop (see above)

BANN (UPPER), RIVER   J 21 40

The Upper Bann rises in the Mourne Mountains and flows north past Rathfriland, Katesbridge, Banbridge, Gilford and Portadown to Lough Neagh. It was a noted dollaghan, brown trout and late-run salmon river until it was adversely affected by the drainage scheme. It has recovered well, but silting is still a problem in certain areas. It flows mainly through pastureland in typical drumlin countryside.

Good quality brown trout are The Upper Bann's chief attraction. Salmon fishing can be good at the end of the season, but the dollaghan fishing is currently of little value. Poor water quality has been a problem in the past, but the four angling clubs are dealing with the problem and are also currently engaged in 'in-river' improvements.

The important fly hatches are large dark and medium olives in spring and blue-winged olive, sedges, reed smuts and the black midge in June and July. The yellow May dun is also making a welcome return. Evening fishing with imitations of BWO spinners and small sedges can be excellent. This is when some of the biggest trout are caught as well as during a fall of black gnats, an event which is always eagerly awaited in these parts.

Favourite salmon fly patterns include Bann Special, Wilkinson Shrimp, Apache Shrimp and Curry's Red Shrimp.

Access is mostly good with well-maintained stiles, steps and bridges and even car parking spaces.

Season
1 March–31 October

There are four angling clubs on the river.

Banbridge Angling Club Ltd
This club has about 10 miles of fishing in the middle section stretching from Hazelbank Weir upstream to the county bridge at Katesbridge.

Enquiries
Mr. Joseph Curran, Hon. Secretary, Banbridge Angling Club, 10 Old Manse Green, Old Manse Road, Banbridge, Co. Down. Tel: 028 40629081

Day permits
Coburn's Ltd, 32 Scarva Street, Banbridge, Co. Down. Tel: 02840 662207
(09.00–17.00, Monday–Saturday)
Anglers Rest, 42 Aughnacloy Road, Katesbridge, Banbridge, Co. Down

Regulations
Flyfishing, worm and spinning
Bag limit: 4 trout; two salmon
Minimum size: 11 inches (trout)

Local tackle shop
Coburn's Ltd, 32 Scarva Street, Banbridge, Co. Down. Tel: 028 40 662207
McIlduff's, Fishing & Field Sports, Unit 2B, Gilpinstown Road, Lurgan, Co. Armagh BT66 8RL. Tel: 028 38349709
Outdoor Experience, 29 Castle Street, Portadown, Co. Armagh BT62 1BA

Gilford Angling Club
The Gilford AC has about seven miles of fishing and is primarily known for its good brown trout fishing.

Day permits
The Spar Shop, 40 Mill Street, Gilford. Tel: 028 38 831087
R. Moffat, Mill Road, Gilford. Tel 028 38 831501

Further information on guides etc.
Mr. Mervyn Magee, 11 Station Road, Scarva, Craigavon, Co. Armagh BT63 6JY. Tel: 02838 831529

Rathfriland Angling Club

The Rathfriland club has about 12 miles of fishing on the Upper Bann.

Rathfriland Angling Club, Mr. John Dougan. Hon. Secretary, 33 Newry Road, Rathfriland, Co. Down. Tel: 02840 638943, email: john@dougan2.freeserve.co.uk

Day permits
Grahams Confectionery & Ice Cream, 11 Downpatrick Street, Rathfriland, Co. Down. Tel: 02840 638179
Bag Limit: 6 fish not to include more than two salmon

Local tackle shop
W. R. Trimble, Downpatrick Street, Rathfriland, Co. Down

Fly casting instructor
Gary Bell, APGAI, 7 White Thorn Grove, Kinallen, Dromara, Co. Down BT25 2DJ. Tel: 02897 533274

Guides and accommodation
Mr. John Dougan, 33 Newry Road, Rathfriland, Co. Down. Tel: 02840 638943
Email: john@dougan2.freeserve.co.uk

Clonduff Angling Club

The Clonduff Angling Club has about 12 miles of water.

Day permits
Downshire Arms Hotel, Main Street, Hilltown, Co. Down. Tel: 02840 638899
Doran's Service Station, Bryansford Road, Hilltown, Co. Down
Killen's Service Station, Hilltown, Co. Down

Regulations
Methods: Flyfishing, spinning and worming
Bag limit: of three trout
Minimum size: 12 inches (trout)

Further information on guides etc
Mr. Danny Mussen, 69 Henry Road, Rathfriland, Co. Down. Mobile: 07752 158361

BLACKWATER (ULSTER), RIVER   H 88 60
AND TRIBUTARIES: THE RIVERS OONA, TORRENT AND
BALLYGAWLEY

The Ulster Blackwater is a big river by the time it reaches Lough Neagh. One branch rises near Clogher, in Co. Tyrone, and the other comes across the border from Co. Monaghan (see Chapter 6). The northern branch flows past Clogher, Augher, Aughnacloy and Caledon before turning northwards past Benburb, Blackwatertown and Moy.

There is a good deal of nice streamy water in the upper reaches from Clogher down to Benburb, which hold some great resident brown trout. The lower reaches, downstream of Blackwatertown, are deep and sluggish.

The Blackwater meanders through farmland from its upper reaches around Clogher to Lough Neagh, providing miles of excellent fishing for trout, salmon and dollaghan. From the headwaters to Favour Royal, the water is in the control of the Clogher and District Angling Club. From there to Caledon (where a good part of the river is in private hands as part of the Caledon Estate) the Aughnacloy and District Anglers have the fishing. Armagh Fisheries and DCAL control fishing around Blackwatertown.

The Ulster Blackwater's tributaries provide river trouting of varying quality. The Oona, which is some of the fishing water controlled by Armagh Anglers, has resident trout to around half-a-pound. The Torrent also has resident trout, but can also see a good run of dollaghan and a few salmon, from July onwards, given suitable water conditions. The brown trout fishing on the Ballygawley River was second-to-none, but a recent road improvement scheme has had a seriously negative impact.

The Blackwater Enhancement Association, a federation of all the clubs and associations involved on the river, is busy working to improve the fishing and habitat on the entire river. The Association encourages anglers to help conserve fish stocks and to practice restraint in killing wild fish.

Season
1 March–31 October

Permits
Fane Valley Supplier, Main Street, Augher, Co. Tyrone. Tel: 02885 548232

Tackle shops
Home Field & Stream, 18 Church Street, Enniskillen, Co. Fermanagh,
Tel: 02866 322114
Dick Kinnan, Venture Sports, Genslough Street, Monaghan. Tel: 047 87495

Ballygawley, Aughnacloy and District Angling Club
McKenna's Food Store, Main Street, Aughnacloy, Co. Tyrone. Tel: 02885 557306
Frankie McPhillips, The Buttermarket, Enniskillen, Co. Fermanagh.
Tel: 02866 324499

Guide
Tom Woods, 190 Aughafad Road, Clogher, Co. Tyrone BT76 UXE.
Mobile: 07743 550804

COLEBROOKE, RIVER   H 34 38

Maguiresbridge and District Angling Club has six miles of wild brown trout fishing on the Colebrooke River in Co. Fermanagh that flows through Maguiresbridge and enters Lough Erne near Lisnaskea. This is an excellent piece of fishing with resident brown trout averaging 12oz and running up to 1lb, not to mention bigger lough trout that run up late in the season. The banks are well developed with stiles and footbridges.

The best fishing on the stretch is from mid-March to the end of June, when fly hatches are prolific. From June, the best fishing is usually in late afternoon and evening.

Best dry flies: Adams, Cul-de-Canard, BWO, Iron Blue, Black Gnat, Hawthorn, all types of emergers, Mayfly, Hoppers, Beetles and Daddies.

Best wet flies: Dark Watchet, Poult Bloa, Waterhen Bloa, Partridge Spider, Black & Silver Spider, Snipe & Purple, Black Pennell.

Upstream of the club water, there is a further three miles of double bank trout fishing in Colebrook Park Estate.

Season
1 March – 30 September

Day permits
Patrick Trotter, APGAI-IRL, Hon. Secretary, Maguirebridge & District Angling Club, 7 Tattinderry Heights, Maguiresbridge, Co. Fermanagh. Tel: 02867 721877
Colebrooke Park Water, The Estate Office, Colebrook Park Estate, Brookeborough, Co. Fermanagh. Tel: 028 89531402, email: alan@colebrookpark.com
Web: www.colebrookpark.com

Regulations
Club Stretch: fly-only
Bag limit: two trout
Minimum size: 12 inches

Local guide and flyfishing instructor
Patrick Trotter, APGAI, 7 Tattinderry Heights, Maguiresbridge, Co. Fermanagh. Tel: 02867 721877

Tackle shops
Frankie McPhillips, The Buttermarket, Enniskillen, Co. Fermanagh.
Tel: 02866 324499
Home Field & Stream, 18 Church Street, Enniskillen, Co. Fermanagh.
Tel: 02866 322114

Erne Tackle, Main Street, Lisnaskea, Co. Fermanagh. Tel: 02867 721969

Local flytyer
Frankie McPhillips, The Buttermarket, Enniskillen, Co. Fermanagh.
Tel: 02866 324499

KILKEEL RIVER   J31 04

The Kilkeel River is primarily a seatrout river and gets a small run of salmon late in the season. The best of the seatrout fishing is in September and October, on a falling spate. Kilkeel Angling Club has about four miles of fishing on the river.

Season
June–31 October

Permits
Kilkeel Sub Post Office, The Square, Kilkeel, Co. Down. Tel: 02841 762225
Kilmorney Arms Hotel, 41 Greencastle Street, Kilkeel, Co. Down.
Tel: 02841 762220

3. Northern Fisheries Region

The Northern Fisheries Region extends from Malin Head in Co. Donegal – the most northerly point in the country – south along the western coast of Donegal to Dunlevy's Point in north Sligo. It stretches far into the north midlands and includes parts of Leitrim, much of Co. Cavan and part of Co. Monaghan.

The Donegal rivers are mostly acid waters draining mountain, moor and bogland. Brown trout are small but the seatrout, grilse and, in many instances, spring salmon make up for lack of brown trout. The Rivers Drowes usually produces the first rod-caught Irish salmon of the season on New Year's Day. Further south, the Upper Erne and its tributaries are totally natural rivers and for the most part unspoiled by arterial drainage schemes. These waters have prolific hatches of olives, mayflies, sedges and black gnats and can give spectacular sport in certain areas for good quality wild brown trout. By good quality, I mean significant stocks of wild brown trout in the size range 1–3lb. Many of these waters are undeveloped, difficult to access and local knowledge is the key to finding the best areas.

I recommend that anglers familiarise themselves with the current situation regarding regulations and bye laws regarding the conservation of salmon and seatrout and when, where and how angling may take place.

At the time of writing, many of the Donegal rivers are closed for angling for salmon (and seatrout over 40cm must be returned), however angling for brown trout and seatrout under 40cm (2¼lb approximately) is permitted. In some instances, the closure may only be temporary and in others it may be more long-term. The rivers so affected are marked thus ** in this guide. For up-to-date information: **www.cfb.ie** or **www.fishinginireland.info**

Visiting anglers should be aware that on certain rivers the owners have a management agreement with local anglers. In some instances this means local anglers book a rod and the maximum number of rods on the beat is not exceeded, eg. Gweebarra River. On other rivers, eg. the Owenea River, fifteen local anglers may fish on any one day throughout the river and it is recommended that they should not overcrowd the better beats.

The Board provides an angling information service. Enquiries to:

Northern Regional Fisheries Board (Headquarters), Station Road, Ballyshannon, Co. Donegal. Tel: 071 9851435, email: info@nrfb.ie. web: www.nrfb.ie

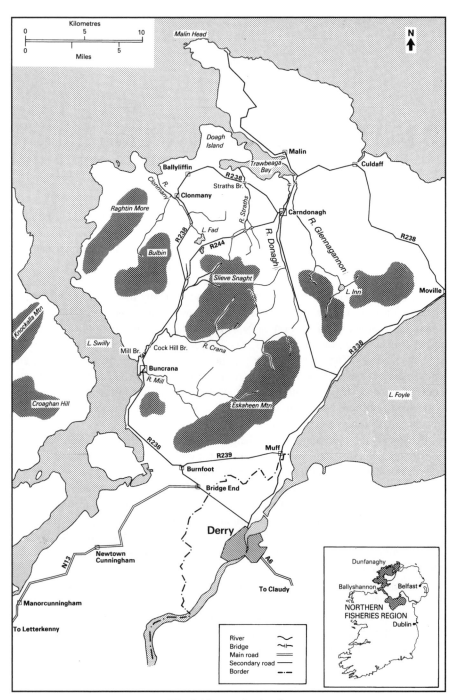

The Inishowen Peninsula

TRAWBREAGA BAY   C 42 51

This is one of the few places in Ireland where you can fish for seatrout in the sea. Stocks are good and it is some of the best seatrout fishing on the Donegal Coast. They are fished at Trawbreaga Bar mouth either from Doagh Island or from the Five Fingers Strand, 3 miles north of Malin. Access is good with a car park near the shore at the Famine Village on Doagh Island and at Lag Church near the Five Fingers Strand. The best fishing is in March and April for big seatrout but there are trout there all season and the peak fishing time is for an hour before and after both high and low-water. Sand eels and spinning silver Devons, silver eels or small spoons are the recommended fishing methods.

Season
2 February–12 October

Licence
A special local State licence is required. The nearest distributor is Inishowen Tourism, The Square, Carndonagh, Co. Donegal.

** GLENNAGANNON, RIVER   C 48 48

This little river flows 10 miles from Lough Inn and drains a 14 sq. mile valley into Trawbreaga Bay. The best fishing is on the last half mile above the tide. It is regarded as one of the better rivers for seatrout and salmon on the Inishowen Peninsula. The seatrout run in July, but expect to catch a seatrout anytime during the season when the water is right. The salmon usually arrive in late August and September.

The best of the fishing water is downstream of the Malin Road Bridge – fishing off the left bank. On a spate, the local anglers fish both banks up to the village of Cardonagh. It can produce some big seatrout – to 61/2lb – and all methods are allowed.

Season
Salmon: 2 February–30 September
Seatrout: 2 February–12 October

Information
Inishowen Tourism, The Square, Carndonagh, Co. Donegal

** DONAGH, RIVER   C 46 46

The Donagh River is 9 miles long and flows through Carndonagh into Trawbreaga Bay. It drains picturesque Glentogher and a 15 sq. mile catchment and holds seatrout from July and grilse from mid August. It is best fished immediately after a spate from the village of Carndonagh downstream. There are some nice pools below Corvish Bridge.

This is a little river with a good deal of potential. Access is off the Malin road and the Corvish road. For salmon, spin a 1¼ inch Devon Minnow or a Mepps No. 2 or 3, or fish a worm. Recommended seatrout patterns are Silver Doctor, Connemara Black, Zulu and Butcher.

Season
Salmon: 2 February–30 September
Seatrout: 2 February–12 October

Information
Inishowen Tourism, The Square, Carndonagh, Co. Donegal

** STRATHS, RIVER   C 43 47

The Straths River enters the west side of Trawbreaga Bay. It drains a 9 sq. mile catchment and is fished for seatrout. The bottom half-mile is regarded as best from June onward but there are some deep pools up in the valley that hold fish.

Season
2 February–12 October

Permission
Riparian owners

** CLONMANY, RIVER   C 35 47

The Clonmany River rises in Lough Fad and flows 7 miles through the village of Clonmany into Tullagh Bay. It gets a fair run of salmon and grilse and a few seatrout.

Season
Salmon: 2 February–30 September
Seatrout: 2 February–12 October

Permission
Fishing permits are not being sold at present.

CRANA, RIVER   C 34 33

The fishing rights of the Crana River (including the netting rights) were purchased by the progressive Buncrana A.A. in 1988. It is a 12-mile long spate river, which rises deep in the mountains of Inishowen and drains a 40 sq. mile catchment into Lough Swilly, just north of Buncrana. The countryside is wild and beautiful, with mountains, rough pasture and some forestry in the upper reaches. The river is characterised by deep pools and a rocky gravel bed. It holds salmon and seatrout from June.

Access is reasonably easy, involving no more than a half mile walk at the furthest point.

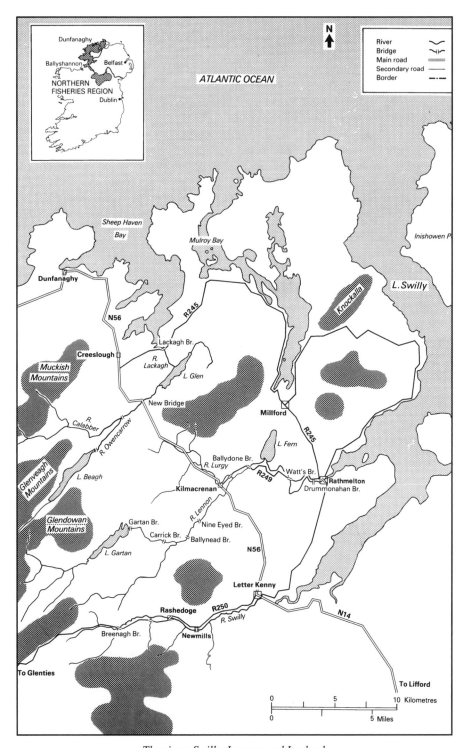

The rivers Swilly, Lennon and Lackagh

The salmon fishing starts with the first spate in late May and peaks with the grilse run in July–August and can be very good when the water is right. The average catch of salmon is 400–600 fish per season.

The river gets a run of fish in September. Some of the best pools for salmon are The Trout Pool, Eye of the Bridge, Willow Pool, (no spinning at any time), Wilson's Pool, McGee's Pool, Hooten's Pool, Cockhill, Ballymangan and Druminderry. Spinning is prohibited in low water, as is 'Bubble & Fly'

This is a river with lovely fly water and favourite flies are Bann Special, Apache Shrimp, Ally's Shrimp, Claret Shrimp and Wilkinson Shrimp – usually in sizes 10–12 and sizes 12–14 in low water. The river fishes best from the top pools downstream after a spate.

The seatrout fishing is very poor. It holds a good stock of brown trout that give good sport on light tackle.

Season
Salmon: 1 March–30 September
Seatrout: 1 March–12 October
Brown Trout: 1 March–12 October

Permits and tackle shop
Buncrana Angling Centre, Castle Lane, Buncrana, Co. Donegal. Tel: 074 9363733 Mobile: 087 2814868, email: buncranaanglersassoc@eircom.net

Office Hours: March to May 10.00–14.00
                    June to September 10.00–18.00

Ten visitor permits are allowed per day. There is no restriction on local anglers. There is no beat system at present and no overcrowding after the first half-mile up river.

Disabled anglers' facility
No specific facilities but some areas of the lower river are suitable for anglers who are partially disabled.

Guides
Can be booked through the Buncrana Angling Centre, as can boats on Fullerton Reservoir.

** MILL RIVER   C 35 31

The Mill River rises north of Buncrana at the base of Grainnes Gap. It then flows in a south-easterly direction through the hills of Inishowen for 9 miles before entering Lough Swilly at Buncrana. This river is spate, spring-fed in summer and has excellent fly hatches. The Mill has high banks but there is good access to the river in most areas. Some rehabilitation was carried out with new fish passes being built in 1998 which has enabled salmon and trout to gain access to the upper stretches of the river. This river is controlled by the Mill Anglers' Association and holds extensive stocks of wild brown trout. The largest trout recorded in recent years was 3lb 8oz. It gets a fair run of seatrout from June onwards.

Location
Co. Donegal. The main town is Buncrana.

Season
March 1–30 September

Fish species
The Mill River is a salmon, seatrout and wild brown trout fishery.

Methods
Flyfishing only; wetfly, dryfly and nymph fishing are all successful.

Best flies
Black Pennell, Connemara Black, Watson's Fancy, Peter Ross.

Angling club
This water is controlled by the Mill Anglers' Association which enforces a policy of catch-and-release.

Permits
Permits for this river are available from:
Brendan McLaughlin (Secretary), 27 Lower Main Street, Buncrana, Co. Donegal
Tel: 074 93 61716, mobile: 086 3564888

** SWILLY, RIVER   C 14 10

This is a substantial little spate river, nearly 26 miles long and draining 112 sq. miles of Donegal mountains and farmland into Lough Swilly at Letterkenny. It was the subject of arterial drainage works some 25 years ago and a spate runs off very fast.

The run of salmon has declined greatly in recent years. The average annual total is about 40 fish and the occasional big seatrout. It is fishable from Old Town for about 7 miles up as far as Breenagh Bridge but the best of it is said to be from Rashedoge to Cornwall graveyard. There are good stiles and footbridges all along the river, so it is very fishable.

Season
Salmon: 2 February–30 September
Seatrout: 2 February–12 October

Permits/local tackle shop
Permits are issued by Swilly & District Anglers' Association and are available from:

John McLoughlin, Lough Swilly Flies & Angling Centre, Rough Park, Ramelton Road, Letterkenny, Co. Donegal. Tel: 074 9168496

Eel Turn on the river Eske (see page 78)

** LENNON (OR LEANNAN), RIVER   C 21 20

Of all the salmon fisheries in Ireland, there are a few that must be considered to be the Premier League. There is Careysville, on the Cork Blackwater; the Ridge Pool, on the Moy; Carnroe, on the Bann – and Watt's Pool, also known as The Ramelton Fishery, on the Lennon, by the town of Ramelton in north east Donegal. The latter remains in private ownership but, for the first time in its history, it was opened for the public to book rods in 2000.

At the time of writing, it is closed for all fishing.

The pool is 750 yards long, situated at the bottom of the river and is flyfishing only. It can produce a fish nearly every day in January. February is probably the peak month and March can be good. April can be fair and May is generally slow. It picks up again in July with the onset of the grilse run.

The whole pool fishes at 2 feet on the gauge, but it can never really be too high and anything between 1ft 9in and 2ft 5in is good. The Cave Hole and the Eel Weir are low water lies. Willie Gunn-type flies are popular, but any yellow tube fly or Waddington will do.

The River Lennon drains the Glendown Mountains in mid-Donegal into Gartan Lough and flows through the village of Kiomacrenan to Lough Fern and on over a series of weirs to meet the tide at Lough Swilly, just below Ramelton. It is 29 miles long and drains 109 sq. miles, including numerous loughs. These loughs play a major role in maintaining good water levels for spring fishing.

Up until 1977, the River Lennon was regarded as one of the great Irish spring salmon rivers. A measure of its former status was the tally of 70 fish taken by anglers up-river on Easter Monday 1975. An outbreak of UDN that same year seriously depleted the stocks in subsequent years. Only in recent seasons has the disease shown signs of waning and the run of spring fish improved.

Watt's Pool nearly always produces a fish on opening day (1 January) and the rest of the river from Drumonahan Bridge above Watt's Pool up to Lough Fern tends to fish best in the cold weather of February and up to 17 March. This stretch is lazy and deep. Woodside, Lagmore, the Black Bridge and the Hawthorn Pool at the bottom of the Long Lane are all noted taking spots. Occasional fish are taken between Lough Fern and Gartan Lough at this time of year too, but this stretch of nearly 8 miles comes into its own from April. There are noted lies at Ballydone Bridge, Coyle's Pool and Harkin's Pool at Kilmacrenan, below the Nine-Eyed Bridge, above and below Ballynead Bridge and above Carrick Bridge. John McLoughlin, Lough Swilly Flies & Angling Centre, Rough Park, Ramelton Road, Letterkenny, Co. Donegal (tel: 074 9168496) always has good and up-to-date knowledge of the state of the fishing in this area.

The Lennon spring fish are good fish, averaging about 9lb. The best fish ever recorded weighed 33lbs. In spring, the fly recommendation is as for Watt's Pool or spin a Yellowbelly, Blue and Silver or Brown and Gold Devon.

The grilse come in late June. Once they leave Watt's Pool, they seem to run hard to Gartan Lough.

The seatrout don't really run up-river and the best of the seatrout fishing is from July at Watt's Pool and below it.

The ownership of the river upstream of Drumonahan Bridge is fragmented and the banks underdeveloped, and it is always best to take a local guide or speak to local riparian owners.

Season
Salmon and seatrout: 1 January–30 September

Permits
There is no permit requirement at present for the Lennon upstream of Watt's Pool. Permission is required to fish Watt's Pool, but it is closed to all fishing at the time of writing.

Information
For up to date information, guiding etc, contact:
John McLoughlin, Lough Swilly Flies & Tackle Shop, Rough Park, Ramelton, Co. Donegal. Tel: 074 9168496, email: jmclswillyflies@eircom.net
Alan Coyle, 22 Manor View, Letterkenny, Co. Donegal. Tel: 074 9167287

** LACKAGH, RIVER   C 10 30

The Lackagh is a short river of less than a mile and drains Glen Lough and a 51 sq. mile catchment into Sheephaven Bay in Donegal. It is crystal clear and flows through rough moorland. The Lackagh is noted for its run of spring salmon, grilse and seatrout, although the spring run has declined in recent times.

The spring run commences in January and peaks in March and some fish continue to run till May. There is a fair run of grilse in June and July when the water is right, as well as a small run of autumn fish in September. The Lackagh spring salmon are noted for how freely they take a fly. They are best fished with a sinking line. A half-inch Willie Gunn tube fly is as good as anything else. Nowadays, spinning is practised on the left bank and the river is heavily fished.

The river has three main pools: the Grilse Pool, which is located at the bottom of a large cascade; the Garden Pool, a long, rather narrow pool and the Eel Weir, a huge wide pool with a narrow fast run at the neck. Further down, there is the Salmon Weir, which can be good for a fish on the rising tide, but the Ivy Rock lie on the left bank has been spoiled by the erection of a fishing stand.

Contrary to popular practice, it is best to fish a slow sinking line on this river up to July.

The river gets a small run of grilse and can be taken after July on a floating or sink tip line. Small shrimp flies work well.

The river gets an excellent run of seatrout from early July and some of the best fishing is in the big pool below the Eel Weir and out into the estuary. The best seatrout fishing is to the fly at night, if you can survive the biting midges.

At the time of writing, I'm advised this is still a great seatrout fishery.

Season
Salmon and seatrout: 1 January–30 September

Permits
This fishery is in disparate ownership. The right bank is privately owned from Glen Lough down to the old Salmon Weir at the end of the Eel Weir Pool. It is flyfishing only and rods are not usually let.

The left bank from Glen Lough out into the estuary below Lackagh Bridge and the right bank from the old Salmon Weir out into the estuary is State owned. It is managed by the Northern Regional Fisheries Board. At the time of writing, permit enquiries should be made to:

The Post Office, Creeslough, Co. Donegal

N.B. By law, a special State licence is required for seatrout fishing in the estuary. The nearest licence distributor is:

The Post Office (see above)

Guides
John Gallagher, Cashel, Creeslough, Co. Donegal. Tel: 074 9138346
Alan Coyle, 22 Manor View, Letterkenny, Co. Donegal. Tel: 074 9167287
John McLoughlin, Lough Swilly Flies & Tackle Shop, Rough Park, Ramelton, Co. Donegal. Tel: 074 9168496, email: jmclswillyflies@eircom.net

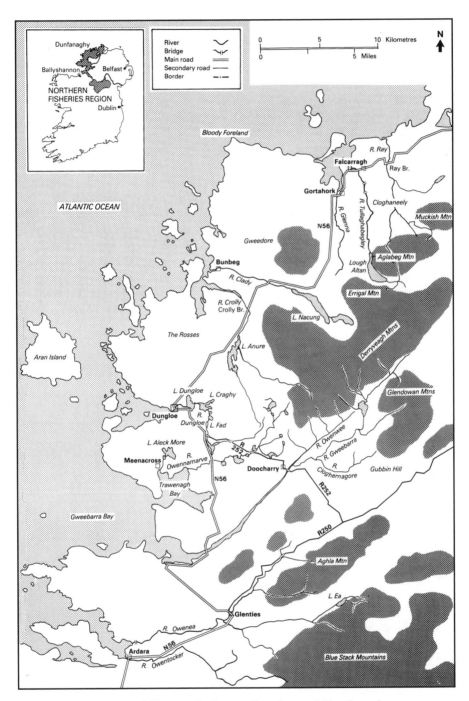

Ardara and Glenties, the Rosses, Gweedore and Cloughaneely

** OWENCARROW, RIVER   C 05 26

The Owencarrow River links Lough Beagh and Glen Lough and is 4½ miles long. It gets runs of salmon and grilse and is still a great seatrout fishery. The lower section, at Glen Lough, is deep and slow and fishes best with a wind to break the surface, while further up there are occasional pools. The banks are developed, with stiles, but access is difficult and involves a lot of walking.

Traditionally, spring salmon did not run the river till it got a flood in late April. In summer, it is a better seatrout than grilse fishery. The best pools and the best of the fishing begin about a mile downstream of Lough Beagh – roughly a mile upstream of the top bridge at Anton O'Donnell's house, where there are two good pools just above the confluence with the Callaber River. From there on, both banks are overgrown with bushes for a distance and then are clear again. Given sufficient water, the river meanders at a nice pace and should be ideal for salmon and seatrout fishing. Access and walking conditions are difficult. From Owencarrow Bridge, on the N56 Creeslough road, there is one stream at the top and the rest of the river is deep glide water with deep pools on bends – about 25 in all – and two long flats before it reaches Glenlough. The country-side is still rough pasture and there are stiles and footbridges for ease of access.

Season
1 January–30 September

Permits
The left bank from the Callaber River downstream is managed by:
Northern Regional Fisheries Board and the same permits apply as for the River Lackagh (see page 64).

The right bank is leased to Letterkenny & District Anglers' Association and permits are available from:
The Log Cabin Bar, Derryfad, Owencarrow Bridge, Creeslough, Co. Donegal.
Tel: 074 9138029

Guides
Alan Coyle, 22 Manor View, Letterkenny, Co. Donegal. Tel: 074 9167287
John McLoughlin, Lough Swilly Flies & Tackle Shop, Rough Park, Ramelton, Co. Donegal. Tel: 074 9168496, email: jmclswillyflies@eircom.net

** RAY, RIVER   B 95 33

The Ray (pronounced Rye) River drains Muckish and Agla Beg Mountains north to the Atlantic west of Horn Head. It is just eight miles long, from source to sea, draining a 21 sq. mile catchment of mountain and rough moorland. The bottom pools are tidal and fish can get up into the river in low water conditions. The lower reaches, below Ray Bridge, are mostly flat and dead. Upstream, it is rough and rocky and fishable only on a spate. Favourite fishing areas are at the Tractor Bridge, the Pots and a couple of nice pools above. On a high spate, it can be fished up for nearly three miles. The Ray is very heavily fished!

A few spring fish run in May, but from mid-June to the end of the season, fish run on every spate. It is a remarkably prolific as well as a beautiful little river and produces an unusually high percentage of 10–12lb fish. The most popular fly is a Curry's Red Shrimp. Natural shrimp is not allowed.

The seatrout run in big numbers from mid-July and are mainly fished at the estuary and below the Tractor Bridge. The best seatrout fishing is at night with a Silver Spider, Peter Ross or Butcher. Access is good by road and some stiles have been erected.

Muckish Mountain Fishery consists of about 1,000 meters of mostly single bank on the upper Ray River. It gets a few spring fish in April and the grilse arrive in mid-June. It has nice fly water on a falling spate and a favourite stretch is between the Steel Bridge and the Foot Bridge.

Season
Salmon: 2 February–30 September
Seatrout: 2 February–12 October

Information
Email: keesw@gofree.indigo.ie, web: www.muckishsalmon.com

Permits
Cloughaneely Angling Association control most of the river and at the time of writing, it is closed for all angling.

Information
John Connaghan. Email: johnconnaghan@eircom.net

** TULLAGHABEGLEY (BAAWAN), RIVER   B 93 30

The Tullaghabegley River is much better known locally as the Baawan River. The Baawan Pool – just above the tide, with its steep waterfall – is known far and wide and is a favourite haunt of worm fishers. The river enters the sea just west of Falcarragh and is a small, insignificant stream, just nine miles long with a 13 sq. mile catchment, which includes Lough Altan and the north slope of Mount Errigal. Despite its size, the Tullaghbegley is a very productive little salmon and seatrout river. The Baawan Pool fishes practically all the time from June onwards, for the fish can ride in on the tide. On a spate, there are four or five nice little pools above the main road bridge with a nice stretch above the old railway bridge and a lovely flat at Meendarragh.

Flies: small Shrimp fly patterns, Black Pennell, or a Donegal Blue. The Baawan Pool is very heavily fished and anglers stand shoulder-to-shoulder.

The Ballyness Estuary, at the mouth of the river, is a favourite with seatrout fishers when the tides are favourable.

Season
Salmon: 2 February–30 September

Seatrout: 2 February–12 October

Permits
Issued by Cloughaneely Anglers' Association
See advice for Ray River on previous page.

** GLENNA, RIVER   B 91 30

The Glenna is only six miles long and drains half a dozen small hill loughs and a 10 sq. mile catchment. It enters the sea at Gortahork. It still gets a late run (September) of good seatrout and big salmon in the 8–9lb class and is worth fishing when the spate is running off. It is still a great little seatrout fishery and well worth fishing.

Season
Salmon: 2 February–30 September
Seatrout: 2 February–12 October

Permission
Riparian owners

** CLADY, RIVER   B 81 23

The Clady and the Crolly Rivers have been joined in anglers' imaginations for genera-tions for the excellence of their salmon and seatrout fishing. Today, they are both excel-lent summer salmon rivers. They are physically joined by a canal, which channels the water from the top of the River Clady, at its outflow from Lough Nacung, and delivers it to a hydroelectric power station situated at the mouth of the Crolly. The hydro dam at the top of the Clady has a fish pass and the flow on the river is euphemistically described as a 'controlled flow'. In addition, a total of eighteen 'freshets' are let down per season to help get the fish up – two in May, six in June, six in July, three in August and one in September. When the hydroelectric power station is generating, the water from the Clady is discharged into the mouth of the Crolly in such quantities that it confuses the homing instincts of the Clady fish and draws them down the estuary to the mouth of the Crolly.

The Clady River, by all accounts, was one of the best little salmon rivers in Ireland. There is a well-confirmed report of about 80 fish being taken in one day during the 2001 season. In spite of its 'controlled flow' and hydro dam, it still gets a fair run of fish and is estimated to produce an average of 300 fish to rod and line in the summer months. The rod fishery extends for a distance of about 3½ miles from Ard Dun Bridge, below the dam, to the sea at the fishing port of Bunbeg. It is a wild moorland river (catchment area 36 sq. miles), characterised by rocky granite outcrops, some deep pools and a deep gorge, and it flows through one of the most densely populated rural communities in western Europe. The main run of grilse is in June, and Whit weekend can be an excellent time to take fish if the water is right. After that, there are good runs in July and some big fish run in late August and September. The best of the salmon fishing is regarded as being on the second day of a 'fishet' from Bunbeg Bridge down to the harbour. It is all fishable when in flood and should be approached from the left bank. Much of the fishing is done with worms but it is worth trying a fly in the Doctor's Pool, the Spinks, the Falls, Diver's Pool and – especially – the pool below Diver's.

The Clady gets only a fair run of seatrout, which peaks at the end of August. The best of the fishing is in the evening from Bunbeg Bridge downstream. Seatrout are also taken, but in lesser numbers, up to the bridge below the dam.

Fishing is not permitted between the dam and the bridge and natural shrimp may not be fished for salmon.

Season
Salmon: 2 February–30 September
Seatrout: 2 February–12 October

Permits
The Clady and Crolly Rivers are fished on the same E.S.B. permit.

C. Boner, The Tackle Shop, The Bridge, Dungloe, Co. Donegal. Tel: 074 9521163
Bunbeg House, The Harbour, Bunbeg, Co. Donegal. Tel: 074 9531305
An Chuirt Hotel, Gweedore, Co. Donegal. Tel: 074 9531101

Note
There are reports that one or two riparian owners whose houses are very close to the river bank do not welcome anglers.

** CROLLY (GWEEDORE), RIVER   B83 20

The River Crolly drains Lough Anure and a number of other loughs in its 23 sq. mile catchment and reports indicate that it fished very well in the 2001 season. It is a narrow, rocky river, with long, deep pools, waterfalls and rocky gorges. The surrounding countryside is wild and beautiful and very thickly populated. Much of it is narrow – 5–7 yards wide. A few spring fish run in March, April and May. The grilse begin to run in early June and fish enter the river, with a spate, right through to September. However, June sees the peak of the run and can give 8 or 9 fish a day. Access is easy, with a road all along the bank, but bankside conditions are rough, as is the case on the Clady.

There are some good lies between Crolly factory and a place upstream called 'The Flag'. There are three pools between Crolly Bridge and the sea and downstream of Lough Anure is said to fish best in August–September.

Late June and July sees a fair run of seatrout and the best fishing is from Crolly down to the estuary.

Season
Salmon: 2 February–30 September
Seatrout: 2 February–12 October

Permits
The Clady and Crolly Rivers are fished on the same E.S.B. permit.

C. Boner, Tackle Shop, The Bridge, Dungloe, Co. Donegal. Tel: 074 9521163
Bunbeg House, The Harbour, Bunbeg, Co. Donegal. Tel: 074 9531305
An Chuirt Hotel, Gweedore, Co. Donegal. Tel: 074 9531101

Guides
Alan Coyle, 22 Manor View, Letterkenny, Co. Donegal. Tel: 074 9167287

** DUNGLOE, RIVER   B 77 11

This small river drains several of the loughs in the Rosses area. It is fished for seatrout in the summer months and the fishing is divided into three parts. The first part stretches from Dungloe Lough to the sea and has some good holding pools. There is good fishing on a spate below the town when the tide is filling. The stretch above the town, from the hospital to Mulhern's Pool, 50 yards below the lough, has some good holding pools for night fishing or for when the surface is rippled by the wind.

The second part of the river, between Dungloe Lough and Craghty Lough, is fished but is very deep. It is only about 600 yards long and can be fished downstream of the bridge.

The third part, the little stream above Lough Fad, has some deep holes and it too can be fished up as far as the bridge.

This river is reported to have had a great run of seatrout in the 2001 season.

Season
Salmon: 2 February–30 September
Seatrout: 2 February–12 October

Permits and tackle shop
C. Boner, Tackle Shop, The Bridge, Dungloe, Co. Donegal. Tel: 074 9521163

** ALECK MORE, RIVER   B 76 07

This short river drains Lough Aleck More into Trawenagh Bay. It is very narrow, but fishable in parts. You can get seatrout at the Bridge Pool at Meenacross in July and August when the tide is full.

Permit
C. Boner, Tackle Shop, The Bridge, Dungloe, Co. Donegal. Tel: 074 9521163

** OWENNAMARVE, RIVER   B 78 07

The Owennamarve is a small, narrow river, which drains about a dozen small lakes and an 8 sq. mile unspoiled, pollution-free catchment west into Trawenagh Bay, south of Dungloe. Its insignificant appearance belies its ability to provide a good day's sport

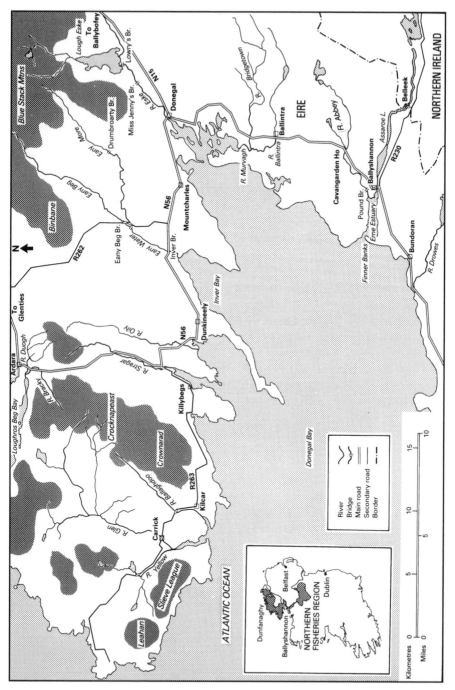

South-West Donegal

with either salmon or seatrout for those who know it. A few spring salmon enter it from March and it gets a heavy run of grilse from mid-June. All methods are allowed, but if conditions are right, small flies – Shrimp Fly, Badger, Teal & Black – can get results. There are several good lies and a long pool about half a mile below the bridge on the N56 Dungloe-Glenties road is one of the favourites. There is another at the second falls about 500 yards above the same bridge.

The river gets a run of good spring seatrout (2–4lb) in May and the summer run peaks in mid-July. It can be fished at several points from the estuary up and the best fishing is either at night, or by day provided there is a fresh west breeze to ripple the surface. Access is at the bridges. The banks are clear but uneven and the setting peaceful.

Permits and tackle shop
C. Boner, Tackle Shop, The Bridge, Dungloe, Co. Donegal. Tel: 074 9521163

GWEEBARRA, RIVER   B 88 05

The Gweebarra is a 20-mile long stretch of spate river which drains Lough Barra and a lonely mountain valley, with Crocknasharragh and Slievesnaght rising up to the north west and Crockastoller and the Glendown Mountains to the east. It drains a 60 sq. mile catchment into Gweebarra Bay and its estuary is all of 10 miles long, as narrow as a medium-sized river and worked by draft nets in June and July up as far as Doochary. Above Doochary, the river and setting are about as remote and beautiful as you will find anywhere. The Gweebarra is a typical medium sized spate river with lovely long, deep pools and shallow rocky stretches in low water. It is especially noted for its prolific spring salmon run.

The fishery consists of 6 beats spread over 8 miles of river plus around 10 miles of estuary fishing. The beats cater for 2 to 4 visitors depending on the beat and time of season. Access has been provided in the form of stiles, walkways, footbridges, access roads and car parks. The Gweebarra has a good run of spring fish during April and May, with grilse running from the end of June and good-sized summer salmon running from August onwards. Seatrout are at their best from July and are usually taken from the estuary and the pools around the Doochary area. Other hot spots on the river are the famous Mayo pool at the confluence of the Cloghernagore River which looks like a small lough and the Fall's pool (beat 4). Any of the traditional Irish shrimp flies work well on the river, as does the popular flying C. The annual salmon catch is normally 350+ fish. The spring fish run from April, the grilse run peaks in late July and continues to run through August and September.

Season
Salmon and seatrout: 1 April–30 September

Permits
I am glad to be able to report that finally, this very fine fishery has been reclaimed for genuine anglers to enjoy and has a management structure in place.

Gweebarra river in its upper reaches

A day permit is required to fish the Gweebarra River. These cost €50 per day (2009) from 1 April to the 17 June inclusive (Spring Salmon permit). From 18 June to the end of the season costs €35 per day (Grilse permit). Day permits are available to fish the estuary and cost €10. This estuary is well worth fishing from July as is the lower part of the river. For information on permits contact:

Owenea Angling Centre, Glenties, Co. Donegal. Tel: 074 9551141
email: nrfbglenties@eircom.net
Northern Regional Fisheries Board, Station Road, Ballyshannon, Co. Donegal.
Tel: 071 9851435, email: info@nrfb.ie, web: www.nrfb.ie

Local tackle shop
Charlie Bonner's Tackle Shop, The Bridge, Dungloe, Co. Donegal. Tel: 074 9521163

Guide
Michael Devine, Classey, Doochary, Co. Donegal.
Tel: 086 8860876, email: mickydevine@hotmail.com

Disabled anglers' facility
A section of Beat 6 below the bridge in Doochary town has been developed to facilitate disabled anglers.

CLOGHERNAGORE, RIVER   B 88 07

The Cloghernagore River joins the Gweebarra from the east at the Mayo Pool. It drains
Lough Nanuroge and several other small lakes under the shadow of Gubbin Hill. This
river has a long, lazy stretch 1½ miles long up in the hills and it holds salmon late in the
season. It now forms part of Beat 4 on the Gweebarra River, see page 72. It is reached
via a winding three-mile forest road, off the R252 Doocharry-Fintown road.

Season
Salmon and seatrout: 1 April–30 September

OWENEA, RIVER   G 74 92

The Owenea is one of Donegal's premier salmon and seatrout rivers. It is a spate river,
16 miles long and drains the mountains of mid-west Donegal and a 45 sq. mile catchment of moorland and some farmland into the sea, one mile north of Ardara. In the
first two miles up from the sea, deep pools alternate with shallow rocky areas, while
further up towards Glenties, deep pools and short streams predominate. The salmon
fishing extends beyond the town of Glenties for three miles to Meenamore Bridge and
the seatrout for another two miles upstream. In all, there are over fifty named pools on
the river. The fishing is all double bank. This is a spate river in an area of high rainfall
and it gives a day or so of 'nice fly water' after a flood.

Forty five rods is the maximum allowed on the river, divided over 9 beats. Visiting
anglers are allocated 30 of these rods – or 3 to a beat – and the local or associate
anglers may fish where they please.

River Owenea rod catch 2001–2008

Year	2001	2002	2003	2004	2005	2006	2007	2008
Salmon	c.750	c.400	c.330	c.370	c.377	c.261	c.330	c.350
Seatrout	N/A	N/A	N/A	N/A	N/A	N/A	N/A	N/A

This is mainly a grilse fishery, with a few spring fish and a diminished run of seatrout.
The peak of the grilse is in August and September.

Favourite beats are 5, 6, 8, 9 for grilse and 2 and 3 for seatrout.

All legitimate angling methods are allowed, except shrimp and prawn. Favourite
grilse flies are John Anthony Shrimp, Curry's Shrimp, Foxford Shrimp, Claret Shrimp
and Silver Stoat's Tail. Fish with small flies (14–16) in low water. Wading is rarely
necessary and nearly all of the river can be fished with a single-handed rod.

Season
Salmon and seatrout: 1 April–30 September

Permits
Owenea Angling Centre, Glenties Hatchery, Glenties, Co. Donegal. Tel: 074 9551141
Office hours (7 days): 1 April–31 May 9.30–13.00, 1 June–30 September 7.00–13.00

Regulations
No shrimp or prawn fishing.
No worm fishing on Beat 5 or 6.
Anglers are requested to return seatrout.

Guides
Alan Coyle, 22 Manor View, Letterkenny, Co. Donegal. Tel: 074 9167287

Local tackle shop
All Kinds of Everything, Main Street, Ardara, Co. Donegal. Tel: 074 9541262

** OWENTOCKER, RIVER   G 74 90

The Owentocker is an extremely spatey river. It is 12 miles long with an 18 sq. mile mountain catchment. It is rocky and shallow and has very few pools to hold fish. The banks are quite overgrown and what fishing there is, is on the last 2 miles, where it flows through farmland. The Ness Pool, under the falls, is its best known pool and gets a lot of attention from worm fishers when the grilse are running after mid-July in a spate.

Season
Salmon: 1 April–30 September
Seatrout: 1 April–30 September

Permits
Owenea Angling Centre, Glenties, Co. Donegal. Tel: 074 9551141
Office hours (7 days): 1 April–31 May 09.30–13.00, 1 June–30 September 07.00–13.00

** BRACKEY, RIVER AND DUOGH, RIVER   G 72 90

The Brackey and the Duogh are two little rivers that converge as they reach the tide at the top of Loughros Beg Bay, about one mile south of Ardara. They look so insignificant that you would pass them by unnoticed, yet they get a run of seatrout and grilse in sufficient quantities to keep three draft nets operating at the mouth. The rod fishery is in three or four small tidal pools below the confluence of the two rivers and on a short stretch – about 300 yards – of the Brackey. It holds grilse and seatrout in July, August and September and is always worth a try if you are passing that way. It is ideal for fly with a wind on the pools, otherwise try a worm. Access is opposite Molloy's Factory on the N56 Ardara-Killybegs road.

Permit
Check with the riparian owners

Middle Beach on the river Crana

| ** GLEN, RIVER | G 60 80 |
| OWENWEE (OR YELLOW) RIVER | G 58 78 |

The **Glen River** drains the mountains of west Donegal, through the village of Carrick and tumbles over a rocky cascade at its mouth into Donegal Bay. The upper reaches down from Meenaneary flow through a treeless moorland valley of smallholdings, whilst from Carrick downstream there is some bank cover. It gets a small run of salmon in May. The big run of grilse comes in early July. August sees the arrival of good summer fish up to about 12lb. The fishing can be very good with fresh fish in the river and a falling spate. The best pools are in the first three miles up from the sea but there are fishable pools up for about six miles. Worming in the Salmon Leap Pool at the sea is a favourite pastime and produces fish even in low water. It is a lovely little river on which to fish a fly on falling water. A short stretch upstream of Carrick is private and not let.

The **Owenwee,** or **Yellow River** shares the same estuary as the Glen River. Its catchment differs from the Glen River in that it drains half a dozen lakes and their effect on the river is to maintain a better flow after a spate. It is fishable about 3 miles up and gets a good run of summer fish. The Owenee is always well worth fishing in August and September. It was closed for angling in 2008–9 because it did not meet its conservation limit but it is thought that the stock recovery should not take long.

Access to both of these rivers is relatively easy, with roads running parallel to the banks in each case.

The Glen and Owenwee Rivers used get a great run of seatrout, but their numbers declined greatly in 1989 and have never really recovered.

The fishery is managed by the Slieve League Angling Company. It consists of 28 miles of spate water, divided into six sections – two of which are private – and while there are no beats and rods are not limited, it is managed on the basis of 'rotation and etiquette'.

Rivers Glen and Owenwee rod catch 2000–2008

Year	2000	2001	2002	2003	2004	2005	2006	2007	2008
Salmon	252	370	280	240	430	375	423	448	430
Seatrout	112	85	55	120	93	114	105	123	119

The Association encourages catch-and-release and the percentage of fish released has increased from 8% in 1995 to 49% in 2008.

This is a late river with little or no activity till June. July–September is peak season, depending on water.

Favourite flies include Foxford Shrimp, Hairy Mary, Black Pennell (very good), Curry's Red Shrimp and Ally's Shrimp.

Season
Salmon and seatrout: 1 March–30 September

Permits
Paddy Maloney, Aughera, Carrick, Co. Donegal. Tel: 074 9739043
Email: dgl1@indigo.ie

Regulations
Seatrout under 10 inches must be returned.
The use of maggots, shrimp and prawn are prohibited.

Guide
Paddy Maloney, Aughera, Carrick, Co. Donegal. Tel: 074 9739043
Email: dgl1@indigo.ie

Tourist accommodation and information
Slieve League Hotel, Carrick, Co. Donegal. Tel: 074 9739043
Web: www.carrickonline.com

Local tackle shop
The Harbour Stores, The Pier, Killybegs, Co. Donegal

EANY WATER   G 82 79

The Eany Water is about 15½ miles long and drains the southern slopes of the Blue Stack Mountains and a 46 sq. mile catchment which includes quite a bit of farmland, some moor and the remains of mature oak and beech woodland at Inver Bay – an offshoot of Donegal Bay. It is managed by the Northern Fisheries Board. The Board ended the controversial draft net licence that permitted a draft net to operate in the river mouth. Fish can now negotiate the river unhindered.

The Eany is a true spate river and can rise and fall very quickly. Fishing is best on falling water when the river begins to clear and the gauge is between 0.6 and 0.3.

The grilse begin running in June but the run doesn't really peak till July and into August. It is a river that can fish well in September, with fish averaging about 7lb. The fishing extends upstream from Inver Bridge to Drumbroarty Bridge on the Eany More water, a distance of approximately seven miles, and as far as Eany Beg Bridge on the smaller Eany Beg western tributary. It is a typical spate river with a gravel and flag bottom and numerous big holding pools. It colours quickly in a spate but clears just as quickly and the fishing can be very good indeed on falling water. The river twists and winds mainly through old pasture. It is possible to get a car fairly close to the water and walking the banks has been made much easier by the erection of numerous well-built stiles and footbridges. Flyfishing, worm and spinning are all practised, but natural shrimp is prohibited. Useful fly patterns include Bann Special and Curry's Red Shrimp and flies with a touch of orange, sizes 8–14.

A Black Pennell also works well for seatrout, as does a Connemara Black, a Teal, Blue & Silver – sizes 10 and 12 and a Donegal Blue.

The peak of the seatrout fishing is in early July. It fishes best at dusk and good seatrout pools include the Devil's Hole, the Carry, the Boat Hole, the Black Hole and Hughie's Pool.

Eany Water rod catch 1999–2008

Year	1999	2000	2001	2002	2003	2004	2005	2006	2007	2008
Salmon	c.350	c.300	c.350	c.450	c.400	c.250	c.332	c.200	c.330	c.300

Season
Salmon: 1 April–30 September
Seatrout and brown trout: 1 March–9 October

Permits
Eany Angling Centre, Gargrim, Frosses, Co. Donegal. Tel: 074 9736559.
Open: May–September 07.00–13.00

Regulations
No shrimp or prawn fishing allowed.

Tackle shops
Doherty's Tackle Shop, Donegal Town. Tel: 074 9737209
Gerard O'Neill, Marine Sports, Main Street, Dunkineely, Co. Donegal.
Tel: 074 9737209

** ESKE, RIVER   G 93 80

The River Eske is a crystal clear river of some 3½ miles that drains Lough Eske and a 41 sq. mile catchment into Donegal Bay at Donegal town.

The fishery is managed by the Northern Regional Fisheries Board. The river still receives a good run of grilse and seatrout. There is a small run of grilse in June and the main run goes through in August and September. Seatrout fishing is best from July onwards. The river is divided into four beats each catering for two visiting anglers. Local anglers may fish where they please. Beats can be rotated at mid-day if required.

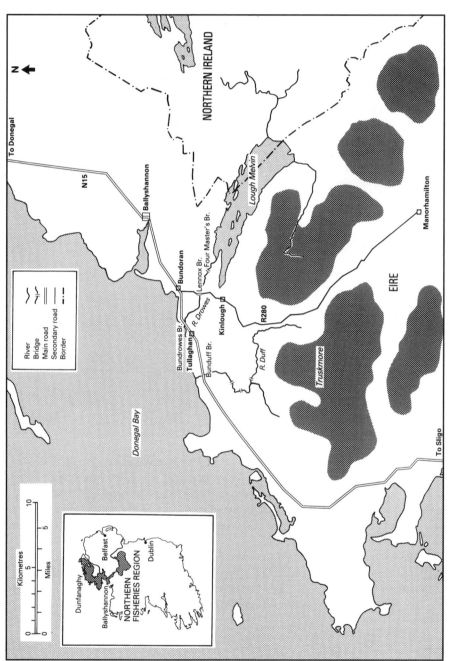

The rivers Duff and Drowes

There are sections of the river that are hard to access and have been left undeveloped to provide effective sanctuary areas for the fish. The fishable waters have been developed to allow good access to anglers with the provision of stiles, footbridges and walkways. The most popular beats are 2 and 4.

There are five boats for hire on Lough Eske and the lough is much more popular with anglers than the river.

River Eske rod catch 2004–2008

Year	2004	2005	2006	2007	2008
Salmon	95	90	100	Closed	Closed
Seatrout	c.200	c.390	c.410	c.50	c.50

Season
1 March–30 September

Permits
The Eske Angling Centre, Lough Esde Demesne (near Harvey's Point), Lough Eske, Donegal Town. Tel: 074 9740781 (in season)
Northern Regional Fisheries Board. Tel: 071 9851435 (closed season).

Regulations
Flyfishing, spinning or worm fishing only.

Disabled anglers' facility
At the Mill Pool in Donegal Town.

Local tackle shop
C. J. Doherty, Main Street, Donegal Town

** MURVAGH (BLACKWATER), RIVER   G 90 72

The Murvagh River and its tributaries, the Rath (Bridgetown) River and the Ballintra River drain a 33 sq. mile catchment of farmland and numerous small loughs into Donegal Bay. The Murvagh holds salmon, seatrout and brown trout. The end of July and the month of August see the peak of the salmon run and the main salmon angling areas are below Murvagh Bridge and in a couple of pools above the bridge. A few fish are also taken in the tributaries.

N.B. This is an excellent seatrout system. The fish begin running at the end of June and the peak is in mid-July and the run continues through August into September.

The Rath River is regarded as a better seatrout river than the Ballintra and trout are taken for two miles up as far as Rath Mill. It also holds brown trout up to a pound and more.

This is a difficult, undeveloped river system with little or no provision made for angler's access.

Season
Salmon: 1 March–30 September
Seatrout: 1 March–9 October

Brown Trout: 1 March–9 October

Permit
Riparian owners.

Local tackle shop
Conor Barrett, Main Street, Bundoran, Co. Donegal. Tel: 071 9842266

DROWES, RIVER   G 80 58

The River Drowes is one of Ireland's premier spring and summer salmon fisheries. Seatrout rarely enter the river, but it holds a good stock of brown trout.

The spring salmon fishing opens on 1 January and rarely does a season pass without a fish being taken on opening day. The peak of the spring run is in April and in some seasons, March can be quite good too. The fishing can be very good in May and June sees the peak of the grilse run. In August and September, anglers are mainly fishing over resident fish.

The Drowes is a delightful little salmon river, some 4 ½ miles long with a catchment of 103 sq. miles. It has 70 named pools. The upper section, down to the Four Masters Bridge, has a lovely series of streams and pools and is usually reserved for anglers staying at Mr. Gallagher's holiday bungalows at Lareen. The middle section to Lennox's Bridge is mostly fast-flowing and fishes best in medium-low water. The third section down to the tide has a mixture of stream, pool and deep, slow water and a very

A promising run on the Owenea river

prolific sea pool, which is always well worth fishing at high tide. It is especially productive on a spring tide. The commercial traps at the mouth were bought out in 1994 and four fishing pools created in their place.

There is no beat system and the number of rods per day is not limited.

All legitimate fishing methods are allowed and the fish take a fly from April. Lady Etna, Cascade, Ally's Shrimp, Bann Special, Silver Doctor, Curry's Red shrimp, Silver Rat, Hairy Mary, Blue Charm, the Badger and the Garry Dog are some of the favourite patterns – fished as small as a size 14, low water double in summer.

The brown trout fishing is largely ignored but good sport can be had with Blue Winged Olives and Sedges on summer evenings.

Season
(between Lough Melvin and the sea)
Salmon and seatrout: 1 January–30 September
Brown trout: 15 February–30 September

Permits
All of the left bank from Lough Melvin to Bundrowes Bridge and most of the right bank is owned by:

Shane Gallagher, The Lareen Estate and Fishery, Edenville, Kinlough, Co. Leitrim
Tel: 071 9841055, mobile: 087 8050806, email: shane@drowessalmonfishery.com
Web: www.drowessalmonfishery.com – very informative

Regulations
All legitimate methods
Minimum size: 11 inches (trout)

Accommodation
The River Cottage Guesthouse and eleven estate cottages. Tel: 071 9841055

Guides
Guides can be arranged through the Fishery office.

DROWES ESTUARY

The Drowes Estuary comprises the three pools downstream of the Bundrowes Bridge in Tullaghan, Co. Leitrim, down to the sea. It gets a good run of spring salmon from 1 January through to April/May with some summer and autumn salmon. The main grilse run starts around the end of May. This is a prolific little fishery since all salmon that run into the Melvin system pass through this section. It is controlled by a syndicate, which issues six permits per day, from 08.00–17.00 and from 18.00–22.00.

Season
Salmon and seatrout: 1 January–30 September

Permits
The Tackle Shop, Lareen Park, Kinlough, Co. Leitrim. Tel: 071 9841055

DUFF (OR BUNDUFF) RIVER   G 75 57

The Duff (or Bunduff) River flows for 14 miles from the Glenade valley to the sea. It is joined by the Ballanaghtrillick River, which runs out of the Horseshoe Pass. The bottom 3½ miles is most fished. This is a prolific little spate river for salmon. The Duff gets a good run of summer salmon and grilse. The fish start to enter the river at the end of May with the peak of the run in July/August. With good water levels it can fish through to the end of September. The Duff is a spate river that can fish very well given the right conditions, especially after a fresh. Most anglers choose the deep pool below the falls close to the sea and consequently this pool can become overcrowded. Once a flood has let fish run the falls, there is some good fishing available above the falls and also some good water upstream of the main road bridge. Anything between 300 and 500 salmon are caught in a season. The river is open from 08.00–21.00. All legitimate methods are allowed but spinning is prohibited in low water.

Season
1 February–30 September inclusive

Permits
There are two separate permits on the river:
• A permit for the right hand bank, from the main road bridge downstream to the sea and 850 yards upstream (same bank) can be purchased on the river bank.
Tel: 086 8135429.
• A permit for the section upstream of this and for the left hand bank from the main road bridge to the sea is available from Barrett's Tackle Shop, Main Street, Bundoran and from McGillan's Supermarket, Cliffoney, Co. Sligo, or from Eamon McSharry.
Tel: 086 8162144.

** ABBEY, RIVER   G 87 82

The Abbey River drains into the Erne Estuary west of Ballyshannon. It is a narrow, fast-flowing stream on which a lot of pools were destroyed by a drainage scheme. Some pools have recovered. It is overgrown and difficult to fish in places.

It still gets a run of seatrout, from ½–2½lb, and the best of the fishing is in July and August. It fishes best with worm after a flood and in a wet season and the best fishing is from Cavangarden House down to Crockacapal – a distance of about 3 miles. It also holds a fair stock of good brown trout and gets a late run of salmon in September. Flyfishing is also worthwhile and local anglers favour Hare's Ear, Blae & Black, Mallard & Claret, Butcher, Blue Dun and Alder, all fished wet.

Season
1 March–30 September

Permit
Riparian owners

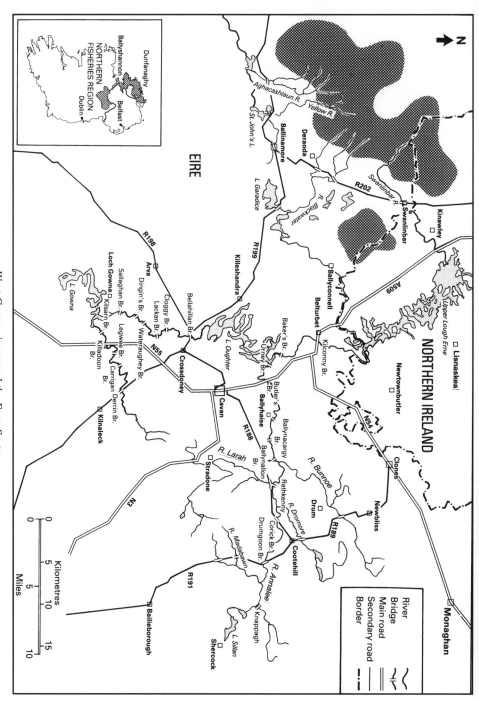

West Cavan rivers and the Erne System

** ERNE, RIVER (AND TRIBUTARIES)   G 93 60

The River Erne rises in Beaghy Lough, two miles south of Stradone in Co. Cavan, and flows 64 miles through Lough Gowna, Lough Oughter and Upper and Lower Lough Erne before meeting the sea at Ballyshannon. In doing so, it crosses the border twice, at Belturbet and again between Beleek and Ballyshannon. For 30 miles from Crossdoney in Co. Cavan to the town of Enniskillen, it is difficult to distinguish the river as it winds its way through a thousand interconnected loughs or parts of loughs nestling among the drumlin hills of Co. Cavan and south Fermanagh.

The Erne has seen many changes to its fish stocks in the last forty years, for it was once a noted salmon and trout river. The building of hydroelectric power stations at Cliff and Ballyshannon (work began in 1945 and the first power station was commissioned in 1950) caused the eight famous salmon beats from Belleek to Ballyshannon to be flooded. The once mighty run of salmon into the Erne has now declined to such a tiny trickle as to be of little angling value except for the few fish that are occasionally caught below Cliff when the power station is generating.

Roach first appeared in the river in 1963 and there was a massive increase in the roach population in 1968. This increase could well have had an adverse effect on trout stocks, which went into decline at that time. Water pollution became a major problem in the 1970s and up to 1987. Since 1987, the pollution problem has been well controlled, the roach population has declined dramatically and trout stocks have made a welcome return and provide exceptionally good angling once more, both on the Erne itself and its tributaries. The status of the salmon stock is dismal.

** ERNE (BALLYSHANNON) ESTUARY

The Erne Estuary at Ballyshannon is an important seatrout feeding ground, teeming with sprat, herring fry, crustacea and the other creatures that support a huge seatrout population and an important seatrout fishery. Fishing extends for two miles from the Mall Quay in Ballyshannon to the bar mouth. The season opens on 1 March but the fishing is best from May, through June and July and it can be very good in August. It is reported to produce well over 2,000 seatrout in a season.

The seatrout range from 1–3lb, though a 32½lb seatrout was reportedly taken in a draft net in the late 1940s. The best of the fishing is for two hours either side of low water, except at Finner Banks and Ramsey Hole at the Old Castle, where one can fish profitably all the time. Anglers have been known to take up to 60 seatrout in a day here. The trout can be taken off the strand, spinning Stucki spoons, Tobys or Mepps. Some prefer to fish the fly and Rogan's Gadget, the Needle Eye, Teal, Blue & Silver, Gosling and Daddy are all used.

There is also good night fishing in summer in the vicinity of the Mall Quay and Stamer Island. Access is at the Mall Quay and there is a path and public access off the Bundoran road near Stamer House.

Fishing from a drifting boat has become popular in recent times. This tactic works well in dull windy conditions but, on brighter days, it is often better to beach the boat and stalk the fish on foot.

Access is at Bundoran road on the south side, Abbey Road, on the north side, at the Mall Quay, Port na Mona, or make the long walk across Tullahan Strand from Bundoran at low water.

Season
Salmon, seatrout and brown trout: 1 March–30 September

Licence
A Special Local Licence is required and anglers with an annual salmon licence can get an extension to that licence for a small fee. A separate permit is not required to fish the estuary.

Licence outlet
The Northern Regional Fisheries Board Office, Station Road, Ballyshannon, Co. Donegal. Tel: 071 9851435
Barrett's Tackle Shop, Main Street, Bundoran, Co. Donegal

Guide and boat hire
Patrick O'Malley, Ernedale Heights, Ballyshannon, Bundoran, Co. Donegal.
Tel: 086 0877137

** ERNE SALMON FISHING

Salmon lie below the power station at Cliff in a stretch of water about a quarter mile long and 100 yards wide. The best fishing is when the station is generating from July through to September and there is a great run of big late-running fish. It is sad to see these hatchery reared fish wallowing about with no place to go. I am reminded of Hugh Falkus The salmon's greatest enemy is man. Access is off the Knather Road from Ballyshannon to Belleek.

ERNE (BELTURBET)

Belturbet TAC has carried out extensive improvements to the river and has three-quarters of a mile of good trout fishing from Kilconny Bridge upstream to the Railway Bridge. The fishing is mainly for wild trout and, over the years, the fishery has built a reputation sufficient to attract return visits from overseas anglers. It is flyfishing only. There are other stretches that hold trout up river at Cornadara, Pogue's Ford and Baker's Bridge between Butlersbridge and Belturbet. The distance between the two towns is about 6 miles and the river is big and wide. The flyfishing does not commence till the water drops and, when it does, this is a stretch of water well worth exploring because it holds an excellent stock of trout. The fishing is with the permission of the riparian owners. The same applies to the stretch downstream of the bridge in Belturbet, where there is also some great fishing in summer with access from both banks.

The river here does not have a mayfly hatch, but it still has a fair hatch of sedges – locally known as the 'Wall Fly' – black gnats, and various olives and midges. Dry fly fishing can be good when the trout are up. The hatch can be sparse at times, when wet-fly and nymph tactics can produce excellent sport.

The local club strongly encourages anglers to practice catch-and-release.

Permits
Railway Bar, The Diamond, Belturbet, Co. Cavan
Robert Morrow, Secretary, Belturbet Angling Club, Ricehill, Crossdoney, Co. Cavan
Tel: 087 2424265

Local tackle shop
McMahon Supply Stores, The Lawn, Belturbet, Co. Cavan

Flycasting instructor and guide
Liam Duffy, APGAI-IRL, FFF, MCI, THCI, Portaliffe, Killeshandra, Co.Cavan
Tel: 049 4334731

ERNE, MIDDLE

By the Middle Erne I mean that part of the river between Sallaghan Bridge, near Loch Gowna, and Bellahillan Bridge, near Crossdoney. This part of the river presently holds a lot of undiscovered riches for the trout fisher. Trout stocks have made a marvellous recovery here and good numbers of fish to over 4lb are to be found in this eight-mile stretch.

The best of the fishing is with wet-fly from April to June. The water drops and is clouded with algae from the loughs in summer, but September fishing can be fair. The river flows through farmland and is completely undeveloped for anglers. Much of it is overgrown and quite difficult to fish. In some instances, the river banks have been fenced off very securely under the R.E.P.S. (Rural Environment Protection Scheme) making access and progress along the banks extremely difficult.

Permission
All the fishing on this part of the Erne is with the permission of the riparian owners.

ERNE, UPPER (RIVER ERNE ANGLERS' CLUB)

The Club fishes most of the headwaters from Lough Gowna upstream. The limits of the club water are from Drumcassidy Bridge near Kilnaleck to Kilsaran Bridge near the village of Gowna, a distance of about 12 miles.

The river holds a good healthy stock of trout with plenty of small fish and good numbers to 2lb and better. This is a natural river with plenty of interesting water, except the stretch between Derrin Bridge and Carrigan Bridge which was drained some years ago. Remedial work has been carried out on this stretch and it has recovered well.

The best of the fishing is early in the season before the weed grows although there is dry-fly fishing in the pools all summer. The main hatches are olives, especially large dark olives, sedges, hawthorn and lots of black gnats.

Permits
Gerry McGauran, Bruskey, Ballinagh, Co. Cavan. Tel: 049 4337198

Local tackle shops
Florence Kinkade, Cornagran, Gowna, Co. Cavan
Sports World, 79 Main Street, Cavan, Co. Cavan
Eamon Donohoe, Dublin Road, Cavan

Taxidermist
Gerry McGauran (previous page)

ANNALEE, RIVER   H 45 12

The Annalee River rises near Lough Egish in Co. Monaghan and flows via Cootehill, Ballyhaise and through Butlersbridge to join the River Erne at Urney. It is 42 miles long. It was along its banks at Lurganboy that I first learned to fish. It was then an exceptionally good trout river and I'm glad to record that after years in decline, due to the introduction of roach and pollution, the trout are back and in most stretches, they are as good as ever.

The river can be divided into two parts. Upstream of Cootehill the river is relatively small, the fly life and the trout have recovered and the river holds some nice trout from Knappagh Bridge downstream past Annsfort Bridge and on to Scarvey Bridge.

The second part, from Cootehill to Butlersbridge, has recovered well. There are big trout at Deredis, some nice stocks of trout at Butlersbridge, and big numbers of small trout and plenty of good trout in the middle reaches, with fair stocks up nearly to Cootehill. The roach have virtually disappeared and fly hatches are good with a fair hatch of Mayfly in places. Local angling clubs have carried out a lot of bank development work in the vicinity of Ballyhaise and Bunnoe in Co. Cavan.

Access is generally good at the bridges, in the Deredis and Butlersbridge areas, at Ballyhaise and Ballynacargy Bridge which is generally regarded as the beginning of the Cavan water.

Season
1 March–30 September

Permits
Cavan Anglers' Club stretch, Donohoe's Bar, Ballyhaise, Co. Cavan
Hon. Secretary, Francis McNally, Cullies, Cavan., Tel: 087 2374503

Some sections require the permission of riparian owners.

Regulations
Flyfishing only
Observe individual club bag limits
Catch-and-release is encouraged

Tackle shops
CJ's Tackle, Bridge Street, Cootehill, Co. Cavan
Eamon Donohoe, Fishing Tackle, Dublin Road, Cavan
Brian Webber, Sports World, Town Hall Street, Cavan

Local flytyer
Patsy Deery, 9 Griffith Park, Cootehill, Co. Cavan. Tel: 049 5552588

LARAGH, RIVER   H 51 04

The Laragh River flows down from Cliffeerna to join the Annalee River at Rathkenny. The fishing is managed by the very progressive Laragh Angling Club which monitors pollution, stocks the river and has had the banks developed through a social employment scheme. There are excellent stocks of trout up to 3lb and good hatches of olives, sedges, black gnats and even some mayfly. The best fishing is in spring, as it tends to run low in summer. In all, there is about five miles of fishing and it isn't heavily fished. Access is good, with stiles in place and it is best approached off the Stradone-Cootehill road. Some of the best stretches are around McShane's Bridge and downstream of Doughty's Bridge.

Season
1 March–30 September

Permits
Edward Kelly, Stragelliff, Cavan. Tel: 049 4331540
Brady's Bar, The Cross, Stradone, Co. Cavan
Kieran Brady, Laragh House, Stradone, Co. Cavan
Philim Donohoe, Cliffeerna, Stradone, Co. Cavan. Tel: 049 4330177

Regulations
Bag Limit: 6 trout, but catch-and-release is encouraged
Minimum size: 10 inches

Tackle shops
CJ's Tackle, Bridge Street, Cootehill, Co. Cavan
Brian Webber, Sports World, Town Hall Street, Cavan
Eamon Donohoe, Fishing Tackle, Dublin Road, Cavan

Local flytyer
Patsy Deery, 9 Griffith Park, Cootehill, Co. Cavan. Tel: 049 5552588

BUNNOE, RIVER   H 51 13

The fishing is reserved for members of Bunnoe Angling Club. There are no day permits available. Part of it is fly-only and it holds a good stock of trout.

DROMORE, RIVER   H 57 13

The Dromore River rises near Ballybay and drains a series of over twenty lakes into the Annalee, at Killycreeny, near Tullyvin on the Cavan-Cootehill road. The last four miles of it are of interest to the trout angler. For long it has been regarded as a coarse/pike fishery but is now being discovered by trout anglers and it holds plenty of trout. Access is difficult and parts of it are virtually inaccessible. Some of the best fishing stretches are at Killycreeny, above and below Ashfield, and at Abbott's Factory on the Cootehill-Monaghan road.

Season
1 March–30 September

Permission
Riparian owners

Local tackle shop
As for Bunnoe River

Local flytyer
Patsy Deery, 9 Griffith Park, Cootehill, Co. Cavan. Tel: 049 5552588

KNAPPAGH WATER   H 68 10

The Knappagh Water is the headwater of the Annalee River. It rises in Lough Egish in Co. Monaghan and flows through Shantonagh, Bawn and the Senator Billy Fox Memorial Park to join the Tacker Water and become the Annalee River. It flows through a series of lakes and the best of the trout fishing is between Bellatrain and Corlat Lake, at the Memorial Park and the two mile stretch from Derragooney Lake down to the confluence. Like a lot of the other Annalee tributaries, it holds very fast-growing trout and some really fine ones have been taken in recent years.

Season
1 March–30 September
Permission
Patrick Boyle, Lacken, Latton Post Office, Co. Monaghan. Tel: 042 9669757

Local tackle shop
Joe Mulligan, Shercock, Co. Cavan

WOODFORD, RIVER   H 27 18

The Woodford River has been developed as a navigable canal, joining the Shannon and the Erne systems.

Trout are now confined to one stretch of about 500 yards, downstream of Ballyconnell, where there is a piece of flowing water. There is public access along one side.

The Sand Hole at Eye of the Bridge pool on the river Crana (see page 58)

Season
1 March–30 September

Flycasting instructor
Liam Duffy, APGAI-IRL, FFF, MCI, THCI, Portaliffe, Killeshandra, Co.Cavan
Tel: 049 4334731, mobile: 086 3647714, email: liamjduffy@hotmail.com

BLACKWATER, RIVER (WEST CAVAN)   H 20 15

This little river drains Benbrack Mountain and a number of loughs into Ballymagauran Lough. It is undeveloped but holds good stocks of trout to 1½lb. It is worth investigating upstream and downstream of Ballymagirril Bridge, as also is the stream that comes down from Derradda.

Season
1 March–30 September

Permission
Riparian owners

YELLOW, RIVER   H 09 12

A small fast-flowing mountain river that drains into St. John's Lake, west of Ballinamore. The river banks are very high in places. It holds fair stocks of half pound trout up to Pollanass Falls, or rather to where the falls once were, because they were swept away in a flood in the mid-1990s.

AGHACASHLAUN, RIVER   H 03 10

The Aghacashlaun River flows down from Slieve Anierin into Lough Scur, mid-way between Ballinamore and Drumshanbo. It is very overgrown but is reported to hold fair stocks of trout to 1¼lb and has some very nice fishing water. Access is mainly from the bridges and there are four road bridges over the last three miles of the river.

Season
1 March–30 September

Permission
Riparian owners

SWANLINBAR, RIVER   H 20 27

This is a spate river, flowing down from the Cuilcagh Mountains of west Cavan. It flows through Swanlinbar and thence across the border into Northern Ireland and into upper Lough Erne. It is a spawning river for lake trout but is also reported to hold occasional brown trout to 2½lb. It is worth fishing from the border up for one mile above Swanlinbar. From the border to the lough, it has been severely drained and is very featureless and unlikely to hold trout.

Permission
Riparian owners

FINN, RIVER (CLONES)   H 50 24

The Finn River rises in West Tyrone/North Fermanagh and flows south across the border into Co. Monaghan and then south west to Lough Erne.

As a trout fishery, it can be summed up in two sentences. Firstly, it was once one of the finest brown trout rivers in the province of Ulster. Secondly, chronic outbreaks of point pollution have left it not worth fishing. If it recovers, fish it at Cummer Bridge, at Scarvey Bridge, on to Creevelea Bridge and to Stonebridge and upstream, where there is some lovely water. Its tributary, the Magnerarny, is a lovely trout stream in its lower reaches. It too has its pollution problems.

Local angling club
Clones Angling Club, Jim Hughes, Hon. Secretary, 32 Beechgrove, Clones,
Co. Monaghan

Flycasting instructor
Liam Duffy, APGAI-IRL, FFF, MCI, THCI, Portaliffe, Killeshandra, Co. Cavan.
Tel: 049 43373, mobile: 086 3647714, email: liamjduffy@hotmail.com

4. North-Western Fisheries Region

The North-Western Fisheries Region stretches from Mullaghmore Point in Co. Sligo to Pidgeon Point near Westport, Co. Mayo. It covers part of Counties Leitrim, Sligo, Roscommon and all of north and west Mayo.

This was a region noted for both the quality and quantity of its game fishing resource. Salmon and seatrout predominated to such an extent that the river brown trout fishing was all but forgotten. This is a mistake on the part of anglers for I have found the brown trout fishing as good here as anywhere else in Ireland. However, the pressures created by modern farming practices, industrial development, etc., have taken their toll. Notwithstanding all this, the River Moy is still the primary salmon river in the region; its estuary provides some superb seatrout fishing and some of its tributaries hold good stocks of brown trout. This is the region that inspired W. H. Maxwell's famous book Wild Sports of the West. Anyone who has ever fished the hauntingly beautiful rivers around Ballycroy and Bangor Erris, or the Easkey in south Co. Sligo, will understand the spell this lovely area can cast, drawing the fisher back to visit time and again.

Ballina, on the Moy, was proclaimed the salmon capital of Ireland in 2008. The river Moy is estimated to have produced an average of more than eight thousand salmon to the rod over the last five years.

The Moy Estuary at Ballina is now regarded as a prime seatrout angling location and Carrowmore Lake – also in this region – is one of the finest spring salmon flyfisheries in the country.

For further information about this region, contact:

North-Western Regional Fisheries Board, Ardnaree House, Abbey Street, Ballina, Co. Mayo. Tel: 096 22788, fax: 096 70543, email: info@nwrfb.com
Web: www.northwestfisheries.ie

Note: Rivers marked ** are – at the time of writing – closed for salmon fishing, and the rivers marked * are catch-and-release for salmon and seatrout over 40cm (this is a measure to conserve the larger breeding fish).

For up-to-date information on these closed and catch-and-release rivers see:
www.cfb.ie (then click on 'Salmon and Sea Trout Fishing in Ireland', then click '2009 Salmon Angling Regulations'). Alternatively, try **www.fishinginireland.info**

** GRANGE, RIVER   G 65 49

The Grange River is a small spate system that drains the northern slopes of Benbulbin and its hinterland through the village of Grange in north Sligo to the sea. The river itself is not worth fishing. However, there is very good seatrout fishing in the estuary, which is extensive and local knowledge is required to get on to the good marks.

Permission
Check with riparian owners

Licence
State salmon and seatrout licence

Season
Salmon: 1 February–30 September
Seatrout: 1 February–30 September
Brown trout: 15 February–30 September

Tackle shops
Barton Smith, Hyde Bridge, Sligo. Tel: 071 9142356, fax: 071 9144196
Doherty's House of Value, Wine Street, Sligo. Tel: 071 9171900
Kingfisher Baits, Pier Road, Enniscrone, Co. Sligo. Tel: 096 36733

DRUMCLIFFE, RIVER   G 68 42

The Drumcliffe River is just over four miles long and drains Glencar Lake and a 26 sq.-mile catchment into Drumcliffe Bay, in Co. Sligo. The character of the banks and river varies greatly along its length. It is partly open and can be fished with fly but in places is quite overgrown. The river itself has some nice streamy pools and a lot of deep, heavy water. Access is at the bridges.

This river gets a small run of spring salmon in January and February and the grilse run in June, July and August. Most are taken either by spinning or on worm. A bye-law prohibits the use of any lure other than artificial fly, for any kind of fish, in the section of river downstream of Drumcliffe Bridge.

The river gets a good run of seatrout averaging 12oz. Fresh trout are reported to run in every month of the season, with some to 3lb.

Season
Salmon: 1 February–30 September
Seatrout: 1 February–12 October
Brown trout: 15 February–12 October

Permits
For information on permits contact:
Sligo Anglers' Association. Tel: 071 9168404

Guide
Ken Henry, Claddagh, Glebe, Dromahair, Co. Leitrim. Tel: 071 9134971
Mobile: 086 8182723, email: henry.ken@itsligo.ie, web: www.pagi.org

* GARAVOGUE, RIVER   G 69 36

The Garavogue River is about 3½ miles long. It drains Lough Gill and its tributaries through the town of Sligo, with a total catchment of 140 sq. miles and carries a huge volume of water in spring. It gets a run of spring salmon and the grilse fishing can be good in June and July. Salmon, seatrout and brown trout can be taken from the Silver Swan Hotel up to Bective. The best of the seatrout fishing is downstream of Hyde (formerly Victoria) Bridge at a location known as the Back River where night fishing can be very productive from June through to August.

Season
Brown Trout: 15 February–30 September
Salmon and Seatrout: 1 January–30 September, 1 February–30 September below 'The Lodge'

Regulations
Catch-and-release until 11 May at the time of writing

Permission
Public fishing

Garavogue rod catch 2003-2008

Year	2003	2004	2005	2006	2007	2008
Salmon	47	31	32	10	N/A	9

* BONET, RIVER   G 80 31

The River Bonet is 28 miles long and rises in Glenade Lough in north Leitrim. It meanders south past Manorhamilton and the ancient village of Dromahair before entering Lough Gill. It can give fair salmon fishing in spring, summer and autumn. It also holds very good stocks of brown trout in certain well-defined areas.

The Office of Public Works completed a drainage scheme in the late 1980s. Since the completion of the drainage works, the water tends to run off very quickly.

The fishing on this river is quite fragmented.

* Subject to catch-and-release till 11 May at the time of writing.

Clooneen Anglers' Club Water
This comprises about seven miles of single and double bank fishing, extending from a mile below Glenade Lough to just below Gortgarrigan Bridge. This fishery holds spring salmon from mid-March and the grilse start running in late June or early July. The fishing can be very good in July and every flood thereafter brings more fish up from Lough Gill, with the result that fishing can be very good in September if water conditions are right.

Access to the fishery is good and stiles and footbridges have been erected by the North-Western Regional Fisheries Board.

The best flies are said to be Silver Doctor, Hairy Mary, Green Peter and Jock Scott. A copper and silver spoon and a copper Toby do well, as does a bunch of worms.

There is some good brown trout fishing on this stretch with trout to a pound from Glenade downstream to Gortinar. The banks are overgrown.

There are very good stocks of trout to 1½lb from Lurganboy for 2½ miles downstream to a Land Commission bridge below the confluence of the Shanvaus River. There are good stocks of trout to 12oz in the Owenmore River up to Manorhamilton. Daisy's Ford provides about 400 yards of good trout fishing.

Fly Hatches
The peak of the brown trout fishing is from late April to mid-June and in late August and September. There are hatches of large dark olives, medium olives and a good Mayfly hatch in some areas. There are big numbers of blue-winged olives and sedges (small red and brown) are very important.

Permits
I am advised that the situation is unclear at the time of writing. It is best to contact the North-Western Regional Fisheries Board for latest information:

North-Western Regional Fisheries Board, Ardnaree House, Abbey Street, Ballina Co. Mayo. Tel: 096 22788, fax: 096 70543, email: info@nwrfb.com
Web: www.northwestfisheries.ie

Dromahair Lodge Fishing
Dromahair Lodge has about nine miles of fishing stretching down to Dromahair. The salmon fishing season is as for the Manorhamilton water above with, perhaps, even better spring salmon fishing in March-April.

There are good trout stocks from Gortgarrigan to Drumlease Glebe. Many of the shallows in this area are newly-exposed and the fishing will improve as time goes on.

There is an arrangement whereby local anglers are allowed to fish this water. Otherwise the fishing is reserved and free to residents staying at:

Dromahair Lodge and Breffni Holiday Cottages, Dromahair, Co. Leitrim
Tel: 071 9164103, email: booking@breffnicottages.com
Web: www.breffnicottages.com

Stanford's Inn
Stanford's Inn, Dromahair, has three-quarters-of-a-mile of double-bank fishing, with three good pools. There is good spring salmon fishing in April and June-July sees the peak of the grilse fishing. This is some of the best fishing on the river. Worm, fly and spinning are allowed.

Permits
Thomas McGowan, Stanford's Inn, Dromahair, Co. Leitrim. Tel: 071 9164140

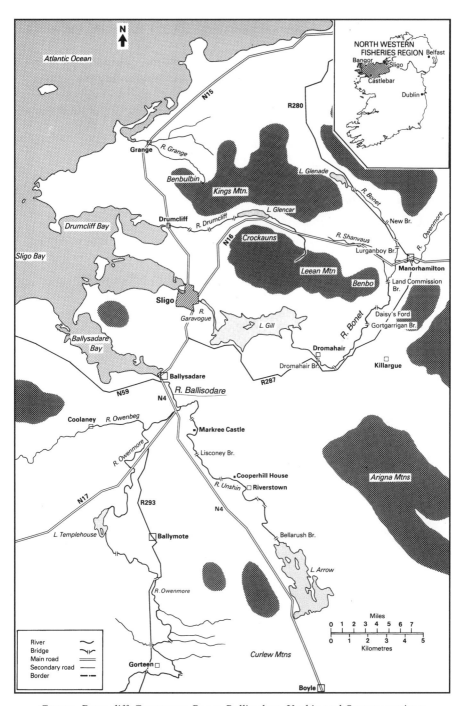

Grange, Drumcliff, Garavogue, Bonet, Ballisodare, Unshin and Owenmore rivers

Dromahair Anglers' Association

Dromahair Anglers' Association controls a stretch at Glebe House. Permits are available from:

Gilmor's Shop, Dromahair, the Blue Devon Pub, Dromahair, Co. Leitrim.
Tel: 071 9164118.

Syndicate Water

There is 1½ miles of syndicate water downstream of Dromahair.

Season

Salmon and seatrout: 1 February–30 September
Brown trout: 15 February–30 September

Regulations

Catch-and-release only for salmon and seatrout until 11 May at the time of writing.

Guide

Ken Henry, Claddagh, Glebe, Dromahair, Co. Leitrim. Tel: 071 9134971
mobile: 086 8182723, email: henry.ken@itsligo.ie, web: www.pagi.org

River Bonet rod catch 2003-2008

Year	2003	2004	2005	2006	2007	2008
Salmon	57	104	24	51	N/A	34

BALLISODARE, RIVER   G 67 29

The Ballisodare River is just five miles long and flows down from Collooney into Ballisodare Bay. With its tributaries, the Unshin River, the Owenmore River and the Owenbeg River, it drains a catchment of 252 sq. miles, which includes Lough Arrow and Templehouse Lake.

The fishing rights for the migratory fish in the system were vested by an act of parliament in the Cooper family of Markree Castle in 1837. This gives the present fishery owners (Ballisodare Fishing Club Ltd) the salmon fishing rights on the whole river including the tributaries. The Coopers then built fish passes at the impassable Ballisodare Falls and introduced salmon to the system. Most of the fishing action takes place in the tidal pools below the 'Butt' of the Falls.

There is a small run of spring salmon from April. June-July sees the peak of the big grilse run and it has been discovered recently that there is very good seatrout fishing in the estuary on the rising tide.

The river above the main road bridge is wide, shallow and overgrown, with some nice pools up as far as Collooney Bridge. This is the best of the salmon fishing above the falls and it holds spring fish as well as grilse. There are good stocks of brown trout averaging 12oz with some to 3lb. One of 6lb was taken in 2001. It has a mayfly hatch. The trout fishing starts in April and the best of it is in May and June. Brown trout fishing can be had with the permission of the riparian owners.

Season
Salmon and seatrout: 1 March–30 September
Brown trout: 15 February–30 September

Permits
Dermot Glennon, Secretary, Ballisodare Fishing Club Ltd, Ballisodare, Co. Sligo
Tel: 071 9130513, mobile: 086 6103423

Guide
Ken Henry, Claddagh, Glebe, Dromahair, Co. Leitrim. Tel: 071 9134971
mobile: 086 8182723, email: henry.ken@itsligo.ie, web: www.pagi.org

Local tackle shop
Barton-Smith Ltd, Hyde Bridge, Sligo. Tel: 071 9146111

UNSHIN, RIVER   G 70 26

The Unshin is a limestone river which drains Lough Arrow and flows north for 15
miles to join the Ballisodare River at Collooney. There is good brown trout fishing, in
parts, all the way up to Lough Arrow. It is very overgrown with a lot of deep water.
Down at Markree Castle the banks are more open and it holds good stocks of trout
from ¾–2lb and two 5lb brown trout were taken in 2001. The best of the fishing is from
the end of April to mid-June, after which it becomes very weeded. There is a prolonged
mayfly hatch and the 'spent gnat' fishing is especially good in the month of May. This
river used to be a treasure but it has been heavily fished in recent years and too many
trout have been killed. Please put your trout back.

Season
15 February–30 September

Permits
With permission of riparian owners

Guides
Ken Henry, Claddagh, Glebe, Dromahair, Co. Leitrim. Tel: 071 9134971
Mobile: 086 8182723, email: henry.ken@itsligo.ie, web: www.pagi.org

OWENMORE, RIVER   G 65 22

The Owenmore River rises near Gorteen in south Co. Sligo and flows through
Templehouse Lake to join the Ballisodare River at Collooney. The trout fishing is
fragmented – interspersed with deep pike water – but the good stretches are very
good. It holds small trout and the banks are clear downstream of the confluence of
the Owenbeg River. There is also a fair stock of trout in a two-mile stretch upstream
of the bridge near Ardkeeran on the R293 Ballymote-Gorteen road. Further up-river
at Moydoo near Greyfield, there is a good stock of trout to a pound and some even to
3lb.

Season
15 February–30 September

Permission
Riparian owners for brown trout

EASKEY, RIVER   G 38 38

The Easkey is primarily a spate salmon river and gets an excellent run of grilse and summer salmon. It is 18 miles long and drains a 41 sq. mile catchment which includes Easkey Lough and the northern slopes of the Ox Mountains. Downstream from the Workhouse Bridge on the N59 Sligo-Ballina road, the river flows through woodland with nice gravel pools and a few, deep, limestone gorges. Upstream of the bridge, the character of the river changes and here it flows through moorland with occasional streams, pools and deep stretches. On a spate, it can be fished up as far as Grants Griddle. Access is good, with roads all along the right bank.

The grilse start running in late June and a prolific run of fish enters the river on every flood to the end of September. It gets a nice run of seatrout in July and August.

The Fortland Fishery – Easkey River
The Fortland Fishery is now the pre-eminent fishery on the river and one of the most picturesque and productive little spate rivers in the north west. The estate and river was purchased by David Cahill in a derelict state in 1999. Following a year of hard work including bankside clearance, refurbishment of roads and bridges and intensive fishery protection, it opened for business in June 2000. The inaugural season was a tremendous success, with many anglers visiting the fishery for the first time and others who knew it in the bad times coming back to admire the transformation. They were not disappointed, for the salmon and seatrout were still there in the kind of numbers one would expect.

The Fortland Fishery consists of three miles of double bank and ¾ mile of single bank fishing with 26 named pools. It is divided into four beats, with a maximum of 16 rods. It has nice fly water. Favourite local patterns include Easkey Gold Shrimp, Bann Special Shrimp, Claret Tailed Bann Special, Wilkinson Shrimp and Collie Dog. To get the best out of the river, it is necessary to wade and this can be a little tricky in places. A wading staff is essential and a life jacket is advised.

Fortland Fishery rod catch 2002–2008

Year	2002	2003	2004	2005	2006	2007	2008
Salmon	347	234	426	256	332	398	353
Seatrout	135	60	71	104	79	107	188

Season
Salmon: February–30 September
Seatrout: 1 February–10 October

Permission

The river is divided in three parts:

From the bridge in Easkey village to the sea is regarded as free fishing.

The Fortland Fishery extends for 3¾ miles from above the bridge in Easkey almost to the Workhouse Bridge.

The fishing upstream of the Workhouse Bridge is strictly controlled and with the permission of the riparian owners.

Permits

Granville Nesbitt, Manager, The Fortland Fishery, Easkey, Co. Sligo. Tel: 086 8032350 Email: info@anglingwestireland.com,web: www.anglingwestireland.com

Guides

Ken Henry, Claddagh, Glebe, Dromahair, Co. Leitrim. Tel: 071 9134971 Mobile: 086 8182723, email: henry.ken@itsligo.ie, web: www.pagi.org Willie McAndrew, 23 Marian Row, Castlebar, Co. Mayo. Tel: 094 9021028 Email: wmcandrew@anu.ie

Lodge

The Ice House and the Gate Lodge, situated on the Fortland Estate. Enquiries to Granville Nesbitt (see above).

Local flytyer

Michael Roulston, Bridge Cottage, Easkey, Co. Sligo. Tel: 096 49445

Resident gillies

Available on request

MOY, RIVER   G 24 18

The Moy is one of the most prolific salmon rivers in the country. It would be impossible to obtain exact figures for rod catches, but the following table of reported rod-caught fish, compiled by the North-Western Regional Fisheries Board, gives some idea of how many fish the river produces.

Estimated total River Moy rod catch 2001–2008

Year	2001	2002	2003	2004	2005	2006	2007	2008
Salmon	6864	6984	5907	9420	8031	9745	8997	7392
Seatrout (Moy Estuary)	N/A	N/A	N/A	c.3000	N/A	N/A	1526	2527

The main channel is 62 miles long and enters the sea at Ballina. With its tributaries, the River Moy drains a catchment of 806 sq. miles, stretching from the Ox Mountains, in the east, to Castlebar, in the south and Loughs Conn, Cullin and the Nephin Beg range of mountains in north Mayo.

The draft nets and the fish traps in Ballina were abolished in the mid-1990s. The old fish traps in Ballina (known locally as 'the Boxes') are a noted landmark for anglers on the Moy. A major arterial drainage scheme was carried out on the river between

1960 and 1970. The drainage works had a devastating effect on the natural character of the river and most of the famous old pools and famous fishing sites were destroyed. It is remarkable that these drainage works did not have a long-term detrimental effect on the potential of the river to produce salmon. Regrettably, however, while the fishing has remained good, the surroundings are aesthetically less pleasing. The banks are high and difficult, much of the river is wide, canal-like and featureless and the natural pool/stream sequence is missing. Major rehabilitation work has been carried out on many of the pools and streams in recent years and has greatly enhanced the fishing. In spite of past vandalism to the river, the Moy still holds large numbers of salmon and gives joy to thousands of anglers every season.

It is said that fresh salmon run the Moy every month of the year. Certainly, if conditions are right – mild weather and the water not too high – salmon can be taken from opening day, 1 February, at Ballina (behind the now-disused fish traps), the Clydagh River and the Manulla (Ballyvary) River. The Pontoon Bridge fishery is closed until 1 June. If conditions are not suitable at first, the fishing picks up as soon as they improve. A run of small spring fish, locally known as 'black backs' used to run in early April and the peak of the spring fishing was from mid-April to mid-May. However, in recent years, the runs are one month later and now the grilse begin running in early June with the peak of the run being from the end of June to early August.

Low water tends to prevent fish from running past the traps in Ballina in summer with the result that there is a huge build-up of fish in the tidal beats in Ballina. The first good flood in late August or September brings more fish up-river and can give excellent back-end fishing with plenty of fish of 7lb-9lb.

The average weight of the spring fish is 9lb, but a fish of 38lb – the best in recent times – was taken in 1983. The grilse range from 1½–6lb and the seatrout average ¾lb.

Popular artificial baits include the Stucki spoon, Swinford spoon, Devons and the Flying 'C'.

Most of the fisheries have stretches suitable for flyfishing. A wide range of flies are used, including some local patterns and are freely available in local tackle shops.

The seatrout fishing is mainly confined to the estuary where it can be very good from April to September. P.J. McNally and Willie McAndrew, of Castlebar, together with this writer, successfully pioneered flyfishing for seatrout from a drifting boat in the estuary in September 1994. Up-river, there is limited night fishing in July in the vicinity of Foxford.

THE MOY FISHERIES

1. MOY ESTUARY

The Moy Estuary is a rich seatrout feeding ground. It teems with sandeel, herring fry, sprat and crustaceans and the seatrout grow rapidly on this rich feeding.

Two spring salmon from the Moy

Seatrout angling in this area dates back some forty to fifty years, with local anglers mainly bait fishing in saltwater for these fish. The popularity of this pursuit waned somewhat from the 1960s onwards and, for many years, only a few anglers pursued this quarry, generally with sandeel and mackerel strip ledgered on light tackle. In the last few years, however, the popularity of saltwater flyfishing for seatrout in the Moy Estuary has increased, mainly due to the ingenuity and passion of local angler and guide, Judd Ruane.

Seatrout of half-a-pound to 4lb are now regularly caught on fly. These fish are in prime condition and are well-known for their superb fighting ability. Bait fishing is still the preferred method under certain conditions, eg. when the water is carrying a little colour. However, the excitement of catching these fish on flyfishing tackle means that this method is becoming more popular.

There are distinct feeding areas which fish best during particular tidal conditions. There are also sandbars and reefs which could prove extremely hazardous. For these reasons, it is strongly recommended that anglers that are new to the Moy Estuary hire an experienced gillie. Areas to concentrate on are the back of Enniscrone beach, the north east shore of Bartra Island, the Walls, the Castle and Rosserk Bay.

Season
17 April–10 October

Regulations
A state licence is required in order to fish for seatrout.
Minimum size: 10 inches
Bag limit: 6 trout

Guide and boat hire
Judd Ruane, 11 Riverside Grove, The Quay Road, Ballina, Co. Mayo. Tel: 096 22183
Email: juddruane@eircom.net

2. MOY FISHERY

The Moy Fishery is owned by the State and managed by the North-Western Regional Fisheries Board. It is the country's premier state-owned fishery and is divided into seven beats, all located in the town of Ballina. Most of it is tidal and fishing may be disrupted for a time by high tide.

Ridge Pool
The most famous Moy Fishery beat is, undoubtedly, the Ridge Pool. Situated at the head of the tidal waters, it is extremely productive and attracts huge interest from the angling fraternity. During peak season, it is fished on a two session per day basis with the first session from sunrise to 14.00 and the second from 14.00 to sunset. Five rotating rods per session are allowed and these must rotate and move constantly along the beat.

In addition to the five rotating rods, an extra space has been added to the Ridge Pool, since the suspension of the salmon trapping at the weir in 1999. This additional 'Weir Pool' rod is fished separately from the rest of the Ridge Pool and can only be booked two days in advance. This single rod operates, however, on the same two session basis.

The Ridge Pool is something that every salmon angler should experience at least once. In good water, it carries the fly beautifully and the fish take freely. It doesn't fish in high water except, maybe, to spinner and worm. However, when the water reaches about 4 inches on the fly-only rock, it will fish the fly on a sinking or sink tip line. Favourite flies at this stage are a Yellow Ally's Shrimp, or a Cascade. As the water drops, a floating line comes into its own and favourite flies include the above-mentioned plus a Thunder Flash, Flame Thrower, Silver Stoat, Goshawk and many others, in sizes ranging 8-14, depending on the water.

In low water, a mini tube skated on the surface can produce excellent results on both the Ridge Pool and The Cathedral Beat.

Ridge Pool rod catch 2001–2008

Year	2001	2002	2003	2004	2005	2006	2007	2008
Salmon	1136	338	1531	839	958	1351	241	469

Season
1 February–30 September

Guide
There are resident guides on the beat.

Cathedral Beat

The Cathedral Beat, immediately downstream of the Ridge Pool, has also become a prolific salmon rod fishery since development works were carried out in 1995. It can accommodate eight anglers per session, provides excellent fly water and has produced over 1,500 salmon in its best season. This beat is also in great demand and booked anglers may commence fishing at sunrise and continue until 18.00, after which time the angling is reserved for locals. A gillie, appointed by the Moy Fishery, is in attendance on this beat to register and advise all booked anglers.

This beat comes in to its own in June when the grilse start running. Experienced anglers on the beat believe that a sinking or sink-tip line is generally the most productive, except in very low summer water.

Season
17 April–30 September

Cathedral Beat rod catch 2001–2008

Year	2001	2002	2003	2004	2005	2006	2007	2008
Salmon	869	273	975	418	546	983	95	225

Beats 1 and 2: 'Polnamonagh' and 'Spring Wells'

These beats are located about 200m downstream of the Lower Bridge in Ballina. Both beats can be very productive. Polnamonagh is deep and slow, making it more suitable for spinning and worming, while Spring Wells consists mostly of shallower water, which is ideal for flyfishing. Although less heavily fished than the Ridge or Cathedral, these beats also require advanced booking and may appeal more to the angler who prefers fishing away from public view. These beats operate on a single session basis, fished from sunrise to sunset. They can accommodate up to eight rods per session.

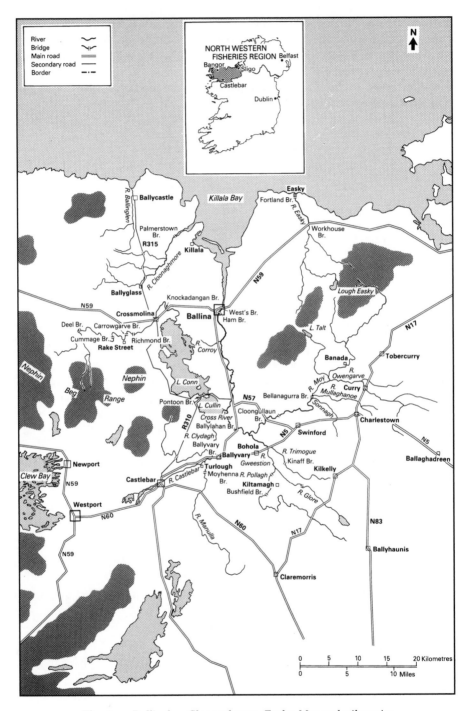

The rivers Ballinglen, Cloonaghmore, Easky, Moy and tributaries

Ash Tree Pool
The Ash Tree Pool is a lovely, tree-lined beat located alongside the town park. It is a haven for the angler who wishes to fish in peaceful surroundings and can be fished with fly, spinner or worm, depending on conditions. A boat and gillie are provided on this beat which can accommodate two rods and a further two rods may fish from the bank. Given its proximity to the estuary, this beat is substantially affected by the tide, so anglers are advised to arrange fishing times with the resident gillie prior to their allocated angling day.

The Point
Located at the mouth of the Brusna (or Bunree) River, the Point is a public beat with no restriction on the number of anglers. It is, nonetheless, a prolific salmon and seatrout fishery, which is popular with locals and visitors alike. Permits are available on a daily, weekly or seasonal basis and can be purchased from local tackle dealers or from fishery staff on duty. Anglers must be in possession of a valid permit before they commence angling.

Freshwater Beat
This beat is located on the left bank immediately upstream of the Ridge Pool and comprises 300m of single bank fishing. It has been developed with four new pools and greatly improved access. It has fished well since the completion of development works, particularly in high water on a falling flood, both for salmon and seatrout. It also fishes well in September.

Season
The season opens on the Ridge Pool and on the Freshwater Beat on 1 February. If water conditions are suitable, salmon can be taken from opening day onwards. On the lower beats, salmon are less inclined to lie until later in the spring when the water usually drops to near summer level. Consequently, the season opens on these beats on 17 April.

The season closes for all angling on the Moy Fishery on 30 September.

Permits, information and booking
River Moy Manager, Moy Fishery Office, The North-Western Regional Fisheries Board, Ardnaree House, Abbey Street, Ballina, Co. Mayo. Tel: 096 21332
Fax: 096 21332, email: info@moyfishery.com or dcooke@moyfishery.com

Angling is available by advance booking (with the exception of The Point). Applications should be submitted on the appropriate forms to the River Moy Manager at the above address before the 31 December each year (forms available at the board office) or as downloaded from the NWRFB website, www.northwestfisheries.ie

Regulations
Flyfishing, spinning and worm fishing depending on beat and water conditions. Ascertain bag limit when applying for permit.

Disabled anglers' facility
There is disabled access at the Freshwater Beat.

Lodge/accommodation

Mrs. Phil Henry, New Lodge, Station Road, Ballina, Co. Mayo. Tel: 096 72693
Email: newlodgehenry@eircom.net

Note

Guides can also be sourced through the individual fisheries and tackle shops
(see listing on page ??).

3. BALLINA SALMON ANGLERS' ASSOCIATION WATER

This Association Water is managed under licence from the Regional Board and from
the Verscoyle family. It comprises approximately three miles of double bank fishing
from the weir in Ballina to the confluence with the Corroy River. There are some newly
developed pools in the Ballina area which are suitable for flyfishing. The remaining
2½ miles consists mainly of deep, slow-flowing water and is suitable for angling with
bait and spinner, although the bubble and fly method can also be very effective here.
Catches on this stretch are estimated at between 1,000 and 2,000 salmon per season.
Seatrout are also regularly caught in this stretch. The number of rods is not limited and
daily or weekly permits are available at a reasonable price from local tackle shops. A
limited number of season permits are also available.

Permits

Available in local tackle shops

4. MOUNT FALCON FISHERIES

This is one of the best-known and most prestigious of the fisheries on this stretch. It
is part of the Mount Falcon estate. The fishery consists of over two miles of double
bank fishing upstream from the Corroy River, including the famous Wall Pool. It also
contains some other pools, such as Connor's Gap, which fish well to a fly on low-to-
moderate water. In all, there are eleven pools.

Mount Falcon Fishery rod catch 2004–2008

Year	2004	2005	2006	2007	2008
Salmon	892	763	582	980	401*

* Excessively high water throughout summer months

Permits and information

The Fishery Manager, Mount Falcon Castle, Ballina, Co. Mayo. Tel: 096 74472
Mobile: 087 2831776, email: info@mountfalconfisheries.com
Web: www.mountfalcon.com

5. ATTYMASS FISHERY

This stretch of river is leased by the Scott-Knox-Gore estate to the Attymass Anglers' Association. It is primarily a bait and spinner fishery, but bubble and fly can be effective too.

Permits and information
Padraig Garrett, Carrowkerribla, Attymass, Ballina, Co. Mayo. Tel: 094 9258151

6. COOLCRONAN FISHERY

This fishery consists of just over one mile of double bank fishing between the Bunnafinglas River to a point near the Yellow River. Access is via the entrance to Coolcronan House, to the assembly point by the Cable Pool. Letting is limited to 20 rods per day, divided into three beats, and advance booking is required. Although considered primarily suited to bait and spinner, there is some good flyfishing at low water, particularly in the Rock Pool. A lot of bank improvements have been carried out in the last 3 years.

Permits and information
Mary Carlisle, Belgarriff, Foxford, Co. Mayo. Tel: 094 9257055, mobile: 087 2398019
Email: salmonrod@gmail.com, web: www.salmonrod.com

7. KNOCKMORE ANGLING CLUB WATER

This club leases two stretches of the left bank. The first is about a mile in length, from the top end of the Wall Pool to opposite the junction with the Bunnafinglas River. The second is from the top of the Coolcronan Fishery to opposite the junction with the Yellow River. Both stretches are generally suited to bait and spinner but the occasional salmon is caught on fly in very low water. Day permits are available.

Permits and information
Martin Kelly, Coolcronan, Foxford, Co. Mayo. Tel: 094 9258287

8. BYRNE'S FISHERY

This is a short stretch comprising about ¾ mile on the left bank, upstream of and opposite the junction with the Yellow River. It has its own parking facility and is accessed via a small road beside the Garden Centre on the Foxford-Ballina road. It is mainly suitable for bait and spinner.

Permits and information
Jim Byrne, Pier Road, Enniscrone, Co. Sligo. Mobile: 086 1600754

9. ARMSTRONG'S FISHERY

Armstrong's Fishery is approximately one and a quarter miles of single-bank fishing, including about 300 yards of nice fly water. The rest is deep holding water and very productive. A limited number of season permits are issued and the remainder of the fishing is let by day permits, approximately 25 rods per day. Spring fish tend to lie at the top of the stretch. All legal fishing methods are allowed.

Permits
George Armstrong, Ballina Road, Foxford, Co. Mayo. Tel: 094 9256580

10. FOXFORD FISHERY (PRIVATE BEATS)

The Foxford Fishery comprises of 1¼ miles of exclusive, private, double bank salmon fishing on the most prolific section of the River Moy. It extends downstream from a point half a mile below Foxford Bridge. The fishing is limited to seven rods per day and guests may fish from bank or boat with the services of three experienced gillies.
In addition, the fishery offers ¾ of a mile of single bank fishing for eight rods a day extending downstream from the Nibb on the east bank.

The Foxford Fishery offers excellent salmon angling throughout the season, with consistent spring fishing mid-April to the end of May, a summer grilse run from June to the end of August and both resident and autumn run fish at the back-end.

The grilse arrive in June and, given suitable water conditions, July and August can provide sensational sport with large bags of fresh fish possible. In summer conditions and good water, flyfishing becomes most productive, with bait and spin fishing coming into their own during summer floods.

Foxford Fishery rod catch 2001–2008

Year	*2001	2002	2003	2003	2005	2006	2007	2008
Salmon	372	523	690	702	646	648	365	342

*Foot and Mouth disease restrictions delayed the start of fishing in 2001

Permits
Granville Nesbitt, Manager, Fortland Fishery, Easkey, Co. Sligo. Mobile: 086 8032350
Email: info@anglingwestireland.com, web: www.anglingwestireland.com

Guides
Two experienced resident guides.

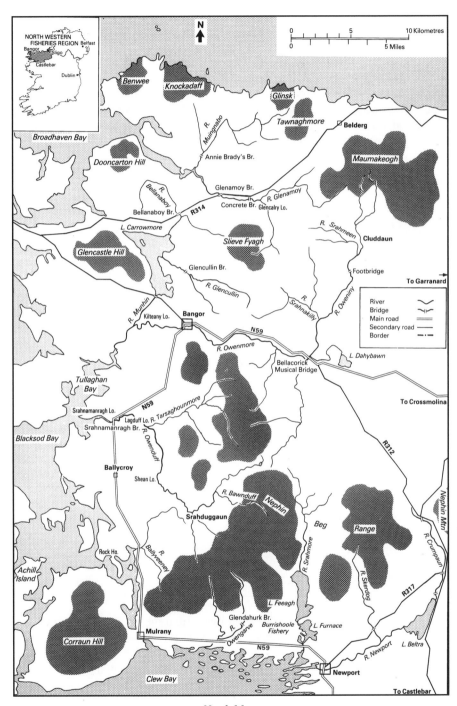

North Mayo

11. GANNON'S FISHERY

This is a section of left bank fishing, approximately 1½ miles in length. It consists largely of slow, bait and spinning water, but in low water, the fly works well around Moran's Rocks and further downstream at the two bends. This is quite a productive fishery, with an average annual catch in the region of 700-800 fish and day permits are available at a reasonable price. Weekly permits are also available by prior arrangement with the owners. Also known as the Beal Easa Fishery.

Permits
Pat Gannon, Post Office, Foxford, Co. Mayo. Tel: 094 9256101

12. FOXFORD SALMON ANGLERS' ASSOCIATION

The Foxford Salmon Anglers' Association has more than ¾ mile of double-bank fishing upstream of the town of Foxford and includes the Leckee Fishery.

In 2002, the State purchased that part of Baker's Fishery upstream of Foxford Bridge and leased it to Foxford Salmon Anglers' Association. This new extended fishery is partly suitable for flyfishing and the rest, more suited to worm fishing and spinning.

The Leckee Fishery, on the right bank upstream of Foxford, is 350 yards long and is leased to Foxford Salmon Anglers' Association.

The Association also had three miles of single bank fishing at Rinnaney on the right bank extending from the Yellow River.

Permits
Tiernan's Tackle Shop, Main Street, Foxford, Co. Mayo. Tel: 094 9256731
Email: pjtiernan@eircom.net

Guides
Declan Hughes. Tel: 094 9256941
Kevin Gallagher. Tel: 096 22718
Michael Tiernan. Tel: 094 9256731

13. BAKER'S NEW FISHERY

This fishery extends for about 400m downstream from the old Eel Weir in Foxford. It has a steep gradient and was formerly not noted as salmon-holding water. However, following major development works carried out by the owner in the summer of 1999, the beat now has some new salmon pools which are suitable for flyfishing from June onwards in low water. Rod numbers are restricted and must be booked in advance.

Permits and information
Tel: 07979 596859 (UK mobile number)

Into the net at last! Jo Hudgell plays and lands a fine Moy salmon

14. CLOONGEE FISHERY

This is an extensive fishery extending to over three miles of single and double bank fishing on the Moy upstream of Foxford and on most of the Lake River (Cross River) where fishing does not commence till 1 June. The Lake River drains Loughs Cullin and Conn. This is a productive salmon fishery for both spring (March) fish and grilse. It has a good variety of fast and slow water and the flyfisher will find plenty of space to test his skills. Water levels are critical and it fishes best to the fly upstream of the Joinings if there is good water coming down from the Upper Moy. The Lake (Cross) River can give good trout fishing especially at mayfly time.

Cloongee Fishery rod catch 2004–2008

Year	2004	2005	2006	2007	2008
Salmon	722	340	231	342	250

Permits
Tiernan's Tackle Shop, Main Street, Foxford, Co. Mayo. Tel: 094 9256731
Email: tiernanbros@eircom.net, web: www.themoy.com

Information
Web: www.northwestfisheries.ie

15. EAST MAYO (SWINFORD) ANGLERS' ASSOCIATION

This is the most extensive fishery on the Moy. It stretches upstream on both banks from the Cloongee Fishery for about 8 miles. Permits are available on a daily or weekly basis. It fishes best in medium-to-high water and can give really excellent results for both spring salmon and grilse when water levels are right. Some of the best flyfishing on the river is above the 'Gub', at the confluence of the Gweestion River, and also Howley's Pool, when the water gauge at Ballylahan Bridge is reading between 5 and 6. The fishery produces approximately 650 fish in a season.

Fishing for spring salmon begins in February, peaks in late April and, depending on water levels, can continue well into May. The grilse appear around the last week of June and, as long as water levels remain moderate-to-high, this stretch can offer excellent fishing.

Permission
The EMAA Offices, Market Street, Swinford, Co. Mayo. Tel: 094 9253955
Mrs Hazel Wills, Ballylahan Bridge, Foxford, Co. Mayo. Tel: 094 9256221

16. BALLINTEMPLE FISHERY

The Ballintemple Fishery comprises two miles of single bank fishing on the left bank of the main Moy channel extending downstream from Cloongullaun Bridge on the Foxford –Swinford road, to the EMAA car park at Oldcastle. This is the main access point to the fishery and anglers with permits for Ballintemple may use this car park. This is a highly attractive stretch of salmon river, with a lovely mixture of streamy water and pools, located in a picturesque rural setting. Accurate catch returns are hard to come by as most fish go unreported. Fishes best in moderate-to-high water.

Permits
Tiernan's Tackle Shop, Main Street, Foxford, Co. Mayo. Tel: 094 9256731

Email: tiernanbros@eircom.net, web: www.themoy.com

17. UPPER MOY

From Ballintemple upstream to Banada, there are several miles of fishable river. It is not heavily fished and, while the banks in some stretches are quite overgrown, it is an ideal location for those who prefer angling off the beaten track. From Cloongullaun Bridge, upstream to Cloonacannana Bridge, there are some good salmon pools which are well worth a visit after a summer spate. Salmon are not known to lie between Cloonacannana Bridge upstream to Cooleen Bridge, but there are some more good salmon pools from Cooleen upstream to Banada.

Access to the river in this stretch is difficult and cannot be guaranteed. Anglers should check locally for permission with riparian owners. At the time of writing, I have reports of a local angling club claiming fishing on parts of the Upper Moy.

18. PONTOON BRIDGE

This fishery is located in the short channel between Lough Conn and Lough Cullin. It is highly regarded as a lie for spring salmon. However, there is a bye-law that prohibits fishing till 1 June. The grilse fishing can be good here, especially in June, but quickly slows up as the water drops. There are anglers who specialise in fishing this stretch. Flyfishing and spinning can take fish. The fishing is adversely affected if a flood in the Moy backs up Lough Cullin and reverses the flow.

Permission
Free

DEEL, RIVER   G13 17

The Deel forms part of the headwaters of the Moy to the west. It rises in north Mayo and flows east for 28 miles past Rake Street, through Crossmolina, and then describes a semicircle round the top of Lough Conn, before entering the lough from the north east.

Possibly because of its free fishing status, the River Deel is very underrated, both as a salmon and brown trout river.

There is very good spring salmon fishing (spinning and worm) from Deel Castle to the river mouth. This fishing commences on 1 February and can last till June or when the lough starts to drop. From June, with a rise in water, the fishing improves up-river for both grilse and salmon. The best stretch has some nice fly water and extends for at least 5 miles from Richmond Bridge (near Rake Street) upstream to Carrowgarve Bridge and on up for about one mile upstream of Commich Bridge. The good fishing in this stretch continues into July and improves again after a flood in late August or September. The top half of this stretch flows through moorland and the remainder through marginal farmland and the banks are undeveloped.

There is about 2 miles of good trout fishing at Knockglass House, north-east of Crossmolina; 5 miles of trout fishing from Ballycarron House upstream past Richmond Bridge and Carrowgarve Bridge and a further mile of fishing immediately upstream of Deel Bridge. Access is restricted on the left bank for one mile upstream of Carrowgarve Bridge.

The resident trout range in size from ½–3½ lb. In May and June, the best fishing is at Knockglass. Later, when the lough trout start running, all areas fish well.

Fly hatches include large dark olives in spring, iron blue dun, a small mayfly (*Ephemera danica*) hatch and sedges and blue winged olives in summer.

Permission
Riparian owners

Season
N.B. This river is closed for any type of fishing from 1 September–31 May. Bye-law C.S. 295, 2008

Guides
Michael Tiernan, PAGI, Tiernan's Tackle Shop, Main Street, Foxford, Co. Mayo.
Tel: 094 9256731, email: tiernanbros@eircom.net, web: www.themoy.com
Gary Crossley, Cloonamoyne Fishery, Enniscoe House, Castlehill Post Office (near Crossmolina), Ballina, Co. Mayo. Tel: 096 31112, fax: 096 31773
Email: gary@cloonamoynefishing.com

Tackle shop
Munnelly's Ltd, Main Street, Crossmolina, Co. Mayo

CLYDAGH, RIVER   M23 97

This is essentially a spate river and the trout tend to be numerous but small. The middle reaches, from Cloonkesh to Parke, are quite overgrown. Further downstream, near the confluence with the Bellavary River, it is deep and slow and the banks are clear. Spring salmon fishing can be taken at this location, mainly with spinners and baits and trout from 1–2lb are also caught during the spring and early summer. The river above Clydagh Bridge, on the R310 Castlebar-Pontoon road, is of little interest to the angler.

Fly hatches include large dark olives, iron blue duns, black gnats, sedges and pale watery duns.

Permits
For information on permits contact:
The North-Western Regional Fisheries Board, Ardnaree House, Abbey Street, Ballina, Co. Mayo. Tel: 096 22788, fax: 096 70543, email: info@nwrfb.com
Web: www.northwestfisheries.ie

CASTLEBAR, RIVER   M20 93

In the past, I have had some great brown trout fishing on this river. A few years later (2001) I received reports of bad pollution, poor water quality and depleted trout stocks upstream of Turlough. It is a rich limestone river and I am hopeful that it still holds a few trout downstream of the waterfall near Turlough village. It is hard to believe they have all disappeared, but it may well be so.

Fly hatches include large dark olives, iron blue duns, black gnats, sedges and pale watery duns, with some mayfly as well.

Permits
For information on permits contact:

The North-Western Regional Fisheries Board, Ardnaree House, Abbey Street, Ballina, Co. Mayo. Tel: 096 22788, fax: 096 70543, Email: info@nwrfb.com
Web: www.northwestfisheries.ie

Local tackle shops
Game Angling Centre, Linenhall Street, Castlebar, Co. Mayo
Island Sports, (Prop. John O'Malley), N5 Business Park, Moneen, Castlebar, Co. Mayo. Tel: 094 9025060, email: jomalley@eircom.net

MANULLA, RIVER   M 23 95

This is another lovely, rich, very clear, limestone river which can offer some good trout fishing, mainly in the stretch from the confluence with the Castlebar River upstream to Moyhenna Bridge. There are patches of streamy water interspersed with pools throughout the stretch between Drumaduff and Gortlahan Bridge. These offer the best wetfly and dryflyfishing. Some of the deeper pools, at the lower end of this stretch, hold trout to 3lb and can offer great sport with dry flies on a summer evening.

Fly hatches are as for the Clydagh and Castlebar Rivers, with a mayfly hatch and spent gnat fishing on occasions – even during the day – in late May and June.

Permits
For information on permits contact:
The North-Western Regional Fisheries Board, Ardnaree House, Abbey Street, Ballina, Co. Mayo. Tel: 096 22788, fax: 096 70543, email: info@nwrfb.com, web: www.north-westfisheries.ie

GWEESTION, RIVER   M 30 97

The Gweestion River is a tributary of the Moy. The Pollagh, Gore and Trimogue rivers are, in turn, tributaries of the Gweestion, which lies between Swinford and Bohola. It is a limestone river and holds occasional grilse in June and an excellent stock of brown trout ranging mostly from 8oz–1½ lb, with some fish to 3½ lb. Stiles and footbridges have been erected up to the confluence of the Glore River. The banks are quite overgrown with alder in places, but it has some nice pools and riffles and prolific fly hatches, including mayfly. The Gweestion can be recommended and it doesn't weed up as many rivers do in summer.

I have had reports of this river being heavily fished in an unsporting manner by groups of greedy bait anglers. I hope that, should they read this, they will desist and allow the trout stocks to recover on this lovely little river.

There are good hatches of large dark olives and iron blue duns in April and May. Black gnats and hawthorns are important in early May and the mayfly hatch is good. Sedges and blue winged olives are common throughout the summer months and there are hatches of pale wateries in July and August.

Permission
Riparian owners

Guide
Michael Tiernan, PAGI, Tiernan's Tackle Shop, Main Street, Foxford, Co. Mayo. Tel: 094 9256731, email: tiernanbros@eircom.net, web: www.themoy.com

POLLAGH, RIVER   M 33 92

The Pollagh River is 10 miles long and holds a great stock of trout from Bushfield Bridge downstream to the confluence. The fish average about 10oz, with some to 2lb. There are some lovely pools in the vicinity of Rathslevin Bridge, on the Bohola to Kiltimagh Road, and again between the two bridges immediately northwest of Kiltimagh. These hold plenty of trout in the 1–2lb size range. Around Ballinamore Bridge, on the Kiltimagh to Balla road, there is some nice streamy water which holds excellent stocks of trout in the 8–12oz range.

There are good hatches of large dark olives and iron blue duns in April and May. Black gnats and hawthorns are important in early May and the mayfly hatch is good. Sedges and blue winged olives are common throughout the summer months and there are hatches of pale wateries in July and August.

Permission
Riparian owners

GLORE, RIVER   M 35 92

The River Glore consists of mainly fast clear water with occasional pools. The trout average about half-a-pound, with some going to 2lb. The best stocks are in a short stretch downstream of the bridge on the Swinford-Kiltimagh Road and above the bridge on the N17 between Kilkelly and Claremorris. My experience is that stocks are sparse. The water is beautifully clear.

There are good hatches of large dark olives and iron blue duns in April and May. Black gnats and hawthorns are important in early May and the mayfly hatch is good. Sedges and blue winged olives are common throughout the summer months and there are hatches of pale wateries in July and August.

Permission
Riparian owners

TRIMOGUE, RIVER   M 33 97

The Trimogue River is about 13 miles long and joins the Gweestion downstream of Ballymiles Bridge. It holds a good stock of trout up to ¾lb upstream from its confluence with the Gweestion to Kinaff Bridge. The average width of the channel is 12 feet and it has some lovely pools. It comes down from Kilkelly and there are some good trout to 2lb in the deeper pools in that area.

There are good hatches of large dark olives and iron blue duns in April and May. Black gnats and hawthorns are important in early May and the mayfly hatch is good. Sedges and blue winged olives are common throughout the summer months and hatches of pale wateries in July and August.

Permission
Riparian owners

SONNAGH, RIVER   M 42 03

The Sonnagh rises south west of Charlestown and joins the Moy downstream of Bellanacurra Bridge. It is no more than 15 feet wide and holds an excellent stock of trout to 1½ lb. It is rarely fished. The best of the fishing is in the two-mile stretch up from the confluence. This is a limestone stream like the Trimogue River (above) and the Mullaghanoe and Owengarve Rivers further to the north, with all the usual fly hatches associated with that type of river.

Permission
Riparian owners

Guide
Michael Tiernan, PAGI, Tiernan's Tackle Shop, Main Street, Foxford, Co. Mayo
Tel: 094 9256731, email: tiernanbros@eircom.net, web: www.themoy.com

MULLAGHANOE, RIVER   G 41 05

The Mullaghanoe rises near Knock then flows through Charlestown and turns west to join the Moy, upstream of Bellanacurra Bridge. It, too, holds excellent stocks of trout to about 1lb. It is a narrow river, only about 12 feet wide. It has recovered well from drainage works and is located in a quiet rural setting. The best of the fishing is for about 1½ miles from the confluence up to Cloonfinish.

Permission
Riparian owners

OWENGARVE, RIVER   G 44 07

The Owengarve flows through the village of Curry and joins the Moy downstream of Cooleen Ford. The three-mile stretch downstream of Curry holds an excellent stock of trout up to 1lb. It has a nice mix of stream and pools. It used to be difficult to access, but the North-Western Fisheries Board has done a good job in clearing the overgrown banks.

In spring, there are plenty of trout surprisingly far up at Shra Lower and Botinny. This is a river that I find fishes well to the dry-fly 'on the blind' (i.e., speculatively). A Klinkhåmer, Adams or small Sedge have all given me good sport in summer.

Permission
Riparian owners

Guide
Michael Tiernan, PAGI, Tiernan's Tackle Shop, Main Street, Foxford, Co. Mayo
Tel: 094 9256731, email: tiernanbros@eircom.net, web: www.themoy.com

EINAGH, RIVER (ACLARE)   G 41 10

The Einagh River flows from Lough Talt through the village of Aclare and enters the Moy just upstream from the confluence with the Owengarve River. The fishing is similar to that of the Mullaghanoe, although it is somewhat spatyer, with a higher gradient. The banks are overgrown in places. It holds a good stock of nice trout.

Permission
Riparian owners

** BUNREE, RIVER   G 26 19

This small river enters the Moy estuary downstream of Ballina. It holds brown trout to 12oz and gets a run of seatrout from late August. An occasional grilse may also be taken on this river in a late season flood.

MOY AND TRIBUTARIES:

Season
Salmon: 1 February–30 September
Seatrout: 15 February–10 October
Brown trout: 15 February–10 October

N.B. There may be exceptions to the above dates on certain waters.

Guides/gillies
Michael Tiernan, PAGI , Tiernan's Tackle Shop, Main Street, Foxford, Co. Mayo.
Tel: 094 9256731, email: tiernanbros@eircom.net, web: www.themoy.com
Jim Murray, PAGI, Curradrish, Foxford, Co. Mayo.
Tel: 094 9257089, mobile: 087 9589896, email: jim_murray@hotmail.com
Declan Hughes, PAGI, Coolegraine, Foxford, Co. Mayo.
Tel: 094 9256941, mobile: 087 7649571
Robert Gillespie, PAGI, Leckee, Foxford, Co. Mayo. Tel: 094 9256874
Padraic Kelly, PAGI, Cloghans Post Office, Ballina, Co. Mayo. Tel: 096 22250
Ken Hall, Lahardaun, Foxford, Co. Mayo. Tel: 086 8846920
Email: kenhallgameangling@hotmail.com, web: www.mayoangling.com
Jack Millet, Pontoon Flyfishing School, Pontoon Bridge Hotel, Pontoon, Co. Mayo
Tel: 094 9256120, email: relax@pontoonbridge.com, web: www.pontoonbridge.com
Ken Henry, Claddagh, Glebe, Dromahair, Co. Leitrim. Tel: 071 9134971
Mobile: 086 8182723, email: henry.ken@itsligo.ie, web: www.pagi.org
Kenny Sloan, 7 Riverside, Foxford, Co. Mayo. Tel: 094 56501, mobile: 087 9670310
Email: ksloan@eircom.net
Gerard Downey, Foxford, Co. Mayo. Tel: 094 9256824
Malcolm McPhearson (Moy Estuary), Killala, Co. Mayo. Mobile: 087 9315712
Paddy McDonnell, Barnacouge, Swinford, Co. Mayo. Tel: 094 9251033
Mobile: 087 4123235
Jackie Barrett, Swinford Road, Foxford, Co. Mayo. Tel: 094 9256162
Ian Wise, Ballybrinque, Castlehill, Ballina, Co. Mayo. Tel: 096 31928
Mobile: 087 7697193
John Sheridan, Clossagh, Foxford, Co. Mayo. Mobile: 087 2067858
Email: johnshrdn@yahoo.com
Judd Ruane (Moy Estuary), Nephin View, The Quay, Ballina, Co. Mayo
Tel: 096 22183, email: judd@juddruane.com, web: www.fishingireland.ie
Gary Crossley (Moy and Lough Conn), Cloonamoyne Fishery, Enniscoe House,
Castlehill, Co. Mayo. Tel: 096 31112, mobile: 087 3148449,
Email: gary@cloonamoynefishery.com, web: www.cloonamoynefishery.com
Harry Feeney, The Foxford Lodge, Pontoon Road, Foxford, Co. Mayo.
Tel: 094 9257777, email: sales@thefoxfordlodge.ie, web: www.thefoxfordlodge.ie

Note
Guides can also be sourced through the individual fisheries and tackle shops

Tackle shops
Ballina Angling Centre, Ridge Pool Road, Ballina, Co. Mayo. Tel/fax: 096 21850
Email: mswartz@oceanfree.net
Tiernan's Tackle Shop, Main Street, Foxford, Co. Mayo. Tel: 094 9256731
Email: tiernanbros@eircom.net, web: www.themoy.com
Island Sports, (Prop. John O'Malley), N5 Business Park, Moneen, Castlebar,
Co. Mayo. Tel: 094 9025060, email: jomalley@eircom.net
Garry Piggott, Ridge Pool Tackle Shop, Cathedral Road, Ballina, Co. Mayo
Tel/fax: 096 72656, mobile: 086 8753648
Edward Doherty, Ridge Pool Bar, Bridge Street, Ballina, Co. Mayo. Tel: 096 21050
Seamus Boland, Bridge Street, Swinford, Co. Mayo
John Walkin, Fishing Tackle, Market Road, Ballina, Co. Mayo. Tel: 096 22442

Lodges/accommodation
Pontoon Bridge Hotel, Pontoon, Co. Mayo. Tel: 094 9256120/9256699
Eeb: www.pontoonbridge.com
Healys Country House Hotel, Foxford, Co. Mayo. Tel: 094 9256443
Email: info@healyspontoon.com, web: www.healyspontoon.com. Member of the
Great Fishing Houses of Ireland Group

Accommodation
New Lodge, Station Road, Ballina, Co. Mayo. Tel: 096 72693
Email: newlodgehenry@eircom.net

Local flytyers
Robert Gillespie, Leckee, Foxford, Co. Mayo. Tel: 094 9256874
Michael Tiernan, PAGI, Tiernan's Tackle Shop, Tackle Shop, Main Street, Foxford
Co. Mayo. Tel: 094 9256731, email: tiernanbros@eircom.net, web: www.themoy.com
Declan Hughes, PAGI, Coolegrane, Foxford, Co. Mayo. Tel: 094 9256941
Mobile: 087 7649571

Information on all aspects of angling in the Moy catchment is available from
The Moy Fishery Office, Ardnaree House, Abbey Street, Ballina, Co. Mayo.
Tel: 096 21332, fax: 096 21332, email: info@moyfishery.com or
dcooke@moyfishery.com

** CLOONAGHMORE (PALMERSTOWN), RIVER   G17 31

The lower reaches of this river are leased by Ballina and Cloghan Angling Club and
the fishing on a stretch up at Owenmore, near Ballyglass, is reserved. The rest of it is
regarded as free fishing. It was a great seatrout river in the past, but now the stocks
are barely surviving. The best chance of a fish now is late in the season. There is some
good fish-holding water up at Doobehy.

Season
Salmon: 1 June–30 September
Seatrout: 1 June–12 October
Brown Trout: 1 June–12 October

Permission
Riparian owners

** BALLINGLEN, RIVER   G1 10 38

The Ballinglen River is near Ballycastle in north Mayo. The better pools are in the lower reaches. It is a small spate river. Further upstream the river is badly overgrown and unfishable. Like the Palmerstown River, above, its run of salmon and seatrout has greatly declined over many years.

Permission
Riparian owners

** MUINGNABO, RIVER   F 88 37

The Muingnabo River is just nine miles long, with a 16 sq. mile catchment. Being so remote, it is rarely fished, but is well worth fishing for seatrout on a spate in September. There are some fine pools for about 1½ miles above Annie Brady's Bridge and it can be fished right to the estuary – when it reopens.

Season
1 May–30 September

Permits
Enquiries to North-Western Regional Fisheries Board, Ardnaree House, Abbey Street, Ballina, Co. Mayo. Tel: 096 21332, fax: 096 21332, email: info@nwrfb.com

* GLENAMOY, RIVER F 89 34

The Glenamoy River has a catchment of 33 sq. miles and is just 14 miles long. Access has been greatly improved with stiles and footbridges built by the North-Western Regional Fisheries Board. This one is a real treasure. The tidal section fishes well for seatrout from late July. In a spate, there is about six miles of fishing from Glencalry Lodge down to the tide. It is basically a seatrout river, fly-only, but I have known anglers to come away from an evening's fishing with half a dozen salmon. Some of the nicest pools are downstream from the graveyard, past the new concrete bridge, where a lot of good development work has been done on pools by the Fishery Board.

Season
Salmon: 1 May–30 September
Seatrout: 1 May–12 October

Permits
Glenamoy Community Angling Association, Angler's Rest Bar, Glenamoy, Co. Mayo. Tel: 097 87961

Disabled anglers' facility
There is disabled anglers' access provided. Check with the North-Western Regional
Fisheries Board.

GLENCULLIN, RIVER   F 85 27

The Glencullin River flows westwards into Carrowmore Lake. It holds a good stock of
seatrout and salmon on a flood. They probably back down to the lake again as the flood
drops. It can be fished from April, but is best from June. The river is crossed by only one
bridge, upstream of which are a few good pools. Downstream, it can look a bit canal-
like, especially near the lake, but this is all good water and well worth fishing when the
wind breaks the surface. It is usually fished by anglers fishing Carrowmore Lake.

Flies
A Black Pennell; Bibio, Watson's Fancy, Shrimp fly, Gary Dog and Hairy Mary in
various sizes will serve the angler well on any of the rivers on the previous pages.

Season
1 May–30 September

Permits
The West End Bar, Bangor Erris, Co. Mayo. Tel: 097 83487/83461

MUNHIN, RIVER   F 83 24

The Munhin River is about 3½ miles long. This river carries a lot of water and it drains
Carrowmore Lake and the Owenmore River into Tullaghan Bay, north of Achill Island.
Formerly, it was overgrown and unfishable. In recent times, the river has been developed and opened up by the North-Western Fisheries Board. The whole river is now
fishable. It usually carries too much water in spring but has the potential for some good
sport with grilse and seatrout in June and July. There is some nice water downstream
of the lake and upstream and downstream of Kiltane Bridge but anglers should consult
when buying a permit regarding whether or not it includes the fishing downstream of
Kiltane Bridge.

Season
1 February–30 September (all species)

Permits
The West End Bar, Bangor Erris, Co. Mayo. Tel: 097 83487/83461

OWENMORE, RIVER F 87 24

The Owenmore drains a large area of the bogs, moorland and mountains of north-west Mayo into the Munhin River, north of Achill Island. It is every inch a brilliant salmon and seatrout fishery. Much of the fishing is reserved and not let. The syndicate waters are:

The Glenmore Syndicate
The Glenalt Syndicate
Finlay's Water

One four-mile stretch in the middle reaches is leased by the Bangor Sporting Club. This is lovely water, well endowed with good pools. A limited number of day permits are available from:

The West End Bar, Bangor Erris, Co. Mayo. Tel: 097 83487/83461

This is really a big spate river, which produces a remarkable number of salmon every season. It holds a few spring fish. The grilse come in early June and it gets another run of big autumn fish from August. A bye-law stipulates that the fishing is fly-only. The Ghost Shrimp, Cascade, Curry's Red Shrimp, Garry Dog, Silver Garry, Thunder & Lightning and Hairy Mary are all good flies on the Owenmore.

The river gets a good run of seatrout from mid-June to the end of September. The average weight is about 12oz and, while most are caught by salmon fishers, they can provide good night fishing in some of the bigger pools.

Season
1 February–30 September

Regulations
Flyfishing only. It is a statutory bye-law.

Guides
Gary Crossley, Cloonamoyne Fishery, Enniscoe House, Castlehill, Near Crossmolina, Co. Mayo. Mobile: 087 3148449, web: www.cloonamoynefishery.com

For others, enquire with
The West End Bar, Bangor Erris, Co. Mayo. Tel: 097 83487/83461

Local tackle shop
O'Maillin Teoranta, American Street, Belmullet, Co. Mayo

OWENINY, RIVER   F 98 21

The Oweniny River is a tributary of the Owenmore. Check with landowners. It flows down for 14 miles from Maumakeogh and joins the main river at Bellacorick Bridge. This is a rugged spate river and holds fine stocks of spring salmon, grilse and seatrout in season.

Permission

The ownership of the fishing rights is very fragmented. It is best to check with the landowners. Glenalt syndicate and the Office of Public Works have about a quarter-of-a-mile upstream from the confluence which is not let. Upstream from here, permission to fish can be obtained from John Gillespie, John Ruddy, Bord na Mona, Tony Cosgrave and Michael McGrath, while Pat Mullarkey gives permission on the Sheskin River which comes in from the west. All the aforementioned have addresses at Srahnakilly, Bellacorick, Co. Mayo.

Access to the lower reaches is up a road at Bellacorrick along the right bank. However, the river stretches for several more miles into the mountains and these upper reaches are best reached via a forestry road off the Crossmoliina-Ballycastle road at Garranard Post Office.

This is a wild moorland river and very remote and all twists and bends. The banks are clear for walking, but go prepared for biting midges. In summer they can be terribly troublesome. The lower reaches can get very stained and dark as treacle with peat from the bogs. This is also a problem on the Owenmore.

This river holds a lot of spring salmon from April, grilse from June and seatrout from July. The fishing extends up to Cluddaun.

From Cluddaun above the Srahmeen confluence, downstream for 1½ miles to the footbridge (at the end of the forest road from Garanard PO) the river consists of streams and pools. Downstream of the footbridge, there is a mile of deep slow water and the rest is a mix of shallow water and pools. It is very much a spate river, but the deep pools can fish well in a strong SSW or NNW wind.

Some anglers have a car drop them off at the footbridge in the morning. They fish all the way downstream and arrange to be collected at Dominic McLoughlin's in the evening. This is a distance of eight miles approximately and it can take more than 12 hours to fish it all. This tactic is only recommended for those fit enough for a long, arduous walk.

Season

1 February–30 September

Guides

Gary Crossley (see Owenmore see previous page)

OWENDUFF, RIVER   F 81 15

This is another of west Mayo's exceptionally attractive and prolific salmon and seatrout fisheries and the fishing is much sought-after.

The river was immortalised in W. H. Maxwell's remarkable book *Wild Sports of the West*, published in 1832. I am glad to report that even at the present time it still weaves its magic for the angler. Many of the pools are still known by the same names and they still hold abundant stocks of spring salmon, grilse and seatrout.

Together with its tributary, the Tarsaghaunmore, the Owenduff River drains a 52 sq. mile catchment of wild moorland and mountain into Tullaghan Bay, a few miles north of Ballycroy. The river is all privately owned, except for the estuary on the left bank only below the weir at Srahnamanragh Bridge. In this estuary (left bank), there is about a mile of free fishing. It can produce a salmon on occasions and the seatrout fishing can be exceptionally good at the turn of the tide. Up river, there are five private fisheries and three fishing lodges – Shrahnamanragh Lodge, Lagduff Lodge and Shean Lodge. A fourth fishery is served by Rock House, near Ballycroy.

The water in the Owenduff is clear and both salmon and seatrout are noted for their free-taking qualities when the water is right. The spring salmon run from 1 February and March is prime time for spring fish at Lagduff and on the bottom of the Shean Lodge water. The grilse come in May, the seatrout run peaks in August and there is a late run of salmon. This is a fly-only river (by law) and useful salmon patterns are Lemon Grey, Silver Stoat, Black Doctor, Thunder and Lightning, various Irish Shrimp flies. For seatrout, Dunkeld, Connemara Black, Invicta and Black Pennell are effective patterns.

Occasionally a week's fishing comes available in one of the following lodges:

Croy Lodge, where W. H. Maxwell, of *Wild Sports in the West* fame, stayed in the 1830s, is still standing but is no longer inhabited.

Shranamanra Lodge is located at the bridge of the same name, at the top of the tidal water. The proprietor is Mr. Colum O'Briain, 'Sheán', Newtown Park Avenue, Blackrock, Co. Dublin *Tel*: 01 2895561

Lagduff Lodge is about two miles further up the river with about three miles of fishing. It fishes four rods for spring fish and five for grilse. It has four double rooms. Information from: Ms. Petra Hancock, 30 Moyola Park, Galway.

Shean Lodge is some four miles further up-river from Lagduff. It has about five miles of fishing (fly-only), divided into 2 beats and takes a maximum of 6 rods on the top beat and 4 on the bottom beat. There is a bag limit of 3 spring salmon, 6 grilse and 6 seatrout per week. The Lodge and fishing is rented on a weekly basis with the top beat, and all services including a gillie. The bottom beat (4 rods) is let separately. There is local accommodation and a gillie is available. Apply to: Mr. J. R. Craigie, Craigie Bros., 'Owenduff', Celbridge, Co. Kildare *Tel/Fax*: 01 6272671. Email: prcraigie@eircom.net

Rock House Fishery

The Rock House Fishery consists of about seven miles of double bank spate water at the top of the Owenduff River. It takes 5 rods. It holds spring fish from late March and grilse from June. The fishing is normally let with accommodation and all services at:

Rock House, Ballycroy, Westport, Co. Mayo. Tel: 098 49137

To book the fishery, contact:
Guy Geffroy, GP Chasse et Peche, 12 Rue de Saussure, 75017 Paris, France. Tel: (0033) 147644747, email: gp.guy.geffroy@wanadoo.fr

Season
Salmon: 1 February–30 September
Seatrout: 1 February–12 October

Day permits
A limited number of day permits may occasionally be available from:

John Noel Campbell, Ballveeney, Ballycroy, Co. Mayo. Tel: 098 49116

BALLYVEENEY, RIVER   F 82 04

This small deep river has about 2,000 yards of fishing water. It gets a run of seatrout and the average size is above normal for this area. A lot of instream development has been carried out and it is worth fishing from July onwards.

Season
Salmon: 1 February–30 September
Seatrout: 1 February–12 October

Permission
The Proprietor, Rock House, Claggan, Ballycroy, Co. Mayo. Tel: 098 49137
Email: gp.guy.geffroy@wanadoo.fr

Day permits
John Noel Campbell, Ballveeney, Ballycroy, Co. Mayo. Tel: 098 49116

** OWENGARVE, RIVER   F 90 97

The Owengarve between Newport and Mulranny holds salmon and seatrout in August and September and fishes best on a wild, stormy day with a good spate on it. It is flyfishing only and Black Pennell, Bibio, Dunkeld and Black and Orange all work well. As a conservation measure, the killing of seatrout is prohibited by law, at present.

Season
Salmon: 1 May–30 September
Seatrout: 1 May–12 October

Permits

Check with the North-Western Regional Fisheries Board when it reopens.

BURRISHOOLE FISHERY   L 96 96

This is really a lough fishery comprising Loughs Furnace and Feeagh. How can I omit it, since it was there that I caught my first salmon and seatrout?

Lough Furnace has four good bank stands for salmon which would earn it the right to be included in this work. They are at the Mill Race, the Salmon Leap, the Back Weir and the Neck, upstream of the seven arch bridge, where it empties into the estuary.

Season

June–30 September

Permits

Mr. Pat Hughes, The Manager, Burrishoole Fishery, Newport, Co. Mayo
Tel: 098 41107

Guides

Resident guides are available at Burrishoole

NEWPORT RIVER   M 05 97

The Newport River drains Lough Beltra and a 56 sq. mile catchment into Clew Bay. This river is something of an enigma: though it holds salmon from opening day, its value as a salmon river is not really appreciated and hence it is quite under-exploited. It gets a run of spring salmon right from the start of the season. Several good fish in the high teens of pounds and one of 22½lb have been taken from the river in recent years. The Newport River seems to be somewhat overshadowed by Lough Beltra and it would appear that most of the patrons of Newport House Hotel prefer the luxury of lough fishing with a gillie to walking the river.

The river is approximately seven miles long and bends and twists its way through rough pasture, bog and woodland. The bottom alternates from gravel to silt and the banks are all negotiable, well maintained with stiles and bridges and it is not necessary to wade. There are numerous access points with car parks strategically placed and nowhere is it necessary to walk more than 200 yards to the river bank.

It is a river that is very well endowed with pools and streams. There are at least 24 named pools and even though it is not divided into beats it could easily take eight or ten rods per day.

The present proprietor, Kieran Thompson, took off the draft net at the river mouth in 1987 as a conservation measure.

The better pools for spring fishing are the Upper and Lower Cement Bridge, the Bush Pool, Sheridan's Pool, the Long Pool (below Sheridan's), the Brigadier's Pool, Welsh's Pool and Upper and Lower Flags. For the grilse, in addition to the above, add the Junction, Jack Mack's Pool and the Road Pools.

The spring fish run from before opening day right up to the end of May and sea-liced fish have been taken in early June.

The grilse begin running on the first flood after 10 June and continue through the summer. There is also a run of bigger autumn fish and this run starts with the first flood at the end of August.

Some would say that this is a river for the experienced salmon fisher. One can fish a stream and a pool down – or back it up – rest it and fish it again and be successful on the second or even the third attempt. Less experienced anglers would really benefit from the services of a guide. A 14-foot double-handed rod is comfortable to use on good water, but when the water runs low a single-handed rod to take a No. 8 or 9 line is adequate. Floating lines are the norm, with a sink-tip being preferred in spring.

Flies

The Newport is a fly-only fishery and the most favoured patterns are Garry Dog, Silver Doctor, Silver Wilkinson, Lemon Grey, Thunder & Lightning and Beltra Badger. McDermott's Badger was popularised by the late Pat McDermott, a gillie on the river for many years. This is a great fly in peaty water, anywhere from Newport to Fermoy. Fly size depends on water height and rarely is anything larger than a size 8 treble or size 4 single required. It is often the angler who dares to err on the small side who takes a fish.

The seatrout begin running in early July and the best of the fishing is through July and August. However, the killing of seatrout is at present prohibited by law due to the collapse in stocks over recent years.

Seatrout can be taken anywhere in the fast water when they are running – even during the day – but the bigger trout are taken at night. The best of the night fishing is from 11.30pm to 1.30am. For daytime fishing, the favourite fly patterns are Green Peter, Silver Stoat's Tail, Delphi Silver (on the point), Bibio (on the bob), Thunder & Lightning, Teal, Blue & Silver (for fresh-running seatrout). On occasions, a Dunkeld can work marvellously well. For night fishing, a Silver Stoat's Tail (10 or 12 single, or 12 and 14 double) is the first choice of many local anglers.

Note: The fishery is subject to catch-and-release regulations until 11 May at the time of writing, in the interests of conservation.

Season
Salmon: 20 March–30 September
Seatrout: 20 March–30 September

Permission
Newport House Hotel, Newport, Co. Mayo. Tel: 098 41222, email: info@newport-house.ie, web: www.newporthouse.ie. Member of the *Great Fishing Houses of Ireland Group*

Accommodation
Enquiries to Newport House Hotel (see above)

5. Western Fisheries Region

The Western Fisheries Region extends from Westport in Clew Bay south to Hags Head in Co. Clare. It covers south Mayo, most of Co. Galway and north Co. Clare. The fisheries in the region are administered by:

Western Regional Fisheries Board, The Weir Lodge, Earl's Island, Galway. Tel: 091 563118, Fax: 091 566335, email: info@wrfb.ie, web: www.wrfb.ie

The region offers a varied and rich choice of game fishing. It is probably true to say that it has a greater number of well-managed fisheries available to the visiting angler than anywhere else in the country. Nearly all the rivers of south Mayo and Galway have runs of salmon – some in spectacular numbers.

The salmon and seatrout fishing of the region was rightly famous for generations, particularly the Connemara district of west Galway, which is especially suited to the production of seatrout. Virtually all of its seatrout fisheries are managed to cater for visiting fishermen. Sadly, in all but a few, the fishing is not what it used to be. While good sport may still be found in some places, others reveal only shadows of their former glories. A sudden decline in seatrout stocks first manifested itself in 1989 and has continued ever since. A major controversy ensued as to whether sea lice from salmon farms in the estuaries might have been responsible for the decline. South Mayo, West and South Connemara were worst affected and anglers should enquire about the current situation. In recent years the situation has improved in some areas, particularly where salmon farms have closed down. Many fisheries have seen an increase in both the numbers and size of the fish and they are cautiously optimistic.

The angling season for seatrout does not commence until 1 June. In an attempt to recover stocks, current regulations decree that all seatrout caught in the Western Fisheries Region during the angling season **must be returned alive to the water**. It is illegal to kill seatrout; to have dead seatrout in one's possession or control; or to sell seatrout; or offer them for sale.

Brown trout: The best of the brown trout fishing is confined to the limestone rivers of east Galway and south Mayo. Some of these rivers have undergone extensive rehabilitation work and hold very good (in some cases, excellent) stocks of good quality brown trout. Fly hatches are excellent on these rich limestone rivers. Prolific hatches of sedge (caddis), upwinged flies (mayflies and olives) and midges offer the prospect of first class dry-fly fishing, when conditions are favourable.

The salmon and seatrout rivers in the west of the region also hold brown trout. These are mainly acid waters and the average size of the trout is small – but there are exceptions.

Note

Rivers marked ** are – at the time of writing – closed for salmon fishing, and seatrout over 40cm must be returned, January 2009. For up-to-date information: **www.cfb.ie** or **www.fishinginireland.info**

Rivers marked * are catch-and-release only for salmon and seatrout over 40cm at the time of writing, January 2009

WESTPORT (OR CARROWBEG) RIVER   M1 84

The Carrowbeg River flows through the town of Westport. It is 10 miles long and drains a 22 sq. mile catchment, including four loughs. It holds a fair stock of wild brown trout and is stocked every year by the Western Fisheries Board. The best of the fishing is in the pools from Westport up to Cooloughra Bridge, where it runs close to the Ballinrobe road for a distance of about 2½ miles. Fish wet-fly in high water and dry-fly (try a Klinkhämer) or nymph in medium- to-low water.

Season

Brown trout: 15 February–12 October

Permits

None is required, but anglers should observe the country code and respect riparian owners' property.

* BELCLARE (OR OWENWEE), RIVER   L95 82

The Belclare is a spate river 2½ miles west of Westport. It is 11 miles long and drains a 20 sq. mile catchment into Clew Bay. It flows through a varied landscape of peat bog, oak woodland, a sitka spruce plantation and small agricultural holdings. It gets a run of spring fish in April/May and grilse in late June–July and summer fish in August/September. The river also gets a small run of seatrout.

The Belclare is not divided into beats and takes about 8–10 rods. It has several long deep pools and they fish best with a good wind from the north-west or south-east. The rest of the river has some nice streams in a falling spate. The Belclare's best salmon in recent years weighed 23lb.

Season

Salmon: 1 February–30 September
Seatrout: 1 June–30 September
Brown trout: 15 February–12 October

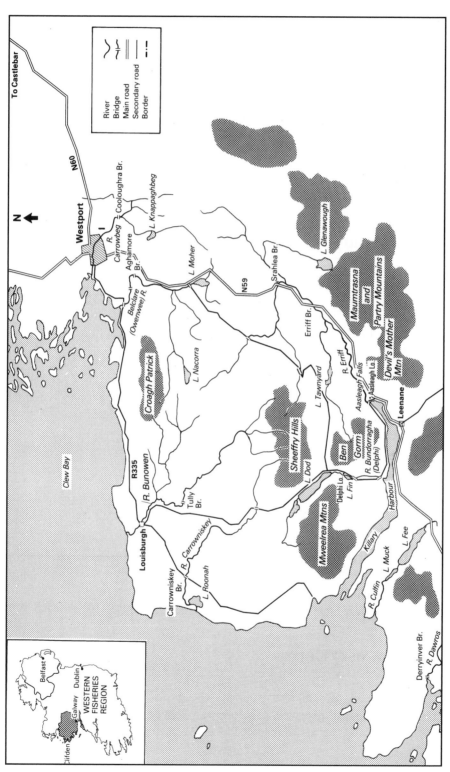

The Erriff, Delphi and south-west Mayo

Permits
Gannon's Garage, Belclare, Westport, Co. Mayo. Tel: 098 25239

Advanced bookings
Tom Bourke. Tel: 086 8331586, email: tombourkefishing@hotmail.com

Regulations
Flyfishing only. Bye-Law no. 721, 1996

Guide
Tom Bourke (details above)

Local tackle shop
Hewetson's, Bridge Street, Westport, Co. Mayo. Tel: 098 26018

---

* BUNOWEN, RIVER   L80 81

The Bunowen River is tidal from the sea up to Louisburgh and drains the Sheeffry Hills and a catchment of 29 sq. miles. It flows through the town of Louisburgh into Clew Bay. Part of it is owned, developed and managed by the Western Regional Fisheries Board and it is that part that is let. It gets a run of grilse from mid-June and holds seatrout from early July. The river is deep and sluggish below the town and there are some nice pools upstream, the best known being Carr's Pool. It is flyfishing only and useful patterns include Silver Doctor, Silver Rat, Hairy Mary, Blue Charm, Black Pennell, Watson's Fancy, Bibio and Bloody Butcher. The best of the fishing is over the mile-and-a-half between Louisburgh and Carr's Pool.

Season
Salmon: 1 April–30 September
Seatrout: 1 June–30 September

Permits
Western Regional Fisheries Board Office, Ballyhip, Louisburgh, Co. Mayo.
Tel: 098 66404

Note
There is a private fishery on the river at Tully Bridge and the fishing is not let.

Local tackle shop
Hewetson's, Bridge Street, Westport, Co. Mayo. Tel: 098 26018

---

* CARROWNISKEY, RIVER   L75 77

The Carrowniskey River flows west into the Atlantic three miles south of Louisburgh. It is very much a spate river, with a catchment of about 14 sq. miles. That part of it that is let is owned, developed and managed by the Western Regional Fisheries Board. It flows into Roonagh Lough before entering the sea and the best of the fishing is on the flats from the lough up to Carrowniskey Bridge. It gets a run of grilse from mid-June and fishes best on a falling spate. It holds seatrout from July.

Season
Salmon: 1 April–30 September
Seatrout: 1 June–30 September

Permits
Western Regional Fisheries Board Office, Ballyhip, Louisburgh, Co. Mayo
Tel: 098 66404

Local tackle shop
Hewetson's, Bridge Street, Westport, Co. Mayo. Tel: 098 26018

BUNDORRAGHA RIVER (DELPHI)   L84 63

The short but exceptionally pretty Bundorragha River is one of the most sought-after salmon rivers in Ireland – and the jewel in the crown of the famous Delphi Fishery. Tumbling out of a spectacular valley formed by the glaciers of the last Ice Age and some of Connacht's highest mountains, the 1½ miles of river contain more than 20 productive pools, some man-made in the 1870s, others completely natural.

The Bundorragha is especially famous for the clarity of its water and it rarely colours for more than a few hours, even after a big flood. This makes it fishable with the fly every day of the (unusually long) season, from February to September. Except perhaps in the most severe of droughts, there is a genuine chance of a salmon on any day of the season.

Spring salmon start running even before the season is under way. Normally ranging from 8 to 12 pounds, these famously short, fat fish are invariably still sea-liced when caught. Springers are taken right through until June, when the average weight is at its peak.

The Delphi Fishery operates a highly successful salmon hatchery, from which about 50,000 smolts a year are released. This has consistently trebled, or better, the natural runs of salmon – including, to the astonishment of many fishery scientists, the spring run.

Delphi Fishery rod catch 2001–2008

Year	2001	2002	2003	2004	2005	2006	2007	2008
Salmon	785	374	474	358	230	584	415	489
Seatrout	519	568	128	174	92	136	280	381

Grilse normally start to enter the river in late June, which is about a month later than used to be the case before 2003. The fish normally range from 2–6 pounds. The run tends to peak in late July and early August and fishing continues in earnest until the end of the season. In the 2008 season, there were only two days between 21 June and 30 September when salmon were not caught at Delphi.

Delphi's seatrout catches used to be the stuff of legend but, like many west coast fisheries, these wonderful fish have largely been destroyed by sea lice from salmon farms. A few finnock are still taken from the river, but not enough to warrant special attention.

The Bundorragha is now divided into two 2-rod beats. The river is fished in rotation with two lovely lakes, Finlough and Doolough, on a half-daily basis. Anglers coming for the normal week of fishing will fish the whole river and each of the lakes four times in the six days. And, within each half day, they will fish both of the river beats, rotating at 11.00 or 16.00 to maximise variety and opportunity.

Fishing is strictly by fly only, but the tackle used varies greatly. Despite the fact the fact that the river is rarely more than 30 feet wide, some anglers in the spring still use double-handed rods to deliver big tube flies in windy conditions. But most use single handed rods throughout the season, often with nothing more than a floating or inter-mediate line and size 8–12 flies.

The Bundorragha contains one of the most important colonies of freshwater mussels in Europe and wading is therefore strictly prohibited (but also quite unneces-sary). Otters and dippers are regularly seen by anglers, with occasional sightings of kingfishers, peregrines and pine martens in the Special Area for Conservation and National Heritage Area.

My favourite pools, starting from the top, are the Bridge Pool from the left bank, especially in high water, the Turn, the Quarry, the Rock, the Holly, Deadman's, Grilse, the Schoolhouse, the Whin, the Waterfall and the Meadow. All of these can be very productive and the Turn Pool is a primary holding pool, with fish present throughout the season. Others are simply pausing points for fresh-running fish, with the tails of the runs deserving particular attention.

The flies used are many and varied. Fishery owner, Peter Mantle, says patience and good fortune are more important than either size or fly pattern. But in recent years the deeper pools have developed a particular reputation as hot spots for nymphing – an exciting new method of salmon angling. My favourite patterns are Collie Dog, Willie Gunn, Vambeck Special, Cascade and a mini tube in low water.

All wild salmon must be released alive, but all tagged fish (of hatchery origin) must be killed to assist research. Normally, over 75% of the salmon taken are tagged.

Advanced booking is strongly recommended, since this little fishery is very popular. Delphi offers luxury accommodation in its main lodge or self-catering in five cottages on the estate.

Season
Salmon: 1 February–30 September
Seatrout: 1 June–30 September

Permits
Delphi Lodge, Leenane, Co. Galway. Tel: 095 42222, fax: 095 42296, email: delfish@ iol.ie, web: www.delphilodge.ie or web: www.delpi-salmon.com. Member of the Great Fishing Houses of Ireland Group

Regulations
Flyfishing only (except Doo Lough). All wild salmon to be returned and all tagged hatchery fish killed.

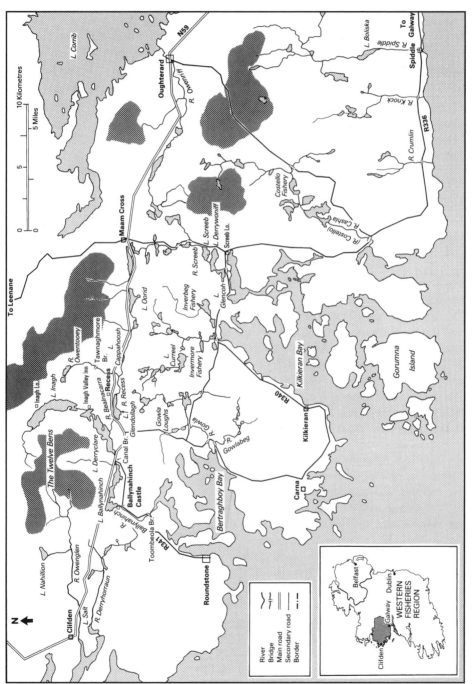

Connemara

Guides
Resident guides are available by prior arrangement.

Fishing lodge
Delphi Lodge (see full details page 136) was completely refurbished in 1994 to cater for anglers. The lodge offers anglers accommodation and has its own rod room and tackle shop, serving all of the angler's needs. 5 self-catering cottages are also available. Open all year round.

Fly casting and flyfishing tuition
Courses in fly casting and flyfishing are available at the fishery, from March to September, conducted by the author, Peter O'Reilly, APGAI-IRL, FFF, MCI and THCI.

Tackle shop
On site. All the salmon flies are Irish made, hand-tied by Peter O'Reilly.

ERRIFF, RIVER   L90 64

The River Erriff enters the sea at the top of Killary Harbour, near the village of Leenane in Co. Galway. It is just over 20 miles long and drains an area of 69 sq. miles. The last eight miles flow through a spectacular and very beautiful glacier-formed valley and it is here that the rod fishery is situated. It is divided into nine beats with a total of 48 named pools and streams. Beats take two or three rods and the total capacity of the main fishery is 22 rods. After a high spate, there is salmon fishing further upstream (above Srahlea Bridge) but this is not regarded as part of the fishery proper. The river is notable for the spectacular Aasleagh Falls, near the sea, and characterized by a series of long, deep pools, glides and streams. The bed consists of stones, sand and glacial deposit, the result of centuries of erosion that appears to be increasing with every passing season.

The Erriff fishery is state-owned and managed by the Western Regional Fisheries Board. The property includes Aasleagh Lodge (completely refurbished in 2001) and two cottages, where anglers are accommodated during the fishing season.

The river is well developed and serviced by stiles and footbridges and access to the banks is easy, with the road running parallel to the bank of the river for its entire length. The banks are good and deep wading is not necessary. The fishery opens on 1 April, by which time there are a small number of spring fish in the river. The peak of the spring run is around mid-May. This fishing can last into June and anglers who fish at this time of year have a chance of a good fish.

The grilse begin running in early June and the peak is in July/August in recent years. Grilse provide most of the sport for the angler for the rest of the season, but there is a fair run of summer salmon, averaging about 9lb and these arrive early in August. The river's heaviest weighed 45lb and was taken on fly in the early 1960s by the late Mrs. Alice Dodds-Marsh, a former lessee of the fishery. The best in recent years was a twenty pounder, taken by Patrick Savage, of Dublin.

River Erriff rod catch 2001–2008

Year	2001	2002	2003	2004	2005	2006	2007	2008
Salmon	546	508	292	293	250	400	270	185
Seatrout	225	202	142	127	79	64	178	140

The Erriff is a productive summer salmon fishery. July is always the best month. June, August and September can also give decent sport when water conditions are suitable. Fly-fishing is the general rule on this fishery, but spinning and worm are allowed for a short period each day.

Fly sizes vary from size 6 trebles down to size 12 doubles, with the smaller patterns fishing best on the higher beats. Popular fly patterns include Cascade, Willie Gunn, Black Pennell, Hairy Mary, Shrimp Fly, Silver Rat, Silver Doctor, Garry Dog, Stoat's Tail, Erriff Green & Gold, Foxford Shrimp and Claret Shrimp. Small flies and mini tubes are essential when the water is low.

Fishing down and across with a floating or intermediate line, is the usual method on the streams in summer. The bigger pools are best fished by backing up, using two flies (invariably with a Black Pennell on the dropper) and using a sink-tip line. For normal flyfishing, a 9½–11ft single-handed rod, capable of casting an 8 or 9 line, is adequate. For high water, a 12–15ft double-handed rod with floating and sinking-tip lines will prove useful.

The river does not get a big run of seatrout and they are generally caught as a by-product of the salmon fishing. I found the slow pools on Beats 1 and 2 as well as the Sea Pool and Coronation Pool and Gowlan to be the most productive areas for seatrout at night. Small flies (10 and 12) seem to work best.

Season
Salmon: 1 April–30 September
Seatrout: 1 June–30 September

Permits
Mr. James Stafford, Manager, Erriff Fishery, Aasleagh Lodge, Leenane, Co. Galway
Tel: 095 42252, email: erriff.fish@iol.ie, web: www.wrfb.ie

Guides
Guides are available but must be booked in advance.

Local tackle shop
Hewetson Bros., Bridge Street, Westport, Co. Mayo. Tel: 098 26018

Lodge
Aasleagh Lodge, Leenane, Co. Galway. Tel: 095 42252, email: erriff.fish@iol.ie
Web: www.wrfb.ie. The lodge was refurbished to a high standard in 2001. Member of the *Great Fishing Houses of Ireland Group*

* CULFIN, RIVER   L74 76

The Culfin River is about a mile long and drains Loughs Muck and Fee and a nine sq. mile catchment. It tumbles down from Lough Muck in a spate. It flows through a bog and the banks are high and access is difficult in places, but there are some nice pools too. It is a lovely peaceful place for a quiet holiday and there are three holiday cottages to let and boats on the loughs. The Culfin River gets a small run of grilse and seatrout.

Season
Salmon: 1 February–30 September
Seatrout: 1 June–30 September

Permits (for the North Bank)
B. Ormsby, Salruck House, Renvyle, Co. Galway. Tel: 095 43997
Email: bowenormsby@eircom.net, web: www.culfin.com

DAWROS, RIVER   L70 59

The Dawros River is about four miles long and drains a catchment of 20 sq. miles, including the Kylemore Loughs, into Ballynakill Harbour. It flows about a mile north of the village of Letterfrack, in Co. Galway and is noted for a small run of spring salmon as well as grilse and seatrout. It is a spate river with a mix of streams and pools, the best known being the Rock Pool, Gavin's Pool, Joyce's Pool and Lavelle's Pool. There are four river beats accommodating two rods per beat. Anglers may also fish the lakes upstream by booking boats.

Kylemore Abbey and Dawros Fishery rod catch 2003–2008

Year	2003	2004	2005	2006	2007	2008
Salmon	72	79	77	119	137	109
Seatrout	248	651	289	248	314	441

Wading is not necessary as all the main pools can be fished from the bank.

Season
Salmon: 1 February–30 September
Seatrout: 1 June–30 September

Permits
Nigel Rush, Moynard, Connemara, Co. Galway. Tel: 095 41178 (office) or
095 41161 (home), email nigelrush@eircom.net, web: www.kylemoreabbeyfishery.net

Regulations
Flyfishing only (Bye-Law No. 721, 1996)

Guide
John Irwin. Tel: 087 6784446

Local tackle shop on site or
Stanley's, Market Street, Clifden, Co. Galway

Lodge
Kylemore House, Kylemore, Co. Galway. Tel: 095 41143

OWENGLIN, RIVER (OR CLIFDEN RIVER)   L68 50

The Clifden River rises in the Twelve Bens mountains in the heart of Connemara and flows due west for 11½ miles to the sea at the town of Clifden. It is an extreme spate river with a catchment of a mere 14 sq. miles. There are three waterfalls on the river: Salmon's Falls, Creggs Falls and the falls at Barnournaun village. The river is well endowed with good pools and when the water is right it can provide some exceptionally good grilse fishing. The first big run comes up on the first flood in June and it is estimated that the river can produce up to 300 grilse in the month of June alone if water levels remain favourable. Grilse continue to run on the spate for the rest of the season and can be taken as far up as Barnornaun – seven miles upstream. A feature of the grilse run is that the fish all tend to be small – averaging 3lb. The river used to be a seatrout fishery. According to local information, salmon were introduced about thirty years ago. The fishing methods allowed are fly and worm. Spinning and shrimp are prohibited. The best patterns are Badger, Silver Badger, Garry Dog, Stoat's Tail, Silver Stoat's Tail, Hairy Mary and small shrimp flies.

The rod catch in the 2001 season was reported as 153 salmon and grilse (mostly taken in June) and 70 seatrout.

The Ivy Pool and the Green Pool are best fished for seatrout at night.

Season
Salmon: 1 February–30 September
Seatrout: 1 February–30 September

Permits/tackle shop
The river is owned by members of the Clifden Anglers' Association and day permits are available from:
John Stanley, Market Street, Clifden. Tel: 095 21039

Regulations
A by-law prohibits fishing with rod and line between Ardbear New Bridge and Ardbear Old Bridge after 15 May each season.

DERRYHORRAUN, RIVER   L68 49

This small stream drains half a dozen loughs into the Salt Lake, just south of Clifden. Occasional salmon run it in summer and it gets a run of seatrout in July. The seatrout mainly run through to the loughs. A by-law prohibits fishing off the Weir Bridge across the Salt Lake, or being in possession of a fishing rod and line on the same bridge.

Season

Salmon: 1 February–30 September
Seatrout: 1 June–30 September

Permits

John Stanley (previous page)

BALLYNAHINCH (OR OWENMORE), RIVER   L76 46

There are eight separate fisheries on the Ballynahinch system. A number of them are private and I shall deal only with those that are available to the general public. The Ballynahinch system is strung like a necklace around The Twelve Bens, in the heart of Connemara. The peaks of Benlettery, Bengower and Bencorr patiently look down on the angler as he drifts the loughs and walks the river banks of one of the most beautiful fisheries in the west of Ireland.

The system is 15 miles long and, from the top of the Inagh valley to the north and Lough Oorid near Maam Cross to the east, it drains a catchment of 68 sq. miles. It once formed part of the sporting estate of the Martin family, one of whose best-known members, 'Humanity Dick' Martin MP, is commemorated by a plaque at Ballynahinch Castle. At the turn of the 19th/20th Century it was owned for a time by The Maharaja Jam Sahib of Nawanagar, better known as Ranji, 'Prince of cricketers'. Ranji spared no expense in developing the fishery by building footbridges and weirs and a feature of the work was the construction of stone-built casting piers which still stands all along the fishery.

A bye-law (No. 714, 1996) prohibits the use of any lure or bait other than artificial fly on the entire Ballynahinch System (it is even illegal to have other than fly tackle in one's possession)

Ballynahinch Castle Hotel Fishery

The Ballynahinch catchment involves a diverse system of interconnected loughs and rivers, drained ultimately by the Ballynahinch River. The river enters the sea at Toombeola Bridge and is two-and-a-half miles long. Its prolific reputation is complemented by the fact that every salmon and seatrout entering the system must run up the river on their migration. The river is well-developed and easily accessible from a road running alongside it. Casting piers were constructed on difficult throws when Maharaja Jam Sahib of Nawanager owned the fishery. The casting piers and fishing huts on every beat enable anglers of all ages and proficiency to enjoy the facility. Complementing the river is the seatrout and grilse lough, Lower Ballynahinch. Traditionally, the lough is fished from a drifting boat, with wet-fly and dapping the methods of choice.

The fishing is let by the beat and may be reserved on an individual basis, or shared with a partner. There is, however, a maximum of two rods per beat. There are seven salmon beats available, which have fishing for fourteen rods; and four 'trout pools' accommodating eight rods. All beats are operated on a strict daily rotation. Ballynahinch Lough has one boat, which can take up to three rods.

The salmon season opens officially on 1 February and extends to 30 September. The effective season, however, begins in late March and spring salmon fishing continues through to May. The catches of 'springers' can be described as occasional, though this may be due to minimal fishing effort at this time of the year. The grilse start running about mid-June, with the main run entering the river in mid-July. The grilse are supplemented by the arrival of the summer salmon in August ensuring a good spread throughout the season.

The seatrout fishing at Ballynahinch declined badly in the early 1990s but has shown a recovery in the last few years due to the closure of the salmon farm in the estuary. At the time of writing, there is a mandatory catch-and-release policy throughout the region as regards seatrout. It is recommended that only barbless hooks be used when specifically after seatrout. The first seatrout begin running in late June/ early July with the arrival of the bigger, more mature trout. Stocks are augmented in August/September by the smaller seatrout, known as 'finnock' or 'harvesters'.

Good brown trout fishing can be had on the upper beats of the fishery and an evening's fishing with an Elk Hair Caddis or a Klinkhåmer can produce a couple of fish in the 2–2½lb bracket. The average weight is just under the pound.

The Ballynahinch River has a consistent flow of water as it is fed by seven loughs. The resulting clean, clear water, is perfect for presenting a fly. Flyfishing is a delight on this well-developed river and the streams are fished in the traditional fashion, allowing the fly to fish round in the current. In the slower, deeper pools, it is necessary for the angler to 'put life' into the fly by retrieving line and this can result in some very exciting fishing. The clarity of the river also allows the angler to experience catching seatrout on wet- and dry-fly during the day – one of the few rivers where seatrout take consistently in daylight hours. Presentation is important and light tackle, a single fly and fine leader are the order of the day.

In recent years, upstream nymphing has produced good sport on the river for brown trout, seatrout and the occasional salmon. It is an effective way of covering some of the more difficult holding areas. Recommended patterns would be weighted Hare's Ears, Pheasant Tail Nymphs and Montanas.

Ballynahinch Castle rod catch 2001–2008

Year	2001	2002	2003	2004	2005	2006	2007	2008
Salmon	79	40	50	73	33	79	97	117
Seatrout	c.400	c.325	275	50	600	650	350	450

A 9½–11ft single-handed rod capable of casting an AFTM 8/9 line is adequate for the grilse fishing in the summer and can also be used for seatrout fishing, although lighter tackle (AFTM 5/6) would be preferred for dry-fly fishing. A 12–15ft double-handed salmon rod would be the favoured weapon for spring salmon fishing and essential against a blustery south-westerly wind at any time of the year. To get the best from this fishery, the angler really should have floating, intermediate and sinking lines to hand. Dapping can be very successful on the loughs during July, August and September. Popular salmon patterns are the Badger, Silver Badger, Hairy Mary, Stoat's Tail, Silver Rat, Collie Dog, Silver Stoat and various shrimp patterns. For seatrout: Butcher, Black Pennell, Peter Ross, Duckfly, Bibio or Connemara Black can all be used, fished on a fine leader. The most effective dry flies are the Elk Hair Caddis, Klinkhåmer, Grey Duster, Pheasant Tail, Daddy longlegs and various sedge patterns. On the loughs, where you may expect salmon or seatrout, the popular local patterns are the Green Peter, Claret Bumble, Bibio, Bluebottle, Muddler Minnow, Delphi Silver, Connemara Black and Daddy.

Season
Salmon: 1 February–30 September
Seatrout: 1 June–30 September

Permits
Ballynahinch Castle Hotel, Recess, Connemara, Co. Galway. Tel: 095 31006, fax: 095 31085, email: bhinch@iol.ie, web: www.ballynahinch-castle.com

Guides
Resident guides available on request.

Tackle shops
On site. All the salmon flies are Irish made, hand-tied by Peter O'Reilly.
Stanleys, Market Street, Clifden, Co. Galway

Lodge
Ballynahinch Castle Hotel, Recess, Connemara, Co. Galway. Tel: 095 31006, fax: 095 31085, email: bhinch@iol.ie, web: www.ballynahinch-castle.com. Member of the *Great Fishing Houses of Ireland Group*

Disabled anglers' facility
Two beats can be fished by disabled anglers, but access is limited and not approved.

Fly casting and flyfishing tuition
Courses at the fishery every season conducted by the author, Peter O'Reilly APGAI-IRL, FFF, MCI, THCI.

INAGH, RIVER (AND LOUGH INAGH FISHERY)   L85 52

The title 'Lough Inagh Fishery' is somewhat misleading. In fact, there are seven river bank beats at the fishery in addition to the lough fishing. These can provide some very interesting and challenging fishing for salmon, seatrout and brown trout, especially for the angler who is prepared to be flexible and adventurous. As an added bonus, it is located against a magnificent backdrop of mountain and woodland in a singularly lovely valley.

The fishery consists of the half-mile-long Inagh River between Loughs Inagh and Derryclare, together with 'butts' – streamy water, mostly outflows of rivers into lakes. Each of the four beats takes two rods. They are quite short, ranging from a couple of pools to 600m.

Lough Inagh Fishery rod catch 2000–2008

Year	2000	2001	2002	2003	2004	2005	2006	2007	2008
Salmon	31	41	51	39	38	8	42	68	85

Seatrout	411	600	255	265	39	547	548	323	759
Brown Trout	170	288	285	N/A	60	402	685	375	231

This fishery has produced some good sport for salmon, seatrout and brown trout in recent seasons.

Derryclare Butts offers the best chance of a spring salmon in medium water in April, but they can be taken here from mid-March. In June and July, all the beats will fish well for grilse in medium water especially Derryclare Butts, Corloo and Glendallogh Butts.

July is the premier month for seatrout and the Trout Pool and Green Point are two of the hot spots. In calm conditions, one can have excellent sport to the dry-fly (especially a Klinkhåmer) and this holds true for brown trout too on the Inagh River and Glendallogh Butts.

Corloo and The Trout Pool make up one beat. Corloo is situated at the outflow of Lough Inagh. Access to the beat is by taking the forestry road 2½ miles south of **Lough Inagh Lodge Hotel**, following it to the river and walking upstream for 600 metres on the right bank (looking downstream). This is the best high water salmon beat on the whole system. There are five casting piers and a hut complete with landing net for the angler's convenience. The beat also holds a good stock of seatrout, conditions permitting, which will take a small wet- or dry-fly. The best piers for salmon are the middle and top ones, although in high water fish can be caught almost anywhere on this beat.

The Trout Pool is situated below Corloo and is fished from the left bank. There is a catwalk adjacent to the pool for easy access and there is a secondary and very productive pool immediately above the Trout Pool and below the rapids. The trout will take dry flies such as Klinkhamers, Adams, sedges, etc. The best wet flies are Butcher, Delphi Silver, Alexandra and Black Pennell, in sizes 10–14.

Derryclare Butts are situated 200 metres downstream of the Trout Pool. Salmon can be taken from April through to September. This is the favourite beat for salmon anglers. It consists of two wall-like structures housing the river flowing into Derryclare Lake. It is delicately fished down from outside the butts and wading is sometimes necessary. The best lie for the fish is at the end of the butts where the flow widens out. Resting the run for 15 minutes after fishing it down is recommended. Favourite patterns include Collie Dog, Badger, Silver Rat and Hairy Mary in the early part of the season. Back-end flies include Silver Stoat's Tail, shrimp flies and Munro Killer. In lower water, sizes as small as 10–14 are advised. There is also a boat on the beat to enable the angler to fish the shorelines each side of the butts. It is important not to disturb the main lie! A friendly hut, complete with landing net, table and chairs and a fireplace provides a welcome respite on a cold, wet day in March or April.

Glendallogh Butts and **Pine Island** make up the next two beats. Glendallogh Butts are accessed along the old railway line 100m south of Pine Island. Drive for about half-a-mile along the coarse gravel road until you come to a 'gorge', where there is a parking place on the left-hand side. The butts are situated 70 metres to the right. Glendallogh Butts are the outflow of the Bealanacrar River into Derryclare Lake. This is mainly a high water salmon lie. There is a wall running adjacent to the flow and salmon lie tight in to this wall. The same flies are recommended as those for Derryclare Butts. This is also a good seatrout beat (wet flies are recommended). July is probably the best month. Pine Island is situated along the N59, 200 metres before the Roundstone turn off. It is uniquely beautiful and possibly the most photographed landscape in Connemara. It is an end-of-season high water salmon beat. It is fished from both banks, from the island downstream. Wind is essential, as there is little flow. There is reasonable trout fishing to be had here too.

Greenpoint is the last beat on the fishery and is the stretch of water upstream of the bridge at the Roundstone turn-off. The beat offers two distinct bits of fishing. One is the seatrout pool, immediately above the bridge. This is fished from both banks below the little island. The other is the salmon lie, 100 metres upstream. There are four piers by the hut to cast from here (the best being the middle two). It is generally a back-end, high water beat and can be very good for seatrout.

To get the best out of the beats, particularly for salmon, it is essential to rest each one for a period – say 15 minutes – before fishing it down again. A Collie Dog, stripped fast on a floating line with a fast sinking leader, can get remarkable results.

During the daytime, a small dry-fly (size 14) can often be successful for seatrout (eg. small sedges, Adams and Klinkhåmers). The Trout Pool is an excellent lie for seatrout and they take a wet-fly well after dark. Biting midges can be troublesome, so be prepared – even during the day!

Season
Salmon: 15 February–30 September
Seatrout: 1 June–30 September
Brown Trout: 1 March–30 September

Permits
Lough Inagh Lodge Hotel, Recess Post Office, Connemara , Co. Galway
Tel: 095 34706

Regulations
Flyfishing only. Catch-and-release for seatrout and brown trout.

Guide
By prior arrangement with the fishery manager at Lough Inagh Lodge Hotel.

Lodge
Lough Inagh Lodge Hotel, Recess, Connemara, Co. Galway. Tel: 095 34706
Fax: 095 34708, email: inagh@iol.ie, web: www.loughinaghlodgehotel.ie
Member of the *Great Fishing Houses of Ireland Group*

THE UPPER BALLYNAHINCH FISHERY   L 86 50

This salmon and seatrout fishery is located between the Canal Bridge (N59 road) and Upper Ballynahinch Lake and on the Bealnacarra River. The fishing is not let.

BALLYNAHINCH, TOP WATERS   L 87 47

This is a river and lough fishery, situated two miles west of Maam Cross, at the village of Recess. It comprises the right bank of the Owentooey River from Tawnaghmore Bridge on the little road up to the Lehanagh Loughs down to the Chapel Pool and the left bank of the Recess River from the top of McCreedy's Pool up to the junction of the Owentooey River and both banks up to Cappahoosh Lough, where the angler may take a boat. There are boats for hire on Derryneen Lake, Shanakeela Lake and Oorid Lake.

This is chiefly a seatrout fishery, with some grilse. Stocks declined greatly in 1989 but improved significantly again in 2008. The best of the fishing is after the first spate in July. The stretch towards the end of the beat at the run into McCreedy's Pool can nearly always be relied upon to produce a grilse in a spate. There are two beats with two rods per beat.

Permits
Leslie Lyons, Tullaboy, Maam Cross, Recess, Co. Galway. Tel: 091 552462
Email: leslielyons@eircom.net, web: www.tullaboy@eircom.net

GOWLA, RIVER   L 81 40

'The Gowla River is over 3 miles long and drains a catchment of 20 sq. miles and a chain of 16 loughs into Bertraghboy Bay. It is mainly a seatrout fishery and gets a small run of grilse. The river is divided into four beats. The lower half of the river has some very good holding pools. Daytime fishing is best in windy conditions and there is excellent night fishing when the seatrout are running. The bigger seatrout run in June, evening fishing is good in July and August and in September, daytime fishing is the best option. Try a Bloody Butcher or Silver Doctor at night and by day, a Bibio, Black Pennell, Watson's Fancy, Camusunary Killer or a Peter Ross.'
I wrote the above nearly 20 years ago for the first edition. Then we had the seatrout collapse and the river was closed for fishing in recent years as a conservation measure. Seatrout stocks were closely monitored and it has now been concluded that there has lately been a good increase both in the size and numbers of fish. Dr. Paddy Gargan of the Central Fisheries Board who directed the surveys is cautiously optimistic about the recovery and prospects for the future.

Consequently, the new owner, Colm Redmond, has decided to reopen both the river and loughs for the 2009 season. He too considers the prognosis to be good and in order to give nature a helping hand he has begun an extensive programme of spawning and nursery stream rehabilitation.

Season
Seatrout: 1 June–30 September

Regulations
Flyfishing only (catch-and-release).

Permits, boat hire and accommodation
The Zetland Hotel, Cashel P.O., Connemara, Co. Galway. Tel: 095 31111
Email: zetland@iol.ie, web: www.zetland.com

GOWLABEG, RIVER   L 82 39

This little river flows north-west into Bertraghboy Bay. It gets a small run of seatrout
from July and there are a few holding pools where the seatrout rest on their way to the
loughs higher up.

Season
Seatrout: 1 June–30 September

Permits
Cashel House Hotel, Cashel, Co. Galway. Tel: 095 31001
Email: info@cashel-house-hotel.com, web: www.cashel-house-hotel.com

INVERMORE, RIVER   L 90 38

This river is closed because of the collapse of the seatrout stock in the late 1980's.

SCREEBE, FISHERY   L 95 40

The Screebe Fishery is situated at the head of Camus Bay, a tortuous winding estuary
located six miles due south from Maam Cross. It consists of an interconnecting series
of about sixteen loughs and, while one might be tempted to conclude it is a lough
fishery, it is surprising to find that there are five bank beats too. Maybe it would be
more correct to call them 'stands', because, with the exception of the river beat, the
others there are short. On their day, however, they can be as productive as many a beat
a mile long.

Screebe is a salmon and seatrout fishery, but the salmon fishing predominates on the river
beats. The fishery is managed by the Burkhart family at Screebe House. It is one of the few
fishery catchments in Connemara unaffected by modern development, such as forestry.
The run of wild salmon is augmented every year by the release of 50,000 smolts reared
in the Screebe hatchery. Even though the Screebe catchment is relatively small – about
22 sq. miles – the river maintains a good flow for five or six days after a flood as a
result of the great volume of water in all of the upstream loughs and the slow release
from the surrounding peat. The fishery gets a small run of spring fish – 11–12lb – in
April and these are usually taken at the Salmon Pool. The grilse begin to run about 20
June and peak in July.

Starting at the top of the fishery and remembering that salmon don't run the
cascade on the river till late in the season, the first spot where an angler might expect
to catch a fish from the bank is at **The Butt at Aasleam**, where the river flows under

the road. This butt is worth knowing about for anyone boat fishing Aasleam Lough. It fishes best with a flood in June, July and August and is totally dependent on the wild fish stocks to provide a salmon for the angler.

The Lady Pool is between the road and the inflow into Cornaree Lake. This pool and Cornaree Butt, some twenty yards below it, give best results in a summer flood. The same holds true of Cornageeragh Butt at the inflow to the next lough down the system.

Next, one comes to **The River Beat,** which extends from the bottom of the cascade at the hatchery to the top of the Salmon Pool. Again, this beat fishes best in a spate in August and September. It is like fishing for salmon in a small trout stream because it is no more than four or five yards wide! There are a few small pools where fish rest and the best one, by far, is Wing's Pool.

We now come to **The Salmon Pool**, also known as Screebe Butt, at the top of Screebe Lake. It is one of the best salmon pools in the west of Ireland. The shape of the river mouth, with its natural rock formation and the two drystone jetties, means that the fishing extends over a distance of 300 yards on both banks. There is also a footbridge to enable the angler to cross over if wind conditions are adverse for casting from one side or other. It is a remarkably productive salmon pool. When I visited it in 1988, the figure was 58 fish in 73 rod days and I had three fish to my own rod in an afternoon. A single-handed rod is adequate to fish this place. In fact, it is *essential*, because the water is practically still at the bottom and stripping the line is required to give the flies some 'life'. It is an ideal location for 'backing up', when a good wind is blowing up river.

For decades, Screebe was a private fishery and was not fished intensively. Some of the better lies were lost or forgotten. Derryvoniff Butt was 'rediscovered' in the late 1980s by the then-Fishery Manager, Philip Clesham. It is located in a most out-of-the way place. It must be approached by boat and the angler runs the gauntlet of all the submerged rocks in Derryvoniff Lough.

Glencoh Butt, between Derryvoniff and Glencoh Loughs, is a very nice place. It is fished – using a taxi boat to get there – in conjunction with **The Road Pool** and **The Sea Stand**. It is tidal and the rising and full tide probably has an effect on the fishing. The tidal Road Pool is half a mile long and located at the top of the estuary. It has proved so productive in recent times that two rods are now fished on it at any one time.

The other two main beats are **The Salmon Pool** and **The River**, which includes Wings Pool, always worth a cast.

Screebe rod catch 2001–2008

Year	2001	2002	2003	2004	2005	2006	2007	2008
Salmon	41	44	45	44	34	139	186	74

Favourite salmon flies for the Screebe Fishery are Lady Etna, Hairy Mary, Thunder & Lightning and any rusty orange shrimp pattern, eg. the Faughan Shrimp. Small sizes (12 and 14) seem to give the best results in summer.

The seatrout fishing is poor but there is good brown trout fishing, particularly on the lakes. They range in size from about 12oz at the top of the system, to 1½lb at the bottom (Road Pool and Glencho Lake).

Season
Salmon: 1 February–30 September
Seatrout: 1 June–30 September
Brown trout: 15 February–12 October

Permits/lodge
Marcus Carey, Screebe House, Rosmuc Post Office, Co. Galway. Tel: 091 574110
Fax: 091 574179, email: info@screebehouse.ie, web: www.screebe-house.ie

Regulations
Flyfishing only
Minimum size: 10 inches (brown trout)
All seatrout must be returned.

Guide
By arrangement with Screebe House

Local tackle shops
Freeney's Tackle, 19 High Street, Galway. Tel: 091 568794
Tuck's Fishing Tackle (for trout flies), Oughterard, Co. Galway. Tel: 091 562335
Hugh Duffy (tackle), Mainguard Street, Galway City. Tel: 091 562367
Corrib Tackle, Liosban Industrial Estate, Tuam Road, Galway. Tel: 091 769974

CASHLA (COSTELLO), RIVER   L 98 26

The Costello Fishery and its famous Cashla River is located near the village of Costello, about 22 miles due west of Galway City. Looked at casually on the map, it appears only a few miles 'out the road' from Galway. But Costello is remote, make no mistake. Situated in bare, boulder-strewn, desolate countryside, it makes the ideal base for piscatorial romantics and fanatical seatrout fishers.

The Cashla River is 3½ miles long and drains a watershed of 32 sq. miles and a chain of 22 lakes, at least 15 of which hold seatrout. It was to Costello that the late T. C. Kingsmill Moore, the father of Irish seatrout fishing, came for twenty years to sample the marvellous 'white trout' fishing.

The river links Glenicmurrin Lake with the sea and is perhaps less well known than the loughs above, but equally deserving of attention. It is a typical moorland river, with a character all of its own. There are huge pools, perhaps forty yards wide – little loughs, really – and short tantalizing streams. The number of the loughs upstream make for a gradual drop in water levels after rain. The flow is now self-regulating. It has some of the finest seatrout pools any angler could wish to clap eyes on: the Cabbage Pool, the Rock Pool, the Round Reedy, Paddy's Stand and the Dinner Pool, to name but a few.

The river is divided into four beats, with two rods allowed on each. The main salmon-taking places are Beat 1 and 2 which probably produce 70% of the salmon, Paddy's Stand, the Butt of Rusheen, the Butt of Formoyle, the Carrick and Clogher Pools, located about 150 yards below Clogher Lough, the Butt of Clogher and the Sea Beat. The salmon catch has almost doubled since the ban on drift netting.

Such is the reputation of the Costello loughs that the river is often forgotten. The fishery opens in March for spring salmon and the first grilse run in late June and July. They continue running in August and there is a run of summer salmon (12–16lb) towards the end of August.

The peak of the seatrout run is around 12 July, though the big seatrout come up earlier, in May. Seatrout hold in the river pools, particularly on river beats 3 and 4.

Flies
The following is a selection of killing sizes and patterns on the river. For grilse, with a good wind on the pools, use a size 10 or 12 Connemara Black on the dropper and a Watson's Fancy on the point. Alternatively, try a Blue Zulu and a Black Pennell. A Jeannie works well on the streams, as do Blue Charm, Ally's Shrimp, Hairy Mary and a small Cascade or a Curry's Red Shrimp. For daytime seatrout fishing, a size 14 or 12 Watson's Fancy has to be the number one choice, fished on a 4lb leader. A small Connemara Black with an orange tag is also highly rated. For night fishing, the choice has to be made between a Blue Zulu, Bibio, Bloody Butcher, Muddlers, Daddy Long Legs and Dabblers (all size 10). A big Black Pennell is often successful, too.

Costello Fishery rod catch 2001–2008

Year	2001	2002	2003	2004	2005	2006	2007	2008
Salmon	41	33	23	22	32	32	56	60
Seatrout	1778	598	N/A	468	864	622	479	1168

Season
Salmon: 1 March–30 September
Seatrout: 1 June–30 September

Permits
Apply to the Manager, Terry Gallagher, Costello & Fermoyle Fisheries, Fishery Office, Bridge Cottage, Costello, Co. Galway. Tel: 091 572196, fax: 091 572366, email: cosfer@iol.ie, web: www.costelloandfermoylefisheries.com

Resident guides
Eamonn Connolly
Colman Keady
Anthony Bollertrum

Regulations
Current seatrout conservation measures require anglers to return all seatrout caught alive to the water (catch-and-release).

Flyfishing only.

Two rods per beat/boat. There are four river beats.

Anglers must be in possession of a valid fishing permit and State Salmon Rod Licence before commencing to fish. State fishing licences can be bought at the Fishery Office. A return of fish caught must be made to the Fishery Office at the end of each day's fishing.

Payment is required at the time of booking in order to secure fishing.

Local guides/gillies
Can be arranged by the Fishery. Guides are employed directly by the angler.

Local tackle shop
Flies and leader material can be purchased at the Fishery Office. Tackle can also be hired by prior arrangement.

Accommodation/lodge
Information at Fishery Office.

CRUMLIN, RIVER   M 03 22

The little Crumlin River is about three miles long and drains a series of nine lakes. It holds small brown trout and gets a run of seatrout and grilse. It has a nice mix of riffles, streams and pools and flows through mainly pristine blanket bog with little or no housing development in the area.

The entire fishery – including the lakes – takes 16 rods and four of these are on the river which is divided into two beats of about 1½ miles each.

Catch records are not available prior to 2004 as they were destroyed in a disastrous fire in the lodge.

July is the best month for grilse and the majority of the seatrout are caught in July, August and September.

The fishery is 'fly only'. Traditional seatrout flies (sizes 10 and 12) work well, particularly the Kingsmill, Bibio, Watson's Fancy and various Bumble patterns, especially the Claret Bumble. August usually brings large falls of various terrestrial insects, including ants and daddy longlegs.

Crumlin Fishery rod catch 2004–2008

Year	2004	2005	2006	2007	2008
Salmon	5	4	6	13	15
Seatrout	214	256	268	394	412

Season
1 June–30 September

Permission
Terry Gallagher, Fishery Manager, Costello & Fermoyle Fisheries Company (Comhlacht Iascaireacht Chasla Agus Faoiremaola), Bridge Cottage, Costello, Co. Galway
Tel: 091 572 196, email: cosfer@iol.ie

Tackle shop
As Costello–Fermoyle, see page 151

** SPIDDAL, RIVER (OWENBOLISKA)   M 9 22

Part of this water is private and part is leased to an angling club. Day permits are not available on the club water.

The Spiddal River is about 3 miles long up to Boliska Lough. There is a further mile of water above Boliska Lough to Derryherk Lough.

Boliska Lough is used as a water supply with a dam at the top of the river. The river gets a fair run of grilse in June-July and seatrout as well. Its main problem is that it is a small river, located close to a big centre of population, with all the attendant problems that creates. The best of the fishing is downstream of the waterfall and there can be quite good fishing on the upper section, above Boliska. Here the banks are clear, unlike the lower river, which is quite overgrown.

Season
Salmon: 1 February–30 September
Seatrout: 1 June–30 September

Guide
Brian Curran, PAGI, Aille, Inverin, Co. Galway. Tel: 091 593860
Mobile: 087 2509722, email: curranb@indigo.ie, web: www.irelandwestangling.com

CORRIB, RIVER (GALWAY FISHERY)   M 29 24

The Corrib River drains Lough Corrib and its tributaries, including Loughs Mask and Carra – a catchment of 1,212 sq. miles – into Galway Bay. It is 5½ miles long and flows through Galway City. It is owned and managed by the Western Regional Fisheries Board. This is one of Ireland's top salmon fisheries, with good spring, grilse and autumn runs of fish. In practice, from an angling viewpoint, it is divided into four distinct sections.

The water level on Lough Corrib is controlled by a weir with fourteen hydraulic gates. This weir is located about 4½ miles below the point where the river flows out of the lough. The first fishery reaches from the Friar's Cut, at the lough, to The Weir. This water is deep and slow. It holds salmon, coarse fish and brown trout. Anglers troll and spin here for salmon and trout and a lot of coarse fishing is done here too. Salmon fishing is with the permission of the Western Regional Fisheries Board.

The next fishery down is what anglers refer to variously as '**The Weir**' or '**The Galway Fishery**'. It stretches some 250 yards down from the Weir itself, to the Salmon Weir Bridge in the heart of the city. It is this stretch of water that, every season, thousands of salmon anglers make their applications to fish. The fishing for spring salmon, which average 12lb, can begin as early as 1 February, depending on the water levels. For good spring fishing conditions, it is necessary that at least six gates in the weir are closed. The peak of the spring run takes place during April and up to the end of the second week in May. Spinning and flyfishing, using tube flies or size 4 treble-hook flies, are the usual methods.

The grilse run from the end of May. They run in big numbers through June and into early July and from mid-July there is a steady run of fresh fish for the rest of the season, with good fishing dependent on a good flow of water. In low water conditions, a fly-only rule applies. Shrimp and spinner may be used when *two or more* gates in the weir are open, with a one-fish limit for spring fish and two for grilse.

Six rods are allowed per 'session' on the fishery. Until 31 May, a fishing session lasts all day. From 1 June until mid-July there are two angling sessions: one from 06.00–13.00; the other from 13.30–20.00. Fishing tactics and equipment are important even on a fishery as prolific as this if good results are to be obtained. It is essential that the angler is able to cast well with a double-handed rod and, furthermore, be able to cast a long line to slow down the speed of the fly. Body waders and a wading staff are essential. A sink-tip line should always be used for the grilse fishing in medium water. A floating line is rarely of any use. It is most important to mend the line well to prevent the fly from skating. The leader should be of at least 12lb strength for grilse and from 15–20lb for spring fish. Line of 25lb strength is not too strong when spinning in spring. In low water conditions the fishing is best in the early morning and late evening. The stream known as the Clonrickard Cut is a favourite in these conditions.

In high water, a black Flying C or a Yellowbelly Devon minnow spun in front of the bridge, or a shrimp fished in the pool at the Weir Lodge is recommended. The favourite daytime flies are Galway Green, Garry Dog, Munro Killer, Green Highlander, Willie Gunn, Tosh, and Black Goldfinch. Dark flies seem to work best in the evening. Fly size is important. A size 10 treble is favoured in summer for grilse, coming down to a size 12 treble in very warm weather.

From 26 July to the end of the season, the fishing reverts to a single all-day session from 09.00–19.00. Half days may be booked at this time.

Evening Fishing (fly-only) starts on April 1 after summer time begins. From June 1 to July 25 (inclusive) the evening fishing is from 20.30–23.00. At all other times: from 19.00–22.00. This evening session is normally booked a day or two before it is required.

The next stretch down is known as **The New Beat**. It extends downstream from the Salmon Weir Bridge to the traps and was first opened in 1989. It takes two rods. It can be booked in advance but there is always the chance of being flooded out. It is also partially tidal for certain periods and a new cat walk was erected on the right bank for the 2002 season.

The final stretch is reserved for local anglers and reaches from McDonagh's turbine to the mouth of the river at Nimmo's Pier. It is bank fishing only. All fishing methods are allowed.

Galway Fishery rod catch 2001–2008

Year	2001	2002	2003	2004	2005	2006	2007	2008
Salmon	776	246	604	1047	891	1251	550	1450
Galway Weir only	N/A	N/A	434	727	691	901	395	1088

N.B. The fishery gets a run of seatrout in August and September

Season
Salmon: 1 February–30 September
Seatrout: 1 June–30 September
Brown trout: 1 March–30 September

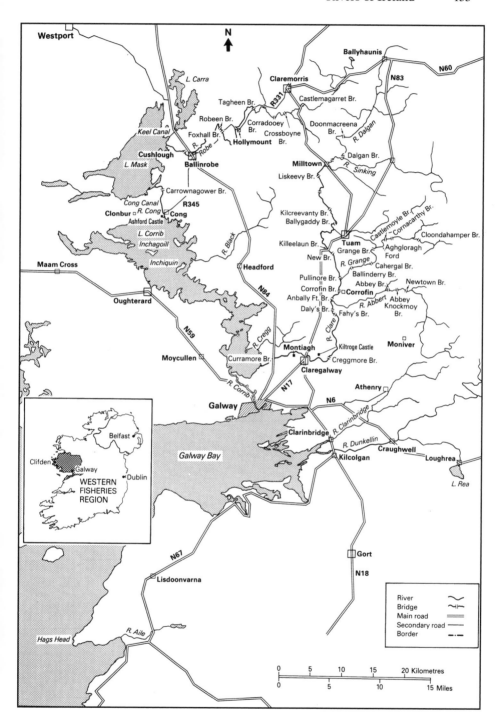

The Corrib system (east) and Galway

Advance bookings
Applications for rod bookings should be made before the start of the season by post, fax or email to:

The Manager, Seamus Hartigan, Galway Fishery, Nun's Island, Galway
Tel: 091 562388, email: shartgalfish@eircom.net

Lodge
Lakeland Country House, Portacarron Bay, Oughterard, Co. Galway. Tel: 091 552121, fax: 091 562930, email: mayfly@eircom.net, web: www.erin.ie/Lakeland. Member of the *Great Fishing Houses of Ireland Group*

Fishery regulations
Licences: Before an angler is permitted to fish on the Fishery, a current State Salmon Angling Licence must be produced. Licences can be purchased from the Fishery Office.

Fly-only rule: During low water conditions (as determined by the Fishery Manager) a fly-only rule will apply.

Polarized glasses: Polarized glasses may only be used by anglers flyfishing on the Fishery.

Foul-Hooked Fish: All foul-hooked fish shall be returned to the river. Fish that cannot be returned through damage or exhaustion must be surrendered to Fishery staff. Anglers failing to comply with this regulation will be banned from the Fishery.

Protocol on the River: Anglers should fish the river taking one step downstream after each cast. On reaching the bridge, anglers should return to the top of the beat and start again.
    Fly anglers wading have right of way while fishing down the river. Anglers must alternate in Jimmy's (weir) pool after one hour's fishing.

N.B. During periods of inclement weather, it is advisable to contact the Fishery for information on water levels and conditions before travelling.

Local guide
Basil Shields, PAGI, Ardnasillagh Lodge, Oughterard, Co. Galway. Tel: 091 552550

Local tackle shops
Hugh Duffy, 5 Mainguard Street, Galway. Tel: 091 562367
Freeney's, 19 High Street, Galway. Tel: 091 562609
The Great Outdoors, Eglinton Street, Galway. Tel: 091 562869
Corrib Tackle, Unit 20, Kilkerrin Park, Liosban Industrial Estate, Tuam Road, Galway
Tel: 091 769974, email: corribtackle@iol.ie

GALWAY CANALS   M29 24

The Galway Canals consist of a network of old mill races and canals on both sides of the Corrib River and located within the city. Some of them hold excellent stocks of wild trout and, being limestone waters, the average size is big, probably 1½lb. In some of them the trout are quite visible in the clear water, against the cream-coloured limestone bottom. They are also stocked by the Western Regional Fisheries Board for the benefit of local children. The canals have all the seasonal hatches of olives, sedges and midges. Access to some is from public footpaths, and flyfishers should beware of catching unwary passers-by on the back cast.

Season
1 March–30 September

Permission
Free

Regulations
Minimum size: 12 inches

OWENRIFF (OUGHTERARD), RIVER   M 12 43

The Oughterard River rises in Shannamona Mountain, south of Maam Cross, and flows east through Oughterard to Lough Corrib, draining on its way a chain of half a dozen loughs. It is approximately four miles long.

It is regarded primarily as a salmon fishery. The resident brown trout are small and it would be quite unsporting to fish for the brown trout that run it from Lough Corrib in September in order to spawn.

The river gets a good run of salmon and grilse. Since it is very much a spate river, with spectacular falls, the runs are dependent on floods to take them up. The first good run coincides with the first good flood in late May or early June. Fish rarely run in July but will run again on a spate in August and September. This river is heavily fished by local anglers when the fish are running.

Season
Salmon: 1 February–30 September
Brown trout: 1 March–30 September

Permits
The fishing is regarded as free for approximately one mile from Lough Corrib up as far as the hatchery opposite Oughterard House Hotel. The rest of the river is privately owned.

Permits are available from
Kathleen Dolly, Waterfall Lodge, Oughterard, Co. Galway. Tel: 091 552168
Web: www.waterfalllodge.net

Tackle shop
Tommy Tuck, Main Street, Oughterard, Co. Galway. Tel: 091 552335

Lodges
Waterfall Lodge, Oughterard, Co. Galway.
Tel: 091 552168, web: www.waterfalllodge.net
Camillaun Angling Centre, Eighterard, Oughterard, Co. Galway. Tel: 091 552678
Email: info@camillaun.com, web: www.camillaun.com. Member of the *Great Fishing Houses of Ireland Group*

OWENWEE, RIVER (SEE CORNAMONA RIVER)	**M 01 47**
JOYCE'S (MAAM), RIVER (SEE CORNAMONA RIVER)	**L 94 53**
BEALANABRACK, RIVER (SEE CORNAMONA RIVER)	**L 90 54**
FARLMORE, RIVER (SEE CORNAMONA RIVER)	**L 95 52**
CORNAMONA, RIVER	**M 01 53**

All these five rivers flow into the north-western end of Lough Corrib. They are spawning and nursery rivers for the lough and the fish that run them are often ripe with spawn. Angling is, therefore, not encouraged on any of these rivers, because it is quite unsporting to take such fish, be they trout or salmon.

CONG, RIVER	**M 13 54**

The Cong River rises in the village of Cong. It is, in fact, the outflow from Lough Mask, further to the north, that escapes and flows through huge cavernous fissures in the limestone and rises again in the village of Cong. Some say it is the biggest spring in the world. It is about one mile long. This is a big, wide river, perhaps 100 yards wide in places, and divided by an island at one point. It pushes down strongly past Ashford Castle. Some of it can be fished off the bank and it is possible to wade it, but more of it is better fished from a boat. To fish it well, the visitor would be well advised to employ a local guide.

The river gets an excellent run of spring salmon and fishing can start on opening day if the water is not too high. The peak of the spring run is in April and then the grilse come in June. July is particularly good, as is early August, and salmon are taken here in lesser numbers for the rest of the season. This is a hugely productive salmon fishery for both spring fish and grilse. To get it in perspective, while there are no official catch records kept, Fishery Board staff believe that the rod catch may be as good or even better than that taken on the Galway Fishery (see page ??). The early-season fish are mostly taken by spinning but the fly can take fish from April onwards.

The river also holds excellent stocks of good brown trout and some are very large. It has good hatches of olives, mayflies, sedges and midge and dry-fly fishing can be especially good. Body waders are very useful when dry-fly fishing, but care should be exercised while wading. Part of the Ashford Castle water is best fished from a boat.

Season
Salmon: 17 March–30 August

Brown trout: 17 March–30 August

Permission and accommodation
Ashford Castle, Cong, Co. Mayo. Tel: 094 9548165, email: ashford@ashford.ie
Web: www.ashford.ie
Grasshopper Cottage, Dooras, Cornamona. Tel: 094 9546003
Email: grasshopper@indigo.ie
Both of the above are Members of the *Great Fishing Houses of Ireland Group*

This permission applies from the Eel Weir Bridge downstream on both banks past
Ashford Castle to the defined mouth of the river at Lough Corrib.

For information on the rest of the river, upstream past the hatchery, contact:

The Manager, Cong Hatchery, Cong, Co. Mayo. Tel: 094 9546049

Local guides
Frank Costello, PAGI, Ashford, Cong, Co. Mayo. Tel: 094 9546348
Mobile: 087 2524253, email: ashfordbay@hotmail.com
John Fahy, Cong Angling Centre, Cong, Co. Mayo. Tel: 094 9546848
Mobile: 087 9096086, email: conganglingcentre@eircom.net

Local tackle shop
John Fahy, Cong Angling Centre (as above)

Disabled anglers' facility
The Hatchery, Cong, Co. Mayo. Tel: 094 9546049

CONG CANAL   M 13 59

The Cong Canal was intended to link Lough Mask with Lough Corrib and extends
from Ballinchalla Bay towards the village of Cong. It is interesting both from an histor-
ical perspective and especially as a superb brown trout fishery. Indeed, it is probably
quite the most remarkable trout fishery in the country. This limestone water is capable
of producing wild brown trout into double figures.
    The canal was proposed by the Board of Public Works in 1844 and work began in
1848. By 1850, 500 men were employed in its construction. Famine was widespread at
the time and the scheme afforded much-needed relief for the men and their families.
The engineer's report for 1848 refers to the greater portion of the men being so desti-
tute and badly nourished that they were unable to realize a wage greater than 3d a day.
By the end of 1853, the main channel was completed.
    The suspension of the work in 1854 gave rise to much speculation over the years.
The porous nature of the limestone through which the canal was cut created considerable difficulty and required much staunching. In 1852, a House of Lords committee
reported that the Board of Public Works at that time was having severe difficulties in
financing such schemes. Moreover, the Committee found that there was unlikely to be

A moored boat on a large side-lake adjoining the Cong Canal (which runs fast behind the stone embankment in this photo)

sufficient traffic on the new canal for it to be viable. This was probably a more likely reason for the navigation work being abandoned as the frequently expressed view that the canal was an engineering failure. The canal was deepened for drainage purposes in 1983. Whatever the reason for its closure as a navigation route, we should remember the distressed and starving workers who gave us a very fine trout fishery.

The canal is about three miles long and the best of the fishing is from Lough Mask down to Carrownagower Bridge. It is approached by the Inishmaine road, which branches off the Ballinrobe-Clonbur road, and the permission of the riparian owners should be sought as necessary. The canal dries up in summer below Carrownagower Bridge and for some distance above it. In springtime, the water flows swiftly and the canal offers good wet-fly fishing and spinning produces several trout over 10lb every year. The Cong Canal trout are beautifully conditioned fish. The average weight of trout caught on wet-fly and dry-fly is marginally under 2lb: one of the highest for any fishery in the country. The canal has all the usual fly hatches associated with an Irish limestone river. Nymph fishing and dry-fly fishing to the sedge are especially good on summer evenings at the canal's outlet from Lough Mask. Plenty of trout are taken here up to 5lb. Many much bigger fish are hooked that are impossible to land. This is popular fishing and it can get crowded. In a wet summer, try further downstream, where the fishing can be just as good.

Season
Brown trout: 1 March–30 September

Permit
Free fishing.

Local guides
Frank Costello, PAGI, Ashford, Cong, Co. Mayo. Tel: 094 9546348
Mobile: 087 2524253, email: ashfordbay@hotmail.com
John Fahy, Cong Angling Centre, Cong, Co. Mayo. Tel: 094 9546848
Mobile: 087 9096086, email: conganglingcentre@eircom.net

Local tackle shops
Fred O'Connor, Cong, Co. Mayo. Tel: 094 9546008
Billy Bourke, Outdoor Pursuits, Glebe Street , Ballinrobe, Co. Mayo.
Tel: 094 9541262
Dermot O'Connor's Fishing Tackle Shop, Market House Tavern, Ballinrobe,
Co. Mayo. Tel: 094 9541083
Cong Angling Centre (as above)

BLACK, RIVER   M 20 48

The Black River flows into Lough Corrib north of Greenfields and Inchiquin Island
after a journey of about 15 miles past Shrule and Headford. It is a rich limestone river,
which was damaged by drainage work in the late 1960s. The river has now recovered
well and much rehabilitation work has been done creating pools downstream of the
village of Shrule. Access is at the bridges and some of them are quite a distance apart.
It holds a good stock of nice trout – some to 3lb and even better. It has the usual fauna
of a rich limestone river, with excellent hatches of olives, sedges, mayflies, black gnat
and plenty of hawthorn flies in May.

Season
Brown trout: 1 March–30 September

Permit and information
Part is free and part can be fished with a Regional Fisheries Board permit, obtainable
from:

The Western Regional Fisheries Board, Weir Lodge, Earl's Island, Galway.
Tel: 091 563118, fax: 091 566335, email: info@wrfb.ie

Regulations
Minimum size: 12 inches

CREGG, RIVER   M 32 35

Much of this river is too deep to hold trout and its upper reaches mainly provide
spawning and nursery waters. There is a lovely stretch of water immediately
downstream of where it rises near Cregg Castle.

CLARE, RIVER   M 32 35

The Clare River rises north of Ballyhaunis in Co. Roscommon and flows south through Tuam before turning west through Claregalway to enter Lower Lough Corrib. It is over 58 miles long (it changes its name to the Dalgan River above Milltown) and together with its tributaries it drains a huge area of East Galway. It is mainly a limestone river and holds excellent stocks of spring salmon, grilse and good-quality brown trout and may well be one of the most under-rated fisheries in the country.

The spring salmon run the river from early in February and the best of the fishing is from 17 March to the end of May. Fish are taken all the way up to and above Tuam, but some of the best of the fishing is in the Claregalway–Corofin area.

The grilse begin running in June, with the best fishing in late June, July and August. As the season progresses, the fish move upstream with every rise in water and fish are sometimes taken on the Dalgan River up near Ballyhaunis.

No records are kept by any of the fisheries or clubs along the river, but all agree that both the summer and spring fishing is very good. The spring salmon average 10–12lb and the grilse 5–6lb. Worm fishing is the most popular angling method and the Flying 'C', Yellowbelly and Toby are popular spinning baits. The Corofin Fishing Association has a fly-only stretch from Daly's Bridge to Anbally footbridge. The most popular salmon flies are Garry Dog, Green Highlander, Munro Killer, Silver Doctor, Hairy Mary, Blue Charm, Stoat's Tail and various shrimp flies.

The quality of the brown trout fishing is first-rate and anglers travel a long way to fish some of the better water. The average weight is about 1½lb and there are reports of trout being taken on fly up to 8½lb. In addition, the river stock is augmented by a run of big trout up from Lough Corrib in July and August when water conditions are right. Photographs on anglers' mantelpieces from Claregalway to Tuam testify to the quality of the trout fishing. Where else could a recent catch of three trout – 5lb, 4lb and 3lb – taken in one evening on a Grey Midge be matched?

The trout fishing begins in April and this can be a good month. May brings the mayfly on several stretches and reed smut are very plentiful and give good fishing. The evening fishing in July and into August can be especially good to sedges, blue-winged olives and white moths, etc. According to Kelly-Quinn and Bracken, in The Distribution of Ephemeroptera in Ireland, there are at least thirteen species of up-winged flies (Ephemeroptera) on the river. They include mayfly (Ephemera danica), purple dun, pale watery, dark olive, iron blue, large dark olive, medium olive, large green olive, late march brown, dark dun, olive upright, yellow may dun, blue-winged olive (BWO) and two species of caenis. Then there are the various sedges, midges, black gnat, reed smut, the hawthorn fly and various other diptera.

Dry fly fishers should equip themselves with a selection of Klinkhåmers, Mosely Mayfly and Spent Gnat, Kite's Imperial, Tupps Indispensable, Pheasant Tail, Orange Quill, Black Gnat and Knotted Midge, in a range of sizes.

CLARE RIVER FISHERIES

The ownership of the fisheries on the river is very scattered and dispersed. There are five major fisheries and I will list them in turn, beginning at the bottom of the river at Lough Corrib and moving upstream.

Western Board Fishery

This fishery is under new ownership. It covers eight miles of the right bank from Lough Corrib up past Curramore Bridge and Claregalway Bridge to a quarter of a mile above Kiltroge Castle and about three miles of the left bank in the vicinity of Claregalway Bridge. The lower section is slow, wide and deep and bank access is difficult. Salmon can be taken near the lake and there is good salmon and trout fishing from Montiagh upstream to above Claregalway Bridge on both banks. Local knowledge is necessary to get the best out of the salmon fishing on the lower stretch, as the lies are very defined and quite far apart. This has to do with how the river was drained and the contours of the river bed.

The upper half of the fishery has a better variety of streams and pools and can give good spring salmon, grilse and brown trout fishing.

Permits and information

The Western Regional Fisheries Board, Weir Lodge, Earl's Island, Galway
Tel: 091 563118, fax: 091 566335, email: wrfb@iol.ie, web: www.wrfb.ie

Corofin Fishing Association

The Corofin Fishing Association Water is in four parts over about nine miles of single and double bank fishing. The first stretch up from Lough Corrib is on the left bank at Curramore Bridge on the Galway–Headford road. This section is slow and deep but is good salmon-holding water. Here again, local knowledge of the lies is necessary.

The second stretch is also on the left bank half a mile up from Claregalway Bridge and extends for nearly two miles.

The third stretch is on both banks below Creggmore Bridge for a mile; and a mile on the left bank upstream of the bridge.

The fourth stretch is quite extensive and consists of nearly three miles of both banks from just above Fahy's Bridge to above Anbally Castle. From Anbally footbridge down to Daly's Bridge is flyfishing only.

The salmon and trout fishing on the latter three stretches are both quite exceptional and some of the very best on the river.

Permit and information

The Western Regional Fisheries Board, Weir Lodge, Earl's Island, Galway. Tel: 091 563118, fax: 091 566335, email: wrfb@iol.ie
Danny Goldrick, Club Secretary, Corofin Fishing Asociation, Spiddal Road, Moycullen, Co. Galway

St. Colman's Angling Club

St. Colman's Angling Club has a couple of miles of excellent salmon and grilse fishing as well as trout fishing on the right bank, from Pullinore Bridge to a point about half a mile below Corofin Bridge. The club also has about 100 yards fishing on the left bank above and below Corofin Bridge.

Permits and information

James Langan, Club Secretary, St. Colman's Angling Club, Toher, Tuam, Co. Galway

Tuam and District Angling Association

Tuam and District Angling Association has extensive fishing rights on the river – either leased or the trespass rights from riparian owners. On sections of this water, there is good and even excellent spring salmon fishing from mid-April; grilse fishing in June, July and August and marvellous brown trout fishing.

The Tuam water begins above Corofin village on the left bank and extends for about 1,000 yards at the junction of the Grange River. This is prime spring salmon, grilse and brown trout fishing.

One mile above Pullinore Bridge, at Cloonkeen, the river holds excellent stocks of trout for about 400 yards. The next worthwhile stretch for brown trout is from the New Bridge up to Killeelaun (Cloonmore) Bridge and the trout stocks are excellent at Gardenfield, one mile above Ballygaddy Bridge.

There is good clean salmon water half a mile above Kilcreevanty Bridge (at the back of the graveyard) and this stretch also fishes well with wet-fly for brown trout.

There is good wet-fly fishing below Lehid and dry-fly fishing from Lehid up to Liskeevy Bridge. This same stretch below Liskeevy Bridge is also noted for spring salmon and grilse. Lastly, quite a few salmon are taken every year downstream of the village of Milltown.

Season

Salmon: 1 February–30 September
Brown trout: 1 March–30 September

Permits

Ian Callander, 3 Ashbrook Avenue, Mountbellew, Co. Galway. Tel: 086 0566405

Regulations

Minimum size: 12 inches (Bye Law 724)

Guide

Brian Curran, Aille, Inverin, Co. Galway. Tel: 091 593860, mobile: 087 2509722
Email: curranb@indigo.ie

Tackle shops

Kevin Duffy, Main Street, Headford, Co. Galway. Tel: 093 35449
Freeney's, 9 High Street, Galway. Tel: 091 562609
Great Outdoors, Eglington Street, Galway. Tel: 091 562869
Corrib Tackle, Unit 20, Kilkerrin Park, Liosban Industrial Estate, Tuam Road, Galway
Tel: 091 769974, email: Corribtackle@iol.ie
Hugh Duffy, 5 Mainguard Street, Galway. Tel: 091 562367
Tommy Cheevers, North Gate Street, Athenry, Co. Galway

Olympic Sports, Dublin Road, Tuam, Co. Galway

DALGAN, RIVER   M 42 64

The Dalgan River is an extension of the River Clare. It has virtually no trout fishing water.

ABBERT, RIVER   M 50 42

The Abbert River is 25 miles long. It flows west from Monivea through Abbeyknockmoy to join the Clare River at Anbally. This was one of the favourite trout streams of J. R. Harris, author of An Angler's Entomology, but it was ravaged by an arterial drainage scheme. A great deal of rehabilitation work has taken place over recent years and there is now a lot of good trout fishing water available, with trout to 3lb or better.

There are at least three different stretches that are worth fishing. The first extends for about three miles downstream and one mile upstream of Abbert Bridge on the Tuam-Claregalway road. There is a piece of good fishing upstream of Abbey Bridge and at the old mill. Finally, there is some nice trout water further upstream, in the vicinity of Newtown Bridge.

Season
Brown trout: 1 March–30 September

Permits and information
Western Regional Fisheries Board, Weir Lodge, Earl's Island, Galway.Tel: 091 563118
Email: info@wrfb.ie
Ian Callander, 3 Ashbrook Avenue, Mountbellew, Co. Galway. Tel: 086 0566405

Regulations
Minimum size: 12 inches

N.B. At the time of writing, there is an application before the Western Regional Fisheries Board to make this river 'fly only'.

GRANGE, RIVER   M 48 50

The Grange River flows west for 17 miles to join the Clare River about three miles south of Tuam. It flows through the bog from Cahergal Bridge down to the confluence and is of no interest to the game angler. It too was affected by an arterial drainage scheme. There is not a sound to be heard now from the famous Ahgloragh Ford (the roaring ford, in Irish). Much rehabilitation work has been carried out by the Western Regional Fisheries Board and the river has recovered well from Grange Bridge upstream. It holds good stocks of brown trout to 3lb and fishes especially well to wet-fly on high water in August and September. It also gets a small run of grilse. The best of the brown trout fishing is from Grange Bridge to Castlemoyle Bridge. The stretch downstream of Cornacartha Bridge holds some very large trout and the tributary coming in from the south is worth fishing from Cloondahamper Bridge downstream.

Season
Brown trout: 1 March–30 September

Permits and information
Western Regional Fisheries Board, Weir Lodge, Earl's Island, Co. Galway
Tel: 091 563118, email: info@wrfb.ie
Ian Callander, 3 Ashbrook Avenue, Mountbellew, Co. Galway. Tel: 086 0566405

Regulations
Minimum size: 12 inches

Bye-Law No. 720 (1996)
It is hereby prohibited: (a) to use a lure other than an artificial fly in angling for fish with rod and line in the section of the Grange River from the Bridge at Conconroe in the County of Galway to the point at which the Imaun stream enters the Grange River, or (b) to have in possession, on or near the banks of the aforesaid section of the Grange River, of a mounted rod to which is attached a lure other than an artificial fly.

SINKING, RIVER   M 50 63

The Sinking River flows through Dunmore and joins the Clare River below Dalgan Bridge. It flows through bog from Dunmore downstream and it has fair-to-good trout fishing upstream of Dunmore. The best of the fishing is up until about mid-June. Thereafter, the river becomes very weedy.

Season
Brown Trout: 1 March–30 September

Permission
Riparian owners

Regulations
Minimum size: 12 inches

ROBE, RIVER   M 20 65

The Robe River is nearly 40 miles long. It rises near Ballyhaunis and flows west past Claremorris through Hollymount and Ballinrobe and enters Lough Mask north of Cushlough. This rich limestone river was drained in the early 1980s and extensive rehabilitation work was carried out on it by the Western Regional Fisheries Board. I am delighted to be able to report that it has made a remarkable recovery. A recent electrical fishing survey found excellent stocks of trout; indeed it is now regarded as one of the trout fishing jewels of the whole region. The staff at WRFB, Cushlough (below) will be glad to advise on where to fish.

A fine trout from the river Robe for a young fisher

Season
Brown trout: 1 March–30 September

Further information
Western Regional Fisheries Board, Weir Lodge, Earl's Island, Co. Galway
Tel: 091 563118
Western Regional Fisheries Board Office, Cushlough, Ballinrobe, Co. Mayo
Tel: 094 9541562

KEEL, CANAL   M 15 68

The Keel Canal is a mile long and links Lough Carra and Lough Mask. Its water is gin-clear and it holds a small stock of timid trout to over 6lb. It flows fast and strong in spring and later has prolific fly hatches of all the usual limestone species, including mayfly. Access is good from Keel Bridge, with stiles and footbridges provided. The lovely silver Keel trout and their clear-water habitat can test even the very best dry-fly anglers. The canal runs low and becomes weedy in summer.

Season
Brown trout: 1 March–30 September

Permit
Free fishing

Regulations
Minimum size: 12 inches

** CLARINBRIDGE, RIVER   M 42 21

The Clarinbridge River is about 12 miles long and comes down past Athenry to the sea at Clarinbridge. It holds a good stock of trout and April to June is the best time to fish as it runs low in summer. Part of the river runs dry due to the porous nature of the limestone bed.

Permission
There is an angling club in Athenry. Most of the fishing requires the permission of riparian owners.

** DUNKELLIN (OR KILCOLGAN) AND RAFORD, RIVERS   M 42 18

The Kilcolgan River is over 30 miles long and drains a catchment of over 140 sq. miles, including Lough Rea. It flows west through the village of Craughwell into Galway Bay. It is a rich limestone river and the porous nature of the bed rock causes part of the river to dry up in summer. It gets a run of salmon and seatrout and holds fair stocks of brown trout in certain areas.

The spring fish run in April and May and the grilse in June and July. The river offers good prospects for flyfishing in the last mile above the tide. It has produced fish to 20lbs in recent years and fish are taken as far as Craughwell and even further upstream.

The best of the seatrout fishing is in July and early August, from the Old Bridge at Kilcolgan down to the top of the estuary. The river gets larger seatrout than those found in Connemara. The best fishing is at night from about 22.00 to 23.30 and again from 01.00 to 04.00. Favourite flies are Bloody Butcher, Silver Doctor and Teal, Blue & Silver.

The Kilcolgan also holds some very big 'slob' trout, but these are rarely taken by conventional flyfishing methods.

The river holds a fair stock of nice brown trout but also some good ones to 3½lb. It can fish well in April, when every half-dozen trout taken will include one or two of a pound or better. April and May see the peak of the brown trout fishing, as the river weeds up in summer. The main stretch for brown trout fishing is from the old bridge up to the waterfall, as far as Dunsandle House and it is very good at Craughwell and on part of the Raford River. The fly hatches are a bit erratic, though the river has all the usual limestone stream insects except mayfly. Upstream, the banks are clear and easy to fish.

Season
Salmon: 1 February–30 September
Seatrout: 1 June–30 September
Brown trout: 17 March–15 September

Regulations
Minimum size: 9 inches (Bye-Law 482)

Permits
The Western Regional Fisheries Board, Earl's Island, Galway (tel: 091 563118) for a short stretch of less than half a mile on the right bank. The rest is strictly with riparian owner's permission. Lough Rea Angling Club has fishing rights on the river that flows out of Lough Rea.

Guide
Brian Curran, Aille, Inverin, Co. Galway. Tel/fax: 091 593860, mobile: 087 2509722
Email: curranb@indigo.ie, web: www.irelandwestangling.com

** AILLE, RIVER   M 10 97

This little river flows down off the Burren, through Lisdoonvarna, to enter the sea at Doolin Strand. It flows in places through deep gorges and is very overgrown. There are several deep holes along its course, both above and below Lisdoonvarna, which hold good brown trout. Access to one of the better stretches is at the old Protestant church above the Spectacle Bridge. The river runs dry in summer, from Roadford downstream, but seatrout and a few grilse are said to run it on a spate. The water is spectacularly clear and clean.

Season
Seatrout: 1 June–12 October
Brown trout: 15 February–12 October

Permission
Riparian owners

Instructors
Ronan Creane, FFF, CI, Roundstone, Co. Galway. Tel: 087 701986
Email: roundstoned@yahoo.co.uk
Ballynahinch Castle Hotel, Recess, Co. Galway. Tel: 095 31006
Web: www.ballynahinch-castle.com
Peter O'Reilly, APGAI-IRL, FFF, MCI, THCI, web: www.oreillyflyfishing.com
Delphi Lodge and Fishery, Leenane, Co. Galway. Tel: 095 42222
Email: delfish@iol.ie, web: www.delphi-salmon.com
Peter O'Reilly, APGAI-IRL, FFF, MCI, THCI, web: www.oreillyflyfishing.com

6. Eastern Fisheries Region

The Eastern Fisheries Region extends from the border with Northern Ireland in Carlingford Lough to Kiln Bay, Co. Wexford. It includes part of Co. Monaghan and Counties Louth, Meath, Westmeath, Dublin, Wicklow, Kildare, Wexford, Offaly and Carlow.

The Fane, Dee, Boyne, Liffey and Slaney are some of its major rivers. With Ireland's capital, Dublin, located right in the middle of the region, one could be forgiven for concluding that the fisheries must all be overcrowded and overfished. This is not the case. There may be some overcrowding in specific areas, at certain times, but there are also miles of river holding decent stocks of good quality wild trout, that are only lightly fished. The reason, perhaps, has been a lack of information on the waters in this region compared with Ireland's more celebrated fisheries in the west.

Eastern Regional Fisheries Board (Headquarters), 15a Main Street, Blackrock, Co. Dublin. Tel: 01 278 7022, fax: 01 278 7025, email: info@erfb.ie
Web: www.fishingireland.net

Note
Rivers marked ** are – at the time of writing – closed for salmon fishing, and any seatrout over 40cm must be returned (this is a policy to conserve the larger breeding fish).
Rivers marked * are catch-and-release for all salmon, and seatrout over 40cm must be returned.

For up-to-date information on these closed and catch-and-release rivers see:
www.fishingireland.net/salmon and seatrout.

Accommodation
For your hotel, lodge and bed and breakfast accommodation, see:

East Midlands (Kildare, Laois, Longford, Louth, Meath, North Offaly, Westmeath, Wicklow), Fáilte Ireland East & Midlands, Dublin Road. Tel: 044 9348761
Fax: 044 9340413, email: eastandmidlandsinfo@failteireland.ie
Web: www.discoverireland.ie/eastcoast
Dublin Tourism, Suffolk Street, Dublin 2. Tel: 01 6057700
Web: www.discoverirlenad.ie/dublin

South East (Carlow, Kilkenny, South Tipperary, Waterford, Wexford), Fáilte Ireland South East, 41 The Quay, Waterford. Tel: 051 875823, fax: 051 877388
Email: southeastinfo@failteireland.ie, web: www.discoverireland.ie/southeast

Guides and local angling contacts

Peter O'Reilly, APGAI-IRL and FFF, MA, THCI, ghillie and angling instructor (River Boyne and Lough Sheelin), Ballybatter House, Boyne Hill, Navan, Co. Meath
Tel: 046 9028210, web: www.oreillyflyfishing.com.

Marc O'Regan, MCG, guide (River Boyne), Cranmor, Dunderry Road, Trim,
Co. Meath. Tel: 046 9431635, email: cranmor@eircom.net, web: www.cranmor.com.

Pat McLoughlin MCG, guide (River Boyne), 64 Magdalene Court, Kells, Co. Meath.
Tel: 046 9241807, mobile: 086 1017415, email:patandtrina@eircom.net
Web: www.fishinginireland.net.

John O'Malley, ghillie (Lough Lene), Carrick Bay, Lough Ennell, Mullingar,
Co. Westmeath. Tel: 044 9349086, mobile: 087 6681672

Tommy Conlon, ghillie (Lough Lene), Addinstown, Delvin, Co. Westmeath
Tel: 046 9430112, mobile: 087 9642659

Tommy Fagan (Lough Lene), Inisfree, Collinstown, Co. Westmeath. Tel: 044 61359

John Higgins, MCG, guide (River Liffey),   Westlakes, Hawfield, Newbridge,
Co. Kildare. Tel: 086 8135497, email: jjhiggins@02.ie

Eamonn Conway, APGAI-IRL and FFF, CI, ghillie and angling instructor (River's Fane and Castletown), 73 Willowdale, Dundalk, Co. Louth. Tel: 042 9337387
Mobile: 086 1242966, email: eamonnconwayflyfishing@hotmail.com

Seamus Lenehan, Ghillie (River Boyne), Clonardon, Garlow Cross, Navan, Co. Meath
Mobile: 086 8140078

** COOLEY, RIVER   J 17 05

It is also known as the Piedmond River or the Big River and the Little River and locals refer to it as the Riverstown River. This is a small spate river, which tumbles down the Cooley Peninsula along a 6 ½ mile course and enters Dundalk Bay, east of Gyles Quay. It holds plenty of small brown trout to about half-a-pound. It gets a good run of seatrout after an August or September spate. These fish range mostly from 8oz–12oz. They lie mainly in the stretch from Riverstown Mill down to the tide. This is a lovely stretch of water – quite fishable and with lots of potential for the development of new pools.

Season
Salmon and seatrout: 1 March–12 October
Brown trout: 1 March–30 September

Permission
Riparian owners

** FLURRY (OR BALLYMASCANLAN) RIVER   J 10 08

The Flurry River, (also known as the Ballymascanlan River) rises on Camlough Mountain west of Newry and flows 13½ miles in a southerly direction into Dundalk Bay. It drains an area of some 37 sq. miles of mainly mountainous countryside. The last four miles flow through old pastureland and woodland consisting of mature oak, ash and beech. This is a beautiful little spate river, about four yards wide, with some nice pools. It has a lovely gravel bed, with clumps of ranunculus. The banks are reasonably clear. It gets a fair run of seatrout and grilse from mid July. The early run of seatrout range from 1lb–3lb. It fishes best after a spate. In all, there are about four miles of fishing that starts at a good pool above Currathir Bridge and continues downstream to Ballymascanlan Bridge. The very best of the fishing is from Ballymascanlon down to the tide and this can be very good indeed.

Season
Salmon and seatrout: 1 March–12 October
Brown trout: 1 March–30 September

Permission
Riparian owners

The Dundalk and District Brown Trout Anglers Association take a deep interest in the well-being of this river. Information from:

Paddy Tennyson, Secretary, Dundalk and District Brown Trout Anglers Association
Mobile: 086 8405653, email: info@browntroutanglers.com
Web: www.browntroutanglers.com

Tackle shops
Mark Sweeney,   Island Fishing Tackle, Park Street, Dundalk, Co. Louth
Tel: 042 9335698
Euro Tackle, Unit 11, Demesne Shopping Centre, Dundalk, Co. Louth
Tel: 042 9240205, web: www.euro-tackle.com
Patsy McArdle, The Bike Doctor/Tackle Shop, Bridge Street, Dundalk, Co. Louth

Instructor/guide
Eamonn Conway APGAI-IRL, FFF, CI. Mobile: 086 1242966
Email: eamonnconwayflyfishing@hotmail.com

** CASTLETOWN RIVER   J 03 09

The Castletown River (also known as the Creggan or Courtbane River) flows into the head of Dundalk Bay. It is quite a sizeable river for, together with its tributaries, the Cully Water (Fallmor or Dungooley River) and the Kilcurry (Forkhill) River, it drains an area of 98 sq. miles. The system holds brown trout and gets a run of salmon and an excellent run of seatrout. It is also stocked with brown trout. This river has heavy angling pressure, particularly when the seatrout are running.

The grilse run with the first flood in July and the seatrout come in late July. This river fishes well through August and September, when the water conditions are right.

The Kilcurry (Forkhill) River is usually fished for seatrout from the Annagh Road Bridge down past Millbrook Bridge to the confluence, a distance of about 2 miles. This is a fast-flowing river, 5–7 yards wide and overgrown with brambles. Mee's Pool is one of the most productive seatrout pools on the river.

Membership is open. Day permits are also available. The Association is very active in developing the waters and co-operates with the Regional Fisheries Board staff in carrying out fishery protection.

Brown trout

The Castletown River flows in a southerly direction from Newtownhamilton and through Cullyhanna, in Co. Armagh. It becomes a worthwhile trout stream from Ballybinaby Bridge downstream just south of the Armagh border. In all, there is about five miles of brown trout fishing, mainly to wet-fly in April, May and June, as it tends to run low in summer.

Seatrout

The seatrout fishing can be very good from early July, through August and September. There is a bag limit of six trout. The best of the seatrout fishing is from Bellew's Bridge (Coffin Bridge) downstream for a distance of about three miles to the estuary. The river is about 10 yards wide at Bellew's Bridge (with its 1674 inscription) and it has a nice sequence of pools and glides over a gravel bottom.

Above Tubberona Bridge is a big pool and a weir and more new pools have been developed downstream. This is a favourite area for seatrout fishing. Most of the fishing is done at night and small silver bodied flies are most popular, eg. Teal, Blue & Silver and Silver Doctor. Angling pressure is very heavy on the river when the seatrout are running and it is good to be able to report that there was a great run of seatrout in the 2001 season.

Salmon

The river gets a small run of salmon. It is considered to be a 'late' river. While some fish enter the river in July, the run doesn't peak until it gets a good spate in autumn when the draft nets go off. The fishing is best after a flood. Working upstream, the main salmon angling areas are: below Tubberona Weir, Tubberona Pool, a few nice pools between Bellew's Bridge and the Court Bridge and, finally, Philipstown Pool. There is a nice long pool about a quarter-of-a-mile above Philipstown Bridge and it is a good place to take a fish on fly from the right bank, especially in a September flood. Shrimp patterns are the most favoured salmon flies on the river.

Season

Salmon and seatrout: 1 March–12 October
Brown trout: 1 March–12 October

N.B. a bye-law prohibits angling in March and April downstream of Toborona Bridge

Permission

The Dundalk and District Brown Trout Anglers Association and the Castletown Salmon Anglers enjoy fishing rights on much of the river by the grace and favour of the riparian owners. Day permits and information:

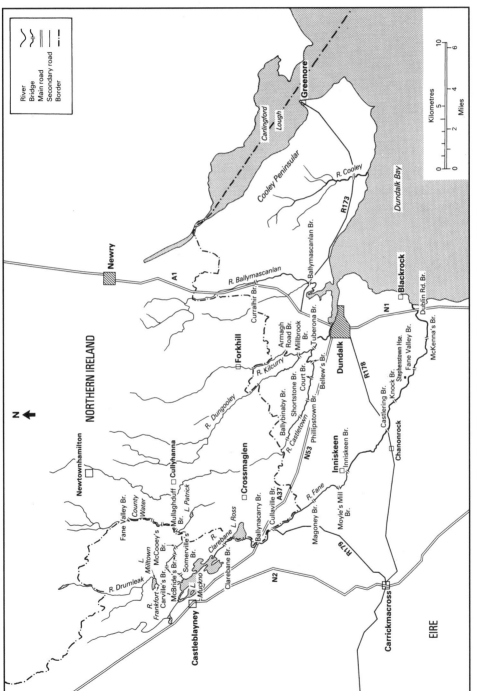

The rivers Fane, Castletown, Ballymascanlon and Cooley

Paddy Tennyson, Secretary, Dundalk and District Brown Trout Anglers Association
Mobile: 086 8405653, email: info@browntroutanglers.com
Web: www.browntroutanglers.com
Mark Sweeney, Island Fishing Tackle, Park Street, Dundalk, Co. Louth
Tel: 042 9335698
Patsy McArdle, The Bike Doctor/Tackle Shop, Bridge Street, Dundalk, Co. Louth

Local tackle shops
Island Tackle, 58 Park Street, Dundalk, Co. Louth. Tel: 042 9335698

Disabled anglers' facility
A facility is being developed at Tubberona Bridge

Instructor/guide
Eamonn Conway APGAI-IRL, FFF, CI. Tel: 086 1242966
Email: eamonnconwayflyfishing@hotmail.com

FANE, RIVER   J 00 02

The River Fane rises north west of Newtown Hamilton, in Co. Armagh, and flows 38
miles to the sea at Blackrock, in Co. Louth. It drains a catchment of 135 sq. miles. Its
upper reaches, before it enters Lough Muckno at Castleblayney, are variously known
as the County Water, the Mullaghduff River and the Little Fane. It flows along the
Monaghan–Armagh border for 6 miles. Another tributary, known as the Drumleak
River, flows into Milltown Lough and the river from Milltown Lough to Lough
Muckno is known as the Frankfort River.

The Clarebane River joins Lough Muckno and Lough Ross in Co. Armagh. From
Lough Ross, the river marks the border between Co. Monaghan and Co. Armagh for
a distance of about five miles and meanders along through drumlin-type countryside towards the stony grey fields of Inniskeen and the country of the poet, Patrick
Kavanagh. From Inniskeen, the gradient lessens and the flow slows as the river makes
its way to meet the tide. The tide can often back up the water as far as Craig's Pool,
below Fane Valley Bridge.

Jurisdiction
In those areas where the river flows along the border between Northern Ireland and
the Republic, the matter of licences and opening and closing dates depends on which
jurisdiction the angler is fishing in. The Northern Ireland season is much longer and it
is illegal for an angler in the Republic to have a fish in his possession on the river after
12 October, even though it might have been legally caught in Northern Ireland.

Salmon
The extent of the salmon fishing depends on water height. In low water, the majority
of the fish are confined to the lower reaches and the best fishing is from Craig's Pool
to the tide below McKenna's Bridge. In high water, salmon fishing extends right up to
Art Hamill weir near Cullaville, though some would contend that the best of it is from
a point about a quarter of a mile above Magoney Bridge. In high water there are at least

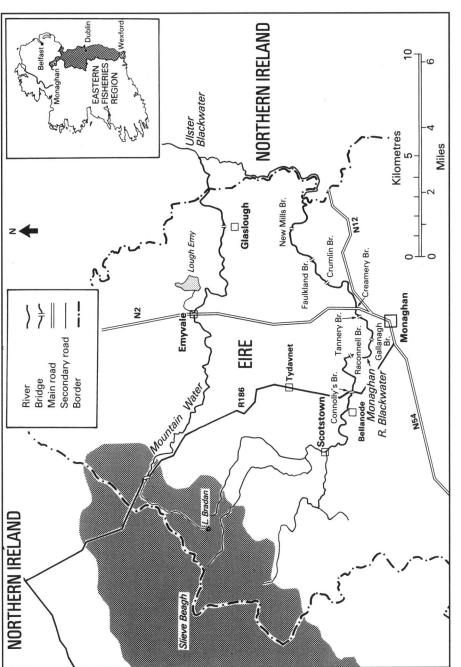

Mountain Water and the Monaghan Blackwater

three good lies from the old mill down to Magoney Bridge. Below Magoney Bridge, the best of the fishing is at the Island Pool, the Flats and the Linnies Pool. Access to this stretch is down along the old railway line, halfway between Blackstaff National School and Magoney Bridge. From Moyles Mill Bridge downstream is particularly noted as nice flyfishing water in a spate.

Passing down from Inniskeen, the first pool of note is the Splink Pool, (which is on the private syndicate water) regarded by many as the most productive high-water pool on the river. The next pools of note are Pepper's Wall and Campbell's Mill Pool, where a 54lb fish was allegedly poached many years ago. The Hall Pool, 100 yards above Castlering Bridge, is the last pool of note on this stretch.

Between Castlering Bridge and Knock Bridge there are half a dozen pools, any one of which could produce a fish. The last of them and probably the best, is McArdle's Pool – a big triple pool. The flat above it is also well worth some attention.

Below Knock Bridge, McGeeney's Pool and Kirk's Pool are favourite throws and, from the weir at Stephenstown House down to Fane Valley Bridge, there are five or six pools, all of which hold fish.

From Fane Valley Bridge downstream it is nearly all deep water except for one shallow stretch and Craig's Pool is a noted lie. This is definitely the most heavily-fished stretch on the whole river.

The Season

The spring run is probably extinct and no one fishes it anymore. The river gets a small run of grilse in June, but it is not significant. The main run – and it can be very substantial, with a lot of big fish in double figures – arrives with the first floods in August. These are the fish, (among them a lot of big two-sea-winter summer salmon), that provide the best of the fishing through September and into October, all the way up to and above Magoney Bridge. The fishing can be very good indeed.

Access

Access to the rivers can be gained at all of the bridges. Other well-defined access points are at the old railway track at Blackstaff, Monahan's Bungalow, Coburn's, Campbell's Lane (remember to park the car at the main road) and Craig's Lane.

Disabled anglers' facility

Stephenstown Bridge (upstream).

Fishing methods

Worm and shrimp fishing are very popular, especially from Fane Valley Bridge downstream. Flyfishing has gained greatly in popularity in recent times and popular patterns are Garry Dog, Green Highlander and various shrimp flies. On good water, the river offers ample opportunities for the fly all the way from Magoney Bridge downstream. Flyfishers should note that water temperatures can drop very fast on this river in autumn, so large flies (sizes 2 and 4) may be called for. The most popular spinning baits are 'Flying Cs', a No. 3 brass Mepps, or a No. 4 copper Mepps.

Seatrout

This river gets a really good run of seatrout, but numbers caught are not reported by anglers and the majority of the anglers concentrate on salmon fishing. The seatrout fishing extends up as far as Knock Bridge and the best of it is from a quarter of a mile below Knock Bridge to Stephenstown House – good fly water, note especially the Mill Pool – and from Craig's Pool to McKenna's Bridge and downstream about a mile to the Fiddler's Hole. From Craig's Pool downstream the river is heavily fished.

The peak of the season is from mid-July through August and both daytime and night flyfishing can be quite good. Many anglers, however, choose to fish maggot and worm. Small flies (size 12) seem to work best and the locals recommend anything with silver in it: Butcher, Bloody Butcher, Teal, Blue & Silver, Dunkeld and Watson's Fancy.

Brown trout

The brown trout fishing on the Fane is generally considered to extend upstream from Knock Bridge to Cullaville Bridge and there is some nice wet-fly fishing in the Stephenstown area in spring. This is a relatively rich river and, while the average size is about 8oz, it holds trout to 2½lb and better. The average weight of the trout in the Castlering Bridge to Knock Bridge stretch is close to 12oz. There is a minimum size limit of 9 inches. The river holds an excellent stock of trout from Cullaville Bridge down to Inniskeen and there is some nice dry-fly water for three-quarters of a mile above the Mill of Moyles. The best daytime fishing is from late April, throughout May and into early June, with very good evening fishing all summer.

The river is reported to have hatches of dark olives, iron blue duns, grey flags, black sedges and black gnats. The river is not heavily fished for brown trout and a visiting angler is likely to find plenty of space, especially mid-week.

Season

Brown trout: 1 March–30 September
Salmon: 1 May–12 October
Seatrout: 1 May–30 September

Permission

Dundalk Salmon Anglers (Secretary, Bernard Devenney. Tel: 042 9334202) have extensive fishing rights on the lower river downstream of Knockbridge to the sea. They also enjoy fishing rights on various other stretches upstream, as do Dundalk Brown Trout Anglers Association (Secretary, Paddy Tennyson. Tel: 086 8405653, email: info@browntroutanglers.com, web: www.browntroutanglers.com) and the Village Anglers, Enniskeen, Co. Monaghan. The Ballintra Anglers have a stretch of private syndicate water too.

For day permits and club information on both the Dundalk Clubs' Waters contact:

Mr. Mark Sweeney, Island Fishing Tackle, 58 Park Street, Dundalk, Co. Louth
Tel: 042 9335698
Euro Tackle, Unit 11, Demesne Shopping Centre, Dundalk, Co. Louth
Tel: 042 9240205, web: www.euro-tackle.com
Mr. Patsy McArdle, The Bike Doctor/Fishing Tackle, Bridge Street, Dundalk,
Co. Louth

The Village Anglers at Inniskeen claim fishing rights on about one mile of water at the village of Inniskeen. Day permits are available at:

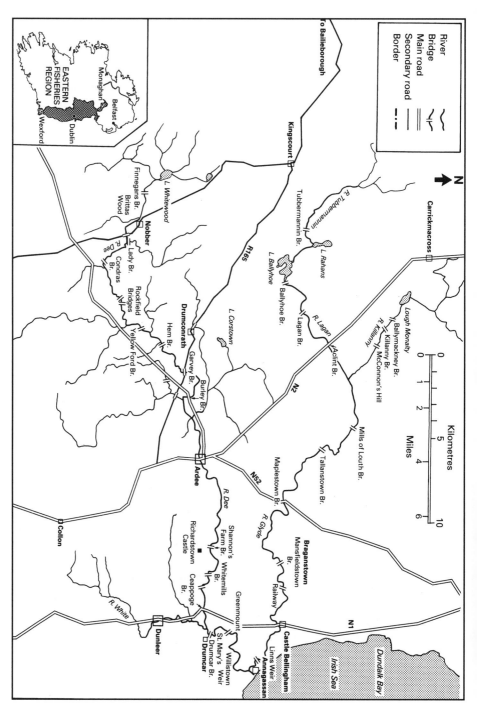

The rivers Glyde and Dee

Ruddy's Filling Station, Inniskeen, Co. Monaghan. Tel: 042 9378139

It is also worth noting that riparian owners exercise their fishing rights on certain stretches.

Local tackle shop
Island Fishing Tackle, 58 Park Street, Dundalk, Co. Louth. Tel: 042 9335698
Euro Tackle, Unit 11, Demesne Shopping Centre, Dundalk, Co. Louth.
Tel: 042 9240205, web: www.euro-tackle.com
Patsy McArdle, The Bike Doctor/Fishing Tackle, Bridge Street, Dundalk, Co. Louth

Instructor/guide
Eamonn Conway APGAI-IRL, FFF, CI.
Mobile: 086 1242966, email: eamonnconwayflyfishing@hotmail.com

CLAREBANE RIVER   H 87 17

The Clarebane River is about 12 miles long and connects Lough Muckno with Lough Ross. Two-thirds of it is in the Republic of Ireland and the lower part flows along the border with Northern Ireland. The access to it is good, with a road close to part of the right bank on the upper reaches and again at Clarebane Bridge roughly halfway along its course.

This is a substantial river, nearly 30 yards wide in places, with firm banks, some nice riffles and glides and some very deep water. It holds an excellent stock of good brown trout with some to 6lb. It is the kind of river that is always likely to produce a couple of nice trout early in the season and it gives really good dry-fly fishing, mainly to sedge but also to small olives and their spinners on summer evenings. A nymph fished deep and slow can give very good results in late April and May.

Season
Brown trout: 1 March–30 September

Permission
From the riparian owners

MULLAGHDUFF (LITTLE FANE) RIVER   H 85 20

The Mullaghduff River rises north-west of Newtownhamilton in Northern Ireland and flows in a southerly direction for about seven miles, forming the border between Northern Ireland and the Republic. It then swings sharply north-west and meanders and glides through drumlin hills for a further 3½ miles to Lough Muckno.

This is a beautiful trout stream, comprising short riffles and glides and innumerable deep holes – ideal for holding brown trout. An angler who fished it all his life once described it as 'a river what you would never get tired of looking at'. It ranges in width from 4–6 yards. It had its problems with pollution some years ago, but I'm glad to report the situation is much improved.

There is good fishing from Fane Valley Bridge (not to be confused with the other Fane Valley Bridge on the River Fane) on the Castleblayney–Newtownhamilton Road down to Mullaghduff Bridge. The fishing can be excellent from Mullaghduff Bridge past McCooey's Bridge, McBride's Bridge and Carville's Bridge to Somerville's Bridge. The stretch from this point to the lake is too deep to hold trout.

Access to the river is from the bridges and the banks are clear for the most part and very fishable. The trout average about 10oz and catches of 8 or 10 trout used be considered normal when the river was pollution-free. It fishes best from April onwards with the best fishing being from 11.00–16.00. The popular early season wet-fly patterns are March Brown, Hare's Ear and Greenwell's Glory. Later in the season dry-fly fishing comes into its own and olive spinners and small sedge patterns are especially useful.

Season
Brown trout: 1 March–30 September

Permission
Riparian owners

FRANKFORT RIVER   H 83 21

This river flows from Milltown Lough for a distance of two miles to Muckno Lough. It holds a fair stock of half pound trout and some better fish – 3lb or more – are always a possibility.

The best fishing is in May and June, when you might be lucky enough to get up to six trout in a day. The better trout are usually taken on dry sedge late in the evening in June and July. The banks are good all along. There is access for the wet-fly fisher at Milltown Lough (fish it down) or from either of the bridges.

Permission
Riparian owners

DRUMLEAK, RIVER   H 85 23

This little river is only about a mile long. It flows into Milltown Lake and holds a nice stock of trout from 8oz. This is really a nursery stream and not a fishery.

Permission
Riparian owners

A well-spotted Boyne brownie for Peter O'Reilly

BLACKWATER (MONAGHAN), RIVER   H 68 35

The Monaghan Blackwater rises on Slieve Beagh on the border between Counties
Tyrone and Monaghan. It flows in a south-easterly direction through Scotstown
towards Monaghan town. From there, it turns north-east towards the border at
Ardgonnell Bridge and Middletown and on to Lough Neagh. From its source to the
border is approximately 25 miles. The river underwent an arterial drainage scheme in
1987.

It is now regarded as one of the most productive trout rivers in the northern part
of the country. Once catches of more than twenty trout per angler per day were not
unheard of. The average size of the trout was about 12oz, with plenty of pound fish and
some to 1½lb. Monaghan Angling Club now maintains a rule that all fish less than 9
inches must be returned to the river. The banks have all been cleared of bushes on one
side and this makes for easier access but the drainage works have also left the banks

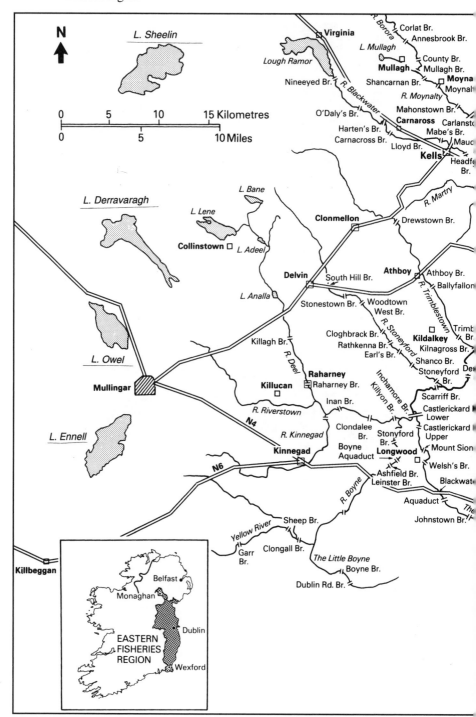

The rivers Boyne, Delvin and Broad Meadow

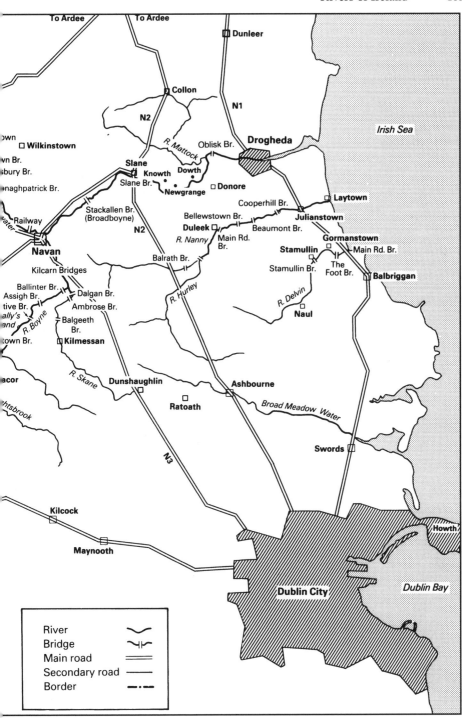

To Ardee

To Ardee

🏛 Dunleer

🏛 Collon

N2

N1

own
🏛 Wilkinstown

Irish Sea

R. Mattock   Oblisk Br.   **Drogheda**

vn Br.

sbury Br.
Slane
🏛 **Knowth**   **Dowth**

naghpatrick Br.
Slane Br.   □ **Donore**
Newgrange

Cooperhill Br.   🏛 **Laytown**

Stackallen Br.
(Broadboyne)   Bellewstown Br.   Julianstown
Railway
ater   N2   **Duleek** □   Beaumont Br.   **Gormanstown**
R. Nanny   Main Rd.   🏛   ⊢Main Rd. Br.
Navan   Br.   **Stamullin**   □
Balrath Br.   Stamullin Br.   The
Kilcarn Bridges   Foot Br.   🏛 **Balbriggan**
Ballinter Br.   Dalgan Br.
Assigh Br.   Ambrose Br.   R. Delvin
tive Br.   R. Hurley   □
ally's   Balgeeth   **Naul**
and   R. Boyne   Br.
town Br.   🏛 **Kilmessan**

acor   R. Skane   **Dunshaughlin**   **Ashbourne**
Broad Meadow Water
htsbrook   □
Ratoath

N3

Swords 🏛

Kilcock
🏛   Howth

Maynooth

Dublin City   Dublin Bay

River	‿
Bridge	⊣⊢
Main road	≡
Secondary road	—
Border	—·—

high in some places. In most instances it is better to wade than to try and fish from the bank. Access to the river is good, with numerous bridges along its course, none of them more than a mile apart.

The Fishery Board has carried out a lot of rehabilitation in recent years building groynes, weirs etc.. There is fishing at Cadden's midway between Scotstown and Ballanode. From Ballanode to Connolly's Bridge and from Connolly's Bridge to Raconnell Bridge, the river is too shallow to hold trout. From Raconnell Bridge to Gallanagh Bridge, there are a few pools that hold trout.

The Tannery Bridge is next downstream and there is a nice pool about 200 yards above it that holds trout. From the Tannery Bridge to the Creamery Bridge – on the N2 Monaghan–Emyvale road – is quite shallow but holds some trout up to ½lb.

There is a lot of shallow water from the Creamery Bridge to Crumlin Bridge and on to Faulkland Bridge, but there are occasional pools which are well worth fishing in springtime. The banks are high here and wading is essential.

The stretch from Faulkland Bridge to New Mills Bridge has some lovely water now, and provides some of the best fishing on the river. It can hold a lot of trout and to fish it properly, it is necessary to wade all the way. From New Mills Bridge to the border the water is mainly deep and heavy. It holds a small stock of big trout but can give good trout fishing.

Now that the drainage scheme is completed and the river rehabilitated, this is a river that recovered quickly. Anglers are reporting good catches. It is clear that rehabilitation work has been a success. It has good hatches of dark olives, and iron blue duns and prolific hatches of sedges. Wet-fly fishing after a flood is now probably the most productive method and popular fly patterns are Hare's Ear, Greenwell's Glory, Olive Quill, Iron Blue and various small sedges. A rehabilitation programme has begun and the Eastern Regional Fisheries Board is anxious that it be continued.

Season
1 March–15 September

Permission
Michael Caufield, Hon. Secretary, Monaghan Angling Club, Carrowhatta, Scotstown, Co. Monaghan. Tel: 047 89756
Also, from riparian owners.

Tackle shop
Dick Kiernan, Venture Sports, 71 Glaslough Street, Co. Monaghan
Tel: 047 81495, email: venturesports@tinet.ie

MOUNTAIN WATER   H 68 43

The Mountain Water rises in Lough Bradan and flows through Emyvale to join the Blackwater two miles north of Glaslough. An arterial drainage scheme was carried out there in the late 1980s and the river now has little or no trout angling potential. It functions as a spawning and nursery stream for Emy Lough.

BLACKWATER (ULSTER), RIVER   H 70 49

The Ulster Blackwater meanders its way along the border from Favor Royal to the point where it meets the Monaghan Blackwater. This is a drained river, with high banks, and it has recovered fairly well. The flow is governed by spates, over a predominantly stony river bed. It holds native brown trout and dollaghan, a strain of lake brown trout found in Lough Neagh. Salmon also come up from Lough Neagh later in the season.

Some of the best brown trout fishing is to sedges and blue-winged olives from June onwards. The dollaghan and salmon are mostly taken on worm or spinner after a flood in August and September.

Season
1 March–30 September

Local Angling Association
Lough More Anglers' Association, Hon. Secretary, Mr. Jim Murphy, Legacurry House, Monaghan, Co. Monaghan. Tel: 047 81402

Regulations
Bag limit: 3 trout
Minimum size: 11 inches

Instructor
Peter O'Reilly APGAI-IRL, FFF. MCI and THCI. Tel: 046 9028210
Email: peter@oreillyflyfishing.com

Local tackle shop/permits/guides
Mr. Dick Kiernan, Venture Sports Equipment, 71A Glaslough Street, Monaghan
Tel: 047 81495, email: venturesports@tinet.ie

** DEE, RIVER   O 8 93

The Dee rises at 1,119 feet above sea level on Loughanlea Mountain, near Bailieborough in Co. Cavan. It flows in an easterly direction for 38 miles, draining a 151 sq. mile catchment, and enters Dundalk Bay at Annagassan where it shares a common estuary with the Glyde.

The tributaries above Whitewood Lake are steep and fast-flowing and have all the appearance and qualities of excellent salmon spawning and nursery streams. The character of the river varies. From Whitewood Lake downstream it is mostly slow-flowing, silted and overgrown, though with a few stretches of fast, streamy water. From the village of Nobber to Garvey Bridge, it is mainly fast-flowing. From Garvey Bridge to Ardee, there is a lot of deep, slow water, but from Ardee to the sea it varies, with a lot of nice streams interspersed with deep, slow flats – ideal holding pools for salmon and occasional big brown trout.

A feature of the river is its high banks, which make the river almost inaccessible in places. These are the result of an arterial drainage scheme that took place between 1950 and 1956. It was one of the first – if indeed not the first – arterial drainage schemes in the country, financed by the Marshall Aid Programme. In those days, drainage schemes were engineers' solutions to flooding and no consideration was given to a river as a fishery.

By 1966, the river was showing good signs of recovery and in the following years, the trout and salmon stocks increased dramatically. At the present time, it is highly regarded as a brown trout, seatrout and salmon fishery.

Fish stocks

The river gets a small run of spring salmon. It has the distinction of being one of the few Irish rivers still getting a run (though very few) of big three-sea-winter salmon ranging from 25lb–35lb. If an angler catches one of these fish, he should not harm or kill it on any account. Because of their rarity, this is a stock that should really be preserved: the genes may well be peculiar to the River Dee salmon. The rod fisheries on the river don't keep records but estimate that about 100 spring salmon and between 250 and 500 grilse are taken annually. Reports from local anglers (the only other gauge available) suggest that the Dee is still a fair spring salmon fishery and the average weight is 12lb–14lb.

The summer grilse fishing is patchy. The first grilse usually show in the river on the first flood after 22 June. They weigh from 5lb to 7lb. The fishing does not really pick up until August, after the nets go off. A heavy run of fish is thought to occur in October, after the season has closed, and some of these fish will come up early if there is a flood in September. The 2003 rod catch was poor (estimated at about 100 grilse) due to the low water.

The Dee gets an excellent run of seatrout from mid-July, through August and September. The first seatrout appear in May. This is usually a small run of good fish from 2lb to 5lb. These big trout continue to come in through June and early July. The river gets a big run of seatrout averaging 1½lb around mid July and enormous numbers of 12oz trout usually arrive around the end of August. Finally, in September, there is a big run of much smaller 7oz–10oz. trout. In some seasons, the majority of these late seatrout are very small indeed. The 2001 rod catch was so poor that some believe that stocks had collapsed.

The Dee holds big stocks of small brown trout, but there are a lot of fish in the 12oz–1½lb class and, occasionally, much bigger trout. This is a very impressive brown trout fishery, with great potential for further development. It currently receives far less attention from anglers than it deserves.

Salmon

The spring salmon fishing is considered to extend upstream from Greenmount Pumping Station on the left bank and the bottom of the St John of God's Fishery on the right bank to Ardee, a distance of approximately 10 miles. The spring fishing lasts from February to May and, while all the fisheries are productive, the section from Cappogue Bridge to the sea is best.

This is a mix of streamy water and deep, slow flats and pools. In low water, fish can be taken on fly from early February – otherwise it is spinning with a Flying 'C' or a Copper Spoon being the popular choice.

The grilse fishing is less extensive and is generally considered to extend from Willistown Weir – and even a bit below it – upstream to Drumcar Weir.

Shrimp fishing, when it is permitted, is very popular over the summer months. A bunch of worms is said to be particularly good in May and from June onwards it is believed that a single worm works best.

For the flyfisher, Stoat's Tail, Green Highlander, various Shrimp flies, Garry Dog and a Collie Dog are recommended.

Seatrout

The best of the seatrout fishing is from Willistown Weir upstream to Cappogue Bridge. Occasional seatrout are caught up as far as Ardee. The choice fishing is from Willistown up to Drumcar Bridge and some claim that the seatrout fishing at Farraher's Fishery, above the weir, is as good as any in Ireland.

All legitimate fishing methods are allowed on the river (but this may change in the near future): worm, spinning, maggot, fly and maggot-and-fly. Night fishing can be excellent and daytime flyfishing in the streams, or when a wind ripples the pools can also be very good. Silver-bodied flies are favoured and the Butcher, Priest, Teal Blue & Silver and Silver Doctor (all size 12), are especially effective by day. For night fishing, try a Bloody Butcher, Connemara Black and Watson's Fancy.

Because of the quality of the seatrout fishing, the better pools become very overcrowded at the peak of the season. It is necessary to find a method of spreading anglers more evenly along all of the productive water, though it is good to be able to report that it is not as crowded as it used to be.

Brown trout

The brown trout fishing on the Dee is mostly from Drumcar up to Whitewood Lake. While the quality of some of it may have diminished in the late 1990's, the consensus among fishery staff and anglers is that it holds an excellent stock of brown trout.

From Whitewood Lake down to Finnegan's Farm Bridge, the river is deep and sluggish. From Finnegan's Bridge to Summerhill (Brittas) Wood, the banks are very overgrown and the channel badly silted but it still holds plenty of trout. Brittas Marsh is again deep and a bit silted, but holds a lot of good trout. There is still good fishing for about 400 yards upstream from Casey's Forge, just south of the village of Nobber. The next good stretch is from Lady's Bridge to a point 300 yards below Condras Bridge. There is some lovely fishing all the way to Rockfield Bridge. The opinion of the local club is that if the stretch from Whitewood Lake to Rockfield Bridge were properly developed, it could take up to 60 anglers. This may be true of evening fishing, but hardly holds true for daytime fishing.

The next good stocks are to be found downstream of Rockfield Bridge (lower) between Yellow Ford Bridge and Hem Bridge and from Burley Bridge all the way to Ardee. There is very good fishing starting a quarter-of-a-mile below Ardee, and from Ardee to Whitemills Bridge, there are five or six good brown trout stretches. There is particularly nice trout-water for a mile above and for some considerable distance below Whitemills Bridge. In July, there is good evening fishing to spent olives and sedges on the stretch below Drumcar Bridge.

Wet flies are favoured for early-season fishing. The river is said to have hatches of march browns, dark olives, iron blues, blue-winged olives, alders, black gnats, mayflies and various sedges. The mayfly fishing can be especially good with a rise in water in June from Hem Bridge upstream and upstream of Ardee. The evening fishing with spent olives and sedges can be very impressive in July and a nymph fished upstream can give marvellous sport.

The Fisheries

Nobber Trout Anglers Club has about seven miles of double bank fishing extending from Whitewood Lake downstream to Bawn (Hem) Bridge. A couple of short stretches are excluded, including both banks between the two bridges at Rockfield.

This is predominantly a brown trout fishery and the club encourages flyfishing, but allows worm and spinning. Fishing with natural minnow or maggots is strictly forbidden and there is a four-trout bag limit.

The river flows through hilly countryside with large land divisions devoted mostly to pasture. The channel was drained in the 1950s leaving some very steep banks in places. The water quality is good and has improved greatly in recent years. The river is characterised by slow, sluggish stretches and a good mix of streamy water, particularly where weirs and groynes have been constructed to enhance the flow. Access along the banks is mostly good. Stiles are provided and maintained. It is necessary to wade to make the most of the fishing and 90% of the river is wadeable.

Trout can be caught throughout the length of the fishery. It holds a good stock of fish between 12oz and 1½lb and every season produces bigger trout to 3lb. The best of the fishing is probably at Aclare, Rockfield and Kilbride. It has a good variety of fly life. Sedges are important and BWOs can bring up big rises on summer evenings.

Season
Salmon and seatrout: 1 February–30 September
Brown trout: 15 February–30 September

Day permits
Nobber Anglers, Derek Primrose, Hon. Secretary, Spiddal, Nobber, Co Meath
The Hardware Store, Nobber, Co. Meath. Tel: 046 9052105
'Shop at Babs', Kilmainhamwood, Co. Meath
Callan's Shop, Drumconrath, Co. Meath

Tackle shops
The Sport's Den, Trimgate Street, Navan, Co. Meath. Tel: 046 9021130
The Flying Sportsman, Kells, Co. Meath

Accommodation
P. J. Keating, Breslinstown, Drumconrath, Co. Meath. Tel: 041 6854213

Private stretches

The fishing rights on the right bank between Yellow Ford Bridge and Hem Bridge are reserved by the riparian owners. The stretch between the two bridges at Rockfield is private fishing. From Cappogue Bridge upstream on the right bank is private fishing for about one mile. From Greenmount Pumping Station on the left bank upstream, for a distance of about four miles to near Whitemills Bridge, is mostly private fishing – some not let and some privately leased. Permission to fish can occasionally be obtained from riparian owners on the stretch downstream of Drumcar Bridge on the left bank.

Dee and Glyde Development Association
The Association has extensive fishing on the river. The following is a guide to where the fisheries are located, a brief description of the fishing and the access routes.

Both banks from a point about ½ mile downstream of Whitemills Bridge to Burley Bridge.
A stretch above and below Shannon's farm bridge near Richardstown Castle.
Access is via a lane 1.9 miles west of Kaig's Crossroads, opposite the Castle.
The **Cappogue Fishery** extends for one mile of the right bank beginning a short distance downstream from Cappoge Bridge.
Very good seatrout and good spring and summer salmon fishing. Most of it is deep and slow-flowing.
Access: Via O'Callaghan's Residence, which is below Cappogue Bridge.
From Willistown Weir on the left bank upstream to Greenmount Pumping Station is known as the Maine Fishery. This is good summer salmon and seatrout fishing with some spring salmon fishing.
Access: Via Greenmount Lane.
The **Drumcar Fishery** (St John of God's Fishery) extends for two miles of the right bank downstream from Drumcar Bridge almost to Willistown House.

This was a prime spring salmon fishery. It still has summer salmon and seatrout and has some brown trout fishing too.

From the field on the right bank at Willistown Weir for a mile upstream is known as Willistown Fishery.
This is a good stretch for summer salmon and seatrout (good daytime fishing).
Access: Via the lane one mile east of entrance to St. Mary's, Drumcar, Co. Louth.

The Ballynagassan and Adamstown Fisheries
The right bank from a point opposite the confluence of the rivers Dee and Glyde upstream to the corner of the field above Willistown Weir. This is a good summer salmon and seatrout stretch.

Permits
Hugh O'Neill Sports, Castle Street, Ardee, Co. Louth. Tel: 041 6853268
Dee & Glyde Fishing Club, Peter Callaghan, Hon. Secretary, Hale Street, Ardee. Co. Louth
Mark Finnegan, Park Street, Dundalk, Co. Louth. Tel: 042 9335698

Accommodation
Aisling on Sea, Coast Road, Salterstown, Annagasson, Co. Louth. Tel: 041 685357

** GLYDE, RIVER (but it is open from 1 July–30 September)   O 6 95

The Glyde rises among the drumlin hills of Counties Cavan and Monaghan in an area between Loughanlea Mountain and Carrickmacross and flows east for 35 miles before joining the River Dee a mile above Annagassan, where it flows into Dundalk Bay. It drains a catchment of approximately 135 sq. miles.

It was the subject of an arterial drainage scheme in the 1950s which has resulted in high banks in places and a general disruption of the fishery. It was a noted spring salmon river before drainage and it still gets a few fish. The River Glyde was once noted for its magnificent seatrout run but no longer gets a worthwhile run.

Salmon

The river still gets a small run of spring fish. The average size is remarkably large, but these days there isn't much hope of a taking fish before the month of May.

The best lies are probably in Clarke's and Meehan's fisheries, downstream and upstream respectively of the bridge at Castlebellingham. There are a few good pools in Meehan's Fishery between Castlebellingham and Bragganstown Bridge but note that this fishery is completely closed.

Most of the fishing on the left bank from Maplestown Bridge to Tallanstown Bridge is strictly private, but there is a bit of good salmon fishing off the right bank that may be had with the riparian owners' permission.

A couple of pools above the weir at Tallanstown hold spring fish and then up to Tully there is a long barren stretch. At Tully, there is good holding water for spring fish below the confluence of the Killanny River at a place called Tully Meadows. Fish are still caught there.

Much of the Glyde is deep and slow and most spring fish are taken by spinning. Favourite baits are the Yellow Belly and brown and gold Devons and a Swinford spoon.

Brown trout

The Glyde still holds good stocks (indeed, some would say very good stocks) of brown trout averaging about a pound in weight. They have a good growth rate and this is attributed by some to the number of minnows in the river. The best of the fishing is early in the season for the river tends to weed up badly in summer. Fishing becomes quite difficult after mid-June and the best seasons are those with lots of rain and high water levels. The river still has a terrific mayfly hatch at the end of May and for the first couple of weeks in June. There is also a good hatch of sedge and the grey flag hatch is especially prolific in those shallower areas with a stony bottom.

The main brown trout fishing stretches are downstream from Bragganstown Bridge, where there is some excellent fishing. The banks are difficult and, in places, very overgrown. There are good trout stocks, too, in stretches downstream of Maplestown Bridge on the N52 Ardee–Dundalk road and there is a lot of good trout water up to Tallanstown. Access is difficult – really only from bridge to bridge – and deep to the right bank below Tallanstown. The last good trout stretch on the Glyde is from McGuinness' Pool which is about 500 yards above the Mills of Louth, right down to Tallanstown where there is about 2½ miles of trout fishing.

Seatrout

The best of the seatrout fishing and it can be very good, is from the village of Castlebellingham downstream to the Linns Weir at the tidal water.

Season

Salmon and seatrout: 1 February–30 September
Brown trout: 1 March–30 September

Permits

Bellingham Castle Hotel has a half mile of double bank fishing in its grounds.
Tel: 042 9372176

The Dee & Glyde Development Association has a two-mile stretch on the north bank, known as Clarke's Fishery. It extends from Castlebellingham downstream to the Linns Weir.

The Association also has Meehan's fishery upstream of Castlebellingham. This is a quarter-mile of double bank fishing and is accessed at the back of the castle, but not through the castle grounds.

The Association also has access to various pieces of fishing between Maplestown Bridge and Tallanstown Bridge.

Permits for the Association Water

Hugh O'Neill Sports, Castle Street, Ardee, Co. Louth. Tel: 041 6853268
Pat Wehrly, Island Fishing Tackle, Park Street, Dundalk, Co. Louth
Tel: 042 9335698

LAGAN, RIVER   N 90 98

The River Lagan is part of the Upper Glyde and flows down from Ballyhoe Lake to become the Glyde at Tully. It is about six miles long and flows under the N2 Carrickmacross road at Aclint Bridge. There are some streamy stretches between Ballyhoe Bridge and Acclint Bridge that hold trout and there are more nice stretches that hold good trout all the way to Tully.

Season

Brown trout: 14 February–30 September

Permission

Riparian owners

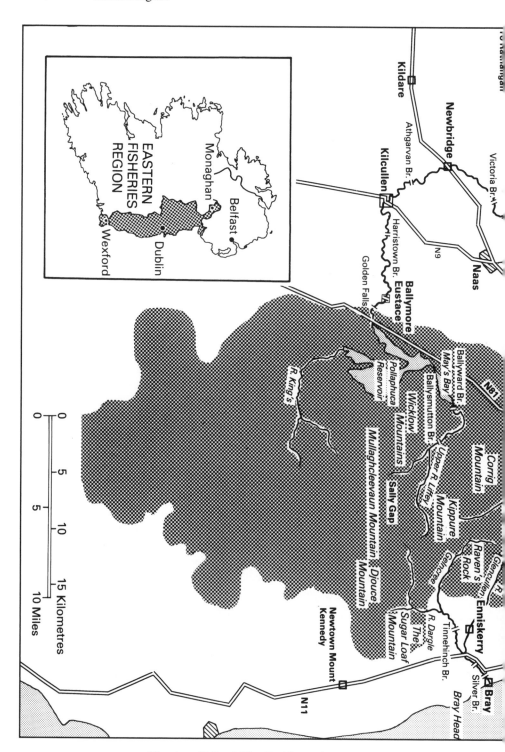

The rivers Tolka, Liffey, Dodder and Dargle

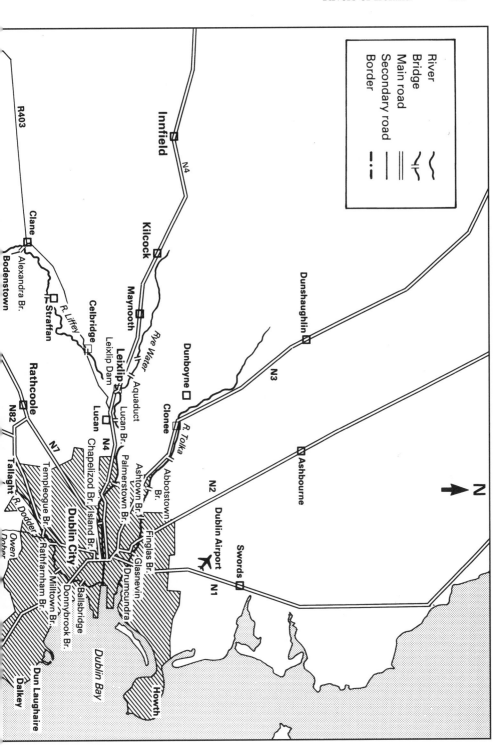

KILLANNY RIVER   N 90 01

The Killanny River flows southeast from Monalty Lake for four miles to join the River Glyde at Tully. In the past, this was a really excellent trout stream with plenty of pound trout and some to 2lb. It is still well worth fishing and a dry sedge in the evening is likely to tempt the better trout. It has a prolific sedge hatch that includes the Murrough, or great red sedge. It is a bit overgrown above Ballymackney Bridge but is reasonably easy to fish from Ballymackney Bridge to a point half-a-mile below McConnon's Mill.

Season
Brown trout: 1 March–30 September

Permission
Riparian owners

TUBBERMANNIN RIVER   N 82 96

The Tubbermannin River flows south from Northlands past Cabra Castle and into Rahan's Lake. Before drainage, it was reputed to be an excellent trout stream, with trout averaging a pound and plenty to 2lb or more. It still has good stocks of trout, with some to 1½lb. The banks are reasonably easy to fish and there are trout to be found from the bridge on the R179 Kingscourt–Carrickmacross road, downstream to Rahan's Lake.

Season
Brown trout: 1 March–30 September

Permission
Not usually required.

** BOYNE, RIVER (AND TRIBUTARIES)   O 07 75

The Boyne rises near Edenderry on the borders of Counties Offaly and Kildare and flows in a north-easterly direction for 70 miles before entering the Irish Sea at Drogheda. Together with its tributaries, it drains a catchment of approximately 1,040 sq. miles.

This magnificent river drains the fertile plains of Royal Meath. Its valley is rich in archaeological remains. The prehistoric burial chambers at Newgrange and the numerous ruins of medieval castles and abbeys bear testament to a colourful history.

It is one of the country's premier game fisheries and both the main river and its tributaries offer a wide range of fishing for spring salmon and grilse, seatrout and brown trout. In all, the Boyne offers something like 100 miles of brown trout fishing, counting the main river and tributaries.

The years 1965 and 1969 were significant dates for angling on the Boyne. The disease, ulcerative dermal necrosis (UDN), appeared in 1965 and decimated salmon stocks. In 1969, an arterial drainage scheme was started on the system and disrupted angling for about 18 years. Both of these events had disastrous effects on all fish stocks and on the character of the river. Fortunately, stocks have recovered quite well since (particularly the brown trout). In some locations, the fishing is thought to be as good, if not better, than before.

The dredging altered the character of the river completely and, in many cases, left very high banks. The main channel from Drogheda upstream to Navan was left untouched, as were a few stretches on the Kells Blackwater.

Salmon

The prime salmon angling water is now found between Navan and Drogheda and on a stretch of the Kells Blackwater, immediately upstream of Navan. Occasional salmon are taken upstream of Navan – provided there is a flood in August or September – at Bective, Trim, Board's Mill below Scarriff Bridge, above and below Inchamore Bridge and on the Kells Blackwater.

Nowadays, the river gets very few of the big three-sea-winter fish from 20lb–30lb. These fish generally arrive early in February and March. Smaller spring fish, averaging about 10lb, arrive in April and early May. Water permitting, the grilse come into the river in July. The river gets a run of autumn fish in late August and September and this run would appear to last long after the season closes.

The early fish run through and the first fish is usually caught between Slane and Navan. Indeed, most of the spring fish are taken from this stretch of river, though some are caught below Slane.

The grilse fishing from July onwards is mostly confined to the fisheries between Slane and Drogheda.

In low water conditions, there can be a big build-up of fish in the fisheries downstream of Slane in late August and September. If a flood comes down in September, there can be excellent salmon fishing all the way up from Drogheda to Navan and good fishing up to Trim and beyond. The distance up-river that the good fishing extends in September appears to be directly related to water levels.

All legitimate fishing methods are allowed for salmon. Spinning is the most popular method for spring fish, followed by worm and shrimp. Occasional fish are taken on fly from mid-April, but only a minority of anglers fish the fly. The salmon fisheries from Navan to Drogheda are made up of streams, glides, pools and stretches of deep water above the various weirs. There is ample water on all of the fisheries and, since it is a big wide river, a 15 foot rod or longer is recommended. The river has a compacted gravel bottom and wading is possible in places.

The most commonly-used baits are Flying 'C's, natural shrimp and worms. Useful flies include Willie Gunn, Garry Dog, Hairy Mary, Blue Charm and Thunder & Lightning, Tosh, Ghost Shrimp and various other shrimp patterns – down to size 10 doubles for summer and autumn fishing.

Boyne Rod Angling Catch 2001–2008

Year	2001	2002	2003	2004	2005	2006	2007	2008
Salmon	476	542	597	665	749	345	n/a	218

Seatrout

The river usually gets an excellent run of seatrout – the 2001 season being an exception and fishing was poor. The fishing extends up as far as Slane Bridge. Seatrout have been found as far as Navan and even Trim, but not in sufficient quantities to warrant fishing specifically for them. The biggest stocks are found downstream of the Obelisk Bridge at Drogheda. The first seatrout are usually taken in April, the run begins to peak in early July and there is good fishing through August and into September.

The various fisheries have different regulations, but some or all of the following fishing methods are allowed: fly, worm, maggot or spinning. The fly produces best results at night and any of the recognised seatrout flies will do: Teal Blue & Silver, Black Pennell, Black & Silver Spider, or even a Grey Duster fished wet.

An interesting fact about the Boyne seatrout is that they feed on river insects on summer evenings and, in particular, on blue winged olives and sedges and I have taken them on various Klinkhåmer patterns up as far as Navan.

Brown trout

The River Boyne and its tributaries hold superb stocks of wild brown trout. There is probably more trout fishing now on the main river than before the drainage schemes were implemented, but some sections of good fishing were lost on the tributaries. Some rehabilitation works have been carried out.

At the present time, there is something in the region of 100 miles of trout angling water spread over the main river and the various tributaries. Details of the various fisheries appear later on under their own sub-headings. I would, however, make the general point that tapping into local knowledge is essential for best results. The best advice for the trout fisher is to fish the fast, streamy water and the glides and avoid the deep flats unless a rise of trout is observed. During the day, the best fly hatches are found in the glides and riffles. But, be warned, this is a big river and avoiding drag with the dry-fly is a problem.

Fly hatches

The river has all the various fly hatches associated with a limestone river and flyfishing can begin about 15 April. On some stretches, certain species are missing. Sedges are especially prolific on the Kells Blackwater. Otherwise, expect to find dark olives, medium olives, iron blues, yellow may dun, alder, simulium, black gnats, mayfly, various sedges, midges, august dun, caenis and blue-winged olives. The grey flag sedge (Hydropsyche spp.) is by far the most important angling insect on the entire catchment at the peak of the daytime and evening trout fishing in May and June. It emerges on open water during the day and at dusk and flutters on the surface. It overlaps with the mayfly – last 2 weeks of May and first two weeks of June – and is taken preferentially to the mayfly where the two species hatch together. The mayfly (Ephemera danica) tends to hatch in pockets and is found on the main channel and some of the tributaries including the Yellow River and the Upper Boyne. The august dun is a very important insect for both trout and angler in August. There is a secondary hatch of iron blues in September which are very small (size 16) and one also encounters large dark olives, medium olives, blue-winged olives, large numbers of small red sedges and some big sedges on the deep flats, all hatching during the day. Of the terrestrials, the hawthorn fly (Bibio marci) is extremely important in May.

Wading

Trout anglers would be well advised to use chest waders and a wading staff, especially in the tributaries, where banks are high. They contribute enormously to the angler's comfort. The bottom is firm and quite safe to wade, with a few important exceptions.

Weed growth

Weed growth can be a problem from mid-June (except in a couple of areas where remedial action is taken) but this is something that the angler has to learn to accept. In fact, angling becomes quite impossible in some areas in August and September.

BOYNE FISHERIES

For those seeking fishing on the Boyne and its tributaries, it is important to understand that there is no right of free fishing on the river and this applies even to the tidal water. Fisheries are either controlled by riparian or fishery owners, or are leased to angling clubs or let to syndicates. A few fishery owners do not allow fishing.

The following are the Boyne's principal fisheries (on both the main river and tributaries), working upstream from the sea at Drogheda.

Drogheda and District Anglers' Club

The Club has fishing on the Rathmullen and Mell Fishery on the tidal water. This is mainly seatrout fishing. It begins at 'Pass', about 1¼ miles below the Obelisk Bridge and extends downstream towards Drogheda.

The club also has fishing for salmon, seatrout and brown trout at McDonnell's Fishery, downstream of Newgrange weir, Fulham's Fishery at Staleen and Donore and part of Law's Fishery.

Enquiries

Mr. John Murphy, Hon. Secretary, Drogheda & District Angling Club, 39 Anneville Crescent, Drogheda, Co. Louth. Tel: 041 9834078

Rossin-Slane and District Angling Club

Rossin-Slane Angling Club has fishing at three locations between Slane and Drogheda. This is excellent fishing for salmon and seatrout, as well as for stocks of good brown trout. The Oldbridge Fishery at Obelisk Bridge, including the famous Curley Hole is mainly salmon and seatrout fishing and extends on both banks for three miles from the confluence with the River Mattock to 'Pass'. The two upper fisheries (Law's and Johnston's) offer occasional salmon, very good seatrout and excellent brown trout fishing, with the trout averaging nearly 1½lb. This water has prolific hatches of mayfly, grey flag sedges and B.W.O. From 1 June, the trout fishing is fly-only. Both club membership and day permits are available.

Note: At the time of writing, the Old Bridge Fishery has been acquired by the State. For up-to-date information, contact the Boyne Fishery Manager. Tel: 046 9073375.

Permission
Brian Herty, Sheephouse, Donore, Drogheda,Co. Louth. Tel: 086 1732379

Dowth Angling Club
This fishery begins at the confluence of the Mattock River, above the Curley Hole. The game angling stretch is about half-a-mile long and is located at the top of the tidal water. This is an extraordinarily productive salmon fishery and also has seatrout.

Enquiries
Dowth Angling Club, Mr. Ciaran Caffrey. Mobile: 086 4015119

Ballinacrad Syndicate Water
This water consists of about two miles of single and double bank fishing at Dowth, downstream of the noted Newgrange megalithic tomb. The river is wide and expansive here and the members fish for spring salmon early in the season, brown trout and seatrout in late spring and summer and it gets a late salmon run in September.

Enquiries
Mr. Gerard Usher, Hon. Secretary, Ballinacrad Angling Club, Huntington, Rackenstown, Dunshaughlin, Co. Meath
Mr. David Whitren, 8 Roc Wood, Stillorgan, Co. Dublin

Law's Fisheries
Law's Fisheries at Rosnaree are let to:
Rossin-Slane and District Angling Club
Drogheda and District Anglers
The Ballinacrad Syndicate

Slane Castle Fishery
The Earl of Mount Charles has extensive salmon and trout fishing at Slane, extending for approximately 3½ miles on both banks upstream as far as Beau Parc. The fishing from the Castle Weir downstream to Scabby Arch is let to a local angling club whose membership is confined to anglers resident within two miles of the village of Slane.

Hayestown Angling Club
This club has about one mile of fishing on the right bank extending from the Beau Parc boundary upstream towards Stackallen (Broadbridge) Bridge. It is noted mainly as a brown trout fishery but also gets a run of seatrout and the seatrout fishing can be very good here on good water in September.

Permission
Mr. Sean Monaghan, Hon. Secretary, Hayestown Angling Club, Kentstown, Navan, Co. Meath. Tel: 046 9025179

Broadbridge Angling Club
The Broadbridge Angling Club water is on the right bank upstream and downstream of Broadbridge – also known locally as Stackallen Bridge. It holds a good stock of brown trout and some seatrout in summer.

Permission
Mr. Patsy Ward, Chairman, Broadbridge Angling Club, Smithstown, Hayes, Navan, Co. Meath. Tel: 046 9024137

Two permits per day are available from
Hayes Post Office, Navan, Co. Meath. Tel: 046 9024187

O'Connor's Fishery
This fishery is situated on the right bank and extends upstream for nearly a mile from Stackallen Bridge. This is good salmon-holding water from early spring. High water in autumn brings up a good late run of salmon. The brown trout fishing, and the fly hatches, are not as good as pre-2000 but it still holds trout to 5lb. The upper half of the fishery is private and the remainder is fished by Broadbridge Angling Club, previous page.

Daly's Fishery
This is a small private fishery on the left bank, extending upstream from Dunmoe Weir for approximately 450 yards. It holds good quality brown trout and occasional seatrout. The fishing is not let.

Navan & District Anglers' Association
Navan Angling Club has access to extensive stretches of the Boyne above and below the town of Navan, totalling about six miles. It also has access to several fisheries on the Kells Blackwater between Bloomsbury's Bridge and Navan. Some are leased and others are fished by reciprocal arrangement with Kilbride Angling Club, giving the club a further six miles of water.

The fishing on the Boyne above Navan extends for over a mile on the right bank and for about 2½ miles on the left bank to Kilcarn. This is all excellent brown trout water and has a few noted salmon lies too.

The club has a further two miles below Navan on both banks, including all but a short stretch of the famous Blackcastle Fishery. Further downstream it has over a mile of the fishing rights on the Dunmoe Fishery. Blackcastle and Dunmoe are prime spring salmon fisheries and have produced salmon to 26lb in recent years. The season peaks here mid-April to mid-May. These fisheries can also provide good fishing in late August and September if there is enough water to bring up the fish.

The trout fishing on this stretch can be superb, but most of the angling effort tends to concentrate on the salmon.

Club membership and/or day permits are available.

Enquiries
Anglers World, Balmorral Business Park, Navan, Co. Meath. Tel: 046 9071866, web: www.anglersworld.ie

Richard Farrelly, Membership Secretary, Balgeeth, Kilmesson Navan, Co. Meath. Tel: 046 9029499, email: rfarrelly@gmail.com

Day permits
The Sports Den, Trimgate Street, Navan, Co. Meath. Tel: 046 9021130

Tuition
Peter O'Reilly, APGAI-IRL, FFF, MCI, THCI. Tel: 046 9028210, email: peter@oreillyflyfishing.com, web: ww.oreillyflyfishing.com

Dalgan Angling Club
Dalgan Angling Club is the next club up river with good trout fishing and occasional salmon on the Boyne from Ballinter down towards Kilcarn.

Enquiries
Joe Lenehan, Clonardon, Garlow Cross, Navan, Co. Meath. Tel: 046 9025787

Bective Angling Club
Bective Angling Club has the fishing at various points from Lally's Island, down past Bective Bridge and Assigh Bridge and almost to Ballinter Bridge. The Club rules that its season opens on the Saturday before 17 March. A lot of rehabilitation work has been carried out in this area and trout stocks are excellent with fish from 12oz to 4lb and even 5lb. Salmon can be taken on this fishery too, above and below Bective Bridge and at Brady's. They are mainly caught in March/April and late August/September. Try fly or a Copper spoon. Club membership is limited, but visiting anglers can usually be accommodated.

Enquiries
Mr. Noel Fitzpatrick, Hon. Secretary, Bective Angling Club, Grange End, Dunshaughlin, Co. Meath. Tel: 01 8259307
Mr. Bill Scorer, Hon. Membership Secretary, Bective Angling Club, 3 Westview Glade, Clonee, Co. Meath. Tel: 01 8255492

Trim, Athboy and District Angling Club
This angling club has access to extensive fishing on the Boyne and Trimblestown River (N 77 56). The fishing on the Boyne extends from Scarriff Bridge downstream past the town of Trim to Lally's Island, with some stretches of private water in-between. The club's rights on the Trimblestown River extend from the village of Athboy to the confluence with the Boyne.

The river here holds occasional salmon and they are taken on worm or spinner in April and May and in September if there is a flood to bring them up. The salmon fishing is mostly on the short stretch below Scarriff Bridge, a short stretch above Board's Mill, a short stretch at the confluence of the Knightsbrook River and a stretch at Lally's Island.

The brown trout fishing on the Trim water of the Boyne can be excellent and as good as or better than any on the river. The average weight is 10oz, but there are plenty of trout to 2lb and 3lb and better. The best trout-holding stretches are for half-a-mile below Scarriff Bridge; from a quarter-of-a-mile above Board's Mill to a point 400 yards downstream of Derrindaly Bridge; a half mile stretch, by the road at Higgins Brook and all the way from Newhaggard to Trim, to Newtown Bridge and downstream to Lally's Island.

Note that there is a soft marl bottom upstream of the Trimblestown confluence and wading is very dangerous.

Club membership is limited at present but visiting anglers can usually be accommodated.

Enquiries
Pat O'Toole, Hon. Secretary, Trim, Athboy & District Angling Club, Unit 1, Duggan Industrial Estate, Athboy Road, Trim, Co. Meath. Mobile: 086 8777039

Longwood Angling Association
Longwood Angling Association has fishing rights on the Boyne between Scarriff Bridge and Leinster Bridge (six miles) and on the Enfield Blackwater (N 71 50) from Johnstown Bridge down to the confluence with the Boyne.

There are trout to 2lb in a one-mile stretch upstream from Scarriff Bridge and in a short quarter mile stretch below Inchamore Bridge. Immediately above and below Stoneyford Bridge, there are trout to a pound and similar-sized fish can be encountered in a quarter mile stretch at Ballinabarney. There is also lovely trout fishing in stretch from the Boyne Aqueduct to a point a quarter-of-a-mile above Ashfield.

Permission:
Mr. Richard Kelly, Carronstown, Ballivor, Co. Meath. Tel: 046 956119
The Post Office, Longwood, Co. Meath
Longwood Anglers Association, David Gorman, Hon. Secretary, Kilrainey, Broadford, Co. Kildare

BLACKWATER (ENFIELD OR LEINSTER), RIVER   N 78 45

There is nearly six miles of fishing on the Enfield Blackwater (N 78 45). The lower reaches, from Longwood down to the confluence with the Boyne, are mainly fast-flowing, with streams, long slow pools and riffles. It holds substantial stocks of trout to 12oz. The best fishing is in the early season – from 15 April onwards.

Upstream of Longwood, the banks are very high and steep, but the river holds a moderate stock of trout, some of which are very big. This is physically difficult fishing – only for the fit and agile. For his efforts, an angler may get only one fish in a day, but it could weigh as much as 5lb. This stretch is not very attractive. It is slow-flowing, deep and difficult to fish. Parts of this river have a weed problem in late summer.

Enquiries
Mr. Richard Kelly, Carronstown, Ballivor, Co. Meath. Tel: 046 956119

Permits
The Post Office, Longwood, Co. Meath

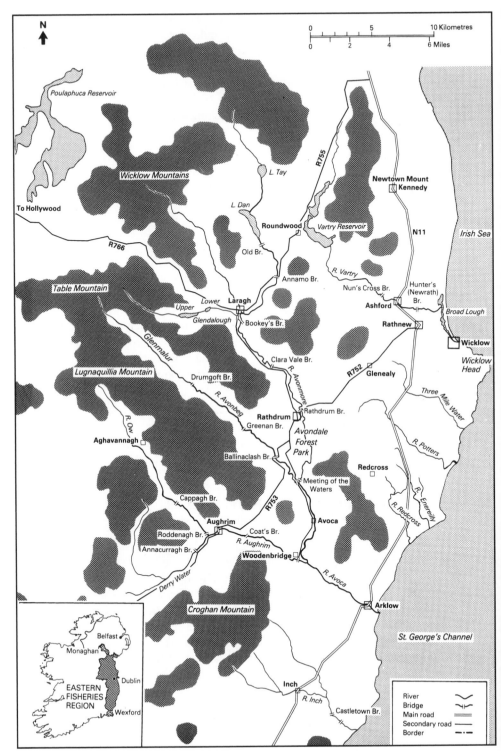

The rivers Vartry, Three Mile Water, Potters, Enereilly, Redcross, Avoca and Inch

Longwood Anglers Association, David Gorman, Hon. Secretary, Kilrainey, Broadford, Co. Kildare

BLACKWATER (KELLS), RIVER   N 74 76

The Kells Blackwater drains Lough Ramor near Virginia in Co. Cavan and flows south-east for 18 miles before joining the Boyne at Navan. It is a medium-sized limestone river and is now recovering from the effects of the arterial drainage scheme. It was noted for its spring salmon fishing and enormous stocks of fat trout. The salmon fishing is poor at present, except on the Mollies Fishery at Navan, where some fish are still taken. The trout fishing varies from good to very good, with fair numbers of trout up to 2lb and better.

Three angling clubs have access to extensive stretches on the river: Kells Angling Club, Kilbride Angling Club and Navan & District Anglers' Association.

There is virtually no trout fishing from Lough Ramor down to O'Daly's Bridge. The best of the fishing is from O'Daly's Bridge to Navan. The section from Lugawooly, below Carnaross Bridge, to Headford Bridge was not drained and can be especially good, with trout to over 2lb. Downstream of Headford Bridge, the river changes in character and is less productive.

The Kells Blackwater has all the usual fly hatches found on a limestone river. Sedge patterns (both pupae and adult) are very important, especially the grey flag. Trout take the yellow May dun here and the flyfisher should have an imitation of the female blue-winged olive when daytime fishing in September.

I would rate the Kells Blackwater as one of the nicest trout streams I have had the privilege to fish. The undrained stretch from above Lloyd Bridge, down past Mabe's Bridge and on to Maudlin Bridge is especially beautiful. Overall, the whole river holds a good head of trout and they are generally free-rising with plenty of small and medium-sized trout and some real trophies too. On the Kilbride/Navan water, the stretch from Donaghpatrick to Liscarton probably offers the best fishing.

The Clubs have erected many stiles and footbridges for the convenience of anglers. Waders are required and some sections of the bottom are very soft.

Bag limits are strictly enforced. For example, Kilbride AC imposes a two trout bag limit and a 12 inch minimum as the takeable size. Catch-and-release of all trout is strongly encouraged.

Permission
Liam McLoughlin, Hon. Secretary, Kells Angling Club, 3 St. Patrick's Terrace, Maudlin, Kells, Co. Meath. Tel: 046 9249472
Desmond Johnston, Hon. Secretary, Kilbride Angling Club, 54 Avondale Park, Raheny, Dublin 5. Tel: 01 8318786
Richard Farrelly, Membership Secretary, Navan and District Anglers' Association, Balgaeth, Kilmessan, Co. Meath. Tel: 046 9029499, email: rjfarrelly@gmail.com

Day permits
The Sports Den, Trimgate Street, Navan, Co. Meath. Tel: 046 9021130
Angler's World, Balmoral Business Park, Navan, Co. Meath. www.anglersworld.ie

BORORA RIVER AND MOYNALTY, RIVER   N 71 83

The Borora River and the Moynalty River flow south from Bailieborough and Mullagh Lough to join the Kells Blackwater at Bloomsbury Bridge. The Borora is the top section and the Moynalty extends downstream from the village of the same name. This river was drained but has now recovered and offers about seven miles of good trout fishing in springtime, from Corlat down to the village of Carlanstown. It is a lovely fast stream with a predominantly gravel bed. It is an especially nice stream in which to fish wet-fly in spring. The trout are small but plentiful and probably average 10oz, with quite a few trout to 1½lb. The best of the fishing is from March to June, as the river runs too low after June.

Unfortunately, there are extensive stretches where the banks are very high and one must wade in order to fish. Access is mainly at the bridges and at a couple of points off the Bellair road. Try a Greenwell's Spider, a Silver Spider or a Hare's Ear in spring and fish dry-fly in summer.

Permission
Gerry Farrell, Moynalty, Kells, Co. Meath. Tel: 046 9244317
Ted Nevin, Hon. Secretary, Borora Angling Club, Carrickspringan, Moynalty, Kells, Co. Meath
Riparian Owners

MARTRY RIVER   N 80 72

The Martry River joins the Kells Blackwater midway between Bloomsbury Bridge and Donaghpatrick Bridge. It is a small stream. The last half-mile has some nice pools and holds trout up to about a pound.

Permission
Riparian owners

ATHBOY (OR TRIMBLESTOWN), RIVER   N 73 62

The Trimblestown River rises west of Ballinlough in Co. Meath and flows south for about 23 miles through Athboy to join the Boyne above Trim. It is a fast-flowing river with a continuous sequence of riffle, pool, and glide. It holds enormous stocks of trout to 12oz from Drewstown House for about six miles, to a point two miles downstream of the village of Athboy, below Ballyfallon Bridge and from Trimblestown Bridge down to the Boyne. Early in the season, you can expect some bigger trout as a lot of fish migrate from the Boyne into the Trimblestown to spawn. This is a spring-fed river and consequently maintains a good volume of water, much like a chalkstream. Parts of the river can become very weedy in summer. The banks are high and wading is necessary but quite safe as the river bed is stony and compacted.

It has an abundance of fly life and has all the ephemeropteran species as described for the Boyne, except mayfly. The fishing is fly-only and opens on 1 April.

Permission
Pat O'Toole, Hon. Secretary, Trim, Athboy & District Angling Club, Unit 1, Duggan Industrial Estate, Athboy Road, Trim, Co. Meath. Mobile: 086 8777039

STONEYFORD, RIVER   N 70 55

The Stoneyford River rises to the east of the village of Fore, in Co. Westmeath, and flows south past Delvin and Ballivor to enter the Boyne below Scarriff Bridge. This is an excellent trout stream with about 10 miles of fishing, starting at South Hill Bridge near Delvin and continuing down to the confluence. It has a marvellous diversity of insect life and a big population of ephemeropterans. Sedge fishing is especially good from Stonetown Bridge to Woodtown Bridge and from Shanco Bridge to the Boyne. This is a spring fed river with chalkstream characteristics and is a favourite stream of mine. It can become very weeded in late summer. It is relatively small and easy to wade. Some sections are a little overgrown and the rest is quite open. It is all excellent trout water but some consider the best of it to be from Rathkenna Bridge, past Earl's Bridge and as far as Shanco Bridge.

Permission
Kieran Burns, Hon. Secretary, Stoneyford Anglers' Association, Trim, Athboy, Co. Meath. Tel: 046 9431455

Day permits
The Post Office, Ballivor, Co. Meath

RIVERSTOWN RIVER   N 60 51

The Riverstown rises near the village of Cloghan, Co. Westmeath and flows in an easterly direction for ten miles before joining the River Deel a mile downstream from the village of Raharney. Since the completion of the drainage scheme this river has re-established its stocks of wild brown trout. It is a difficult river to fish, with high overgrown banks and poor access, involving long walks. The rewards can be justified, however, by the angler willing to brave these obstacles. The Riverstown River holds stocks of fish up to 13/4lb. The best fishing is to be had by wading and chest waders are essential. There are good stretches from Thomastown Bridge to Stonetown Bridge and from Ballyhaw Bridge to the Deel confluence. Parking and access are located close to the road bridges. The river offers good fishing throughout the season, but it can get very weedy in summer.

The fishing is controlled by the Deel and Boyne Angling Association and may be closed to fishing from time to time to conserve trout stocks.

Permits
Paddy Connaughton, Joristown, Raharney, Mullingar, Co. Westmeath. Tel: 044 32118

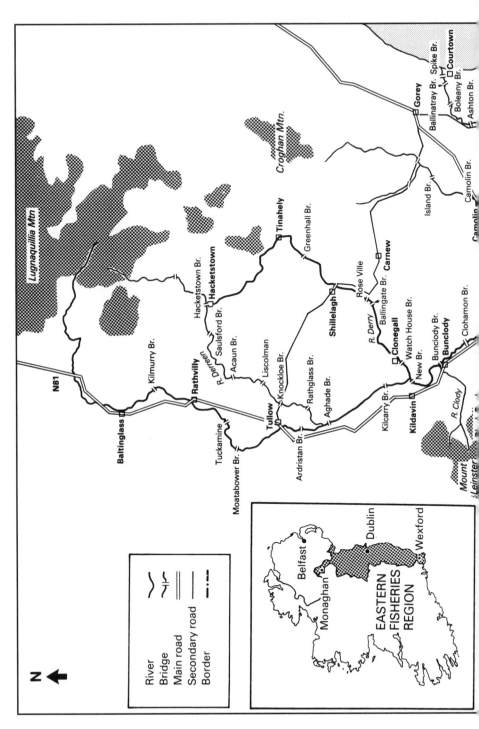

The rivers Slaney, Sow, Owenvorragh and the Bridgetown Canal

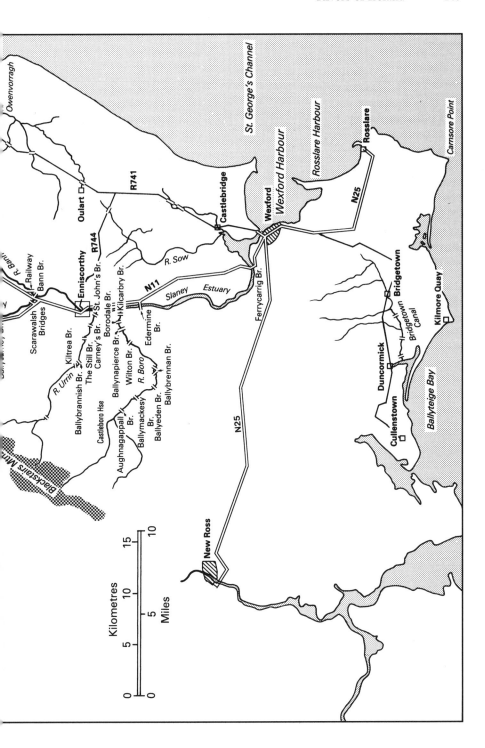

DEEL, RIVER   N 60 53

The River Deel rises in Lough Lene and flows south through Raharney to join the Boyne above Inchamore Bridge. The Deel and Boyne Angling Club has extensive fishing on it down to the Boyne. The Club has also about two miles of fishing on the left bank of the Boyne, from Stoneyford Bridge downstream to the confluence of the Deel. This is another spring-fed river. This once great trout and salmon river suffered greatly as a result of the arterial drainage scheme and some of it will never recover. A rehabilitation programme has been carried out and there is a lot of good fishing now for trout to a pound, but mostly during high water in March and April and up to mid-June. The best stretches are for 500 yards downstream of the bridge on the Delvin–Mullingar road, a 500 yards stretch immediately above Killagh Bridge, from Killagh Bridge down to the confluence of the Riverstown River, and from Clondalee Bridge to the Boyne. The stretch from Killagh Bridge to Raharney was rehabilitated in 1989 and should now hold good stocks of trout. The banks of the lower Deel are not too difficult to fish and a secondary bank has formed. There are, however, many stretches where full chest waders are necessary to fish it properly. It has all the fly hatches one expects to find on a limestone river, including a small hatch of mayfly.

Permission
Paddy Connaughton, Joristown, Raharney, Mullingar, Co. Westmeath. Tel: 044 32118

YELLOW RIVER   N 60 37

The Yellow River rises to the north of Daingean, Co. Offaly, and flows in an easterly direction for approximately 13 miles before entering the Boyne three miles above Ballyboggan Bridge. This river has a good stock of generally small trout, but the stretch below Clongall Bridge holds bigger fish of up to 2lb in weight. The river is fishable from Garr Bridge to its confluence with the Boyne. The Edenderry and Castlejordan Angling Association controls the fishing.

Joe Enright, Hon. Secretary, Edenderry and Castlejordan Angling Association, 37 Fr. Paul Murphy Street, Edenderry, Co. Offaly

MONGAGH RIVER   N 59 39

The Mongagh River rises near Tyrrellspass and Rochforthbridge and it flows for 12 miles through Co. Westmeath in an easterly direction before joining with the Yellow River just upstream of Clongall Bridge, near Castlejordan. This river holds a good stock of small wild brown trout and a few much better fish up to 2lb. The Edenderry and Castlejordan Angling Association controls the fishing, the best of which is from Castlejordan Bridge to the Yellow River confluence. The early season can produce good results.

Permits
Joe Enright, Hon. Secretary, Edenderry and Castlejordan Angling Association, 37 Fr. Paul Murphy Street, Edenderry, Co. Offaly

LITTLE BOYNE RIVER   N 60 37

The Little Boyne is strictly a spring fishery for trout. The best of the fishing is from the Boyne Bridge downstream to the confluence – a distance of about three miles. It holds trout of up to a pound, but is not very attractive fishing since arterial drainage works left it little more than a weedy ditch. It is not a river I can recommend.

SKANE, RIVER   N 90 56

The Skane rises near Dunshaughlin and flows northwards through Kilmessan and past the Hill of Tara before entering the Boyne at Dalgan Park. It is a lovely trout stream from the village of Kilmessan to the confluence and is at its best in spring as a wet-fly stream. After the drainage, it did not have adequate pool areas, but that situation has since been remedied by the erection of a series of small weirs. It has now taken on quite a natural character, especially as the drainage work was less destructive than elsewhere. The Skane flows through pasture and tillage land and even Royal Tara Golf Course before entering the Boyne at Dalgan Park College. It has a good mix of stream, glide and deep water and, in season, it suits both wet and dry-fly fishing. The fishing extends almost as far up as Dunsany but the best of it is probably from Balgeeth to Dalgan Park. It is an excellent spawning river with lots of stone and gravel. It holds big stocks of trout to about a pound and a few better ones. Its one major fault is that the quality of the water is generally not good and can, at times, be quite poor. The club normally reserves the fishing for junior club members.

Permission
Joe Lenehan, Dalgan Angling Club, Clonardon, Garlow Cross, Navan, Co. Meath
Richard Farrelly, Balgeeth, Kilmessan, Co. Meath. Tel: 046 9029499

BOYCETOWN RIVER   N 90 56

The little Boycetown River is about 10 miles long, flowing down from Grange to join the Boyne about a mile east of Trim. It may appear insignificant but the last mile holds some nice trout.

Permission
Riparian owners

KNIGHTSBROOK RIVER   N 81 54

The Knightsbrook River flows down from Summerhill and joins the Boyne two miles below Trim. It is difficult to get permission to fish from the riparian owners. This river holds a good stock of brown trout up to a pound. The fish are mainly concentrated in a 2¼ mile stretch from Laracor to the confluence with the Boyne.

Permission
Riparian owners

Useful information and addresses for the River Boyne and its tributaries

Season
Salmon and seatrout: 1 March–30 September
Brown trout: 1 March–30 September
The above are the statutory seasons, but local regulations often differ. Please remember to check individual Angling Club rules. For example, The Longwood Waters open on 17 March, while Trim, Athboy and District doesn't open until 1 April and the brown trout fishing closes on 15 September.

Permission and information
There is no free fishing on the Boyne system. Anglers should ensure that they have the necessary permission. Tourist anglers will find up-to-date information from:

Angling adviser
Ashley Hayden, Eastern Regional Fisheries Board. Mobile: 087 2746127
Email: Ashley.hayden@erfb.ie

Regulations
All of the fisheries, clubs and syndicates have regulations governing bag limits, minimum size and fishing methods. Catch-and-release is encouraged and some clubs make this a condition of issuing a visitor permit.

Local guides
Pat McLoughlin, 64 Magdalene Court, Kells, Co. Meath.
Tel/fax: 046 9241807, mobile: 086 1017415, email: patandtrina@eircom.net
Marc O'Regan, Crannmór Guest House, Dunderry Road, Trim, Co. Meath.
Tel: 046 9431635, email: cranmor@eircom.net, web: www.crannmor.com
Seamus Lenehan, Clonardran, Garlow Cross, Navan, Co. Meath.
Tel: 046 9025787, mobile: 086 8140078
Paul O'Callaghan, Balmoral Business Park, Navan, Co. Meath. Tel: 046 9071866
Pat Murphy, Hill of Ward, Athboy, Co. Meath. Tel: 046 9432343
Brian Herrity, Sheephouse, Donore, Co. Meath. Tel: 041 9842472
Tom Conlon, Addinstown, Devlin, Co. Westmeath.
Tel: 046 9430112, mobile: 087 9642659

Fly casting and flytying instruction
Peter O'Reilly, APGAI, FFF, MI, THCI, Ballybatter House, Boyne Hill, Navan

Peter O'Reilly returns a Boyne salmon

Co. Meath. Tel: 046 9028210, email: peter@oreillyflyfishng.com

Local tackle shops
The Flying Sportsman, Carrick Street, Kells, Co. Meath. Tel: 046 9241743
Anglers World, Balmoral Business Park, Navan, Co. Meath. Tel: 046 9071866
Clarke's Sports Den, Trimgate Street, Navan, Co. Meath. Tel: 046 9021130
Drogheda Angling Centre, Fair Green, Drogheda, Co. Louth. Tel: 041 9845442
The Sports Gallery, Castle Street, Kells, Co. Meath. Tel: 046 9240114

Fishing lodge/accommodation
Mrs. Paula Casserley, Boyne Dale, Slane Road, Navan, Co. Meath. Tel: 046 9028015
Email: boynedale@iolfree.ie
The Station House Hotel, Kilmessan, Co. Meath. Tel: 046 9025239
Email: stationhousehotel@eircom.net
Ita McDonnell, Roughgrange Farm, Donore, Co. Meath. Tel: 041 9823147
Newgrange Hotel, Bridge Street, Navan, Co. Meath. Tel: 046 9074100
Email: info@newgrangehotel.ie
Brogan's Guesthouse, High Street, Trim, Co. Meath. Tel: 046 9431237
Email: brogangh@iol.ie
Crannmór Guest House, Dunderry Road, Trim, Co. Meath. Tel: 046 9431635
Email: cranmor@eircom.net, web: www.crannmor.com
Highfield House, Maudlin Road, Trim, Co. Meath. Tel: 046 9436386,
Mary Lydon (self-catering accommodation), Kiltale House & Cottage, Kiltale, Trim,
Co. Meath. Tel: 046 9436679, email: mmlydon@eircom.net
Beechwood Lodge, Enfield Road, Trim, Co. Meath. Tel: 046 9436926
Email: beechwoodlodge@esatclear.ie
Headford Arms Hotel, Kells, Co. Meath. Tel: 046 9240063
Email: headfordarms@eircom.net
Anne Finnegan, Woodtown House, Athboy, Co. Meath. Tel: 046 9435022
Email: woodtown@iol.ie

NANNY AND HURLEY, RIVERS   O 10 70

The River Nanny rises near Kentstown and flows east through Duleek and Julianstown
to enter the sea at Laytown. It gets a good run of nice seatrout up to the pool at the
back of the mill at Julianstown and the rest of the fishing is for brown trout averaging
12oz, of which a fair number are wild trout. The river is also stocked and more than
half the trout taken every year are these stocked fish. The trout fishing extends up to
a mile above Balrath Bridge on the Nanny and to Dean's Bridge on its tributary, the
Hurley River, where there are trout to a pound. The peak of the trout fishing is March
to May. There is a fly-only stretch above Bellewstown Bridge.

Season
1 March–15 September

Permission
Pat Gallagher, Duleek Angling Club, Railway View, Downstown, Duleek, Co. Meath
Tel: 041 9823054, email: duleekanglers@eircom.net,
web: www.community.meath.ie/duleekanglers/
Dominick Gallagher, Duleek Angling Club, Downstown, Duleek, Co. Meath
Julianstown Anglers' Association (Membership reserved)

N.B. There are prohibited areas at Kilsharvan House and a small area at Rockbellow,
Julianstown, Co. Meath

Local tackle shop
ARRO, EEC Hardware, Stephenstown Industrial Estate, Balbriggan, Co. Dublin

Regulations
Bag: two trout per day
Minimum size: 12 inches

DELVIN, RIVER   O 18 86

This little river is just 10 miles long and drains a catchment of 27 sq. miles. It enters the sea less than two miles north of Balbriggan and is stocked annually by the local angling club to augment the small stock of native brown trout. This is a small narrow river, very overgrown and difficult to fish with fly. It is best suited to bait fishing and can be fished all the way up as far as the Nail. Access is reasonably good and some stiles are provided.

It used to get an excellent run of big seatrout (1½lb –4½lb) but these have declined in recent years. Small numbers of seatrout are still taken there from August onwards and the pool at the main road bridge, which is now filling in with gravel, is regarded as a prime location. The best fishing is at night. Occasional seatrout are also taken in the stretch at the footbridge and at the back of Gormanstown College.

Season
Seatrout and brown trout: 1 March–15 September

Enquiries and permits
Ciaran McDonald, Hon. Secretary, Gormanstown and District Anglers' Association, 1 Knightswood Park, Balrothery, Balbriggan, Co. Dublin. Mobile: 087 2311017, web: www.gormanstownanglers.com

BROAD MEADOW WATER   O 18 47

The Broad Meadow Water, once famous for its magnificent seatrout, was reduced to a ditch by ongoing drainage work. It has, however, made a recovery in recent years and now has an angling club again

John J Brody, Hon. Secretary, Broadmeadows Anglers' Association, 64 Valley View, off Boelentown Avenue, Swords, Co. Dublin

WARD RIVER O 18 45

The Ward River is 13 miles long and drains a 69 sq. mile catchment. It is a small river with a good flow in spring. It is relatively clean and doesn't run dry in summer.

A recent Eastern Regional Fisheries Board survey revealed that it holds brown trout and still gets a run of seatrout up to Tubberbur. It may even be possible to take a seatrout in the park in Swords.

Season
1 March–15 September

Permission
Riparian owners

TOLKA, RIVER   O 12 37

The River Tolka rises near Dunshaughlin, in Co. Meath, and flows east via Dunboyne, Clonee, Blanchardstown and Finglas, before entering the sea at Clontarf on the north side of Dublin City. For nearly half its length, it flows through urban sprawl and, ironically, the only trout fishing left is within the urban area. There are seatrout in the lower reaches at Clonliffe and up to the Botanic Gardens, where there are wild trout to 3lb. The Tolka flows through some of the most fertile land in Ireland and is an extremely rich river. In the 1950s, it regularly produced trout up to 6lb and trout of 4lb were frequently taken at Ashtown. There are still wild trout to be found up to Black Bull Bridge on the Trim road. Today, it holds some wild trout but it is drained and eutrophic and is really a put-and-take fishery, stocked by Tolka Anglers' Club. The best of the fishing is from The Royal Oak at Finglas Bridge to Mullhuddart – a distance of about three miles. The river still gets hatches of spring olives, midges, black gnats and a big hatch of blue-winged olives. It has no iron blue duns and the sedge hatch is patchy.

Season
Seatrout and brown trout: 17 March–15 September

Permission and Dublin tackle shops
Henry's Tackle Shop, 19 Ballybough Road, Dublin 3. Tel: 01 8745691
Rory's Tackle Shop, Temple Bar, Dublin 2
ABC Tackle, 15 St. Mary's Abbey, Dublin 7

Enquiries
John Hennessy, The Tolka River Environmental Alliance. Mobile: 086 8873141
Eamon Lynch, 46 Donard Avenue, Navan Road, Dublin 7. Tel: 01 838 9630
Mobile: 087 7747350

Elsewhere, permission should be sought from riparian owners.

** LIFFEY, RIVER   O 10 34

The Liffey rises only 12 miles south of Dublin and flows in a huge crescent for over 82 miles before entering the sea at Dublin Bay. Along its course, it drains a catchment of nearly 530 sq. miles. This is a big and very interesting river, with a great diversity of character. It starts as a poor acid mountain river and is transformed into an extraordinarily rich trout stream as it glides and meanders through the plains of Co. Kildare. It flows over a range of differing geology: from granite, to sandstone, to sandstone-limestone and, finally, to pure limestone. Dr Michael Kennedy, formerly of the Inland Fisheries Trust, observed some of the fastest-growing brown trout ever recorded in Ireland in the river near Lucan.

It goes without saying that a river which flows through a capital city the size of Dublin cannot avoid the undesirable effects and demands of such a thickly-populated and heavily-industrialised area. It has been dammed at Pollaphuca to form one of the largest reservoirs in Europe and there is a second reservoir at Leixlip (Leixlip means 'salmon leap', from the Norse lax, salmon). Water abstraction is a huge and growing problem for the Liffey. There are three hydro-electric power stations along its course. Consequently, the flow is controlled artificially and the river is subject to artificial spates, which bear no relation to or connection with the natural rainfall.

The lower stretches, from the city out to beyond Leixlip, tend to be slow and deep, with a series of old mill weirs. Out in the country beyond Celbridge, the river takes on a more natural character. Access to the river downstream of Leixlip can be difficult in places and the banks are undeveloped. Upstream of Straffan to Ballymore Eustace, a lot of good work has been done by the Eastern Regional Fisheries Board which organized a social employment scheme. Under this scheme there has been a lot of bank clearance and construction of stiles and footbridges.

Most of the fishing on the Liffey is controlled by clubs or private interests. There is free fishing at the Memorial Park at Islandbridge and on the left bank immediately above Leixlip Bridge to the River Rye confluence. The latter can provide useful summer grilse fishing and the access to it is via the car park of the Ryevale Hotel.

Salmon

Spring salmon can be taken from early January and grilse run from June, with July providing the peak of the run. It is very difficult to quantify catches, but all indications are that they are very much in decline. Most Liffey salmon are taken either by spinning or on worms. Most of the spring fish are taken at Islandbridge, while the grilse tend to run through and most are taken on the fisheries up to Leixlip and the rest upstream of the Leixlip dam in late August and September – water permitting. It takes a natural flood rather than an artificial spate to get the salmon to run up-river and, of course, they cannot pass the dam at Golden Falls above Ballymore Eustace.

Seatrout

The river gets a small run of seatrout. The best of the fishing is in July on the Dublin and District Salmon and Trout Anglers' Association water, immediately above and below the bridge at Islandbridge. Flyfishing at night is said to be most productive. Useful flies are Peter Ross, Butcher, Bloody Butcher and Teal, Blue & Silver.

Brown trout

The Liffey brown trout in the upper reaches are not terribly big but they are there in good numbers and the water is extremely clean. Trout are found above Islandbridge, but the best of the trout fishing is above Leixlip and all the way to Ballymore Eustace. In some areas it can be quite brilliant. The average weight at Clane is about 10oz and one in six would weigh around a pound. A 3lb trout would be considered an exception. It is thought that the average size is declining on the river, as a whole, but it is noticeable that the size of the trout increases the further downstream you fish.

The Liffey has all the usual fly hatches associated with a rich river. There are plenty of dark olives in spring but the iron blue hatch is patchy and mayflies are scarce. The best fishing of the season is in May and after that September can be very good. There are excellent hatches of sedges – including grey flags. The trout are not too particular and any small brown sedge pattern seems to work. The river has a heavy hatch of yellow evening duns around Clane. The trout take the hatching insect freely but are incredibly difficult to catch on summer evenings. Blue-winged olives are present, which are taken spasmodically. It is important to note that the Liffey blue-winged olive has a very dark wing. A successful imitation is an Orange Quill with a very dark blue dun hackle.

Season
Salmon and Seatrout: 1 January–30 September
Brown trout: 1 March–30 September
For an update on opening times, please check the website: www.fishinginireland.net

LIFFEY ANGLING CLUBS

Dublin and District Salmon Anglers' Association
The club has extensive water at Islandbridge, opposite the Wren's Nest Bar, at C.P.I., a stretch between Lucan and Leixlip and a stretch at Castletown near Celbridge. Membership of this club is open and may be purchased at Rory's Fishing Tackle (see below)

Enquiries
Pat O'Molloy, Hon. Secretary, Dublin and District Salmon Anglers' Assocication, B1 Wellington Park, Whitehall Cross, Terenure, Dublin 6
Paul Devereux, Hon. Secretary, Chapelizod Anglers' Association, 23 St. Laurence's Road, Chapelizod, Dublin 20
Matt Cunningham, Leixlip and District Anglers' Association, 4 Sli an Chanail, Leixlip, Co. Kildare
Michael Brown, Kilcullen Trout & Salmon Anglers, 3164 Avondale Drive, Kilcullen, Co. Kildare
Tallaght Rod & Gun, Unit 2, Castletymon Shopping Centre, Tallaght, Dublin 24
Tel: 01 4526522

Dublin tackle shops
ABC Fishing Tackle, 15 St. Mary's Abbey, Dublin 7. Tel: 01 8731525
Henry's Tackle Shop, 19 Ballybough Road, Dublin 3. Tel: 01 8555216
Rory's Fishing Tackle, 17A Temple Bar, Dublin 2. Tel: 01 6772351, fax: 01 6719986
South Side Angling, Unit D, Southgate, Cork Street, Dublin 8. Tel: 01 4530266
Baumanns of Stillorgan. Old Dublin Road, Stillorgan, Co. Dublin. Tel: 01 2884021

LIFFEY (UPPER), RIVER   O 17 05

The Upper Liffey flows down from the Sally Gap past Manor Kilbride and enters May's Bay on Pollaphuca Reservoir. The trout here average less than half-a-pound and the river tends to drop quickly. It is really a spate river, suitable for wet-fly fishing. An occasional larger trout might be taken early in the season.

This is a fast-flowing rocky river passing through hilly countryside, with wild trout and beautiful scenery. The water quality is excellent, clear and peaty. April to June is the peak of the season, after which the water runs low. Fly hatches consist mainly of stonefly and sedges. Wet-fly and evening sedge fishing give best results.

Permission
Des Johnston, Hon. Secretary, Kilbride Angling Club, 54 Avondale Park, Raheny, Dublin 5

Regulations
Minimum size: 10 inches
Bag limit: 4 trout

Accommodation
Poulaphouca House Hotel, Poulaphouca, Co. Dublin

Ballymore Eustace Angling Association
This club has about 4 ½ miles of river. It is subject to sudden artificial floods, involving a rise in level of up to 3 feet. The wild trout have increased in size since the treatment plant was commissioned and trout over 1lb are now a regular feature.

Enquiries
Thomas Deegan, Hon. Treasurer, Ballymore Eustace A.A., River Grove, Broadleas, Ballymore Eustace , Co. Kildare. Tel: 045 864477

Day permits
Deegan's Daybreak, Ballymore Eustace, Co. Kildare
Costcutters, Ballymore Eustace, Co. Kildare
Mick Murphy's Pub, Ballymore Eustace, Co. Kildare
Also, see the website: www.kildare.ie/ballymoreanglers

North Kildare Trout & Salmon Angling Association
This club has over 15 miles of fishing on the river which has a natural character but the dams at Poolaphouca and Leixlip allow floods to be released when the former gets full and the latter runs low. The banks are quite overgrown. The flow is classic trout water over a gravel, silt, and stony bottom. Weed growth is a problem in summer especially in the town of Newbridge. The water quality has improved since the Osberstown treatment plant was upgraded. Trout are plentiful all along the fishing with the smaller trout further up and the big trout at Millicent which produces trout between 5 and 6 ½lb every season. Fly hatches include dark olives, some mayfly (Ephemera danica), blue-

winged olives, yellow may dun, sedges and black gnat. May, June and July is best and the dry-fly is the preferred method. Adams, Hares Ear and various Olive and Sedge patterns are favoured. Access is not difficult and chest waders are recommended.

There are three prohibited areas:
Newbridge College – 300 yards
St. Patrick's Well, Barrettstown to Victoria Bridge
The right bank at Millicent Bridge for 100 yards

Season
1 March–30 September

Regulations
Minimum size: 20cm (8 inches)

Mike Weaver fishes the river Deel

Bag limit: 6 trout

Catch-and-release is encouraged

Artificial fly-only: no ground bait or maggots

Permission

Rory's Fishing Tackle Shop, Temple Bar, Dublin 2. Tel: 01 6772351

Paddy Fleming, New Road, Naas, Co. Kildare

Mick Deely, Hon. Secretary, North Kildare Trout & Salmon Angling Association, 32 Langton Park, Newbridge, Co. Kildare

Cleere's Tackle Shop, 16b Clane Business Park, Kilcock Road, Clane, Co. Kildare. Tel: 045 893551

Southside Angling, Unit D, Southgate, Cork Street, Dublin 8. Tel: 01 4530266

Guide

John Higgins. Mobile: 086 8135497,email: jjhiggins@02.ie

The K Club Water

This fishery consists of almost a mile-and-a-quarter of double bank fishing. It holds an excellent stock of brown trout and occasional salmon in a woodland and golf course setting.

The peak of the brown trout season is May through to August, with seasonal hatches of mayfly, hawthorn, blue-winged olives, black gnat and various sedges. The best of the fishing is in low water conditions in the evening.

The river takes eight rods and larger groups can alternate between the river and the stocked ponds on the estate.

All the water can be accessed from the bank. Wading is safe in the shallower, sandy areas but can be difficult in the rocky fast water. There is a good variety of water consisting of deep glides, fast water, streams, deep pool and a weir pool.

Permission

The Kildare Hotel and Country Club, Straffan, Co. Kildare. Tel: 01 6017200

Web: www.kclub.ie

Local tackle shop

Countryman Angling, Pacelli Road, Naas, Co. Kildare. Tel: 045 879341

Regulations

Methods: flyfishing and spinning (certain areas are fly-only)

Bag limit: 2 fish

Guides

Resident guides are available at the fishery

email: resortsales@kclub.ie

Lodge/accommodation

The Kildare Hotel & Country Club, Straffan, Co. Kildare. Tel: 01 601 7200, email: hotel@kclub.ie, web: www.kclub.ie. Member of the Great Fishing Houses of Ireland Group

Clane Angling Club

The club has nearly four miles of natural limestone river extending from 300 yards below Millicent bridge, to Tayler Wall above Straffan on the left bank. Most of it is easily accessible. The Club's water is characterized by nice fast glides and slow pools over a sandy bottom. There are few obstacles and one can wade with normal care. In the summer months, water abstraction can sometimes be a problem. Some stretches can get weedy in summer, but most of the river remains fishable.

This particular stretch of water is noted for its large trout and, as a result, there is a waiting list for club membership. Day permits are available, however. The average size of trout range from 1lb–1½lb, but quite a number of fish in the 3lb to 5lb bracket are recorded every season. It is usually the serious dry-fly fishers that hook the bigger trout.

Above Victoria Bridge, at Clane village, the river is quite slow-moving but the average size is fairly large. This is a very productive stretch, with very little barren water. This is predominantly a dry-fly stretch.

Mid-April to the end of June is probably the peak season for the yellow May dun. In June/July there are prolific hatches of blue-winged olives and in August, the sedges come into their own. Unfortunately, hatches of the grey flag sedge (Hydropsyche spp.) have declined considerably. Pale wateries, black gnats and reed smuts are also important.

Season

1 March–30 September

Permission

Joseph Doherty, Hon. Secretary, Clane Angling Club, Corkeragh, Staplestown, Donadea, Co. Kildare

Day permits/tackle shops

Cleere's Tackle Shop, 16b Clane Business Park, Kilcock Road, Clane, Co. Kildare. Tel: 045 893551, web: www.fishingirelandcentre.com

Regulations

Bag limit: 2 trout (catch-and-release is encouraged)
Minimum size: 10 inches

Access

Car parking can be a problem on the Dublin road. Most anglers tend to park at or near the bridge in Clane village.

Local tackle shops

Angling & Shooting Centre, Ballydowd, Lucan, Co. Dublin
Patrick A. Fleming, New Row, Naas, Co. Kildare
Finn McCarthy & Son Ltd, Downings North, Prosperous, Co. Kildare. Tel: 045 841752, email: fishingmccarthys@gmail.com

Dublin Trout Anglers' Association

Dublin Trout Anglers' Association has three separate fisheries on the Liffey.

The first stretch consists of approximately 4½ miles at Straffan/Celbridge. This is a good trout fishery, close to Dublin, with easy access. It has stiles and footbridges in place. The trout average 12oz with some to 2lb and occasional three pounders each season. It is flyfishing only below Gallagher's Lane and all legal methods are allowed elsewhere. Wading is fairly safe, but use a staff. Fly hatches include spring olives, iron blue, black gnat, some mayfly (Ephemera danica), blue-winged olives, yellow may dun and various sedges.

The second stretch consists of 1½ miles of the south bank at Clane. This is good fly water, with good access, stiles and footbridges, and the average size of the trout is good with fish to 2lb and some to 3lb. Fly hatches are as at Straffan/Celbridge and dry-fly probably gives best results.

The third stretch consists of approximately one mile of double bank fishing on the Upper Liffey, at Ballyward Bridge. This is a mountain stream-type water. It holds moderate stocks of small trout up to a pound and gets a late run of spawning trout from Poulaphouca Reservoir with a rise in water in the autumn. Spider patterns, various nymphs and particularly Gold-Head nymphs work well. It is flyfishing only on this stretch. Waders are necessary.

Season
1 March–30 September

Permission
Membership of the Dublin Trout Anglers' Association is full at the time of writing.
Mr. J.R. Miley, Hon. Secretary, Dublin Trout Anglers' Association, 4 Dodder Park Road, Dublin 14. Tel: 01 4902163
Craul's Shop, Manor Kilbride, Co. Wicklow

Day permits
Angling and Shooting Centre, Ballydowd, Lucan, Co. Dublin
Dan O'Brien, New Road, Blackhall, Clane, Co. Kildare
Charles Camping, Blessington, Co. Wicklow

Regulations
Bag limit: 3 trout
Minimum size: 10 inches

KING'S RIVER   N 99 03

The King's River is about 10 miles long with about half a dozen tributaries. It is best described as a wild mountain stream, flowing down from the Sally Gap and entering the southern bay of Poulaphouca Reservoir at Valleymount Bay. The countryside is mountain moorland. There is a lot of forestry and this can cause a problem for water quality with a silt run off at times of heavy rain.

The fishing extends for about three miles from Grana Beg Bridge down to the reservoir. Amidst idyllic scenery, anglers can fish for numerous small trout early in the season. If there is a flood in August/September, some bigger trout (up to 2lb) run up from the lake.

Permission
Dublin Trout Anglers' Association members only.
Mr. J.R. Miley, Hon. Secretary, Dublin Trout Anglers' Association, 4 Dodder Park Road, Dublin 14. Tel: 01 4902163

Regulations
Minimum size: 9 inches

CAMAC RIVER   0 06 31

The Camac River is about 10 miles long. It rises at Brittas Ponds, between Mount Seskin and Saggart Hill, and flows north-west through Saggart, Rathcoole, and Clondalkin and joins the Liffey at Islandbridge. Don't be surprised if you cannot find it from Clondalkin downstream for it is culverted for several miles. Yet, miracle of miracles, proving the tenacity of wild creatures, it was found by the Eastern Regional Fisheries Board development staff to hold seatrout and brown trout to 2lb in April, 2001.

It is fishable above Nangor Road and at Corkagh Park, which is public parkland.

RYE WATER   N 99 37

The fast-flowing Rye Water rises near Kilcock, in Co. Kildare, and flows east past Maynooth to join the Liffey at Leixlip. It holds occasional salmon but is notable for its propensity to grow brown trout at a phenomenal rate.

The fishing extends from Carton Estate downstream to the confluence with the Liffey. The fishing is moderate at present. The stock of bigger trout has decreased but there are plenty of trout to 1lb and some to 2lb.

The upper Rye has hatches of dark olives and the iron blue hatch is more dependable than on the Liffey. It has a very early hatch of blue-winged olives in May and very consistent hatches in July and August. The angler should note that the blue-winged olive found on the Rye has much paler blue/grey wings than its cousin on the Liffey. An imitation of the female BWO is a great fly on the river in September. There are good hatches of sedges and lots of alders on the Rye. Access is good and waders are required.

Season
Brown trout: 1 March–30 September

Day permits
Leixlip Amenities Centre, Collinstown, Maynooth Road, Leixlip, Co. Kildare. Tel: 01 6243050
Mattie Cunningham, Club Secretary, Leixlip and District Angling Club,
4 Sli an Chanail, Leixlip, Co. Kildare

Regulations
Catch-and-release

DODDER, RIVER   O 10 30

The Dodder starts as three streams in the Dublin Mountains above Bohernabreena Reservoir. In that area, it is a typical mountain stream, flowing over granite and sandstone and has very good stocks of trout up to about 8oz. It changes dramatically between Oldbawn and Tallaght, where it flows over limestone, and from Firhouse to the sea the trout become relatively fast-growing and average around 10oz, with plenty to 1¼lb.

The River Dodder is a quite remarkable river in that it flows right through the city of Dublin and yet is well worth fishing for brown trout and seatrout. It is a great tribute to those who care for it that its fish stocks still survive. However, be warned: visually, the river may be in an appalling condition due to the illegal dumping of household rubbish, goods and burned out cars. The Dodder Anglers' Club has a special interest in the river and there is a policy of making visitors welcome for a day's fishing. Membership of the club is open to all.

The Dodder has put most of its pollution problems behind it and the water is now quite clean. In all, there are nearly eight miles of good fishing from Firhouse down to Ballsbridge. It still holds trout to 3lb and these are usually found in the weir pools. The severe pollution in the past killed off many of the insect species, but it still has good hatches of olives and various midges. It has very few sedges or other large flies. The fly angler has to fish very small (sizes 18-20). It is a very difficult river on which to learn to flyfish and anyone who really cracks it is something of a master.

The seatrout seem to migrate in and out and can give quite good fishing in July, August and September. From the estuary up to the bus garage at Beaver Row, Donnybrook, fishing can be very good and seatrout can be taken too at Clonskea, Milltown and Templeogue. It is difficult to fish during the day with so many people about, but at dusk and into the night it can be good.

Access is reasonably good with public parkland stretching for miles on both banks.

Season
Brown trout: 17 March–30 September

Enquiries
Redmond O'Hanlon, Hon. Secretary, Dodder Anglers' Club, 82 Braemor Road, Churchtown, Dublin 14
Des Chew, Eastern Regional Fisheries Board, 15A Main Street, Blackrock, Co. Dublin. Tel: 01 2787022, email: des.chew@erfb.ie

Membership
Rory's Tackle Shop, Temple Bar, Dublin 2. Tel: 01 6772351
Baumann's of Stillorgan, Old Dublin Road, Stillorgan, Co. Dublin. Tel: 01 2884021
Southside Angling, Unit D, Southgate, Cork Street, Dublin 8. Tel: 0 4530266
Also in most fishing tackle shops on the south side of the city and in Tallaght

OWENDOHER RIVER   O 13 24

This is an extraordinary productive little river flowing down from the mountain through residential housing estates and Marley Grange to join the Dodder at Templeogue. It holds lots of small trout and has good hatches of olives and some sedges. It is one of the main nursery streams for the Dodder.

** DARGLE, RIVER   O 26 19

The River Dargle is 12 miles long and with its tributaries, the Glencree River and Glencullen River, drains a catchment of 47 sq. miles. It rises in the Wicklow Mountains and flows east through Enniskerry and enters the Irish Sea at Bray. It is a rather small river, coming off bare mountain and weathered granite cliffs, and is subject to violent spates. It flows through a deep valley from the confluence of the Glencree River down to Enniskerry and is well-endowed with deep holding pools, some of which are very inaccessible.

This is one of Ireland's prime seatrout rivers and comes closest to the famous Welsh rivers in its capacity to produce big seatrout. I don't know of any other river in Ireland that can match it for producing double figure seatrout and one of the biggest seatrout ever recorded from fresh water in Ireland, came from the Dargle. It weighed 16lb 6oz.

The big seatrout come in May and the run increases through June, July and August, with plenty of 2lb-4lb seatrout. The best of the seatrout fishing is above the confluence of the Glencullen River. This is a deep valley with fantastic big holding pools. There is beautiful water in Powerscourt Demesne and this is a beautiful place to fish. The upper limit of good seatrout fishing on the Dargle is at the top end of Powerscourt at the confluence of the Glencree River.

The Tinnehinch Fishery (Hugh Duff) provides night seatrout fishing. It is flyfishing only and is limited to a maximum of eight rods at a time.

On club water, a single worm, spinner and fly are all used for seatrout. Some anglers have a preference for dark flies, such as Connemara Black, Zulu and Black Pennell, but a Teal, Blue & Silver is also favoured.

The Dargle can get a good run of salmon, though some seasons are disappointing. The peak of the salmon run is at the end of April and early in May. The grilse fishing can be good in a wet season, with the best of the fishing in August. The best of the salmon fishing is in the valley from the bottom of the Tinnehinch Fishery to the Silver Bridge.

This is a most productive river in a beautiful setting. Unfortunately, being situated so close to a densely populated area, it is much-abused and heavily poached.

Season
Salmon: 1 February–30 September
Seatrout: 1 February–12 October
Brown trout: 1 March–30 September

Permits

The Tinnehinch Private Seatrout Fishery offers season permits and day permits. Contact:

Hugh Duff, Tinnehinch House, Enniskerry, Co. Wicklow. Tel: 01 2766089 or 2868652

There is now a new lake fishery at Tinnehinch House which is quite lovely and doing well.

Dargle Anglers' Club day permits

Viking Tackle, 79 Castle Street, Bray, Co. Wicklow. Tel: 01 2869215
Web: www.vikingtackle.com
Anthony D. Grehan, Hon. Secretary, Dargle Anglers' Club, 45 Boden Park, Rathfarnham, Dublin 16

N.B. River maps are available from Viking Tackle

Tackle shops

Viking Tackle (see above)
Eddie Roe Tackle Shop, 107 Patrick Street, Dunlaoghaire, Co. Dublin.

Further information

Des Chew, 15A Main Street, Blackrock, Co. Dublin. Email: des.chew@erfb.ie

** VARTRY, RIVER   T 30 96

The Lower Vartry River rises in Vartry Reservoir. It belongs to Dublin Corporation and no provision is made for compensation water in times of low flow. It flows down the Devil's Glen, through the village of Ashford and Mount Usher Gardens, before meeting the tide at Broad Lough. It is a small, narrow river, 20 miles long, with a catchment of about 60 sq. miles. The upper reaches are overgrown and unfishable. From Nun's Cross Bridge to Ashford, the river flows through a densely populated area with private gardens, including Mount Usher Gardens. The only fishing available is the Vartry Angling Club water, which is downstream of Ashford. The club has developed a couple of miles of fishing. Club membership is limited.

The Vartry gets a small run of salmon but is primarily a seatrout river. The seatrout run late on a flood and it is usually August before the run begins and it continues through to the end of the season. The seatrout average about a pound, but the river produces a lot of nice seatrout up to about 4lb.

Night fishing is by far the best and while all legal methods are allowed, flyfishing is regarded as being most effective. Useful patterns include Wicklow Killer, Teal, Blue & Silver, Peter Ross, Zulu, Bibio, Black Pennell and Green Peter. Size 10 is considered best.

Season
Seatrout: 1 February–12 October
Salmon: 1 February–30 September

Enquiries
Sean McDevitt, Hon. Secretary, Vartry Angling Club, 50 Wicklow Heights, Wicklow

THREE MILE WATER   T 32 87

The Three Mile Water rises east of Glenealy and enters the sea just south of Ardmore Point. It holds small brown trout and gets a run of seatrout. Very few people fish it, probably because it is almost completely overgrown and nearly impossible to fish.

Season
Seatrout: 1 February–12 October
Brown trout: 1 March–30 September

Permission
Riparian owners

POTTER'S RIVER   T 30 84
ENEREILLY RIVER   T 29 80

The Potters River enters the sea a little over two miles south of Ardmore Point. It has brown trout, seatrout and even a small late run of salmon. Most of the seatrout fishing is done in the last half mile above the tide and there are brown trout upstream and downstream of Ballinameesda Bridge and on down to Castletimor Bridge.

Season
Seatrout: 1 February–12 October
Brown trout: 1 March–30 September

The Enereilly River comes down from Jack White's Crossroads and enters the sea south of Mizen Head. It gets a small run of seatrout after a flood in late summer and it's important to be there at the right time.

Permission
Vartry Angling Club and Riparian owners.

Local contact
Paul McDevitt, Vartry Angling Club. Tel: 0404 69683

REDCROSS RIVER   T 28 79

The Redcross river comes down past the village of Redcross and enters the sea between Mizen Head and Arklow. This is a very productive trout river: teeming with fry and fingerlings, according to a Fishery Board survey. It holds brown trout and seatrout in season and is reported to have fished well in recent seasons, particularly close to the tide.

Season
Seatrout: 1 February–12 October
Brown trout: 1 March–30 September

Permission
Riparian owners

WEBB'S RIVER   T 35 75

This is a small river that runs into the sea about a mile north of Arklow. It is only a tiny stream but holds brown trout and seatrout to 2lbs, according to the results of a recent survey. The best of the fishing is just up from the tide. There is a caravan park at the mouth.

Season
Seatrout: 1 February–12 October
Brown Trout: 1 March–30 September

Permission
Riparian owners

** AVOCA, RIVER (AND TRIBUTARIES)   T 20 76

The Avoca River and its tributaries drain a catchment of 252 sq. miles from the Sally Gap down to Arklow. This is a magnificent and very beautiful river system, world famous for its lovely setting among the Wicklow Mountains.

The Avoca River itself begins at the meeting of the Avonmore River and the Avonbeg River and is joined below Woodenbridge by the Aughrim River. There is a lot of pollution because the water is poisoned by the run-off from the disused sulphur and copper mines in the area. Migratory fish hold up in the tidal water and have learned to take their chance and run up into the clear water rivers above on a flood.

This is a river with the potential to be among the five top salmon rivers in the country and it was beginning to show some improvement before it was closed.

There is a special bye law for this river, see web: www.erfb.ie

Season
15 March–30 September

** AVONMORE, RIVER   T 19 89

The Avonmore flows down from Lough Tay and Lough Dan, through the villages of Laragh and Rathdrum, to join the Avoca River – a distance of 22 miles. This is a lovely wide river with streams, glides and deep pools. It is very clean, except for one short stretch, with little industry or agriculture to pollute it. Wading can be dangerous and it is no place for children. The fishing extends from Clara Bridge to the White Bridge at Avoca.

There is an active Angling Club – Rathdrum Trout Anglers Club. New members are always welcome and the club spends a lot of money on the river, clearing banks and providing stiles and bridges.

The river holds big stocks (some would say too many) of small brown trout of 7 to 8 inches. It also holds trout of 1lb–1 ½lb and every year can produce trout of 3lb–5lb, though these are probably seatrout. Some of the best fishing is in Avondale Forest Park, downstream of Rathdrum. There are good hatches of olives – including blue-winged olives – sedges and black gnats. The best of the fishing is usually after a flood in May, June and July using wet-fly, dry-fly, Czech nymph and New Zealand dry-fly.

Access is good and mostly at the bridges. There is a car park at Avondale House, but one must pay a fee.

Biting midges can be incredibly troublesome here in summer. Be warned!

Season
1 March–30 September

Permission
Riparian owners
Mr. Pat Cullen, Hon. Secretary, Rathdrum Trout Anglers' Association, Main Street, Rathdrum, Co. Wicklow. Tel: 0404 43142
Kelly's Service Station, Main Street, Rathdrum, Co. Wicklow
Gala News, Main Street, Rathdrum, Co. Wicklow
Rathdrum Tourist Information Centre, Main Street, Rathdrum, Co. Wicklow

Regulations
Minimum size: 8 inches

Accommodation
Hill Top B & B, Glasnarget, Rathdrum, Co. Wicklow. Tel: 040 446304

AVONBEG RIVER   T 17 85

The Avonbeg River is 17 miles long and flows down through beautiful, untouched scenic countryside past Glenmalur, Greenan, and Ballinaclash, to join the Avonmore above Avoca. It holds big stocks of small trout all the way down from the top of the glen to below Ballinaclash. It is very overgrown at Ballynaclash and virtually unfishable, while farther up at Grennan there is no cover and it is easy to spook the trout in the clear water. On this river, one can have lots of fun fishing for small trout in beautiful countryside. For flyfishing, try a small Wickham's Fancy or a Klinkhåmer.

Permission
Riparian owners

OW RIVER   T 10 81

The Ow River is 12 miles long and flows down from Lugnaquillia Mountain through a heavily-wooded valley. Access is very difficult and the trout are small, though one can turn up the occasional good trout to 12oz in the deeper pools.

Permission
Riparian owners

DERRY WATER   T 10 76

The Derry Water rises near Knockanana in west Wicklow and flows south and then north-eastwards to join the Ow River and from there onwards it becomes the Aughrim River. It is a superb little trout stream. I'm told the reason is that it flows over probably the only little bit of limestone in Co. Wicklow. It holds good stocks of brown trout to a pound at Annacurra and, reportedly, it is not heavily fished.

Permission
Mr. Arie Vandereel, Hon. Secretary, Aughrim and District Trout Angling Club, Ow Valley House, Cappagh, Aughrim, Co. Wicklow. Tel: 087 9202751

Day permits
Lawless's Hotel, Aughrim, Co. Wicklow. Tel: 040 236146

Local accommodation
Lawless's Hotel (see above)

AUGHRIM, RIVER   T 14 79

The River Aughrim begins at the confluence of the Derry Water and the Ow River, about a mile west of Aughrim.

The average size of the trout is 8oz–12oz. Bigger fish, to 4lb, are usually caught at night, but these are possibly seatrout. There are three fish farms on the river and there is always the possibility of catching a few escapee rainbow trout. The club rule is that fish under 8 inches should be returned. The best fishing is in April to July and in September, with a chance of good night fishing in September for seatrout.

The best of the fishing is from Roddenagh Bridge on the Ow River, down through the village of Aughrim to Coat's Bridge and down as far as Woodenbridge.

Access is by the football field on the left bank at Roddenagh Bridge. There is a short stretch below the village of Aughrim which was shamefully dredged in September 2000. All of the natural character and boulders were removed and the landowner doesn't allow fishing. This is followed by a fishable stretch, but then there is a problematic stretch with heavy bank cover for about a mile from the Woodfab Factory to Coat's Bridge. There is no fishing allowed along by the fish farm at Coat's Bridge but below this there is a stretch known locally as the 'Slaney', with good access and good fishing down as far as the big fish farm at Woodenbridge (where access is also possible). The Aughrim Road (R747) closely parallels the river, crossing it at Coats Bridge.

The Aughrim River has probably the most prolific fly hatches of all the Wicklow rivers, especially olives and sedges. Some of the best fishing is to sedges on summer evenings. A Greenwell's Spider is a favourite early season pattern. A Coachman works well fished wet at night, or try fishing a dry White Moth.

N.B. The Eastern Regional Fisheries Board is looking at the implications of the E.U. Water Framework Directive with this river in mind. It may be possible greatly to enhance the potential of this river as a salmonid producing fishery.

Permission
Mr. Arie Vandereel, Hon. Secretary, Aughrim and District Trout Angling Club, Ow Valley House, Cappagh, Aughrim, Co. Wicklow. Tel: 087 9202751

Day permits
Lawless's Hotel, Aughrim, Co. Wicklow. Tel: 040 236146
Brook Lodge Hotel, Aughrim, Co. Wicklow
Woodenbridge Hotel, Woodenbridge, Co. Wicklow
Power Sound Tackle, Arklow, Co. Wicklow

INCH RIVER   T 64 23

The Inch River and its tributaries drain a catchment of approximately 27 sq. miles in North Wexford into Courtown Harbour at Clone. The Inch is affected by intermittent water pollution but its condition is beginning to improve. It still gets a good run of seatrout in July. The main fishing area is in the fields immediately upstream and downstream of Castletown Bridge. The water is deep and slow and good fishing depends on a flood, an upstream wind, or fishing at night.

Season
15 March–30 September

Permission
Riparian owners

OWENAVORRAGH RIVER   T 20 56

The Owenvorragh River is 18 miles long and drains a catchment of 63 sq. miles, south of Gorey, into Courtown Harbour. The water quality is poor due to the leaching of mainly agricultural nutrients. It was drained in 1975 and is relatively featureless and slow-flowing and very overgrown, except where the anglers have cleared the banks.

It holds salmon after the first flood in August and gets a very good run of seatrout up to 4lb from July. The Angling Club stocks brown trout each season and some of these are known to run to sea and return as seatrout. The best of the seatrout fishing is from mid-June through to August and the river is usually heavily fished at this time. All legitimate methods are allowed, including maggot and spinner. The best of the fishing is at night and, for the flyfisher, dark flies get best results: Zulu, Butcher, Black Pennell and Connemara Black (sizes 12-14). The seatrout here are thick and short and take best after a spate. The main fishing area is from Ballycanew to the mouth.

Season
All species: 15 March–30 September

Permission
There is an active Owenavarragh Angling Club which leases part of the stretch from the tide up to a point about a mile above Boleany Bridge, a distance of about three miles. The rest of the fishing is with the permission of the riparian owners. Day permits and a State licence are available on the Angling Club water from:

Whitmore's Jewellers Shop, Main Street, Gorey, Co. Wexford. Tel: 055 21351
Brian Miller, Hon. Secretary, Owenavorragh Angling Club, Gorey, Co. Wexford.
Tel: 086 2616905

Local tackle shop
John Murphy, 82 North Main Street, Wexford, Co. Wexford

** SLANEY, RIVER   S 97 40

See web: www.erfb.ie

The River Slaney rises in the Glen of Imaal in Co. Wicklow and flows south through Baltinglass, Co. Wicklow, Rathvilly and Tullow, in Co. Carlow and Bunlcody and Enniscorthy, in Co. Wexford, where it meets the tide. It is 73 miles long and drains a catchment of approximately 680 sq. miles. In spring, it is a beautiful, big, fast-flowing river, ideally suited for salmon fishing. Later in the season the water tends to run off rather quickly due to the extensive land drainage works carried out by farmers. The Slaney holds salmon, seatrout and brown trout.

Salmon
The Slaney is primarily a spring salmon fishery and was once regarded as one of Ireland's the top rivers for early spring salmon fishing. It used to be known as 'The Queen of Irish Rivers', but its salmon are now probably an endangered species.

The peak of the spring salmon fishing is from opening day (10 March) to the end of March. The fishing can be fair-to-good in April and even into May. In fact, the biggest run of fish comes in May, but the majority of these are taken by the nets. Water temperature determines how far upstream the spring salmon fishing extends. With snow water the fish tend to lie below Bunclody, but in mild weather they can be caught up to Tullow, in Co. Carlow. Very few grilse are taken on the rod in the Slaney. The average weight of salmon is 10lb and the usual size range is from 7lb to over 20lb.

Spinning is the most popular early season fishing method. The most popular baits are yellow belly, brown & gold and blue & silver Devons – in that order. Sizes range from 3 inches maximum, down to 1¼ inches. The majority of the fisheries don't allow worm or shrimp.

Upstream of Ballycarney Bridge, it is flyfishing only from 1 April. Yellow flies are popular, including yellow tube flies, Garry Dog and Yellow Shrimp. In April, when the water is low and warm, Blue Charm and Hairy Mary work well by day and a Thunder & Lightning is a favourite at dusk. Fly size depends on water temperature and height and can range from a tube fly or a Waddington to a size 4 double down to size 10. I particularly like a yellow or lemon shrimp fly.

Most of the fishing is done from the bank. Wading is not usually allowed, except where a fishery owner owns both banks.

The Slaney is a river with a very long, narrow estuary. It is over 12 miles from Enniscorthy Bridge to Ferrycarrig Bridge and a total of 75 nets operate from 1 April along the estuary. Many anglers believe that the 48-hour period each week when the nets are closed is too short to allow fish to run in low water conditions. The river, too, is not without its problems. Water abstraction takes place above Rathvilly and Clohamon Weir, where a new fish pass, installed by ministerial order in 1989, is a cause of concern to anglers.

Seatrout

The river gets a very good run of seatrout. They begin to run around 20 June and peak in the first two weeks of July. The fishing remains good through July and into August when river fog often puts the trout off.

Certain stretches are especially good and include the free fishing from Enniscorthy Bridge down to the mouth of the River Urrin; from Scarawalsh Old Bridge down to the mouth of the River Bann; from Clohamon Weir down to Moyeady; the stretch opposite the cemetery at Bunclody; the stretch at Ballina Park downstream of Bunclody; the right bank opposite the mouth of the River Derry down to the confluence of the Kildavin Stream and the stretch at Caherdavin can give great sport. Some of these stretches are private and some do not issue permits.

The fishing methods can vary from fishery to fishery and may include fly, worm and maggot. The most popular flies are Killdevil Spider, Greenwell's Spider, Bibio, Butcher, Priest, Sooty Olive and Peter Ross (sizes 10-12). The full range of fly line density can be employed, according to conditions. A slow retrieve is said to work best.

Brown trout

The river holds plenty of brown trout averaging 6oz. Anglers rarely bother fishing for them, except upstream of Tullow where there are good stocks of trout up to a pound up as far as Baltinglass. Among the fly hatches observed in early spring are what appears to be the true March Brown.

Season

Salmon and seatrout: 10 March–31 August upstream of Enniscorthy Bridge and to 15 September downstream of the same bridge.

Statutory regulations

Artificial fly only after 1 April, between Ballycarney Bridge and Aghade Bridge.

Artificial fly only after 1 May, upstream of Enniscorthy Bridge and on all tributaries, except on the River Bann above the Railway Bridge.

Permission

The Slaney Rod Fishers' Association represents the private fisheries and riparian owners which let rods mainly on a seasonal basis. Day rods occasionally become available.

Mr. Leslie White, Hon. Secretary, Slaney Rod Fisher's Association, White & Co., The Square, Tullow, Co. Carlow. Tel: 059 9151482

Free fishing

The salmon and seatrout fishing is free on the downstream side of the old bridge in Enniscorthy to a point 200 yards below the River Urrin confluence. It has produced up to 100 spring fish in recent years and a lot of seatrout during the summer.

Ballin Temple Fishery

The Ballin Temple Fishery holds salmon, seatrout and brown trout in season. It is located midway between Tullow and Bunclody. It is 2½ miles of double bank fishing. It lies in a secluded valley and is unspoiled, surrounded by mature woodland. The fishery takes six rods, it has 22 named pools and is not divided in beats.

Rods are let on either a seasonal, weekly or daily basis but always limited to six rods fishing, to ensure a harmonious balance. Visitors are always welcome.

Spinning is allowed in March, but this is nice fly water and prospective anglers should be able to spey cast. This is a distinct advantage and you should use a sinking tip line up to late April. Favourite flies are: Blue and Yellow Badgers and various shrimp patterns. Noted pools are: The Four Black Rocks, Smelly Well, the House Pool and the Trout Stream, Half Moon and Wilson's.

Season

10 March–31 August

Permission

Mr. Robin Eustace-Harvey, Mill Park, Kilbride, Nr Tallow, Co. Carlow
Tel: 059 9155612. web: www.ballintemple.com

Regulations

Spinning allowed in March only

Local guide

Tony Sweeney, 28 Parkmore, Baltingcass, Co. Wicklow. Tel: 059 6481240

Local tackle shop

Liam O'Connor, The Square, Tullow, Co. Carlow. Tel: 059 9151337

Local flytyer

Tony Sweeney. Tel: 059 6481240

Accommodation

Ballin Temple Cottages, Ardattin, Nr Tullow, Co. Carlow. Tel: 059 9155037
Email: manager@ballintemple.com, web: www.ballintemple.com. Member of the *Great Fishing Houses of Ireland Group*

Permits

John O'Brien, Tullow Salmon and Trout Anglers' Association, Ballybritt Big, Rathvilly, Co. Carlow

Patrick Lacey, Salsboro Angling Club, Dolphin House, Bellfield, Enniscorthy, Co. Wexford. Tel: 054 35822

Bernard Cash, Hon. Secretary, Salsboro Angling Club, Kilbeggan, Bree, Enniscorthy, Co. Wexford

Jim Murphy, Enniscorthy & District Angling Club, 24 Fr. Cullen's Terrace, Enniscorthy, Co. Wexford. Tel: 054 37405

Derek Nally, Chairman, Mount Leinster Anglers. Tel: 054 77801

Arthur Kavanagh, Hon. Secretary, Mount Leinster Anglers.

Jason Sheridan, Island Angling Club, 78 Slaney View Park, Enniscorthy, Co. Wexford
Tel: 054 37405

CARRIGGOWER, RIVER   S 91 95

This is the most northerly tributary of the River Slaney. It comes down from Hollywood Glen, south of Hollywood for about six miles to join the Slaney about a mile east of Stratford. It is a spate river with a gravel bottom and the margins are boggy with rough grazing and rushes. It holds a stock of nice brown trout upstream of Whitestown Bridge which is located near the confluence.

Season

10 March–30 September

Permission

Riparian owners

DERREEN, RIVER   S 86 70

The River Derreen is 25 miles long. It holds salmon in spring and was once considered by some anglers to be a better salmon fishery than the Slaney itself, above the confluence. It fishes best in high water when the water temperature rises. It flows through rich agricultural land and holds good quality brown trout. There are good stocks of 12oz trout here and some even reach 3lb. The best fishing is in March, April, May and June and there are good hatches of the various olives. It is a small river, easy to wade and a short fly rod is recommended.

Tullow Salmon and Trout Anglers' Association (see John O'Brien, above) has a short stretch on the right bank, at the confluence with the Slaney. Upstream of that there is private fishing, and above Rathglass Bridge, fishing can be obtained with the permission of the riparian owners.

Hacketstown and Rathvily Trout Anglers Association disbanded following serious pollution and a fish kill that occurred at Hacketstown. Those that still fish the river prefer to do their trout fishing upstream of Hacketstown and on towards Rathangan.

Season and regulations
As for the River Slaney

Permission
Riparian owners

DERRY, RIVER   S 90 60

The River Derry rises north-west of Tinahely, in Co. Wicklow, and flows south-west for 21 miles through Shillelagh to join the Slaney at Kildavin. It is close to the road and access is relatively easy up to Shillelagh. It holds occasional salmon and a fairly good stock of brown trout to a pound or better. It is a nice little river, but very overgrown and is, perhaps, best left that way because it is very important as a spawning and nursery river for Slaney salmon.

Permission
Riparian owners

BANN, RIVER   S 98 45

The River Bann rises in north Co. Wexford and flows south-west for 28 miles, past the towns of Gorey, Camolin and Ferns, to join the Slaney below Scarawalsh Bridge. It is regarded mainly as a seatrout fishery and holds lots of brown trout up to about a pound. The banks are overgrown and the river gets very weedy in summer. The three best places for the seatrout fishing are: at the confluence, Doran's Bridge (Ferns area) and at the village of Camolin. There are some good pools in these areas and the fishing can be great from mid July to the end of August. Access to the rest of the river is difficult and the banks are very overgrown.

Season
10 March–31 August

Permission
Riparian owners
River Bannn Angling Club, Padric Bolger, Hon. Secretary, St. Aidan's, Ferns, Co. Wexford.

N.B. Artificial fly-only up to the Railway Bridge after 1 May

URRIN, RIVER   S 96 39

The River Urrin is 14 miles long and flows from the west into the Slaney estuary one mile south of Enniscorthy. It is regarded as an excellent seatrout river. The fishing can be very good with lots of seatrout from 12oz–1½lb. The season is at its best from around the first week in July to the end of the season. The best fishing extends from the mouth up to the weir at Kiltrea, a distance of about four miles. This is a nice river – averaging about 10 yards wide – with good banks and relatively easy access, once you have gained some local knowledge. It has nice, deep pools. All legitimate angling methods are allowed.

The Eastern Regional Fisheries Board carried out a lot of instream development work to aid both spawning and angling on this river.

Season
10 March–15 September

Permission
Myles Kehoe, Castle Street, Enniscorthy, Co.Wexford
Charles Cullen, Tackle Shop, 14 Templeshannon, Enniscorthy, Co. Wexford
Murphy's Fishing Tackle, Main Street, Wexford

Regulations
Minimum size: 9 inches
Bag limit: 4 trout
All legitimate methods

BORO, RIVER   S 97 35

The Boro River is an impressive fast-flowing productive seatrout fishery, 18 miles long, with some lovely streams and pools. Some of the best fishing is developed by the Eastern Regional Fisheries Board. A lot of good work has been done improving access and removing fallen trees from pools. The river is well signed and provided with car parks, stiles, paths and foot bridges. The main seatrout angling water reaches from the mouth up as far as Castleboro, a distance of about nine miles. The river retains its natural character, with open banks, farmland and some forestry, but no drainage works. The seatrout fishing can be excellent with lots of fish up to 1½lb. They begin running around the last week of June. The peak of the season is around the third week in July, and good fishing can continue until about mid-August. The best of the early-season fishing is from the mouth to Victoria Bridge, up to Wilton Bridge and as far as Ballybrennan, a distance of six miles. From mid-August, the better fishing is farther upstream and good local knowledge of the pools is necessary. This river is heavily fished with maggots.

Season
10 March–15 September

Permission
Ger Carthy, Boro Angling Club, 2 Market Square, Enniscorthy, Co. Wexford

Regulations
Minimum size: 9 inches
Bag limit: 4 trout
All legitimate methods allowed

SOW, RIVER   T 5 26

The River Sow drains a 34 sq. mile catchment into Wexford Harbour at Castlebridge.
It is regarded primarily as a seatrout fishery with about a mile of tidal fishing located
below the waterworks dam at Castlebridge. The best of the fishing is downstream of
the waterworks to the Vale Bridge. Access is difficult, with high reeds. Nonetheless,
this stretch produces 200-300 seatrout every year, from mid-June onwards. This part
of the river is tidal.

Season
15 March–30 September

Permission
Riparian owners

BRIDGETOWN, CANAL   S 93 8

The Bridgetown Canal flows into the estuary about four miles north-west of
Kilmore Quay in south Wexford. Further west, the estuary discharges into the sea at
Cullenstown. The tide rushes through a narrow neck at Cullenstown and this location
is known to produce good seatrout to 5lb in April and May. They are fished for by
spinning as the tide floods through. The most recent information indicates that stocks
are still excellent.

Season
Seatrout: 15 March–30 September

Permission
Riparian owners

7. Shannon Fisheries Region

The Shannon Fisheries Region comprises all the rivers that flow into the sea between Hags Head in Co. Clare and Kerry Head.

This is a huge region, extending from north Kerry in the south virtually to the border with Northern Ireland. The Shannon River is the biggest in these islands and drains the entire central plain. Most of it is on limestone and it has the characteristics required to produce and nurture huge numbers of fish of all the species it hosts.

The fisheries are described later, in detail, but a brief word is necessary on the Shannon itself, the greatest river of them all.

Traditionally, it is reputed to have produced large numbers of big salmon. In 1929, a hydroelectric power station was commissioned at Ardnacrusha, near Limerick. A fish pass was incorporated in the regulating weir at Parteen. There are many that claim that relatively few salmon ran through this fish pass. In 1935, the Shannon Fisheries Act gave over the entire fishing rights of the Shannon to the Electricity Supply Board. In 1959, a Boreland lift was built at Ardnacrusha power station in order to get the salmon up the river.

At the present time, the Electricity Supply Board controls all of the salmon fishing on the river. The company actively manages the fisheries on the lower river at Limerick – that is Castleconnell and the Mulcair River – and extensive stocking takes place. However, an Electricity Supply Board permit is required to fish for salmon anywhere on the Shannon or its tributaries.

The run of fish has declined steadily in recent years. As a result, anglers will find salmon scarce, particularly in the tributaries with the exception of the River Mulcair and of course, the River Feale.

Rivers marked ** are – at time of writing – closed for salmon fishing, and seatrout over 40cm must be returned (a measure designed to preserve the larger breeding fish).
Rivers marked * are catch-and-release only for all salmon, and seatrout over 40cm must be returned.

The trout fishing on a number of its tributaries – including the Suck, Inny, Brosna, Little Brosna and Camlin, etc. – is leased to the Central Fisheries Board and managed by the Shannon Regional Fisheries Board. A Shannon Regional Fisheries Board trout fishing permit (available in tackle shops, etc.) is required on these rivers.

Since the Shannon Fisheries Region is the largest in the country, I have divided it into two for the purpose of easier reference. The Lower Shannon area consists of the main channel of the Shannon south of the town of Portumna, together with all its tributaries as well as the rivers of north Kerry and west Clare. The Upper Shannon area incorporates the tributaries that drain east Co. Galway and Counties Roscommon, Leitrim, Longford, Cavan and Westmeath.

Accommodation

For your hotel, lodge and bed and breakfast accommodation, see:

East & Midlands (Kildare, Laois, Longford, Louth, Meath, North Offaly, Westmeath, Wicklow) Fáilte Ireland East & Midlands, Dublin Road, Mullingar, Co. Westmeath. Tel: 044 9348761, fax: 044 9340413, email: eastandmidlandsinfo@failteireland.ie Web: www.discoverireland.ie/eastcoast
South West (Cork, Kerry) Fáilte Ireland South West, Áras Fáilte, Grand Parade, Cork Tel: 021 4255100, fax: 021 4255199, email: corkkerryinfo@failteireland.ie Web: www.discoverireland.ie/southwest
Shannon Development (Clare, Limerick, South Offaly, North Tipperary) Shannon Development-Heritage & Tourism, Shannon Town Centre, Co. Clare Tel: 061 361555, fax: 061 363180 email: tourisminfo@shannondev.ie Web: www.discoverireland.ie/shannon
Ireland West (Galway, Mayo, Roscommon) Fáilte Ireland Western, Forster Street, Galway. Tel: 091 537700, fax: 091 537733, email: irelandwestinfo@failteireland.ie Web: www.discoverireland.ie/west

THE LOWER SHANNON

The Lower Shannon consists of the main channel south of Portumna together with all its tributaries and the rivers of west Co. Clare. We begin with the River Feale, which is the most southerly fishery, and then work our way northwards.

FEALE (CASHEN), RIVER   Q 99 33

The River Feale and its tributaries constitute the most important salmon and seatrout river in those parts of north Kerry and west Limerick lying south of the Shannon estuary. The Feale rises in the mountains of north Cork, near Rock Chapel, flows for 46 miles through the towns of Abbeyfeale and Listowel and enters the sea south of Ballybunnion. For the last six miles of its course it is known as the Cashen River. It drains a catchment of approximately 450 sq. miles. Even though it drains such a large area, it is a typical fast-flowing spate river, subject to huge floods. The lower section is dominated by large, deep fish-holding pools. An important feature of the upper river and its tributaries is the number of holding pools, which is presumably the reason that it is such a good fishery so far upstream. The lower part of the river is tidal, almost to Finuge Bridge.

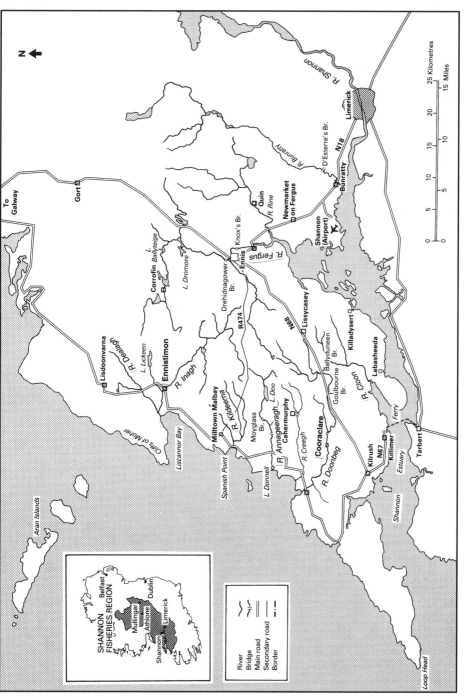

The rivers of County Clare

The Feale gets equally good runs of salmon and seatrout. In a good season – with frequent spates to bring the fish up and high winds to hamper the commercial netting – it is estimated to produce 1,500 salmon and grilse and well over 2,000 seatrout to rod and line.

There are fish in the river from opening day on 1 March and the best of the spring fishing is from then until mid-May, depending on water levels. Small grilse begin showing in the river about mid-June and there is always a dramatic improvement after the draft nets go off at the end of July. There can be very good fishing for the bigger summer fish from mid-August through September in suitable weather conditions. The spring and autumn salmon average about 9lb and the grilse about 4lb.

All legitimate angling methods are allowed (except shrimp and prawn), with spinning, worm and fly being most popular. For salmon, Devon Minnows are still favoured by traditional anglers, while the Flying C is the probably now the most widely-used spinning lure. The most popular salmon flies are the Ally's Shrimp, Garry Dog, Thunder & Lightning, Hairy Mary, Blue Charm, Wilkinson and The Halpin. This local fly was the creation of the late John Joe Halpin of Listowel and is dressed as follows:

The Halpin
Tag: fine oval silver
Tail: none
Butt: red wool or seal's fur well teased out
Rib: oval silver
Body: black floss silk
Body hackle: dyed bright red cock
Hackle: white cock
Wing: fibres of cock pheasant tail, with grey mallard (or teal) flank over
Head: red varnish

N.B. This is still a great fly on the river, particularly upstream of Listowel when the water is dark and peat-stained on a falling spate.

Seatrout
There are two main runs of seatrout. The first occurs in April/May and brings a run of what locals refer to as 'Spring Whites'. These are larger fish in the 2–5lb range. They can be slow takers but put up a memorable fight when hooked.

The main runs of seatrout occur from mid-May to mid-August and these fish are in the 8oz–3lb bracket and are much more plentiful than the earlier fish. The lower-to-middle stretches fare best in June, while the upper stretches enjoy better returns as the season progresses. In high water conditions, spinning and worming are the most rewarding methods. The most productive spinning lures for seatrout fishing are the Mepps, small Devon Minnows and the Lane Minnow (known locally as the Lane 'bait'). Lane Minnows are available from all the local tackle dealers in sizes from 1 inch to 5 inches.

In normal water levels, flyfishing for seatrout comes into its own. Early morning and late evening are the peak times for seatrout flyfishing. However, those anglers who are willing to fish on into the night are often well rewarded for their efforts.

Dark flies are best for daytime fishing: Zulu, Black Pennell, Bibio, Mallard & Claret and Wickham's Fancy (sizes 10-14).

At night, silver-bodied flies are best, the most popular being: Bloody Butcher, Silver Doctor, Teal Blue & Silver; Priest; Jungle Cock & Silver (sizes 10-14).

Season
1 March–15 September

Permission
Most of the fishing is controlled by five angling clubs, some is let to rods annually by private owners and there are a few short stretches that are regarded as free fishing

Local tackle shop
Landers Outdoor World, Mile Height, Tralee, Co. Kerry. Tel: 066 7126644
Web: www.landers.ie
Jim Halpin, Shooting Supplies Ltd, William Street, Listowel, Co. Kerry
Tel: 068 22392, wwww.halpins.net
Ryan Bros, New Street, Abbeyfeale, Co. Limerick. Tel: 068 31411

Killocrim-Finuge Club
This club has three miles of water downstream of Listowel. It fishes best after a spate and has good salmon and grilse fishing and fair seatrout fishing as the fish run through. Day permits from:
Mr. Dan Joy, Hon. Secretary, The Killocrim-Finuge Club, Killocrim, Listowel, Co. Kerry. Tel: 068 40310

North Kerry Anglers' Association
The association is based in Listowel and has access to about nine miles of fishing on both the River Feale and its main tributary, the Smearlagh River. The fisheries are spread in an urban rural divide in the lower-to-middle reaches of the Feale. The urban fishery is about 2½ miles from tidal waters. The rural fisheries, which are about three miles east of Listowel town, comprise of the Kilmorna/Trienereagh/Bunagaragh stretches on the Feale and also about four miles of fishing on the River Smearlagh. Under the Tourism Angling Measure (TAM) the association undertook a major development programme on its fisheries which resulted in a marked improvement in the fishing. Four salmon-holding pools were refurbished and a programme of riverbank stabilisation was carried out. These have been complemented by new car parking facilities and improved access. Day or weekly permits and annual membership are available. Accommodation and guides can be arranged with prior notice.

Permits
Mr. Jim Halpin, Shooting Supplies Ltd, William Street, Listowel, Co. Kerry
Tel: 068 22392, web: www.halpins.net

Tralee and District Anglers' Association

Tralee and District A.A. has over two miles of fishing located downstream of Kilmorna Bridge. This is nice salmon water with 15 named pools. This is a first-class flyfishery and holds salmon and seatrout. There is a car park about 600 m from the river and good access. Chest waders are essential.

Popular salmon patterns are Ally's Shrimp, Garry Dog, Munro Killer, Willie Gun and Halpin. For seatrout: Silver & Blue, Coachman, Wickham's Fancy, Dusty Miller and White Moth.

Day permits

Matthew Doody, Colbert's Terrace, Abbeyfeale, Co. Limerick. Tel: 068 31983
Joseph O'Keeffe, Glenview, Kilmorna, Co. Kerry. Tel: 068 45189
Landers Outdoor World, Mile Height, Tralee, Co. Kerry. Tel: 066 7126644
Web: www.landers.ie

Abbeyfeale Anglers' Association

Abbeyfeale Anglers' Association has about four miles of fishing, the greater part of which is located downstream of the town. It offers good seatrout fishing from June and salmon fishing in August and September. The best of the fishing is upstream of Kilmorna Bridge and Duagh Bridge. Access is good and body waders are required.

Popular salmon flies

Wye Bug, Foxford Shrimp, Cascade Shrimp, Garry Dog and Red, Yellow and Purple Shrimps. For seatrout, Bloody Butcher, Peter Ross, Black & Silver Beach Spider and Red, Black & Silver Jungle Cock.

Enquiries

Mr. Denis P. Dennison, Hon. Secretary, Abbeyfeale Anglers' Association, Glenashrone, Abbeyfeale, Co. Limerick. Tel: 068 31118

Day permits

Ryan Bros. Fishing Tackle, New Street, Abbeyfeale, Co. Limerick. Tel: 068 31411

Brosna-Mountcollins Angling Club

The Brosna-Mountcollins Angling Club controls approximately eight miles of double-bank fishing from a point a quarter-of-a-mile below the Owveg River confluence up past Mountcollins to within half-a-mile of Ahane Bridge. This stretch produces a small catch of grilse but excels as a seatrout fishery. However, the rod catch has declined greatly since 2006. The seatrout fishing here is from mid-May to September. There is a 10 inch size limit. It is flyfishing and spinning only and maggots and clear-water worming are not allowed.

Access is good, with stiles, footbridges and ladders provided. The river is mostly close to the road.

Enquiries

Mr. Patrick Danaher, Hon. Secretary, Brosna-Mountcollins Angling Club, Mountcollins, Abbeyfeale, Co. Limerick. Tel: 068 44281/44456

Pool Beg on the Castleconnell Fishery

Day permits
Mr. Patrick Danaher (see previous page)
Mr. Dan Shine, Brosna, Co. Kerry. Tel: 068 44251

Regulations
The various clubs have specific regulations regarding minimum size, bag limits, fishing methods, etc. These should be carefully observed.
All of the above clubs have a ban on shrimp or prawn fishing.
    There is a statutory ban on fishing or carrying a rod on the bank of the river for 60 metres above and below Scartleigh Weir, which is located downstream of Listowel.
    Fly-only is the rule on a stretch of the Killocrim-Finuge Club water at the tide.

Gillies/guides
All of the above clubs should be able to arrange gillies if given advance notice, contact:

Martin Hurley, Marine & Countryside Guide, 8 Urban Terrace, Boherbee, Tralee, Co. Kerry. Tel: 066 7121639
Paddy Dunworth, Celtic Angling, The Commons, Ballingarry, Nr. Adare, Co. Limerick. Tel: 069 68202, fax: 069 68202, mobile: 087 6525687
Email: info@celticangling.com, Web: www.celticangling.com

Local tackle shops
Ryan Bros, Fishing Tackle, New Street, Abbeyfeale, Co. Limerick. Tel: 068 31411
Jim Halpin, Shooting Supplies Ltd, William Street, Listowel, Co. Kerry
Tel: 068 22392
Landers Outdoor World, Mile Height, Tralee, Co. Kerry. Tel: 066 7126644
Web: www.landers.ie

Local flytyer
Alan Griffin, Clahane, Tralee, Co. Kerry. Tel: 066 7128539
David Curtin, Acres, Mountcollins, Abbeyfeale, Co. Limerick. Tel: 068 44530

Local tackle manufacturer
The Lane Minnow Co, New Street, Abbeyfeale, Co. Limerick. Tel: 068 31121
Fax: 068 32550

Accommodation
Niall Stack, Ceol na h-Abhainn, Ballygrennan, Listowel, Co. Kerry. Tel: 068 21345
Leen's Hotel, Abbeyfeale, Co. Limerick. Tel: 068 31121
Joseph & Eileen Brown, Brosna, Co. Kerry

SMEARLAGH, RIVER   R 02 33

The River Smearlagh, which is about seven miles long, rises in the Stacks Mountains
and joins the Feale at Inchymagilleragh about three miles east of Listowel Town. The
North Kerry Anglers Association (page 245) controls most of the fishing up to Foran's
Bridge (about four miles in all). This is a fast-flowing river with good salmon and
seatrout fishing. There is a certain wildness about the Smearlagh with a different scene
to greet the angler around every bend. An exciting challenge is offered to resourceful
anglers who can adapt their tactics to suit the prevailing conditions. The Smearlagh
can yield rich rewards to those who rise to its challenge and will lure them back time
and again. The most popular spots are 'The Joinings' (confluence of the Feale &
Smearlagh); and about two miles upstream, there is a small waterfall known locally
as 'The Rock'. First time visiting anglers are well advised to avail themselves of an
angling guide. This is a great seatrout river.

Daily or weekly permits and annual club membership available. Accommodation and
guides can be arranged with prior notice.

Enquiries
Jim Halpin, Shooting Supplies Ltd, William Street, Listowel, Co. Kerry
Tel: 068 23848, fax: 068 21900, email: jahorgan@eircom.net

CLYDAGH, RIVER   R 13 18

This is a small spate stream which flows down through Brosna. It can give a bit of
seatrout fishing on a falling spate to a worm by day, or a fly at night.

ALLAGHAUN, RIVER   R 12 28

The Allaghaun River is 16 miles long and flows from the east to join the Feale downstream of Abbeyfeale. The fishing is regarded as free. The seatrout fishing is fair and it produces an occasional grilse, when water conditions are right. The fishing extends up as far as Barber's Bridge.

FEALE (UPPER), RIVER   R 17 16

There are two places upstream of Ahane Bridge where the fishing is regarded as free. These are Walsh's Flat and Nookra and seatrout can be taken there on high water.

Permission
Riparian owners

GALEY, RIVER   Q 99 37

The Galey River (pronounced locally as 'Gale' river) is 27 miles long and the longest of the River Feale tributaries. It flows west through Athea in west Co. Limerick and enters the River Feale five miles west of Listowel. It flows over flagstone, sandstone and limestone in its lower reaches. It is regarded primarily as a brown trout river and is fished mainly by local anglers using small spinners and worms. It is a lovely wild river with a gravel bottom and nice streams and pools. The majority of the trout range from a half to three quarters of a pound with the occasional one to 3lb and better. Access is from bridge to bridge and it can be fished all the way down from Ahavoher Bridge. Some anglers claim to have had nice trout fishing upstream of Athea. It gets a run of estuary trout up as far as Shrone Bridge from February to April and these average half-a-pound. There is also a run of seatrout in August and September.

Season
1 March–30 September

Permission
Anglers fish with the goodwill of the riparian owners.

Athea, Moyvane & District Anglers' Association Club Secretary/local guide
Jerry Brouder, Galeview, Athea, Co. Limerick. Tel: 068 42342

Tackle shop
Jim Halpin, Shooting Supplies Ltd, William Street, Listowel, Co. Kerry
Tel: 068 22392

Local flytyer
Terry Caffrey. Tel: 068 22298

OWVEG, RIVER   R 08 22

The Owveg enters the Feale about three miles south of Abbeyfeale and flows close
to the N21 Castleisland-Abbeyfeale Road. It gets a small run of seatrout on a spate in
August and September.

** DEEL, RIVER (CO. LIMERICK)   R 37 40

The River Deel rises near Drumina in north Cork and flows north through Co.
Limerick to the tide at Askeaton on the Shannon estuary. The river is 40 miles long
and its innumerable tributaries drain the hills of west Limerick around Newcastle
West. In 1913 Grimble wrote of a weir at Askeaton that impeded the run of salmon and
the situation remains virtually the same today. Beacause of this impediment, the Deel
is a brown trout river only, and one with a lot of potential. Unfortunately, it has been
subjected to extensive drainage work that has left the banks very high and caused the
usual problems to the fishery associated with drainage work.

The river holds a fair stock of brown trout. It is a limestone river, so growth rate is
good and the average size is around a pound, while trout to 5lb are taken every season.
In addition to the wild fish, the local clubs stock fry and some adult trout.

Before drainage, the local Anglers' Association was very proud of the river and
flyfishing was very much the rule. Even now, there are fly-only stretches. One is from
Deel Bridge downstream to the Black Bridge at Newcastle West.

The peak of the season is from mid-May to mid-June, with good evening fishing to
the blue-winged olive through the summer. The chief insect hatches are olives, sedges,
black gnat and hawthorn fly. Useful daytime flies are the Light Olive, Gold Ribbed
Hare's Ear, Tup's Indispensable and Red, Orange and Ginger Quills. For night fishing,
the locals use Black & Silver Spider, Black Pennell, Silver Sedge, Brown Sedge,
Greenwell's Glory and Orange & Grouse.

The Newcastle West Club has 12 miles of river from Belville Bridge downstream
to the Slawnaun Bridge, at Reens Pike. There is some good fishing at Belville early
in the season, but the best of the fishing is considered to be from the confluence of
the Bunoke River downstream to Castlemahon and from Deel Bridge all the way to
Reens Pike. From Reens Pike, past Courtmatrix the river is deep and sluggish as far as
Rathkeale, but for those who know the river there is some nice fishing below Rathkeale
at the Castle, the Glen, Kilcool Bridge and Newbridge. The Deel is a difficult river to
fish after May, unless you know exactly where to go.

Access is at the bridges. The road runs conveniently close to the river in the
Newcastle West area and the clubs are on good terms with the local farmers.

Season
Brown trout: 15 February–30 September

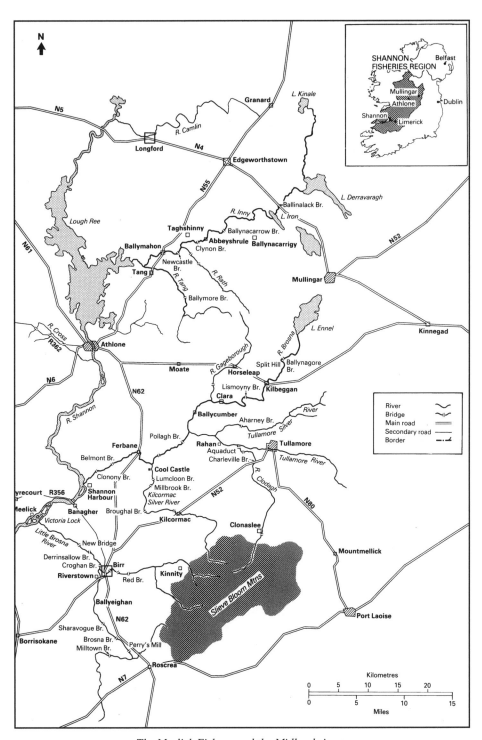

The Meelick Fishery and the Midland rivers

Permission

Most of the fishing is controlled by the Deel Anglers' Association with clubs in Newcastle West, Rathkeale and Askeaton. Newcastle West Angling Club has the fishing from Belville Bridge downstream to Reens Pike; and Rathkeale Angling Club takes it from there down to Newbridge.

For permission to fish the Newcastle West Association water, contact:
Mr. Michael Dee, West End Service Station, Killarney Road, Newcastle West,
Co. Limerick. Tel: 069 62318
Mr. Mike Sheehy, Bridge Street, Newcastle West, Co. Limerick
Tel: 069 62620/61291

Weekly permits are available on the Askeaton/Deel Anglers' Association Water, contact:

Brian Whelan, The Tower, Main Street, Askeaton, Co. Limerick. Tel: 061 398880

For information on Rathkeale and Deel Anglers' Association contact:
Christy Jones, 22 St. Mary's Park, Rathkeale, Co. Limerick or Jim Dollery, Kylpaun, Rathbeale, Co. Limerick. Tel: 069 64422.

Guide

Paddy Dunworth, The Commons, Ballingarry (Nr. Adare), Co. Limerick
Tel: 069 68202, mobile: 087 6525687, email: info@celticangling.com
Web: www.celticangling.com.
Paddy guides for brown trout, salmon and sea bass with the fly.

Regulations

No live bait allowed

** MAIGUE, RIVER   R 52 41

The River Maigue rises south of Bruree and flows north through Croom and Adare in Co. Limerick into the Shannon estuary. This is a rich limestone river and, together with its tributaries, the Camoge, the Morning Star and the Loobagh, it drains the lush pastures of Limerick's Golden Vale.

Writing in 1913, Grimble said of the Maigue: "It is worthy of mention that the Maigue throughout its upper waters can hardly be surpassed as a trout river in regard to the size and quality of its fish". It was regarded as one of Ireland's premier trout rivers up to the starting of an arterial drainage scheme in the 1970s. The drainage works ravaged and canalized the channels, destroying their natural character and it now looks like any other drained river. A certain amount of rehabilitation work has been carried out by the Shannon Regional Fisheries Board and trout stocks have made a comeback in certain areas. Some sections hold a nice stock of trout averaging 12oz–1lb and there are certainly larger trout, even as big as 3lb.

The Maigue has all the fly hatches one associates with a limestone river, including mayfly. The peak of the trout fishing season is in May and up to mid-June. For early season wet-fly fishing, an Orange & Grouse, Greenwell's Glory and Silver Spider are recommended.

The salmon fishing, particularly in spring, appears to have worsened in recent seasons.

Season
Salmon: 1 February–30 September
Brown trout: 15 February–30 September

Permits
The fishing rights are either privately owned or controlled by angling clubs. Understandably, with their fishing now curtailed, some do not let day permits. There is some limited fishing available and enquiries should be made to:

The Recreation Manager, Adare Manor Hotel, Adare, Co. Limerick.
Tel: 061 86566

Adare Manor Hotel has three miles of water with a mix of stream and pool water and some slow, sluggish stretches. It holds spring salmon, some grilse and brown trout. The Manor grounds are private and the fishery manager advises anglers on procedure. Enquiries should be made at the hotel reception.

Hotel guide
Jim Robinson, Bellview Court, Father Russell Road, Dooradoyle, Co. Limerick.
Mobile: 087 2339999, email: jimrob@iol.ie, web: www.iol.ie/~jimrob

The fishing below Adare Bridge and for about 200 metres below the railway bridge is free.
To fish the Maigue at Croom, contact Seamus Sheehan, Tel: 061 397155 to arrange permits for trout fishing.

Local guide (for brown trout, salmon and sea bass with the fly)
Paddy Dunworth, The Commons, Ballingarry (Nr. Adare), Co. Limerick
Tel: 069 68202, mobile: 087 6525687, email: info@celticangling.com
Web: www.celticangling.com

CAMOGUE, RIVER   R 55 41

The Camogue flows west and joins the Maigue upstream of Croom. Camogue Angling Club controls about eight miles of the river, from the confluence at Cloghanduff upstream to the Iron Bridge, a short distance downstream of Glenogra Bridge. This is an exceptionally rich river and the trout grow remarkably fast. The average weight is probably close to 1½lb. A certain amount of rehabilitation work has been carried out since a drainage scheme despoiled the river. The banks have been replanted and small weirs constructed. Nevertheless, it still bears the scars.

The river is strictly flyfishing only (Bye-law 712). There is a 10 inch minimum size rule and a five trout bag limit. The Camogue can be a difficult river to fish even when conditions seem right. The big trout are a terrific attraction and evening fishing in summer to the sedge and blue-winged olive can be very good. The peak of the season is from mid-April to mid-June. The fly hatches are prolific. The mayfly, however, is nearly extinct on this river and the alder is very important in May.

The Camogue Angling Club does not let day permits and club membership is limited. All enquiries regarding the Club's waters should be directed to:

Mr. John Quain, Hon. Secretary, Camogue Angling Club, Lacca, Manister, Croom, Co. Limerick. Mobile: 087 6311411

MORNINGSTAR, RIVER   R 55 33

The Morningstar River comes down from Bruff, past Athlacea and joins the Maigue about 2 miles north of Bruree. It suffered badly as a result of drainage, but has made a recovery and is now worth fishing again. It has a good gradient, except in the mid-section where it is sluggish. It has a mayfly hatch and holds some good trout.

Permission and information
Joe Ring. Tel: 063 90957

LOOBAGH, RIVER   R 55 27

The Loobagh flows west from Kilmallock to join the Maigue 2 miles south of Brunee. It is an excellent little trout stream with especially good summer time sedge hatches. The trout average ½lb with some to 1lb.

Enquiries and permits
Mr. Michael Garvey, Hon Secretary, Kilmallock & Kilfinane Anglers' Association, Gotoon, Kilmallock, Co. Limerick. Tel: 063 98566

Regulations
9 inch size limit and please respect farmers property

CROAGH, RIVER   R 42 43

The Croagh River joins the Maigue from the west, downstream of Adare. As you cross Drehidnaman Bridge on the N21 road, between Adare and Rathkeale, remember that here was a little river that at one time could produce a dozen trout for a father and son in an afternoon. That is the story the son gave me in 1998 and I have no reason to disbelieve it. Then it was drained. My information is that it now has good nursery water and holds small trout.

** (DEALAGH) KILSHANNY, RIVER   R 10 90

The Kilshanny River rises in The Burren and flows south-west for 10 miles into Liscannor Bay where it shares a common estuary with the Inagh River. It flows through farmland and the banks are mostly clear. It is a spate river and has some nice deep holes for holding fish. It holds brown trout up to 10oz and gets a run of grilse and seatrout in June and July. Traditionally, the estuary of the Kilshanny and the Inagh River supported seven draft nets. The falls at Ennistimon were impassable, so the majority of the fish were probably of Kilshanny River origin. It can be fished up as far as the bridge on the N67 Ennistimon–Lisdoonvarna road. Try a small Garry Dog or a worm for the grilse. If the water is coloured after a spate, the seatrout can be fished during the day, otherwise the best fishing is at night. The Kilshanny gets seatrout up to 3lb.

Season
1 March–30 September

Permission
Free/riparian owners.

** INAGH (CULLENAGH), RIVER   R 12 88

This river is overrun with rudd and pike since the 1960s and it has little to offer the game angler. There is a fair stock of small brown trout in a two mile stretch above the town of Ennistimon and for a similar distance upstream of the village of Inagh.

Season
15 February–30 September

Permission
Free/riparian owners

** KILDEEMA (BEALACLUGGA) RIVER   R 04 75

This little spate river enters the sea south of Spanish Point. It gets a few grilse and an excellent run of seatrout to over 3lb on a spate in the months of June and July. The fishing is on the south bank in a half mile stretch from Bealaclugga Bridge up to the waterfall. Fish a fly or spinner by day, but the best seatrout fishing is from dusk till dawn. Try a size 12 Silver Doctor, Bibio or Peter Ross.

Season
Salmon, Seatrout, Brown trout: 1 March–30 September

Permission
Free/riparian owners

** ANNAGEERAGH, RIVER   R 02 71

The Annageeragh River in west Clare drains a 25 sq. mile catchment. It used to be a great grilse river and it also gets a good run of big seatrout to 4lb in May and June. It can still give fair-to-good seatrout fishing with the chance of a grilse on a spate from late June through to August. The best of the fishing is in the deep water for about a mile upstream of Lough Donnell and in the pools up as far as Moyglass Bridge. The Grave Yard Hole, half-a-mile downstream of Lisseyneillan Bridge is regarded as one of the best pools on the river.

Season
1 March–30 September

Permission
Free/riparian owners

** CREEGH (CREE OR SKIVILEEN), RIVER   Q 99 66

This little spate river enters the sea two miles north of Doonbeg. It gets a small run of grilse on a flood from mid-June and a marvellous run of seatrout in July and August. It is a small stream, only 15–25 feet wide. Access by road is good, the banks are relatively clear and on a spate it can be fished all the way to the bridge at Cahermurphy with either fly or worm.

Season
1 March–30 September

Permission
Free/riparian owners

** DOONBEG, RIVER   Q 98 65

This was one of the most underestimated salmon and seatrout fisheries in the country. It rises near Lissycasey and flows west for 26 miles and drains a 52 sq. mile catchment into the sea at Doonbeg. The locals reckon it is worth fishing for spring salmon from 10 April if there is plenty of water and the spring run peaks in the first two weeks of May. The grilse are in the river from early July; and September is a good month for both salmon and seatrout. It has suffered a lot of indiscriminate drainage work in recent years.

The Doonbeg is perhaps as good a seatrout river as any in the country with a run of spring seatrout in the 2–4lb range arriving in April and early May. The smaller summer seatrout come in late June and the river peaks in mid-July, with finnock to follow later.

A Hairy Mary and shrimp flies are popular for salmon. The Dunkeld is a favourite seatrout fly and Teal, Blue & Silver, Watson's Fancy, Peter Ross and Black Pennell are also popular in sizes 10 and 12. Bait fishing is widely practised. The best of the salmon fishing is from approximately three miles below Cooraclare up to a point one mile above Goulbourne Bridge. Seatrout are taken up to Ballyduneen Bridge. The early seatrout run straight through to the upper reaches. The fishing is not easy, with the banks being high, difficult to walk and overgrown in many places.

Season
1 March–30 September

Permission
Free/riparian owners

Local tackle shops
Michael Burke, Kilrush Road, Kilkee, Co. Clare

** CLOON, RIVER   R 12 55

The Cloon River enters the Shannon Estuary two miles north-west of Labasheeda. It gets a run of seatrout in June and July and can be fished in places for about two miles upstream to the New Bridge. It is overgrown and inaccessible and not many bother to fish it.

Season
1 February–30 September

Permission
Regarded as being free

** FERGUS, RIVER   R 35 75

The River Fergus in Co. Clare is 37 miles long and drains a rich limestone catchment of 402 sq. miles which includes many interconnected loughs. It rises north-west of Corofin and enters the tide at Ennis. It is a noted brown trout dry-fly river and was a worthwhile spring salmon fishery in its lower reaches. The banks are high and difficult in the middle reaches. It is tidal up as far as Knox's Bridge at Ennis.

The brown trout average 12oz, with some to 4lb (8-inch minimum size for trout). The water is gin clear and it is a river that will test the skill of the best angler. It has good hatches of early olives, iron blues, blue-winged olives and sedges, but no mayfly.

The best trout fishing stretches are at Knox's Bridge; the stream opposite the Vocational School in Ennis; above and below Drehidnagower Bridge; the Cut, 1½miles upstream of Ennis; the Upper Cut, below Templemaley Bridge; Addroon Bridge, upstream to Ballyteigue Lough; Ballyteigue Lough, upstream to Ballyogan Bridge;

Atedaun Lough, upstream to Inchiquin Lough; Inchiquin Lough to Kilnaboy Bridge; and Kilnaboy Bridge, upstream to Elmvale. The banks are overgrown in places and the river runs low and becomes weeded in summer.

The Fergus was said to produce about 200 salmon and grilse every year, though numbers of spring fish have declined in recent years. The best spring fishing is from opening day through February and March. Anglers no longer stand shoulder-to-shoulder at such well-known taking places as the Post Office Field, the Sandy Hole and The Meadow, all near the town of Ennis. The grilse come in mid-June and there is always the possibility of taking one right through to September in good water conditions. Some of the Fergus's pools are deep and sluggish and worm fishing and spinning are the favourite fishing methods.

Season
Salmon and seatrout: 1 February–30 September
Brown trout: 15 February–30 September

Permission
Generally regarded as free

Local tackle shops
Tierney's, 17 Abbey Street, Ennis, Co. Clare

Local Club
Mr. John Connors, Hon. Secretary, Ennis & District Anglers' Association, Cloonteen, Ballyolla, Ennis, Co. Clare. Tel : 065 6840076

** RINE (OR QUIN), RIVER   R 40 72

The Quin River rises in the East Clare Lakes and flows south-west through the village of Quin to the Fergus estuary. It is a nice clean little river, partly overgrown and part flowing through open pasture and parkland. It gets a small run of grilse and some seatrout in July and there are six recognized pools and a number of flats from Dromoland to above Quin village. The best of it is probably from Ballykilty Manor up to the village of Quin. The straight stretch above the Black Weir is said to hold some nice trout. It is fished mostly by locals after a flood using worms or spinner.

It has a fair stock of brown trout averaging half-a-pound. It is a limestone river, and has good hatches of fly. Useful wet-fly patterns are Partridge & Orange, Grouse & Green, William's Favourite and Waterhen Bloa.

Season
Salmon and seatrout: 1 February–30 September
Brown trout: 15 February–30 September

Permission
Partly free. For those parts that flow through the grounds of Dromoland Castle, contact:
The Recreation Manager, Dromoland Castle, Newmarket-on-Fergus, Co. Clare. Tel: 061 368144

** BUNRATTY, RIVER   R 46 72

The Bunratty River enters the Shannon estuary near the well-known medieval Bunratty Castle. It is a fair-sized river and drains several lakes in east Co. Clare. Access is either at the castle or on a few miles upstream at D'Esterre's Bridge, off the Cratloe–Sixmilebridge road. The banks are difficult to walk, rocky and undeveloped. It holds brown trout to 2lb and used to get a small run of grilse and a fair run of seatrout. The best fishing is from mid June through July. There is some slob trout fishing at the tide. The best of the fishing extends upstream for about three miles to D'Esterre's Bridge and on up to the village of Sixmilebridge.

Season
Salmon and seatrout: 1 February–30 September
Brown trout: 15 February–30 September

Permission
Free/Riparian owners

** SHANNON, RIVER   R 62 57

The Shannon is the largest river in these islands. It rises in the mountains of West Cavan and flows south for 160 miles to the tide at Limerick. The total catchment of the main river and its tributaries is approximately 6,060 sq. miles. For the most part, this is a big, sluggish river, which connects the three great loughs – Lough Allen, Lough Ree and Lough Derg. The Shannon is a great mixed fishery and holds a wide range of coarse fish and pike as well as trout and salmon. Indeed, the fishing for the latter species is quite limited on the main channel and much better stocks are found in the tributaries. On the main river, there are three main areas where game anglers might concentrate their efforts: the Upper Shannon, Meelick, and at Limerick. However, it is but a shadow of its former self and confirms Hugh Forkins statement that 'the Solomon's greatest enemy is man'. The Shannon Scheme, extensive drainage schemes, canalisation, intensive farming, afforestation and water pollution have all impacted negatively on the stocks.

However, there is extensive fishing on the Shannon's tributaries – see later.

Season
Salmon and seatrout: 1 February–30 September
Brown trout: 15 February–30 September

THE LIMERICK FISHERIES

*PLASSEY & THE LONG SHORE   R 61 59

An unlimited number of annual permits are issued at reasonable prices. They are widely availed of by local anglers and the fishing can get crowded at peak runs. Both of these fisheries offer spring and summer salmon fishing. The Plassey stretch has fishing on both banks of the river near the University of Limerick. The Long Shore is on the right bank, downstream of the tailrace from Ardnacrusha Power Station.

Plassey is a lovely fishery with fast streamy water. There are several miles of fishing here. The 'Cut' starts below the confluence of the Mulcair River and offers two miles of spring and grilse fishing. Then there is about three-quarters of a mile of good fly water from Plassey Falls to the Black bridge. 'Plassey Deep' is below the Black Bridge and is regarded as good spinning water. The fishing at Corbally Weir is only fished on a falling tide but offer's opportunities for both flyfishing and spinning.

The Long Shore was very highly regarded as a spring fishery. At this point, anglers are fishing the full width of the mighty Shannon, at nearly a quarter of a mile wide and deep as well. The spring salmon tend to run in late March and April and much of the fishing effort is concentrated on the Long Shore. No records are available, but probably something in the region of 500 fish used to be taken each year.

The Shannon, rising in the mountains of West Cavan to become Ireland's largest river

The grilse begin running in May and the Plassey stretch becomes very popular for it holds not only the Shannon fish but also the big runs of grilse for the Mulcair River. Again, no records are available for the summer fishing, but estimates put the rod catch at 1,000 fish.

Visiting anglers are strongly advised to avail themselves of the services of a local guide when fishing these waters.

Season

1 February–30 September

Permits

Bonds Fishing Tackle, Wickham Street, Limerick
John Doherty, Newstop Shop, Mulgrave Street, Limerick
Paddy Guerin, Kingfisher Angling Centre, Castleconnell, Co. Limerick

Local guide

Mick Doherty, 56 Pineview Gardens, Moyross, Limerick. Tel: 086 3087370
Paddy Guerin, Kingfisher Angling Centre, Castleconnell, Limerick. Tel: 061 3774071
Richard Keays, Millbank Angling Centre. Tel: 061 386115
Email: info@millbankhouse.com
Paddy Dunworth. Tel: 069 68202, Mobile: 087 6525687
Web: www.celticangling.com

Tackle shops

Limerick Angling Centre, John Street, Limerick
Bond's Tackle Shop, 40 Wickham Street, Limerick
Steve's Fishing Tackle, 7 Denmark Street, Limerick

---

* CASTLECONNELL, FISHERY   R 66 62

This famous and prestigious salmon fishery lies close by the ancient village of Castleconnell, seven miles north-west of Limerick City. It is owned and managed by the Electricity Supply Board. The construction of a hydroelectric dam up-river at Parteen greatly reduced the volume of the flow of the old river. The present fishery has been reconstructed to take account of the reduced volume of water. New streams and pools have been imaginatively created and many of the old pools retained, with their lovely evocative names, derived from the Irish – Fall na Hassa (Cliff of the Waterfall), Thraw-na-Knock (Strand of the Horses), Balchraheen (Place of the Rapids), to name but a few. The pools are varied and interesting and most can be fished from the bank. Boats are provided to give access to some of the lies. A controlled flow is maintained from the dam to ensure that the water never runs too low.

The fishery is divided into 6 beats, each about half-a-mile long. The beats are rotated daily. All legitimate fishing methods are allowed, except shrimp fishing. A small double-handed rod (14 feet) is advised, but a single handed rod will suffice for grilse on some beats. A wading staff is necessary.

The season opens on 1 March and the fishery gets a few big spring fish in March. In the past, the Shannon was famous for its big fish – up to 45lb, with some beats averaging an unbelievable 21lb (*The Salmon Rivers of Ireland*, Augustus Grimble, 1913). The spring average is now about 10lb, though fish of over 20lb are taken occasionally. The month of April sees an improved run of fish averaging 10lb and known locally as 'April fliers'. These fish provide good sport through April and the first two weeks of May.

The peak of the grilse season is reckoned to fall between mid-May and the end of June-early July. Resting fish can be found in some of the bigger pools right through the season and fresh fish move up from the estuary with a rise in the water. In good seasons, with suitable conditions, good sport can be had right up to the closing date of 30 September. But it has to be acknowledged that the fishing, both here and on the Shannon in general, has declined greatly in recent years.

Fishing methods
Spinning is the most productive method up to 17 March. After that date, some anglers prefer to fish a fly or a worm. The most popular early season baits are 3 inch Blue & Silver Devons and 17g Copper or Silver Orklas and 'Flying Cs'. In March, local anglers prefer 3 inch Lane Minnows and drop down to 2 inch Minnows as temperatures rise. Wooden Minnows and Mepps baits are not considered useful.

There is a short list of well-tried fly patterns used at the fishery: Collie Dog, Black Goldfinch, Silver Doctor, Hairy Mary, Garry Dog and Mephisto (Curry's Red Shrimp). Sizes range from 4–10. For this river, the big spring flies tend to be very heavily dressed.

Season
Salmon: 1 February–30 September
Brown trout: 15 February–30 September

Permits
E.S.B. Fisheries Conservation, Ardnacrusha, Co. Clare
Email: mary.omeara@esb.ie, tel: 061 350598, mobile: 087 9066099
Email: peter.gallagher@esb.ie, tel: 061 350538, mobile: 087 0525103

Guides
Richard Keays, Millbank House & Angling Centre, Murroe, Co. Limerick
Tel/fax: 061 386115, email: info@millbankhouse.com,
web: www.millbankhouse.com
Paddy Guerin, Kingfisher Angling Centre, Castleconnell, Co. Limerick
Tel: 061 3774071, fax: 061 3774071, web: www.stormloader.com/kingfisher/
Mick Doherty, 56 Pineview Gardens, Moyross, Limerick. Tel: 086 3087370
Paddy Dunworth. Tel: 069 68202, mobile: 087 6525687, web: www.celticangling.com

Regulations
No shrimp or prawn fishing

Lodge/hotel
Richard Keays, Millbank House & Angling Centre, Murroe, Co. Limerick
Tel: 061 386115, fax: 061 386115, email: info@millbankhouse.com
Web: www.millbankhouse.com

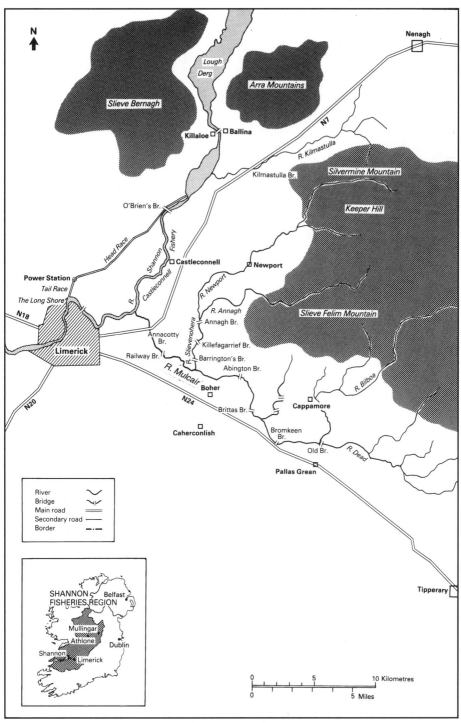

The Limerick Fisheries

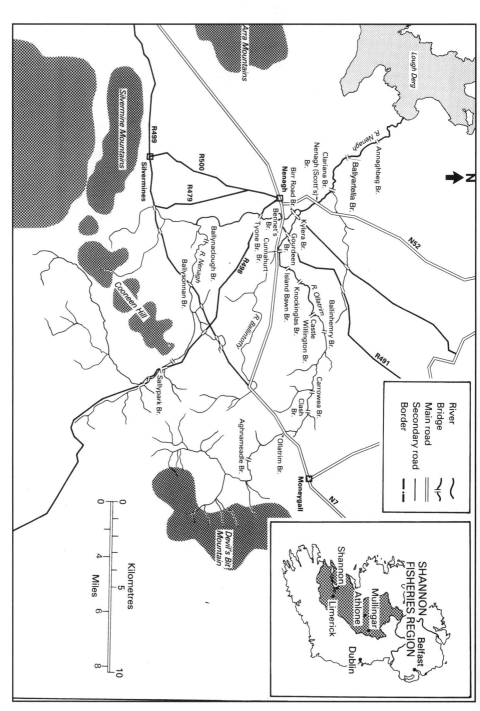

The Nenagh river

Castle Oaks Hotel, Castleconnell, Co. Limerick. Tel: 061 377666
Web: www.castle-oaks.com

** MEELICK, FISHERY   M 94 13

The salmon fishery at Meelick on the Shannon is situated approximately five miles downstream of the bridge at Banagher. The river here is very wide, with several islands. In the channel between the islands the water is relatively shallow and streamy with some nice salmon fishing stretches. The water level above the fishery is controlled by weirs and this can determine the quality of the fishing. In low water, with all the sluice gates closed, the extent of the fishing water is greatly reduced. With a good flow of water, this is a handsome river, and when the salmon are running the fishing can be exceptionally good. There are no records kept but local opinion puts the annual catch somewhere between 100 and 200 fish.

It is a fishery that is heavily fished at the peak of the season. For the first-time visitor it presents an awesome prospect, such is the huge scale of the water. It is one place where a gillie would be really useful, but none is available. The next best thing is to observe the locals. The fishery can be divided into two parts: the right bank, or Eyrecourt side and the left bank, or Offaly side.

Access to the right bank is off the Banagher–Eyrecourt road at Kilnaborris and thence to the pumphouse at the riverside. The water here is streamy and wading (with a staff!) is possible in places, but some locals use a boat to fish the runs and eel gaps. Two prime locations when fish are running are above the pumphouse, where the electric wires cross the river, and immediately above the weir.

Access to the left bank is from the town of Banagher, via Lusmagh village to Victoria Lock. A boat is virtually a necessity to fish this side. With a few gates open in Shaughnessy's Weir, fishing can be excellent in the pool under the weir and at the mouth of the Little Brosna River.

The salmon begin running at Meelick about the third week in May and the run tends to peak around the last week in June and early July. The fishing tends to be quiet in late July and August but can improve again at the back end, in September, with a rise in the water.

All fishing methods are allowed, including spinning and worm. For flyfishing, try a size 8 single or size 10 double Silver Doctor, Blue Charm or Thunder & Lightning (size 6) in high water, or a Garry Dog (size 12) in low water

There are no permit agents in this area.

MULCAIR, RIVER	**R 65 55**
DEAD, RIVER	**R 81 47**
NEWPORT, RIVER	**R 70 62**
BILBOA, RIVER	**R 80 51**

The Mulcair is a big spate river with lots of character, some lively streams and plenty of good holding water in the form of long, deep flats. It rises north of Tipperary town and flows north west to join the Shannon downstream of Annacotty. Together with its tributaries, the Newport, the Dead and the Bilboa rivers, it drains an extensive catchment.

It is regarded primarily as a grilse river but it also gets a small run of spring salmon and provides fair-to-good brown trout fishing.

The salmon angling season runs from 1 March–30 September. It holds a few spring salmon by mid-March and the best of the spring fishing is from mid-April onwards. The run, however, is small. It is as a grilse fishery that the river excels. They begin arriving in big numbers in the last week of May, and the first two weeks of June can be excellent. With every rise in water, new fish move into the river right to the end of the season. The annual rod catch for the Mulcair and its tributary, the **Newport River**, in recent years is estimated to be between 1,000 and 3,000 fish.

Access to the river is at recognized entrances to the left bank and at the bridges. There is one unfishable stretch from Boher to Abington Bridge. Otherwise, in high water, the river can be fished right up to Cappamore, giving at least 17 miles of fishing.

All fishing methods are allowed except shrimp and prawn. Baits favoured by local anglers include the Orkla, Flying 'C' and a copper and silver spoon. Favourite fly patterns include Hairy Mary, Black Goldfinch, Garry Dog, Ally's Shrimp and two local patterns, the Michaelangelo and Silver Shrimp.

In low water, the Long Field and the Haunt hold a lot of fish. In good water you can expect to meet a fish anywhere, but many favour Walsh's Streams and Scart.

Another feature of this river and its tributaries is the very good stock of brown trout. There are a lot of trout from 10–14 inches on the main river and to 11 inches on the **Bilboa River**, up at Cappamore. The Bilboa is a beautiful river with big numbers of brown trout. It is very accessible and a lovely place to fish the dry-fly.

The **Dead River** is mostly canal-like and not very interesting to fish. However, the trout are bigger than on the Mulcair and the dry-fly or upstream nymph gets best results.

Season
Salmon: 1 March–30 September
Brown trout: 17 March–30 September

Permits
Bond's Fishing Tackle, Wickham Street, Limerick
John Doherty, Newstop Shop, Mulgrave Street, Limerick
Kingfisher Angling Centre, Castleconnell, Co. Limerick
Richard Keays, Millbank House & Angling Centre, Murroe, Co. Limerick. Tel: 061 386115, fax: 061 386115, email: info@millbankhouse.com
web: www.millbankhouse.com
NB: Richard Keays provides permits for guests at his lodge only.

Lodge
Richard Keays, Millbank House & Angling Centre (see details above)

Guides
Richard Keays , Millbank House & Angling Centre (see above)
Paddy Guerin, Kingfisher Angling Centre, Castleconnell, Co. Limerick. Tel: 061
3774071, fax: 061 3774071, web: www.stormloader.com/kingfisher/
Mick Doherty, 56 Pineview Gardens, Moyross, Limerick. Tel: 086 3087370
Paddy Dunworth. Tel: 069 68202, mobile: 087 6525687, web: www.celticangling.com

SLIEVENOHERA, RIVER (see ANNAGH RIVER)	**R 68 54**
NEWPORT, RIVER (see ANNAGH RIVER)	**R 70 62**
ANNAGH, RIVER (CLARE RIVER) Newport River tributary	**R 70 59**

The Slievenohera, Newport and Annagh rivers converge and join the Mulcair on
the north bank two miles upstream of Ballyclough. The Newport River is really an
extension of the Slievenohera River, while the Annagh is a tributary. This system gets
an excellent run of grilse on a flood from late June at the same time as the Mulcair.
The fishing can be really good. Fishing is best on a falling spate because the fish
are alleged to become very nervous and scarce as a result of poaching in low water.
There is a nice pool-stream sequence up to Barrington's Bridge. Barrington's Bridge
to Killeenagarriff Bridge is deep and slow flowing, then there are more streams
and pools followed by a deep stretch up to Annagh Bridge. It can be fished up to
Martin Hearn's bar on the road to Newport and as far as Gamalta and Killoscully
in high water. There are about 200 yards of fishing at the bottom of the Clare (or
Annagh) River. In addition to the flies recommended for the Mulcair, try a Thunder
& Lightning.
    The brown trout fishing is excellent with the trout averaging half-a-pound. It has a
gravel bottom and the wading is easy. The trout are in great condition in summer. The
main fly hatches are olives, black gnats and sedges.

N.B. Beware of hog-weed on these rivers in summer.

Season
Salmon: 1 March–30 September
Brown trout: 17 March–30 September

Permits/guides/lodge
As for River Mulcair previous page.

KILMASTULLA, RIVER   R 75 70

The Kilmastulla River is 14 miles long. It rises south of Nenagh and empties into the
Shannon at Parteen Weir. It is a river that has been drained and is maintained fairly
regularly. The banks are very high in places – up to 10 feet – and much of the channel is
shallow and featureless. It holds some good trout – 2lb plus – at Shalee and a moderate
stock of trout to 1lb, upstream of Kilmastulla Bridge on the N7 Nenagh–Limerick
road. Weed growth makes fishing difficult from June onwards.

Season
Brown trout: 17 March–30 September

NENAGH, RIVER   R 86 83

The Nenagh and Ollatrim Rivers are leased by the Ormond Anglers' Association from the Electricity Supply Board. The Nenagh River is 28 miles long. It rises in the Silvermine Mountains, in Co. Tipperary, and flows north-west through the town of Nenagh to join Lough Derg at Dromineer. It has two main tributaries, the Ollatrim River (described below), itself no mean trout fishery and the Ballintotty River, which is really a spawning stream. This is a spring-fed system so the rivers maintain quite good flows in periods of low rainfall, except in periods of prolonged drought.

These rivers are primarily brown trout fisheries but have a few grilse in the autumn. They hold really excellent stocks of trout. The majority are in the 6–12oz range, but trout up to 5lb are a possibility. The system holds two distinct kinds of trout: a very big stock of indigenous river trout and migratory lake trout from Lough Derg. The latter begin to run the river with the first summer flood in June or July.

Access to the river bank is mostly at the bridges and is good. Stiles and footbridges have been erected all along the angling water, though some are in a poor state of repair.

The river was the subject of an arterial drainage scheme in the past and while the banks are of normal height in the upper reaches, they are up to 15 feet high in the lower parts. Wading with body waders is essential for fishing these stretches and, even then, should only be attempted by the athletic. Barbed wire fences are a nuisance in many places.

The river has hatches of dark olives, iron blues, *simulium* and various diptera, mayfly, pale wateries, pale evening duns, blue-winged olives, yellow may duns and a prolific sedge hatch on summer evenings. The mayfly hatch can sometimes begin in late April. In July, the big evening hatches of sedges – locally known as 'rails' – give excellent sport at dusk.

Trout Stock Distribution on the Nenagh River
The angling water on the Nenagh River begins approximately opposite Young's bar on the Nenagh–Thurles road. This stretch holds good stocks up to half-a-pound. The two-mile stretch Ballysonnan Bridge to Ballynaclough Bridge holds good stocks of 10oz trout. The bank conditions vary: good in places; terribly high in others; and badly overgrown, elsewhere.

The stretch from Ballynaclough Bridge downstream to Tyone Bridge is five miles long. Permission for access to fish downstream on the right bank can be obtained at Bayly Farm. A beautiful stretch, with lovely pools and nice holding water for trout, it holds excellent stocks of 8–10oz trout, with some to 2lb. The fishing here involves a long walk.

Between Tyone Bridge and Bennett's Bridge there is an excellent stock of trout from 8oz–2½lb in the stretch immediately above the railway bridge, but it is slow-flowing and the trout are hard to tempt. From Bennett's Bridge to the Birr Road Bridge the river is not worth fishing.

From Birr Road Bridge to Scott's Bridge there are excellent stocks of trout from 9–11 inches and is an especially good area for the lake trout after the first summer floods. From Scott's Bridge to Clarianna Bridge trout stocks are poor-to-moderate. A few salmon might be found in the 400 yard stretch above Clarianna Bridge.

The stretch between Clarianna Bridge and Ballyartella Bridge is a lovely one with big stocks of 8–14 inch trout. The renowned Violet Banks water is in this stretch, which holds lake trout in summer. Approach the upper section by the left bank and use body waders.

Between Ballyartella Bridge and Annaghbeg Bridge, the river consists of fast, streamy water, deep glides, pools and flats. It holds excellent stocks of trout from 10–15 inches and is one of the best stretches for lake trout. The banks are very high and covered with tall foliage in summer. From Annaghbeg Bridge to Lough Derg the river is deep and sluggish. It holds virtually no trout, though perhaps an occasional salmon will lie up on the bends.

Season
Brown trout: 17 March–30 September

Permits
Open Season Tackle Shop, 45 Pearse Street, Nenagh, Co. Tipperary. Tel: 067 31774
Web: www.openseason.ie

N.B. The Club makes associate membership available to visitors. It does not let day permits.

Regulations
Minimum size: 10 inches
Bag limit: 4 trout
Bye-Laws prohibit the use of maggots and fishing between Ballyartella Bridge and Ballyartella Weir.

Accommodation
Abbey Court Hotel, Dublin Road, Nenagh, Co. Tipperary. Tel: 067 41111

OLLATRIM, RIVER   R 90 79

The Ollatrim River joins the Nenagh River downstream of the town of Nenagh. The gravel nature of its channel has enabled it to recover well from the effects of arterial drainage. It offers what can best be described as 'small stream fishing', with a channel that is only 3 yards wide in the upper reaches and 15 yards wide at the confluence. The majority of the trout are in the 8–10 inch size range but there are some to 18 inches or 2½lb. Overall stocks are good.

From Carrowea Bridge to Ballinhemry Bridge the river is 3–5 yards wide, with lovely water in the middle reaches and plenty of trout to 12oz. Stay on the left bank. The stretch from Ballinahemry Bridge to Castlewillington Bridge is about a mile long with riffles and small pools and a fair stock of 8oz trout.

The stretch from Castlewillington Bridge to Knockinglas Bridge offers fair prospects for wet-fly in spring, but runs too low in summer. The same applies for the next stretch to Islandbawn Bridge. At the top of the stretch from Islandbawn Bridge to Cunnahurt Bridge there are a few pools, which hold fair stocks of 8–10 inch trout. Approach it from Islandbawn Bridge.

Between Cunnahurt Bridge and Gurdeen Bridge the river is about 12 yards wide. There is a good pool above the confluence of the Ballintotty River; and from Lisbunny Castle downstream there are nice glides and pools. The trout average about half-a-pound, with some to 12oz.

From Gurdeen Bridge to Kylera Bridge the Ollatrim holds excellent stocks of half pounders, with some to 1½lb. This is attractive water, best fished off the left bank. The railway embankment is high and difficult to climb.

Season
Brown trout: 17 March–30 September

Permits
Open Season Tackle Shop, 45 Pearse Street, Nenagh, Co. Tipperary. Tel: 067 31774
Web: www.openseason.ie

N.B. The Club makes associate membership available to visitors. It does not let day permits.

Regulations
Minimum size: 10 inches.
Bag limit: 4 trout.

N.B. Bye-Laws prohibit the use of maggots or any fishing between Ballyartella Bridge and Ballyartella Weir.

Accommodation
Abbey Court Hotel, Dublin Road, Nenagh, Co. Tipperary. Tel: 067 41111

BALLYFINBOY, RIVER   R 89 94

This once-lovely prolific little trout river has been badly damaged by an arterial drainage scheme. It holds small pockets of trout, but much of it is featureless and it weeds up badly in summer. The most promising stretch is downstream of Ballinderry towards Lough Derg.

Season
17 March–30 September

WOODFORD, RIVER   M 77 98

The Woodford River holds a moderate stock of trout, but the latest information I have is that it is so overgrown and weedy that it is not worth fishing after June.

Season
17 March–30 September

Local tackle shop
Garry Kenny, Palmerstown Stores, Portumna, Co. Galway

CAPPAGH, RIVER   M 79 04

The Cappagh River rises near Loughrea and flows south-east into the Killimor River less than a mile up from Lough Derg. It is a nice fast-flowing river. It used to hold a nice stock of pound trout and had a good mayfly hatch. However, according to a local Fishery Board Officer, a recent drainage scheme has caused great damage and there is a possibility of more to come. Nonetheless, it is worth a try early in the season.

Season
17 March–30 September

Permission
Free

Local tackle shop
Garry Kenny, Palmerstown Stores, Portumna, Co. Galway

KILCROW (KILLIMOR), RIVER   M 79 10

The Killimor River, as it is best known, flows south from Kiltormer, through Killimor into the top of Lough Derg. It is a medium-sized fast-flowing limestone river in spring, winding through rich pastureland, and can provide exciting trout fishing early in the season. It becomes difficult to fish in summer when the weed comes up. It holds a fair stock of trout, averaging about a pound. The fishing water is in a stretch from Oxford Bridge downstream for 10 miles approximately to Ballyshrule Bridge on the R352 Portumna-Gort road. Access is at the bridges and off the side roads. Local anglers regard it as a spring river only.

Season
17 March–30 September

Permission
Free

Local tackle shop
Garry Kenny, Palmerstown Stores, Portumna, Co. Galway

LISDUFF, RIVER   M 78 13

The Lisduff River joins the Killimor River from the west. It used to provide good early season wet-fly fishing from Gortymadden downstream. However, it is subject to drainage maintenance work from time to time.

LITTLE BROSNA RIVER   M 99 10

The Little Brosna rises near Roscrea and flows north-west past the town of Birr to join the Shannon at Meelick. It is a limestone river and holds good stocks of brown trout and fair stocks of salmon in summer in the lower reaches. The grilse arrive in late June or early July, depending on water and a few nice fish arrive with every flood to the end of the season. The salmon fishing is confined to the deep water downstream of the Angler's Rest bar at New Bridge. It is fished mainly by local anglers and worm, shrimp and spinner are the usual fishing methods.

Nowadays, it is as a brown trout fishery that the river is best known with plenty of trout averaging a pound and some to 3lb and better. In summer, the river gets a run of lake trout, locally known as 'croneen'.

The trout fishing is in two sections: from Milltown Bridge to Sharavogue Bridge and from Purcell's Drain – one mile above Riverstown – downstream to Derrinsallow Bridge, at Bunrevan House.

After opening day in March, there is very good fishing in the vicinity of Roscrea and from Fanure to Brosna Bridge. Other productive stretches are to be found at Perry's Mills, upstream and downstream of Riverstown and at Derrinsallow. At mayfly time, some of the best fishing is to be had at Riverstown and from Ballyeighan up to Sharavogue Bridge.

The river weeds up quite badly after June, but open water will be found upstream of Sharavogue Bridge all the way past Perry's Mills and Fanure, or downstream at Croghan, Derrinsallow and New Bridge (Angler's Rest).

The river has all the usual fly hatches associated with a limestone river including mayfly (*Ephemera danica*). Sedges are very important in June/July for evening fishing and can account for some of the big 'croneen' in the deep pools around Derrinsallow.

The river gets a small run of grilse in June and July and fishing for them is usually confined to the lower river downstream of New Bridge (Angler's Rest).

Season
1 March–30 September

Permits
Chris Brummell, Roscrea Road, Birr, Co. Offaly. Tel: 091 22082
Mobile: 086 3858221
Michael Madden, Townsend Street, Birr, Co. Offaly. Tel: 057 9120135
J.J. Percival Stores, Castle Street, Roscrea, Co. Tipperary. Tel: 057 9121586
Permits may be purchased online at: www.shannon-fishery-board.ie

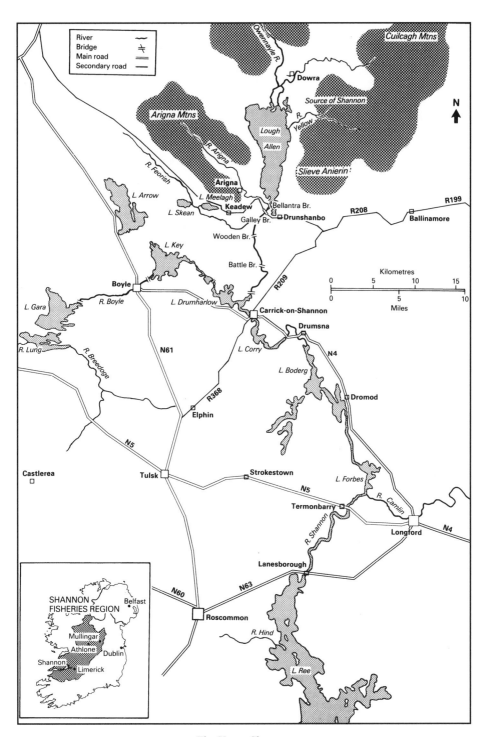

The Upper Shannon

Regulations
Minimum size: 9 inches
Bag Limit: 6 trout
Fishing is not permitted in Birr Castle demesne.

CAMCOR RIVER   N 10 04

The Camcor River rises on the western slopes of the Slieve Bloom mountains and is the principal tributary of the Little Brosna River. It is a spate river, about 12 miles in length from its source to where it joins the Little Brosna, in the castle grounds at Birr. The river meanders quite a bit immediately above Birr, then alternates between long flats with occasional broken riffles, glides and pools. Its gravel bed makes it an ideal spawning river for both salmon and trout. There are resident trout of a pound or so, but most are generally smaller at about 8–12oz. The main interest is the migratory runs of large Lough Derg trout, locally known as 'croneen', on route to spawn. There are usually a few summer grilse accompanying these lake trout. The first summer floods see fish entering the river upstream of Birr, where the angling is best. All pools from Birr – Syngefield, Sandymount, and Palmers Flats – as far as Killyon, are good holding areas. With drainage work undertaken on the river some years ago, the steep banks upstream of Clonbrone (Red) Bridge can be difficult. The 'croneen' average nearly 1½lb, with fish of 3–4lb and sometimes larger possible. Being a spate river, most angling activity is confined to a dropping flood when good fishing is had by spinning and worming.

Wet-fly fishing is also very effective on a clearing flood and, thereafter, at night-time when fish tend to shoal back into the pools exhibiting similar habits to seatrout. Bloody Butcher, Peter Ross, Silver Invicta and Black Pennell (sizes 8-10) are all effective. The larger sizes are used while the water is fining down and also after dark. Use a smaller fly (size10) during a dry spell and low water conditions. Medium or fast sink-tip lines often prove useful. Alternatively, try a floating line and a 'wake fly', such as a sedge, slowly skated across the surface. The best time of year is between late June and September.

Season
1 March–30 September

Permission
As Little Brosna River (page 272)

Regulations
Minimum size: 9 inches
Bag Limit: 6 trout
Fishing is not permitted in the grounds of Birr Castle.

BROSNA, RIVER   N 11 24

The River Brosna rises in Lough Ennell and flows south west through Kilbeggan, Clare, Ballycumber and Ferbane to join the Shannon at Shannon Harbour. It has a number of important angling tributaries and, together, they provide extensive fishing for both brown trout and salmon fishing. The water quality is generally poor, however. In the late 1960s, the river was subjected to an arterial drainage scheme which has left the banks very high. Moreover, the Brosna also flows through one of the largest areas of peat bog and active peat harvesting in the country. As a consequence, the river often suffers from problems of peat silt and sediment.

The grilse run depends on water flow but the first salmon of the season usually begin showing at the end of May and the run increases through June. The peak of the run such as it is, is in the first two weeks of July. The river usually runs low in summer but a rise in water in September generally brings in some more salmon. However, the Brosna is no longer considered a worthwhile salmon river. Local knowledge of the best stretches is all-important and Jim Griffin, of the Tackle Shop in Rahan, is usually the source of much helpful information. There are really four areas to consider: downstream of Clonony Bridge, where there are some nice runs, pools and glides but the banks are high and overgrown; the streams and pools for a mile below Belmont Weir; a short stretch downstream of Ferbane; and at a place called the Rock, a mile below Pollagh Bridge. Some of the runs are suitable for fly, but worm and spinner are the usual methods and float-fished shrimp (allowed after 1 June). A brass spoon is very good, as is a copper & silver spoon, or a No. 3 red-spotted Mepps.

The River Brosna and its tributaries offer quite good wet and dry-fly fishing for trout in many areas. It is a limestone system and the river trout grow big – to 3lb plus. In addition, the Brosna gets a run of 'croneen' from the Shannon in late July and August, when there is a rise in the water. Access is difficult in places and weed growth is a problem during the summer. The following is a breakdown of the Brosna's current trout stocks, starting at the bottom of the river and working upstream.

The river is wide and swift at Clonony and the best trout fishing is immediately above and below the bridge. Access is difficult and the river is very overhung with bushes. From Clonony to Ferbane, the access is bad, banks difficult to negotiate and trout stocks poor. Give it a miss.

From Ferbane up to Pollagh, the Brosna is a not very attractive river, with a lot of spoil and bog. Nevertheless, the banks are reasonably good along this six-mile stretch and so too is the fishing, with trout averaging about 12oz. Weed is a problem in summer.

From Ballycumber up to Clara the access is fair-to-good, even if the banks are not great, but the stocks are good and 12oz trout are fairly plentiful. Between Clara and Lismoyny Bridge, the river has been drained recently. It has a lot of weed and should be given a miss.

The stretch from Lismoyny Bridge to Kilbeggan is about four miles. There are excellent stocks of 12oz trout in the two miles below Kilbeggan and even some to 1½lb. Between Split Hill and Ballynagore Bridge the trout are small and between Ballynagore Bridge and Lough Ennell there are few trout except in high water in March.

It is always possible to find somewhere to fish on the Brosna, but it has to be said that the best of the fishing is in spring and early summer before the weed comes up in June.

Season
Salmon and trout: 1 March–30 September

Permits
Jim Griffin, The Tackle Shop, Clara, Tullamore, Co. Offaly. Tel: 057 9155979
Dermot Kenny, Bridge Street, West End, Co. Offaly. Tel: 057 9131866
Raymond Duthie, The Old Forge Tackle, Birchwood, Banagher, Co. Offaly
Tel: 057 9151504
John Cunningham, Cunningham Tackle, Rahan, Kilclare, Durrow, Co. Offaly
Tel: 057 9331851

Regulations
Minimum size: 9 inches
Bag Limit: 6 trout
No shrimp fishing for salmon before 1 June

Tackle shops
Jim Griffin, The Tackle Shop, Rahan, Tullamore, Co. Offaly. Tel: 0506 55979
Raymond Duthie, The Old Forge Tackle, West End, Banagher, Co. Offaly
Tel: 057 9151504

KILCORMAC SILVER, RIVER   N 14 20

The Kilcormac Silver River is a tributary of the Brosna. It rises in the Slieve Bloom Mountains and flows north for 24 miles through Kilcormac in Co. Offaly to join the main river just east of Ferbane. It flows almost entirely through bog and this presents the angler with many problems regarding access, difficult banks and dangerous wading conditions. For all that, it is a limestone river and holds fair stocks of brown trout.

The river can be divided in four sections for angling purposes. Starting at the bottom, there are fair stocks of half pound trout, with some nice fish to 1¼lb from Coole Castle upstream to Lumcloon Bridge. Access is at Lumcloon power station, but the banks are difficult and the water is sometimes discoloured by peat sediment. This situation is improving. There are some nice streamy sections here where it is possible to wade. From Lumcloon Bridge up to Millbrook Bridge the stocks are much as in the last section, but the banks are high. Do not attempt to wade due to the soft, treacherous nature of the bottom!

From Millbrook Bridge upstream to Broughal Bridge is nearly three miles. There is a good stock of trout here averaging 8oz. Again, the bottom is soft, so do not wade. Weed becomes a problem here from June. Sedges are important and there is a mayfly hatch in the Broughal area. Finally, there is some fast water between the village of Kilcormac and Broughal Bridge. It holds a good stock of trout, especially at the Broughal end. Wading is possible here with care.

Season
Salmon and trout: 1 March–30 September

Permits
Jim Griffin, The Tackle Shop, Clara, Tullamore, Co. Offaly. Tel: 057 9155979
Dermot Kenny, Bridge Street, West End, Co. Offaly. Tel: 057 9131866
Raymond Duthie, The Old Forge Tackle,Birchwood, Banagher, Co. Offaly
Tel: 057 9151504
John Cunningham, Cunningham Tackle, Rahan, Kilclare, Durrow, Co. Offaly
Tel: 057 9331851

Regulations
Minimum size: 9 inches
Bag Limit: 6 trout
No shrimp fishing for salmon before 1 June

Tackle shop
Jim Griffin, The Tackle Shop, Rahan, Tullamore, Co. Offaly. Tel: 0506 55979
Raymond Duthie, The Old Forge Tackle, West End, Banagher, Co. Offaly
Tel: 057 9151504

CLODIAGH, RIVER   N 25 25

The Clodiagh River is 25 miles long. It rises in the Slieve Bloom Mountains and flows north through Clonaslee and Rahan to the River Brosna. It is another drained river with high, steep banks in places. The Clodiagh holds some good trout stocks and gets a good run of salmon.

The fishing can be divided in four sections. The stretch from the confluence with the Brosna up to Rahan is nearly five miles long. The river is deep (no wading) and 20 feet wide and the banks are high. This stretch holds a very good stock of 12oz trout with many to 2lb. This stretch was renowned for holding a good head of croneen which run up from the Shannon after a mid-summer flood, but numbers have declined in recent years.

From Rahan to the junction of the Tullamore River, the Clodiagh provides some of the best brown trout fishing in the whole of the River Brosna catchment. The banks are high, the water is fast and, for the most part, you cannot wade. The trout average about a pound. The best access is along the left bank. The short stretch from the Tullamore River confluence up to the aqueduct is overgrown, but has fair stocks of fish. The rest of the river is mainly spawning water, except for a short stretch above and below Charleville Bridge on the N52.

Season
Salmon and trout: 1 March–30 September

Permits
Jim Griffin, The Tackle Shop, Clara, Tullamore, Co. Offaly. Tel: 057 9155979
Dermot Kenny, Bridge Street, West End, Co. Offaly. Tel: 057 9131866
Raymond Duthie, The Old Forge Tackle,Birchwood, Banagher, Co. Offaly

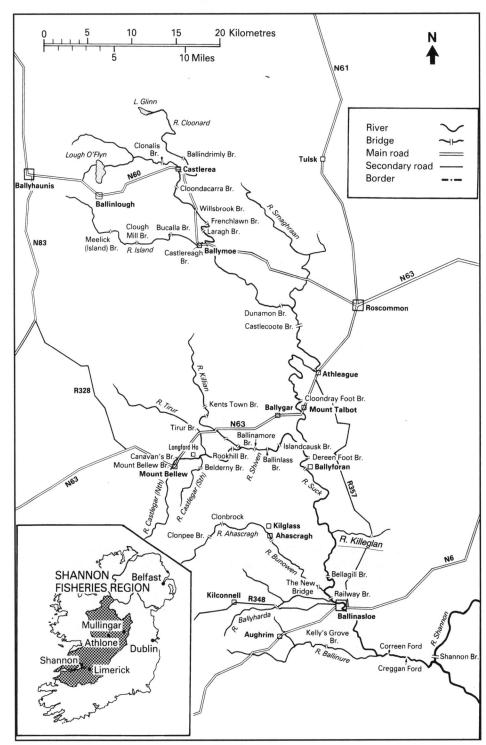

River Suck system

Tel: 057 9151504
John Cunningham, Cunningham Tackle, Rahan, Kilclare, Durrow, Co. Offaly
Tel: 057 9331851
Joe Power, Chairman, Tullamore District Anglers' Association. Tel: 057 9351351

Regulations
Minimum size: 9 inches
Bag Limit: 6 trout
No shrimp fishing for salmon before 1 June

Tackle shops
Jim Griffin, The Tackle Shop, Rahan, Tullamore, Co. Offaly. Tel: 0506 55979
Raymond Duthie, The Old Forge Tackle, West End, Banagher, Co. Offaly
Tel: 057 9151504

TULLAMORE RIVER   N 28 28

The lower section of this river above the confluence with the R. Clodiagh holds good-
sized trout. There are also good stocks of ½–¾lb trout upstream and downstream of
Tullamore. Unfortunately, I'm informed that it is due for drainage maintenance work.

Permits
Joe Power, Chairman, Tullamore District Anglers' Association. Tel: 057 9351351

TULLAMORE SILVER, RIVER   N 28 28

The Tullamore Silver River flows west to join the Clodiagh River downstream of
Rahan. It holds plentiful stocks of trout averaging 6oz with some up to a pound. It
can be fished, early in the season, from its confluence with the Clodiagh up as far as
Aharney Bridge. It is a limestone stream with a very good mayfly hatch. Unfortunately,
weed takes over in June and makes fishing difficult. Access is fairly good along the
banks.

Season
Salmon and trout: 1 March–30 September

Permits
Jim Griffin, The Tackle Shop, Clara, Tullamore, Co. Offaly. Tel: 057 9155979
Dermot Kenny, Bridge Street, West End, Co. Offaly. Tel: 057 9131866
Raymond Duthie, The Old Forge Tackle,Birchwood, Banagher, Co. Offaly
Tel: 057 9151504
John Cunningham, Cunningham Tackle, Rahan, Kilclare, Durrow, Co. Offaly
Tel: 057 9331851
Joe Power, Chairman, Tullamore District Anglers' Association. Tel: 057 9351351

Regulations
Minimum size: 9 inches

Bag limit: 6 trout
No shrimp fishing for salmon before 1 June

Tackle shops
Jim Griffin, The Tackle Shop, Rahan, Tullamore, Co. Offaly. Tel: 0506 55979
Raymond Duthie, The Old Forge Tackle, West End, Banagher, Co. Offaly
Tel: 057 9151504

GAGEBOROUGH, RIVER   N 24 35

The Gageborough River is a small stream which flows south from Horseleap and joins
the River Brosna a mile downstream of Clara, in Co. Offaly. It can be fished for about
three miles up from the confluence and the trout stocks and conditions are on a par
with the Tullamore Silver River, previous page.

Season
Salmon and trout: 1 March–30 September

Permits
Jim Griffin, The Tackle Shop, Clara, Tullamore, Co. Offaly. Tel: 057 9155979
Dermot Kenny, Bridge Street, West End, Co. Offaly. Tel: 057 9131866
Raymond Duthie, The Old Forge Tackle,Birchwood, Banagher, Co. Offaly
Tel: 057 9151504
John Cunningham, Cunningham Tackle, Rahan, Kilclare, Durrow, Co. Offaly
Tel: 057 9331851
Joe Power, Chairman, Tullamore District Anglers' Association. Tel: 057 9351351

Regulations
Minimum size: 9 inches
Bag limit: 6 trout
No shrimp fishing for salmon before 1 June

Tackle shops
Jim Griffin, The Tackle Shop, Rahan, Tullamore, Co. Offaly. Tel: 0506 55979
Raymond Duthie, The Old Forge Tackle, West End, Banagher, Co. Offaly
Tel: 057 9151504

INNY, RIVER   N 17 56

The Inny is over 55 miles long and drains a catchment of 486 sq. miles. It rises near
Oldcastle, in Co. Meath, and drains several midland lakes including Lough Sheelin,
noted for its mayfly hatch and big brown trout. It then flows west, through Ballymahon
in south Longford, into Lough Ree. An arterial drainage scheme in the 1960s left the

banks very high. At present it is best described as a mixed fishery. It holds trout, has a big head of coarse fish and presently holds large stocks of roach. Some areas hold pike, and chub were introduced in recent years. The Sh.R.F.B. has made a big effort to remove them by electrical fishing.

There is a small stock of trout above and below Ballynacarrow Bridge on the R393 Ballynacarrigy–Ardagh road. The banks are good here and I have been told it fishes well in low water. The next stretch worth fishing is the streamy water extending for about a mile above and below Abbeyshrule Bridge. This stretch is fishable all season and holds a fair stock of 12oz trout. The banks are very high. Keep to the left bank.

Downstream of Abbeyshrule there is a mile of trout fishing above Clynan (Tenalick) Bridge and about two miles below it at Taghshinny. Stay on the right bank above the bridge and try to find a patch under the bushes on the left bank below the bridge. There are a lot of large trout to 6lb below Newcastle Bridge and a fair stock of 12oz trout from Newcastle Bridge downstream through Ballymahon to the confluence of the Tang River. Finally, there is a nice stretch at Derragh (pronounced Derá), downstream of a lough of the same name that holds a good stock of trout, down to Camagh Bridge. It is accessed by a minor road from Abbeylara, Co. Longford.

The river has all the usual hatches associated with a limestone river, including mayfly (*Ephemera danica*).

Season
1 March–12 October

Permits
Mr. Jim Roche, The Cottage, Buttlersbridge, Mullingar, Co. Westmeath
Tel: 044 40314
Ms. Geraldine Clarke, Finea, Mullingar, Co. Westmeath. Tel: 043 81158
Ian Jameson, Aim and Swing, Killyfassey, Mount Nugent, Co. Cavan
Eamon Donohoe, Tackle Shop, Dublin Road, Cavan

Shannon Fisheries Office, Tudenham Lodge, Mullingar,. Co. Westmeath
Tel: 044 9348769, web: www.shrfb.com (09.00–13.00 only)
Tom Fox, Inny Bay, Ballymahon, Co. Longford
Finea Post Office, Mullingar, Co. Westmeath. Tel: 043 81101

Guide
Michael Flanagan. Mobile: 087 2797270, email: mick@midlandangling.com

Regulations
Minimum size: 12 inches

Tackle shops
David O'Malley, 33 Dominick Steet, Mullingar, Co. Westmeath. Tel: 044 48300
Email: dpomalley@eircom.net
Denninston's Central Stores, Centenary Square, Longford. Tel: 043 46345
Eamon Donohoe, Tackle Shop, Dublin Road, Cavan
Ms. Geraldine Clarke, Finea, Mullingar, Co. Westmeath. Tel: 043 81158 (for flies)
Ian Jameson, Aim and Swing, Killyfassey, Mount Nugent, Co. Cavan

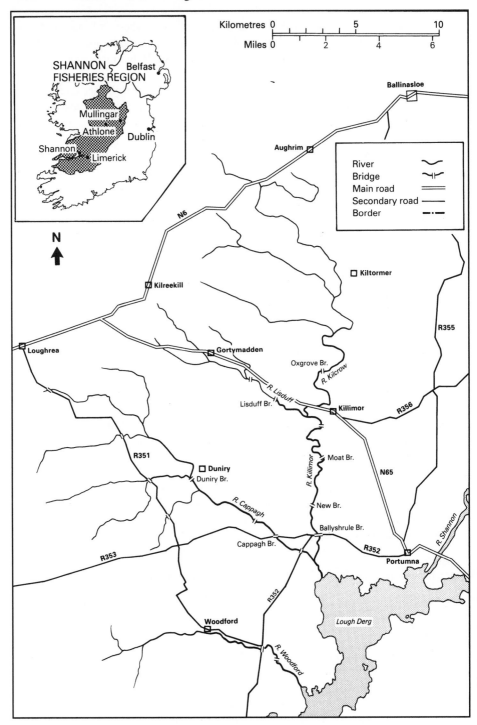

East Galway: Killimor, Lisduff, Cappagh and Woodford rivers

TANG RIVER   N 15 54

The Tang River joins the Inny from the south between Ballymahon and Lough Ree. Like the main river, a drainage scheme has left high banks which are wild and uncared for and well-nigh impassable. The Tang holds some good trout up as far as Ballymore but after June it runs low and weeds up.

Season
1 March–12 October

Permits/tackle shops/guide
As River Inny (page 280)

GLORE RIVER   N47 73

The Glore River rises in the lough of the same name and flows west to join the River Inny north of Castlepollard. It has good stocks of trout to 1lb. The best of the fishing is on the top two miles where there is road access at five points. It is really a spring/early summer river as it weeds up later on.

Permits/tackle shop/guide
As River Inny (page 280)

Regulations
Minimum size: 12 inches

RATH RIVER   N20 56

The Rath River joins the Inny just over two miles upstream of Ballymahon. It has a stock of trout up to about 8 inches and a very occasional trout to 12oz. Most of these fish are concentrated in the mile-and-a-half stretch from the confluence upstream to the first bridge at Newcastle. It is best fished in high water in March and April because thereafter it runs very low. It is very overgrown and difficult to fish. Stay on the right bank.

Permits/tackle shop/guide
As River Inny (page 280)

Regulations
Minimum size: 12 inches

CAMLIN RIVER   N 75 12

The Calmin River rises west of Granard and flows for 26 miles through Ballinalee and Longford before joining the Shannon a few miles north of Termonbarry. It holds a fair stock of trout throughout its length with some big ones. The best fish I know of weighed 10lb 2oz. The river is best suited to dry-fly fishing and heavy weed growth becomes a problem in summer.

The middle section from Ballykenny Bridge upstream to Ballinalee is regarded as the main fishing area with hot spots at Longford and from the Bypass Bridge to Mullagh Bridge. It is a limestone river and has all the usual fly hatches, including mayfly. You are also likely to find people bait fishing.

Season
1 March–30 September

Permits
Not usually required

Tackle shops
As River Inny (page 280)

A Shannon Regional Fisheries Board trout permit is required. There are no permit outlets in Longford Town.

Disabled anglers' facility
At the Mall Complex in Longford Town.

Local Angling Club
Michael Galvin, Hon. Secretary, Camlin & District Angling Club, Tarmonbarry, Co. Longford

SHANNON (UPPER), RIVER   M 94 00

The first stretch of the Upper Shannon extends for a distance of about six miles from Bellantra Bridge (the Baily Bridge) at Lough Allen to just below Battle Bridge near Leitrim village and the fishing is free. This stretch holds fair stocks of brown trout to 2lb. Occasionally, trout as big 9lb are taken on spinners. Fly hatches include olives, sedges, black gnats and some mayfly above Battle Bridge. This stretch is not heavily fished for trout. Roach have spread to this part of the river in recent years and quite a bit of coarse fishing takes place here. The best trout fishing water is: for a mile below Galley Bridge (access fair); a short stretch above Wooden Bridge (access very difficult); midway between Wooden Bridge and Battle Bridge (access very difficult); above and below Battle Bridge (access fair), this being a developed coarse fishing stretch. The final piece of water suited for trout fishing on this part of the river is at the village of Jamestown. There is a weir here and a stretch of about 200 yards that usually holds trout. It is conveniently located by the roadside and access is easy.

Season
1 March–30 September

Permit
Not usually required

Tackle shops
Shannon Tackle, Jamestown, Carrick on Shannon, Co. Leitrim
Ciaran Fallon, Rooskey Quay, Rooskey, Co. Roscommon
Tooman Tackle, The Bridge, Carrick-on-Shannon, Co. Leitrim

YELLOW RIVER   N 00 23

The Yellow River enters the northern end of Lough Allen from the east. It is a spate, mountain river and holds good brown trout to 1½lb in the deep pools downstream of the bridge on the Dowra-Drumshanbo road.

Season
1 March–30 September

Permit
Not usually required

OWENNAYLE, RIVER   M 97 27

The Owennayle is another spate river that enters Lough Allen from the north. It is reputed to hold some of the best stocks of trout in the Lough Allen catchment. There are plenty to half-a-pound and occasional bigger trout to 2lb in the pools.

The banks are partly clear and partly overgrown and the pools are always likely to give up a trout or two, especially after a spate. I also have reports of anglers having success with a dry-fly and some describe it as a super trout river.

Season
1 March–30 September

Permit
Free

CLOON RIVER   N13 97

This river is located between Mohill and Carrigallen in Co. Leitrim. It has had a lot of rehabilitation work carried out and is now a lovely trout stream with lots of ½ and ¾lb trout.

Permit
Riparian owners

ARIGNA RIVER   G 93 13

The Arigna River drains a steep valley in the Arigna mountains into Lough Allen. It holds a small stock of small trout in the pools in its lower reaches – downstream of the Iron Bridge. This river is in a poor state at present, suffering from pollution from various sources as well as being highly acidic.

Season
Trout: 1 March–30 September

Permission
Not usually required

FEORISH, RIVER   N 02 78

This small limestone river comes down from Lough Na Bo, past Geevagh and Ballyfarnan in north Roscommon, and joins the Shannon upstream of Wooden Bridge. It is a fair-sized stream and the pools are well worth fishing for trout. A 2008 fishery survey revealed that stocks are good, with trout to 1½lb. It has good hatches of olives, sedges, mayfly, black gnat and reed smut (simulium).

Season
Trout: 1 March–30 September

Permission
Not usually required

BOYLE, RIVER   G 80 02

The River Boyle rises in Lough Gara and the stretch of interest to trout anglers is between Lough Gara and Lough Key, from a point two miles above the town of Boyle and 1½ miles below it.

The trout average 8oz, and there are a lot of them, with some fish to 2lb and there are plenty of small fish. Access is reasonably good off the roads to the right bank and the best fishing is said to be upstream of Boyle. There is also some nice water downstream of the town, as far as Lough Key and access is good with a road close to the left bank. This is a limestone river, with some nice streamy water. The fly hatches are prolific. It has a great mayfly hatch and sedges are very important.

Season
Trout: 1 March–30 September

Permit
Not usually required

LUNG, RIVER   M 65 95

The Lung River, near Ballaghadereen, is usually considered to be a coarse and pike fishery. The most up-to-date information on trout stocks indicate that it cannot be recommended for trout fishing.

Season
Trout: 1 March–30 September

Permit
Not usually required

Tackle Shop
Abbey Marine, Carrick Road, Boyle, Co. Roscommon

BREEDOGE, RIVER   M 74 95

The Breedoge River flows into Lough Gara down past Ballanagare on the N5 Tulsk to Ballaghaderreen road. I met a man recently who described it as a super river. It holds a good stock of trout to about 14 inches in the stretch from Loughbally Bridge, downstream to Bella Bridge and upstream of Breedoge chapel. The river is in a pretty derelict state in some places and the best prospects for fishing are early in the season.

Season
Trout: 1 March–30 September

Permit
Not usually required

Regulations
Minimum size: 10 inches

Tackle Shop
Trapper John, Castlerea Road, Tulsk via Sligo, Co. Roscommon

KILLUKIN, RIVER   M 93 97

This is a nice little trout stream that drains Loughs Canbo, Corbally and Lisdaly into the Shannon from the west just south of Carrick on Shannon. It is rarely, if ever fished, but Fisheries Board staff in the area describe it as having some lovely trout water from Deerpark downstream.

Season
Trout: 1 March–30 September

Permit
Not usually required

Regulations
Minimum size: 10 inches

Tackle shop
Toomin Tackle, The Bridge, Carrick-on-Shannon, Co. Leitrim

MOUNTAIN RIVER   M 94 85

The Mountain River (part of it is known as the Scramoge River) drains a big catchment, extending from Tulsk in the north to Roscommon town in the south, into Kilglas Lake. Fisheries Board staff in the area report that it is a lovely spring-fed river and completely unfished but that it appears to be a river with a lot of trout fishing potential in several parts. It is completely pollution-free.

Season
Trout: 1 March–30 September

Permit
Not usually required

Regulations
Minimum size: 10 inches

NB. While the rivers Mountain, Killukin, Breedoge, Lung, Boyle, Feorish, Arigna, Owennayle, Yellow and Upper Shannon are generally regarded as 'free fishing', it is as well to consult the riparian owners, just to make sure.

HIND, RIVER   M 88 61

The River Hind flows through the town of Roscommon into Lough Ree. It is about 11 miles long. It is once more a marvellous trout river and well worth a visit. It holds quite a good stock of trout – some between 2½lb and 5lb. It tends to run low late in the summer and this gives rise to a problem with weeds. Roscommon Rod & Gun Club is active on the river.

Season
Brown Trout: 1 March–30 September

Permission
Mr. Gabriel Finn, Main Street, Roscommon. Mobile: 087 2251906

** SUCK, RIVER   M 60 80

The River Suck is an extensive tributary system of the Shannon and drains large areas of Counties Galway and Roscommon. Upstream of Ballymoe, there is a mixture of streamy water and deep, sluggish stretches. Downstream of Ballymoe, to its confluence with the Shannon, the Suck is a big river, mostly deep and slow and more suited to coarse fishing, except for a few streamy sections to the fords. These areas still hold trout. Most of the Suck's tributaries hold trout and some have marvellous potential as trout rivers. Practically all of the Suck catchment is on limestone and fly hatches are prolific, including mayfly in certain areas.

But, before proceeding further, let's set the record straight and not mislead anyone. This system could accurately be described as the 'forgotten river'. It has been raped by unsupervised, unsympathetic drainage works; the stiles have been neglected and the footbridges are rotting and falling down. The Suck's trout stocks, together with those of most of its tributaries, have been greatly depleted from the fine trout fisheries I once knew.

Salmon
The river gets a small run of grilse from about the end of May but can no longer be regarded as a salmon fishery. The river was dredged in the early 1990s to allow river cruisers upstream to Ballinasloe and all the fords were removed. Salmon fishing is confined to a 600 metre man-made fishery at Poolboy Mill, near Ballinasloe.

Brown trout
There is about seven miles of trout fishing in spring and early summer from the bridge on the Castlerea-Kilkelly road (near Clonalis House) downstream past Castlerea, Cloondacarra Bridge, Willsbrook Bridge, Frenchlawn Bridge and on to a point half-a-mile downstream of Laragh Bridge. The river here is 7-9 yards wide and was drained. The best of the trout fishing is near the bridges. The banks are high and stiles and footbridges are provided by the Shannon Regional Fisheries Board. The trout range from 8–12oz and the better fish are downstream of Frenchlawn Bridge. This is an early season fishery and it weeds up after May. It is fairly heavily fished by local anglers, using all methods. There is a good mayfly hatch.

Information on the fishing is available from:

Mr. John Ryan, Fisheries Inspector, Ballinlough, Co. Roscommon. Tel: 094 9640103

Moving downstream, the next piece of trout fishing is at Dunamon Bridge. Then there is a mile of fishing at Castlecoote. Most of it is upstream of the bridge and access is on the left bank. There is another mile of trout water at Cloondray Footbridge. This footbridge is about 1½ miles upstream of Mount Talbot, with access off the Mount Talbot-Athleague road. At Ballyforan, there is a stretch of trout water at Deereen Footbridge, upstream of the village.

Further downstream, trout are to be found on the fords at Derrycahill Bridge, Daly's Grove and the confluence of the Killeglan River. Here there can be some good dry-fly fishing at mayfly time, but you must have a local guide to find it (see below). In the Ballinasloe area, there is trout fishing at Bellagill Bridge, the confluence of the Bunowen River and the Railway Bridge above the town and at Poolboy downstream.

Season
Salmon & Trout: 1 March–30 September

Trout permits
Salmon's Shop, Main Street, Ballinasloe, Co. Galway
Giblin Bros, Kilconnell, Ballinasloe, Co. Galway

Local tackle shop
Barry's Cycles, Sarsfield Road, Ballinasloe, Co. Galway

CLOONARD, RIVER   M 67 82

This river is formed by the confluence of the Lough Glinn stream and the Frances River and offers about eight miles of trout fishing before joining the River Suck at Castlerea. It is crossed by six bridges, hence access is reasonably good. This is a good trout river, especially from Ballindrimley Bridge downstream to Termon Bridge and all the way downstream to Castlerea. It holds a lot of trout to 1½lb. The stretch upstream of Castlerea swimming pool is especially good.

It runs low in late summer.

Season
Trout: 1 March–30 September

Permits
John Hunt, Patrick Street, Castlerea, Co. Roscommon
Shannon Fishery Board Office, Lough O'Flynn, Ballinlough, Co. Roscommon
Tel: 094 9640103
Breege Comer, Ballinlough, Co. Roscomon

Guides
Mr. Bernard Mannion, Knockroe, Castlerea, Co. Roscommon. Tel: 094 9620976
Mr. Matthew Foley, Main Street, Castlerea, Co. Roscommon. Tel: 04 9621531
Tom Flynn, The Square, Castlerea, Co. Roscommon

Information
John Ryan, Shannon Regional Fisheries Board, Ballinlough, Co. Roscommon
Tel: 094 964103

Regulations
Minimum size: 10 inches

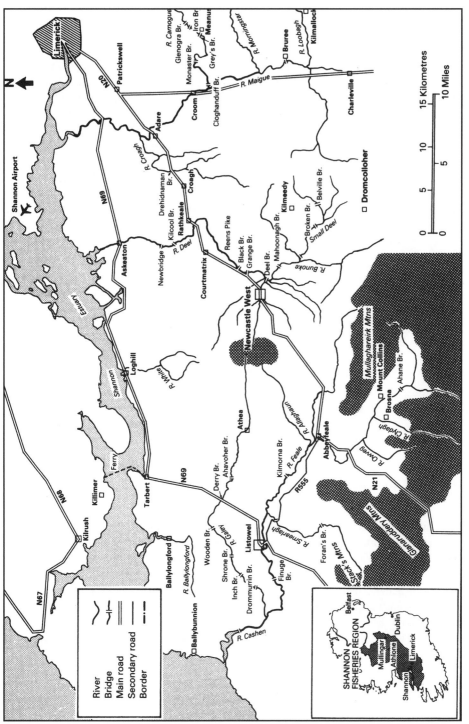

North Kerry and the Golden Vale

ISLAND RIVER   M 68 72

The Island River rises south of Ballinlough in Co. Roscommon and flows east to the River Suck at Ballymoe. It is primarily a spring-fed river, over limestone, and the water is crystal clear. It is slow-flowing in many parts, but with a few livelier sections. Overall, however, it has all the signs of a drained river. The peak season is from March to May before it weeds up badly in summer. It holds a huge stock of trout to half-a-pound, a fair number to 1½lb and the deep pools hold trout to 3lb. These are beautiful deep trout. It can be fished all the way from Island Bridge, past the Mill of Clough and on to Buchalla. Try a wet-fly in spring, down to the Mill of Clough. There are some nice pools for dry-fly from the Mill of Clough to Buchalla Bridge and another good stretch at Ballymoe from a point one mile upstream of Castlereagh Bridge down to the confluence. The channel varies in width from 4 to 40 metres.

For the greater part of its journey, this river flows through rough pasture, marshy areas and cut-away bog and access along the banks is difficult.

Season
Trout: 1 March–30 September

Permits
John Hunt, Patrick Street, Castlerea, Co. Roscommon
Shannon Fishery Board Office, Lough O'Flynn, Ballinlough, Co. Roscommon
Tel: 094 9640103
Breege Comer, Ballinlough, Co. Roscomon

Guides
Mr. Bernard Mannion, Knockroe, Castlerea, Co. Roscommon. Tel: 094 9620976
Mr. Matthew Foley, Main Street, Castlerea, Co. Roscommon. Tel: 04 9621531
Tom Flynn, The Square, Castlerea, Co. Roscommon

SMAGHRAAN, RIVER   M 80 65

The Smaghraan River rises six miles west of Roscommon town and joins the River Suck from the north a mile downstream of Dunamon Castle. It was famous once for its big fat trout, until it was drained. It now weeds up terribly in summer. It now holds a big stock of mostly small trout, though occasionally turns up some good ones to 3lb (16 inches), or better. The trout seem to be found in specific areas or hot spots. One such location is upstream and, especially, downstream of the bridge at Oran on the N60. Another is in the one mile stretch between the Railway Bridge and the Suck confluence. Access to the right bank is by a small lane, a short distance north of Dunamon Bridge.

Season
Trout: 1 March–30 September

Permits
John Hunt, Patrick Street, Castlerea, Co. Roscommon
Shannon Fishery Board Office, Lough O'Flynn, Ballinlough, Co. Roscommon

Tel: 094 9640103
Breege Comer, Ballinlough, Co. Roscomon

Guides
Mr. Bernard Mannion, Knockroe, Castlerea, Co. Roscommon. Tel: 094 9620976
Mr. Matthew Foley, Main Street, Castlerea, Co. Roscommon. Tel: 04 9621531
Tom Flynn, The Square, Castlerea, Co. Roscommon

SPRINGFIELD, RIVER

This is a beautiful little stream with lots of trout averaging 10 inches and better ones too, up to 16 inches. It is one of my favourite trout streams. It is spring-fed – hence the name – but in recent years (2000) is beginning to show signs of nutrient enrichment (eutrophication).

It is a tributary of the Island River, which it joins about three miles west of the village of Ballymoe. I have only fished the two mile stretch downstream from Ballaghaugeag Bridge on the Ballymoe to Dunmore road. It is a real gem and a delightful place to fish a dry-fly. It has good hatches of olives, sedges and black gnats.

Despite the fact that it has a good gradient, it has not escaped the attention of the drainage machines and, as a result, part of it weeds up in summer. What a shame!

Season
1 March–30 September

Permits
John Hunt, Patrick Street, Castlerea, Co. Roscommon
Shannon Fishery Board Office, Lough O'Flynn, Ballinlough, Co. Roscommon
Tel: 094 9640103
Breege Comer, Ballinlough, Co. Roscomon

Guides
Mr. Bernard Mannion, Knockroe, Castlerea, Co. Roscommon. Tel: 094 9620976
Mr. Matthew Foley, Main Street, Castlerea, Co. Roscommon. Tel: 04 9621531
Tom Flynn, The Square, Castlerea, Co. Roscommon

SHIVEN, RIVER   M 78 48

The River Shiven receives a number of tributaries and drains into the River Suck from the west between Ballygar, Co. Galway and Ballyforan in Co. Roscommon. It flows over limestone and is very rich in fly life. At one time it was regarded as one of the leading trout fisheries in the country. Now, sadly, it is another one of those 'forgotten' rivers. No development work has taken place for nearly twenty years: stiles and footbridges are neglected and this makes negotiating the banks difficult. Some stretches have a serious peat silt problem. The river has also been drained and it runs low in summer. The best of the fishing is early in the season – up to about the end of May – as it becomes heavily weeded in summer. The trout average about 12oz, but they are scarce and hard to locate. The best of the mayfly hatch is from Rookhill downstream and there is an excellent hatch of olives at the Tirur River confluence.

Season
1 March–30 September

Permission
Tommy Salmon, Department Store, Main Street, Ballinasloe, Co. Galway
Tel: 090 9642120
Giblin Bros. Ltd, General Merchants, Kilconnell, Ballinasloe, Co. Galway
Tel: 090 9686646

Regulations
Minimum size: 10 inches

TIRUR, RIVER   M 70 49

The Tirur is 7½ miles long and joins the River Shiven to the east of Mount Bellew Bridge. It is a typical, featureless, drained channel. However, there is a very good stock of trout downstream of Tirur Bridge with a fair proportion of them that are over 10 inches. The river weeds up badly from the end of May and is difficult to fish.

Season
1 March–30 September

Regulations
Minimum size: 10 inches

Permission
Tommy Salmon, Department Store, Main Street, Ballinasloe, Co. Galway
Tel: 090 9642120
Giblin Bros. Ltd, General Merchants, Kilconnell, Ballinasloe, Co. Galway
Tel: 090 9686646

CASTLEGAR (NORTH), RIVER   M 70 48

This stream flows down past Mountbellew and joins the Shiven three miles further on. It is mainly a featureless drained river with a good gradient and a lot of glide water. It holds some good trout up to 3lb and is worth a visit. Here again, this is mostly an early-season fishery as it tends to become heavily weeded in summer. The only access is at Canavan's Bridge on the N63 Mountbellew-Ballygar road. The banks are difficult to negotiate and there are no stiles.

Season
1 March–30 September

Permission

Tommy Salmon, Department Store, Main Street, Ballinasloe, Co. Galway
Tel: 090 9642120

Giblin Bros. Ltd, General Merchants, Kilconnell, Ballinasloe, Co. Galway
Tel: 090 9686646

Regulations

Minimum size: 10 inches

CASTLEGAR (SOUTH), RIVER   M 70 47

This is a small weedy stream flowing in a northerly direction from Castleblakeney.
There is some glide water above the confluence and access is by the left bank at
Cloonfaris Bridge. It has very few, if any, trout at all. Don't bother to fish it.

KILLEGLAN, RIVER   M 86 39

The Killeglan stream joins the River Suck from the east, three miles north of
Ballinasloe. It is a lovely, small, spring-fed river with gin clear water over limestone
and is very rich in insect life. It holds moderate stocks of trout averaging half-a-pound,
with some to 2lb. It fishes very well up to June, after which, much of the river becomes
very weedy. The upper limit of the fishing is at Finneron's Bar (now gone; also know at
'Patsy Jacks') on the R357 Ballinasloe-Thomas Street road and access is at the bridges
downstream.

Season

1 March–30 September

Permission

Tommy Salmon, Department Store, Main Street, Ballinasloe, Co. Galway
Tel: 090 9642120

Giblin Bros. Ltd, General Merchants, Kilconnell, Ballinasloe, Co. Galway
Tel: 090 9686646

Regulations

Minimum size: 10 inches

BUNOWEN (AHASCRAGH), RIVER   M 80 36

The Bunowen River flows through Clonbrock and Ahascragh in east Galway and joins
the River Suck two miles north of Ballinasloe. It is a medium-sized river that flows
over limestone and has the potential to be one of the finest trout rivers in the country.
Its course is mainly through pastureland, but it has no stiles and footbridges. The trout
average around 12oz and the lower reaches can hold trout to 2lb. The best stretches

are from half-a-mile upstream of Clonpee Bridge, downstream for nearly three miles past Clonbrock House (in ruins), which has lots of small trout. A mile long productive stretch downstream of Ahascragh Bridge was dredged recently and a two-mile stretch, from Sonnagh down past Killure Castle, has a fair stock of trout to 16 inches (3lb).

The town of Ballinasloe has a big angling population and the river is heavily fished. The Inland Fisheries Trust used to have a fly-only rule upstream of Ahascragh Bridge. It is something I would dearly like to see anglers continuing to observe. There are excellent hatches of fly and a good mayfly hatch downstream of Sonnagh.

(Permissions etc. as for the Shiven river, see page 293)

BALLYARDA, RIVER   M 82 32

The little Ballyarda River joins the River Suck from the west, a short distance upstream of Ballinasloe. It flows east from Kilconnell and has trout from 8oz–3lb (16 inches) in the last four miles. Access is at the bridges. This is a relatively productive little stream with a fair stock over 10 inches. It weeds up and is unfishable after May and there is a stretch up in the bog that is overgrown with willows and impossible to fish.

Season
1 March–30 September

Permission
Tommy Salmon, Department Store, Main Street, Ballinasloe, Co. Galway.
Tel: 090 9642120
Giblin Bros. Ltd, General Merchants, Kilconnell, Ballinasloe, Co. Galway.
Tel: 090 9686646

Regulations
Minimum size: 10 inches

BALLINURE, RIVER   M 86 26

The Ballinure River drains the Bloody Hollow and the site of the Battle of Aughrim and flows east into the River Suck downstream of Correen Ford. It is a limestone river holding moderate stocks of 12oz–1lb trout. There are no stiles or footbridges worth a visit.

Local tackle shop
James J. Killeen, Shannonbridge, Athlone, Co. Westmeath

Permits
Tommy Salmon, Main Street, Ballinasloe, Co. Galway. Tel: 090 9642120

CROSS, RIVER   M 99 42

This lovely little limestone stream has trout ranging from 8oz–12oz. It is on the Roscommon side of Athlone and enters the Shannon downstream of the town. The best of the fishing is from the Mill Bar, on the Athlone-Tuam road, downstream to the bridge on the N6 Ballinasloe road. A lot of rehabilitation work has gone into this river and it has proved worthwhile.

Season
Trout: 1 March–30 September

Permission
Free

There is an active angling club on the river and the chairman is:

Mr. Tom Egan, Chairman, Cross River Anglers' Association, Villa Maria, Monksland, Athlone, Co. Roscommon. Tel: 090 6492578

8. Southern Fisheries Region

The Southern Fisheries Region stretches from Kiln Bay, east of Bannow Bay, to the southern tip of Ballycotton Bay. It comprises the catchments of four major rivers, the Barrow, Nore, Suir and Munster Blackwater, and a number of smaller streams, which can be productive in season.

Southern Regional Fisheries Board (Head Office), Anglesea Street, Clonmel, Co. Tipperary. Tel: 052 80055, email: enquiries@srfb.ie, web: www.srfb.ie

Rivers marked ** are closed for salmon and seatrout fishing at the time of writing. Rivers marked * are catch-and-release only for salmon, and seatrout over 40cm must be returned. For up-to-date information: **www.cfb.ie** or **www.fishinginireland.info**

Instructors/guides
Glenda Powell, APGAI-IRL S/H, D/H (River Blackwater), Blackwater Lodge, Upper Ballyduff, Co. Waterford. Tel: 058 60235, email: info@ireland-salmon-fishing.net Web: www.ireland-salmon-fishing.net
Andrew Ryan, APGAI-IRL S/H FFF Master (River Suir), Clonanav Flyfishing Lodge & School, Nire Valley, Ballymacarbry, Clonmel, Co. Tipperary. Tel: 052 9136141 Email: andrew@flyfishingireland.net, web: www.flyfishingireland.com
John Woodside, APGAI-IRL, S/H/ D/H (River Blackwater), Murwood School of Salmon and Trout Angling, Shean Road, Upper Ballyduff, Co. Waterford Tel: 058 60414. mobile: 0877644618
Michael Drinan, G.A.I.A. (River Blackwater), Dunbullogue, Carrignavar, Co. Cork Tel: 087 2353885, email: michaeldrinan@eircom.net, web: www.flyfishingireland.net

Guides / Ghillies
Maurice Cahill (River Blackwater), Gofish Trout & Salmon Guide, Castlemartyr, Co. Cork. Tel: 021 4667798, email: gofish@eircom.net
Connie Corcoran (River Blackwater), Station Road, Upper Ballyduff, Co. Waterford Tel: 058 00146
Paul Whelan (River Blackwater), Fortwilliam Road, Upper Ballyduff, Co. Waterford Tel: 087 8292077, email: info @Fortwilliamfishing.net
John Brady (River Nore), 8 Hill View, Bennetsbridge, Co. Kilkenny
Jim Brown (River Nore), Rose Bank Lodge, Mount Alto, Inistioge, Co. Kilkenny.

Tel: 056 7758419 or 087 2498619, email: jimmbrown@eircom.net, web: www.noresalmon.com

Norman Gillett (River Blackwater), Main Street, Lismore, Co. Waterford. Tel: 058 53325 or 086 1233148

Blackwater Lodge (River Blackwater), Blackwater Lodge, Upper Ballyduff, Co. Waterford. Tel: 058 60235, email: info@ireland-salmon-fishing.net, web: www.ireland-salmon-fishing.net

Ballyvolane House & Blackwater Salmon Fishery (River Blackwater), Castlelyons, Near Fermoy, Co. Cork. Tel: 025 36349, email: info@ballyvolanehouse.ie, web: www.ballyvolanehouse.ie

Longueville House (River Blackwater), Mallow, Co. Cork. Tel: 022 47156, email: info@longuevillehouse.ie, web: www.longuevillehouse.ie

Careysville House and Fishery (River Blackwater), c/o Lismore Castle, Lismore, Co. Waterford.
Tel: 058 54424, email: lismoreestates@eircom.net

Mount Juliet Conrad Hotel (River Nore), Thomastown, Co. Kilkenny. Tel: 056 7773000, email: info@mountjuliet.ie, web: www.mountjuliet.ie. Contact: Eamonn Holohan, Estate Host. Tel: 086 3838115

Accommodation

For your hotel, lodge and bed and breakfast accommodation, see:

South East (Carlow, Kilkenny, South Tipperary, Waterford, Wexford) Fáilte Ireland South East, 41 The Quay, Waterford. Tel: 051 875823, fax: 051 877388
Email:southeastinfo@failteireland.ie, web: www.discoverireland.ie/southwest

Shannon Development (Clare, Limerick, South Offaly, North Tipperary) Shannon Development-Heritage & Tourism, Shannon Town Centre, Co. Clare
Tel: 061 361555, fax: 061 363180 email: tourisminfo@shannondev.ie
Web: www.discoverireland.ie/shannon

** BARROW, RIVER   S 71 44

The River Barrow rises in the Slieve Bloom Mountains in Co. Laois and flows north and then east through the Bog of Allen towards Portarlington. At Monasterevin, it turns southwards and makes its way through the rich tillage and pasturelands of Counties Kildare, Carlow and Kilkenny. From the town of Borris, the adjoining landscape changes to a scenic wooded valley as the river makes its way to the tide in Waterford Harbour, where it shares a common estuary with the River Nore and River Suir. In all, it is 120 miles long and drains a catchment of 1,185 sq. miles.

The river has been developed as a navigable waterway from Athy downstream to St. Mullins and the fishing rights are vested in Waterways Ireland with access from the towpath from which the fishing is regarded as free. The locks and weirs on that 35-mile stretch have greatly altered the character of the river, making it more suitable for coarse fish and pike than for trout and salmon. It doesn't yet have heavy cruisers, but boat traffic is increasing.

At present it is a fair-to-good salmon river. A number of fish are taken every year below the weir at St Mullins, at Graiguenamanagh and a few at Borris.

The trout fishing is also described as fair-to-good with the average size of the trout probably reaching 12oz but with trout to 2½lb. The best trout fishing is considered to be upstream of Monasterevin and on the tributaries, where fishing was excellent in the past and can still be so. There are plenty of smaller trout downstream, too, as far as St Mullins with very good brown trout fishing at Milford, Borris and Goresbridge.

Season
Salmon: 17 March–30 September
Seatrout: 17 March–30 September
Brown trout: 17 March–30 September

These opening and closing dates apply also to all tributaries of the Barrow.

THE BARROW FISHERIES

St. Mullins Angling Club
St Mullins Angling Club has about four miles of water extending downstream from St Mullins Weir, past the island, to St Mullins quay. It holds brown trout, seatrout and salmon. This is very much a mixed fishery with trout, salmon as well as coarse fish (bream and dace).

The trout are small – averaging half-a-pound – but fairly plentiful and there is a brilliant blue-winged olive hatch.

There are said to be salmon in the river from April but the best salmon fishing is considered to be in June and September. Occasionally, June can produce good grilse fishing – referred to locally as 'gilleen'. Try the tidal pool by Odlum's Old Mill.

A feature of the river at St Mullins is the run of shad, every year in May. Anglers come from far and wide to fish for them and they will take many baits, including a fly.

Day permits
Blanchfields Bar, St. Mullins, Co. Carlow. Tel: 051 424745

Regulations
The trout fishing is fly-only

Fishing accommodation
Helen Blanchfield, The Green, St. Mullins, Co. Carlow. Tel: 051 424745

Graiguenamanagh Angling Club
Graiguenamanagh Angling Club has about two miles of water on the right bank, from Cahill's field up to Joyce's Marsh. The brown trout average about 10oz and the fishing can be very good in May and June. Anglers with local knowledge do very well indeed and can take trout to 2lb on the evening rise. There is some nice streamy water downstream of the town and it is there that most of the fishing is done. The grilse fishing is best in July.

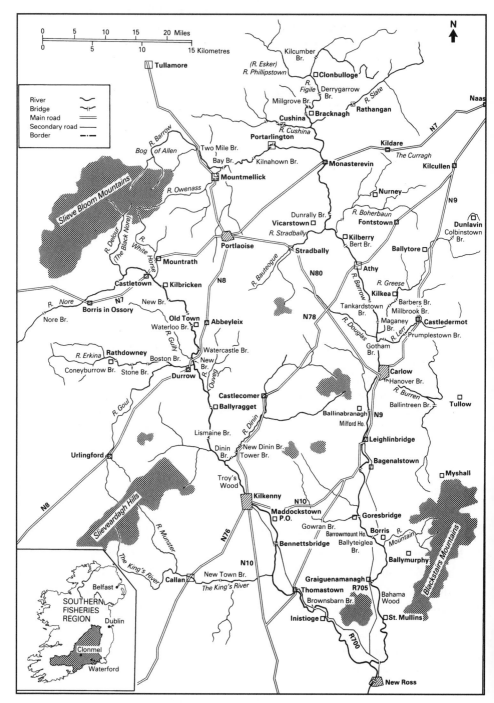

The rivers Barrow and Nore

Enquiries/permits
Shane Byrne. Mobile: 085 1577391
Doyle's Bar, Main Street, Graiguenamanagh, Co. Kilkenny

Clashganna Angling Club
Clashganna Angling Club has fishing from Cloghasty Weir to Bun na hAbhana Bridge. It consists of a small piece of streamy water. The trout are very small and the river is over-run with dace.

Enquiries
Frank Hynes, Cournellan, Borris, Co. Carlow. Tel: 059 9773423

Borris Angling Club
Borris Angling Club has about three miles of fishing on the left bank, extending downstream from Ballyteiglea Bridge to below the weir at Clashganna. This is a mixed fishery with trout, salmon and coarse fishing. The trout fishing can be very good, as too can the salmon fishing on occasions. Boats trolling up and down the river can be a source of great annoyance to trout flyfishers who may find it better to stick to the shallow water below the weirs.

Enquiries andpermits
The Green Drake Inn, Borris, Co. Carlow
Fintan Ryan, Bog Lane, Borris, Co. Carlow. Tel: 0503 71904

The Milltown Fishery
The Milltown Fishery is located downstream of Ballyteiglea Bridge. It is strictly private.

Goresbridge Salmon & Trout Angling Association
Goresbridge Salmon and Trout Angling Association has the goodwill of the fishing on approximately 2½ miles of water, extending from Fenniscourt, upstream of Goresbridge on the Carlow border, downstream as far as Barrowmount House. The trout fishing can be very good in this area. There is a good stock of wild and stocked trout but local knowledge is essential.

Day permits and tackle shop
William O'Neill, Barrow Breeze, Goresbridge, Co. Kilkenny

Killinane Anglers' Association Water
This fishery is about one mile long on one side of the river opposite Baganalstown. It is one of the nicest stretches of the Barrow. Downstream of a confluence, the river is fast-flowing and streamy at this point, in a natural channel. This section of the river is not used for navigation.

This is especially nice trout water and the natural brown trout stocks are sometimes augmented by stocking. The best of the fishing is from May onwards. It has a reasonably good mayfly hatch as well as sedges, olives and black gnat. Access is good and it is possible to wade at low water. Excessive weed growth makes fishing difficult from mid-summer.

Permits and further information
Mr Jim Browne, Killinane Farm, Baganalstown, Co. Carlow. Tel: 087 2494115 or 059 9721359

Regulations
Trout: fly-only after 1 May
Barbless hooks, size 10 minimum

Vicarstown Angling Club
Vicarstown Angling Club members fish extensively on the Stradbally River, the Killenny River and on the main river. Most of the water is better suited to coarse fish, except the Stradbally River. It holds a good stock of fine brown trout.

Further information
James Crean, Vicarstown Inn, Vicarstown, Portlaoise. Tel: 057 8625189

Athy and District Anglers' Club
Athy and District Anglers' Club has access to an extensive stretch of the River Barrow. This water is fished for salmon late in the season and the trout fishing is regarded as being only fair.

Enquiries about fishing and club membership to:

Enquiries
Tom Bradbury. Tel: 086 8383115

Local tackle shop
Griffin Hawe Ltd, 22 Duke Street, Athy, Co. Kildare

Belin Angling Club
The club has about 10 miles of fishing stretching from Dunrally Bridge up to Sally Island. This water produces about half a dozen salmon every season, but the trout fishing is mostly good over the whole stretch. The average weight is 12oz, with some to 4lb. It is necessary to wade to make the most of the fishing. Stiles are in place. There are good hatches of sedge and blue-winged olive and there is a mayfly hatch.

Enquiries
John Corcoran. Tel: 086 2230120

Local accommodation and information
Fishermans Inn, Fisherstown, Co. Laois. Tel: 057 86 26488

Monasterevin and District Anglers' Association

This club has almost 10 miles of fishing, mostly dry-fly. Stocks are reasonably good and the average size is about a pound. Hatches include olives, mayfly, hawthorn, sedges and black gnat. Access is good. All parts can be accessed from the road and by crossing a field or two.

Permits/tackle shop

Finlays Tackle Shop (Beside the Shell Filling Station), St. Evin's Park, Monasterevin, Co. Kildare.Tel: 045 525331

Regulations

Minimum size: 11 inches
Bag limit: 4

Local flytyer

Tony Finlay, Passlands, Monasterevin, Co. Kildare

Portarlington Angling Club

Portarlington Angling Club's waters on the Barrow extend from Kilnahown Bridge, some three miles upstream of Portarlington (towards Mountmellick), to the footbridge four miles downstream of the town. In all, about eight miles.

The club has access to both banks. The river is 30 to 40 feet wide at this point. It flows over limestone and has stretches of stony, sandy bottom. The river habitat provides good natural cover for trout. Roughly 90 per cent of the banks are low and clear, while the remainder was damaged by a drainage scheme. A lot of work has been done providing stiles and footbridges.

Very few salmon reach this stretch of river during the angling season but, in the past, the waters around Lea Castle provided excellent spring salmon fishing from mid-March.

The club waters usually hold decent stocks of wild brown trout and stocked trout ranging from 12oz–4lb. The fishing is only fair at present as it is still recovering from a serious pollution spill in 1987. It is hoped that it will soon return to its former high quality. The best stretches for trout include the Pump House, the Widow's Hill, Lawnsdowne Bridge, Quinn's Sharp, Maker's Ford, the Footstick, the Mill Island and Green's Flat.

The trout-fishing season begins in early March, when the spun natural minnow is widely used and juvenile members fish a floated worm. A slow-sinking line with a team of wet flies – March Brown, Alexandra and Bloody Butcher – can also get results at this time.

The first fly hatches occur around midday in April and a wet Waterhen Bloa or a Pale Watery are suggested. The principal fly hatches are blue-winged olive, alder, grey flag sedge, mayfly (limited) and black gnat. Favourite wet flies include a Gold-ribbed Hare's Ear, Greenwell's Glory, Waterhen Bloa, Coachman, Red Spinner and Black & Peacock Spider. Most flyfishing activity takes place from May to August.

The visiting angler would be well advised to visit Finlay's Bar, where the proprietor will only be too glad to supply information on 'what they're on'.

Permits

Finlay's Bar, Bracklane Street, Portarlington, Co. Laois. Tel: 057 8623173

Christy Finlay, Station Road, Portarlington, Co. Laois. Tel: 087 2483261

Mountmellick Angling Club

This club has the rights from Two-Mile Bridge to Kilnahown Bridge, a distance of 12 miles. This stretch includes the Garryhinch Fishery which has recently been developed by the Southern Regional Fisheries Board. There is really good trout fishing here with the occasional salmon. Access is good with well developed paths and stiles.

Permits

Brian Lynch, Secretary, Mountmellick Angling Club,,Cox's Hardware, The Square, Mountmellick, Co. Laois, Tel: 057 86 24904

THE BARROW TRIBUTARIES

BURREN, RIVER   S 74 75

The River Burren rises near Myshall in Co. Carlow and flows in a semicircle to join the Barrow at the town of Carlow. It is a brilliant trout river with an excellent head of wild brown trout, supplemented by annual stocking with fingerlings. The Barrow Anglers' Club leases 8 miles of the river from the Southern Regional Fisheries Board. This stretch reaches from Hanover Bridge in Carlow town up to Ballintrean Bridge at Rathtoe, near Tullow. The better trout range from 12oz to a pound and they are lovely, slim specimens. The banks are generally low and a drainage committee carries out weed cutting. This is a limestone river and has all the usual flies associated with that kind of water, including mayfly. It is a good dry-fly river.

Permission and for membership of the club contact

Mr Eamon A. Moore, Hon. Secretary, Barrow Anglers' Club, Link Road, Chapelstown, Carlow. Tel: 059 9142225, email: e.amoore@unison.ie

Murph's (membership only),Tullow Street, Carlow

Regulations

Fly-only

Minimum size: 8 inches

Local guides

Michael and Garry Brennan

Burrin Road, Carlow

Tel: 059 9140995

LERR, RIVER   S 72 82

The River Lerr is a lovely, clear, small stream, which comes down from Castledermot and joins the Barrow three miles upstream of Carlow. It holds beautiful, deep, heavily-spotted pink-fleshed trout. Stocks are excellent and the average size is over a pound. They seem to prefer a wet-fly, but the dry can also do well on its day. The Lerr has an especially good hatch of iron blues and plenty of sedges (caddis). The banks are artificially built and overgrown in places. The fishing is leased in sections up to Prumplestown by Barrow Angling Club and permission to fish can be obtained from the same contacts as for the River Burren, above.

Permission and for membership of the club contact
Mr Eamon A. Moore, Secretary, Barrow Anglers' Club, Link Road, Chapelstown, Carlow. Tel: 059 9142225, email: e.amoore@unison.ie
Murph's (membership only), Tullow Street, Carlow

Regulations
Fly-only
Minimum size: 8 inches

Local guides
Michael and Garry Brennan, Burrin Road, Carlow. Tel: 059 9140995

GREESE, RIVER   S 79 96

The River Greese rises near Dunlavin, Co. Wicklow, and joins the Barrow north of Carlow. It is a clear, fast-flowing limestone stream with some deeper, slow stretches, ideal for holding trout. It holds a very good stock of trout from 8oz–1½lb and in recent years has produced trout to 6½lb.

The Barrow Anglers' Association is active on the river, developing the banks and protecting the trout stocks. The club water stretches for about five miles, from Colbinstown Bridge down through Ballytore Village to Barber's Bridge near Kilkee Castle.

Season
1 March–30 September

Club Secretary
Mr Eamon A. Moore, Secretary, Barrow Anglers' Club, Link Road, Chapelstown, Carlow. Tel: 059 9142225, email: e.amoore@unison.ie
Murph's (membership only), Tullow Street, Carlow

Regulations
Fly-only and single worm

BOHERBAUN, RIVER   N 02 67

The Kilberry-Cloney and Boherbaun Angling Club has fishing on the Boherbaun River which flows down from Nurney and joins the Barrow near Kilberry. Despite drainage works and pollution, it still has the potential to be a great trout river. It is mainly a limestone river with gravel and a lovely white marl bottom. Bianconi, the legendary coachman of the 1800s, once described it as the Irish Test. The banks are good and stiles are in place.

When the river is in good conditions, the trout average 1–2lb and the fishing can be very good. Fly hatches are good and all the usual limestone river species are present, including mayfly. The peak of the fishing is in May-June, but this river can produce a trout right through from April to September.

Permits and information
Mr Eoin Day, 28 Greenhills, Athy, Co. Kildare

SLATE, RIVER   N 62 17

The Slate River rises near Robertstown in Co. Kildare and flows west through Rathangan to join the Figile River two miles south of Bracknagh. It holds good stocks of trout but is mainly an early season river. It was drained some time in the past and consequently runs low and becomes weeded in places in summer. The banks are high. The fishing can be very good around Rathangan and the trout are of a good average size, wild and free-rising.

Information
Mr Lar Martin, Chairman, Rathangan Angling Club, Bonaghmore, Rathangan, Co. Kildare
Murt Loughlin, Hon. Secretary, Rathangan Angling Club, Kilmoney South, Rathangan, Co. Kildare

CUSHINA, RIVER   N 60 15

The Cushina River flows through Clonsast Bog north of Portarlington and joins the Figile River, a tributary of the Barrow, in the middle of Derrylea Bog about two miles south of Bracknagh. It flows over limestone, has a marl bottom and has excellent spawning grounds. It is mostly a wild, deep, narrow river with lots of pools and some streamy water. The banks are generally clear but, as can be appreciated, such a remote river can have its wild, overgrown stretches. It holds trout all along the five-mile stretch downstream from Cushina Bridge to the confluence. The average size is a little under the pound and there are trout there to 5½lb. The fish are very wild and catching them on fly is a real thrill. It is best to wait till dusk and stalk them with great care.

In a wet summer the Cushina can fish well right through the season, though from time to time it does suffer problems with bog silt.

Permits and information
Peter Dunne, Clonsast, Rathangan, Co. Kildare. Tel: 050 223020

OWENASS, RIVER   N 45 06

The Owenass River rises in the Slieve Bloom Mountains and joins the Barrow at Bay Bridge, downstream of Mountmellick. It holds a very big stock of small trout. It is only worth fishing downstream of the town. Here, the trout can reach a pound and can provide pleasant evening fishing in June and July, when a Cinnamon Sedge is likely to account for a nice trout.

Permits
Mr Brian Lynch, Hon. Secretary, Mountmellick Angling Club, Cox's Hardware, The Square, Mountmellick, Co. Laois. Tel: 050 224904

FIGILE, RIVER   N 61 20

The Figile River rises a few miles south of Edenderry in Co. Offaly and flows in a southerly direction through the village of Clonbulloge to join the Barrow just north of Monasterevin. It flows almost entirely through bog, and peat silt can be a problem. Indeed, it may become a greater problem when a new peat-fuelled power station is built here. The Figile holds brown trout to 2lb from Kilcumber Bridge down to Clonbulloge Bridge. This stretch runs entirely through bog. There used to be trout at Bracknagh before recent drainage work was carried out. Some excellent trout have been taken on the fly at Millsgrove Bridge. This river holds large stocks of bream, perch and pike.

Permission
Fishing with consent of the landowners

PHILLIPSTOWN, RIVER   N 55 27

The Phillipstown River joins the Figile River from the west at Clonbulloge. It is mainly a coarse fishery and heavily peat silted, but there are fair numbers of trout in a half-mile stretch up and downstream of Esker Bridge.

* NORE, RIVER   S 51 56

The River Nore rises on the eastern slopes of the Devil's Bit Mountain in Co. Tipperary and, at first, flows east through Borris-in-Ossory, Durrow, then turns south through Co. Kilkenny, passing through Ballyragget, Kilkenny City, Bennettsbridge and Thomastown, before meeting the tide at the lovely village of Inistioge. It is 87 miles long and drains a total catchment of 977 square miles. It rises on a sandstone base but the catchment soon turns to limestone over the rest of its course to the sea. The countryside is one of mixed farming, with some tillage, quite a bit of pasture and dairying and some bloodstock. The river has a fairly steep gradient but the flow is checked by innumerable weirs. Shallow glides are the predominant feature. Wading is usually safe but take care. Chest waders are necessary in many parts for the trout fishing. The banks are lined with trees in many places. There is less aquatic vegetation than in its sister rivers, the Barrow and Suir.

The best of the salmon fishing extends up as far as the confluence of the River Dinin. The best trout fishing is all the way upstream of Thomastown, though there is some below it too. The Nore was once one of the finest salmon rivers in the country. It declined badly in the second half of the 20th Century but I'm glad to say it is making a great recovery and the August/September fishing in particular can be brilliant and is much sought-after. I would go so far to say that it is probably the best salmon river in the country at this time. It gets a small run of spring salmon. The peak of the grilse fishing is from mid-June to early July and the autumn run arrives some time after mid-August. The latter can be big fish – from 12–20lb – and the run has been very good in recent years.

Recent stock surveys revealed an excellent stock of brown trout, with huge numbers found in some areas. The average size is 10oz–12oz, with few fish over a pound. The best of the trout fishing is from early season to mid-June on the tributaries and throughout the season on the main river.

The ownership of the fisheries is well-defined in most cases and the fishing rights are either exercised by individual owners or leased to angling clubs and associations.

Season
Salmon: 17 March–30 September
Seatrout: 17 March–30 September
Brown trout: 1 March–30 September

THE NORE FISHERIES

Tighe Fishery
The Tighe fishery at Inistioge consists of about 4 miles fresh and tidal water. It is reported to be a good salmon fishery but the situation regarding letting is unclear at the time of writing.

Kilkenny Anglers' Association
Kilkenny A.A. has extensive fishing rights (approximately 15 miles) on the Nore, extending upstream from Brownsbarn Bridge to Ballyraggett Bridge. Part of it is double bank and part single bank. These waters hold salmon and brown trout as well as some coarse fish and pike. The spring salmon fishing is poor and there is a small run of grilse from June. It is interesting to note that in the 2002 season the back-end run (September) was one of the best seen on the river in the last 25 years according to a report from the Club Secretary, Ed Stack. Much of the club water is fast and streamy and ideal for the fly. In fact, the club hopes to make some stretches fly-only. Shrimp fishing is not encouraged.

The best of the brown trout fishing is from Bennetsbridge upstream to Ballyragget. The trout average 12oz, with some to 1½lb and occasional fish to 4lb. There is very good trout fishing downstream of Maddockstown and the water downstream of the Dinin confluence holds some of the best stocks of trout on the entire river. Maggot fishing is strictly prohibited.

At the time of writing, a flood relief scheme is in progress above and below Kilkenny City. This will have an adverse effect on angling in that area and downstream.

Enquiries
Mr Ed Stack, Bleach Road, Kilkenny. Tel: 056 7765220
Luke Boyle, 8 Loreto Avenue, Riverside Drive, Kilkenny. Tel: 056 7722489

Permits
The Clubhouse Hotel, Patrick Street, Kilkenny

Local tackle shops
J.J. Carrigan, The Sports Shop, 82 High Street, Kilkenny, Co. Kilkenny
Tel: 056 7759878

Local guide/flytyer/fishing tackle
John Mealy, Dublin Road, Kilkenny. Tel: 056 7721532

Coolmore Estate Fishery
This is a private fishery.

Thomastown Angling Club
Thomastown Angling Club has 4 miles of double bank fishing upstream and downstream of the town. This stretch is said to have some of the nicest pools and some of the best salmon fishing on the River Nore. There is a lot of streamy water and it is an especially nice spring-salmon fishery. It fishes particularly well in August and September. Flyfishing, worming and spinning are the allowed angling methods.

This water also holds excellent stocks of brown trout, but a club regulation does not permit trout fishing until April and only flyfishing and worming are allowed for trout. Ten salmon permits and ten trout permits are available per day.

Permits
Tracey's Hardware, Thomastown, Co. Kilkenny

Mount Juliet Hotel and Country Club
Mount Juliet has two miles of double-bank fishing and two miles of single bank on the Nore upstream of Thomastown and on the right bank of the King's River, upstream from the confluence. The salmon fishing is mostly for grilse and autumn fishing which can also be very good.

Mount Juliet rod catch 2001–2008

Year	2001	2002	2003	2004	2005	2006	2007	2008
Salmon	57	N/A	39	40	54	53	83	232

The brown trout fishing is very good on this stretch in April and the evening fishing can be magic through July and August.

Salmon rods are let by the day and there are evening permits for the trout fishing. Gillies are available by prior arrangement and fishing tackle can be hired. The fishing can be booked through:

The Fishery Manager, Mount Juliet Conrad Hotel, Thomastown, Co. Kilkenny. Tel: 056 7773000, mobile: 086 3833115, email: info@mountjuliet.ie, web: www.mountjuliet.com

Lodge/accommodation
Mount Juliet Conrad Hotel, Thomastown, Co. Kilkenny. Tel: 056 7773000
Email: info@conradhotels.com. Member of the *Great Fishing Houses of Ireland Group*

Bennettsbridge Angling Club
The club has fishing on about two miles of good trout water. In addition to the natural stocks, it is stocked annually with fingerling trout. The access to the water is only a short distance from the road. The principal fly hatches are olives, sedges and midges.

Enquiries
Pat Quigley, Hon. Secretary, Bennettsbridge Angling Club, Cairn, Dunbell, Kilkenny. Tel: 056 7727614

Guide
John Brady, 8 Hill View, Bennettsbridge, Co. Kilkenny

Day permits
Cullen's Centra Shop, Bennettsbridge, Co. Kilkenny

Regulations
Flyfishing only for trout.
Minimum size: 10 inches
6 trout bag limit

Kilkenny Corporation Fishery
Kilkenny Corporation has ancient riparian rights on the Nore, extending upstream on the right bank from opposite Maddockstown to Talbots Inch, a distance of about five miles. It also has rights on the left bank. The fishing is regarded as 'free'. Very overgrown and mainly trout fishing.

Deen & Dinan Angling Club
The Club has about 10 miles of trout fishing on the rivers Deen and Dinan that extends from Massford Bridge, down through the town of Castlecomer and on as far as Tower Bridge near Jenkinstown Park.

If you travel from Castlecomer towards Clogh, you will see the little river meander its way through the fields along the road. Don't be misled by its size. It is a wonderful river to fish and you will not be disappointed with your time spent there. The trout are as fat as butter, with bright red spots and they are remarkable fighters.

It also holds a good stock of bigger trout downstream of Castlecomer. There is often a good evening rise here to sedges that sometimes goes on until after midnight.

Season

17 March–30 September

Permission

Hon. Secretary, Ballyhemmon, Castlecomer, Co. Kilkenny. Tel: 056 4440199
Ms. Helen Rothwell, Hennessey's Gift Shop, The Square, Castlecomer, Co. Kilkenny

Ballyraggett Angling Club

The club has a couple of miles of trout fishing extending upstream to the Ouveg River confluence. Some areas hold good stocks of trout.

Permits

O'Shea's, The Square, Ballyraggett, Co. Kilkenny

Durrow & District Angling Association

Durrow and District Anglers' Association has extensive fishing on the **River Nore**, extending from Watercastle Bridge downstream to the confluence of the Ouveg River; on the Erkina River from Boston Bridge downstream to the old mill at Durrow; on the River Goul from Boden's Hole to the confluence with the Erkina River and on the lower reaches of the Ouveg River.

The River Nore is about 18 yards wide at this point. It has deep pools and fast streamy water with a good gravel bottom. The trout stocks are very good. This is interesting fishing with big hatches of iron blue duns and black gnats.

The **Erkina River** is about 16 feet wide and is slow moving, with a silt bottom and occasional gravel-bottomed streams. It holds good stocks of trout to 3½lb. The best fishing is early in the season.
The **River Goul** joins the Erkina River. It is a fast-flowing deep stream and holds lots of trout from 8oz–3lb probably better than the Erkina.

The **Oubeg River** is a feeder stream of the Nore. It is a fast-flowing gravel stream and fishes especially well for trout to the wet-fly in high water. The banks are relatively clear, but there is a lot of natural woodland in the Durrow area and fishing is difficult where the river flows through the wood. Any angler fishing this river would be well advised to take along body waders.

Permits

The Gala Stores, The Square, Durrow, Co. Laois. Tel: 050 236234
Jimmy Tyrrell, Abbeyleix, Co. Laois. Mobile: 086 8451257, www.irishflycraft.com

Guide and flytyer
Peter Dunne, The Course, Durrow, Co. Laois. Tel: 050 236181

Guide/fishing tackle/flytyer
Jimmy Tyrrell (above)

Rathdowney Angling Club
Rathdowney Angling Club has about 2½ miles of fishing on the Erkina River, extending downstream from Coneyborow Bridge to Boston Bridge. Access is good, the banks are relatively clean and the river at this point is narrow and has a nice sequence of pool, riffle and glide. There are good stocks of trout in this stretch averaging between 10oz and 12oz, with occasional fish going as big as 3lb, It fishes best early in the season as it runs low in summer.

Permits
W. Hayes, Hon. Secretary, Rathdowney Angling Club, 30 Quigley Park, Rathdowney, Co. Laois.
Michael White, Moorville, Rathdowney
Co. Laois

Abbeyleix Angling Club
Abbeyleix Angling Club has about four miles of water on the River Nore, extending downstream from the New Bridge at Donore House to Waterloo Bridge at Old Town. The river holds good stocks of trout ranging in size from 8oz–1lb. Access to the banks is quite difficult, especially on the upper stretches as the river is a long distance from the nearest road.

Permits
Liam Dunn, Hardware Shop, Abbeyleix, Co. Laois

Guide/flytyer/fishing tackle
Jimmy Tyrrell, Abbeyleix, Co. Laois. Tel: 086 8451257
Email: irishflycraft@eircom.net, web: www.irishflycraft.com

Mountrath and District Anglers' Club
Mountrath and District Anglers' Club has fishing on the **River Nore**, the **Delour River** (known locally as the **Black Nore**) and the **Mountrath River** (known locally as the **White Horse River**). The trout in the Black Nore tend to be small. On the main River Nore, the best of the Club's trout fishing extends from Kilbricken downstream to New Bridge. The White Horse River has substantial numbers of trout, averaging 10oz, downstream of the town of Mountrath. Chest waders are a great boon for flyfishing here.

Permits and information
Mr Thomas Watkins, 6 St Finan's Terrace, Mountrath, Co. Laois. Tel: 050 232540
Kelly's Tackle Shop, Main Street, Mountrath, Co. Laois

Local tackle shop
Kelly's Tackle Shop (above)
D. Lawlor, Main Street, Mountrath, Co. Laois

KING'S, RIVER   S 41 43

Callan and District Anglers' Association has approximately five miles of fishing
on the King's River. This river – like its tributary, the Munster River – rises in the
Slieveardagh Hill in Co. Tipperary and flows east through Callan, in Co. Kilkenny, to
join the Nore north-west of Thomastown. This is a rich limestone river, 15–20 yards
wide with a gravel bottom and occasional 'swallow holes', which cause stretches to
go dry in summer. The Callan and District Anglers' Association fishing extends from
the Metal Bridge, located about 2½ miles upstream of the town. There is a lot of nice
streamy water, especially early in the season, and some of the best fishing is from April
to June. This river was drained and the banks are high in places. The trout average
12oz, with trout to 3½lb and better. Wet-fly is most popular method from March to
May and there is good evening dry-fly fishing in summer. Fly hatches include various
olives, mayflies, stoneflies, black gnats, midges and various sedges.

Permits and information
David Byrne, Hon. Secretary, Callan and District Anglers' Association, 8 Clonmel
Road, Callan, Co. Kilkenny
John Roche, 323 Mile Street, Callan, Co. Kilkenny. Tel: 056 7755046

Kells Anglers' Association
The Kells Anglers' Association has fishing further downstream.

Information
Mr Matt White, Vipers Cottage, Kells, Co. Kilkenny

DININ, RIVER   S 69 54

The Kilkenny Angling Club Water on the River Dinin extends upstream from where
the river joins the Nore for 1½ miles on the left bank and there is about half-a-mile on
the right bank, downstream of the New Dinin Bridge.

Information
John Dalton, Dun Ard, Bishops Hill, Kilkenny City. Tel: 056 7762354

* SUIR, RIVER (AND TRIBUTARIES) S 20 22

The River Suir (pronounced 'sure') rises in the Devil's Bit Mountain in Co. Tipperary and flows south and then north and east to join the Barrow and the Nore in Waterford Harbour. It is 115 miles long and, together with its tributaries, drains a total catchment of 1,394 square miles.

The main river lies entirely on limestone except for a few miles at the source and all the tributaries are on limestone, with the exception of the Nire, the Clodiagh and the upper reaches of the Multeen, which comes in from the west near Cashel. The flow in the main river is characterized by deep and shallow glides interrupted by shallow riffles. Its width increases as it proceeds downstream and the sequence of relatively shallow glide and riffle is maintained.

This combination of a rich limestone base and huge areas of relatively shallow glides makes the Suir ideal for the production of brown trout. There is massive recruitment of young trout from the extensive system of tributaries and the trout survive and grow in what is a near-perfect environment. They have few predators in the form of pike, and other coarse fish are almost entirely absent. It is really a river for the skilled flyfisher rather than for the beginner.

The Suir is one of Ireland's premier brown trout fisheries. Only a handful of rivers can compare with it in terms of trout density and I doubt if any river can equal it in terms of the overall numbers of trout that it produces and that are available to the angler.

The trout range in size from 12oz–2lb in different areas, depending on the habitat. Their lifespan is relatively short and few live to much older than four years.

Season
Salmon: 17 March–30 September
Seatrout : 17 March–30 September
Brown trout: 1 March–30 September
Note: Some fisheries and angling clubs may defer the opening date.

Fly life
The relative uniformity of the river bed over the Suir's entire length means that the dominant fly hatches are more or less similar along the course of the river. Mayflies, however, are found only between Camus Bridge and Golden and stoneflies are confined to fast shallow sections of the river. Otherwise, from March to late April, there are large dark olives around midday. From late April to mid-May, there are medium olives, iron blues and stoneflies (early browns). From mid-May to mid-June, there are alders, medium olives, reed smuts and midges, mayfly, pale wateries, blue-winged olive (BWO), caenis, hawthorn, black gnat, yellow stoneflies and various sedges, including Murroughs and grey flags. From mid-June to the end of July sees BWO, pale wateries and pale evening duns, small dark olives, a variety of sedges (including Murrough, cinnamon sedge, red sedge and silverhorns) and ants on occasions. August has similar hatches. The BWO is very important in the evening, as are various sedges and trout take small black and green midges by day. In September, the trout take BWOs during the day and on mild evenings. Midges, olives and small sedges and the cinnamon sedge are also important.

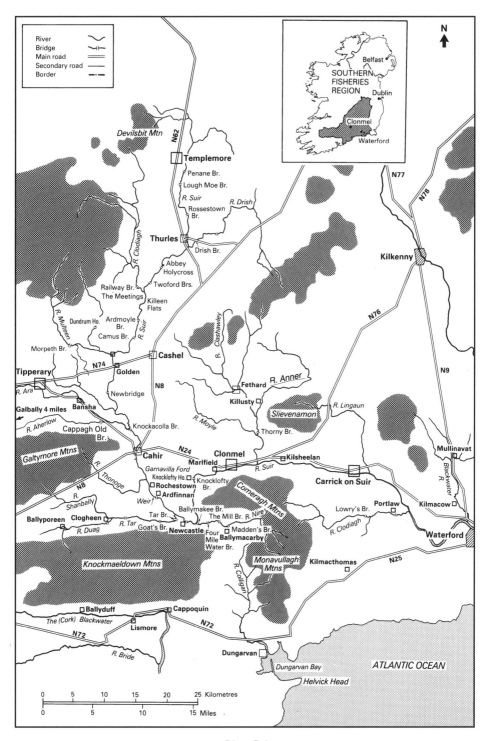

River Suir

The peak of the trout fishing is from early May to mid-June for day-long fishing, at dusk for the rest of the summer and during both day and evening in September. At these times, there is usually no shortage of feeding trout.

It is good to be able to report that, at the time of writing (2002), the mayfly (*Ephemera danica*) has become re-established in many sections of the Suir, due to an improvement in water quality. Anglers can expect to see trout feeding on them in certain areas during the May-June mayfly season.

Wading

Body waders and a wading staff are essential for fishing the main channel of the Suir and its tributaries. In most areas, the bottom is firm and consists of stone, gravel or sand. This is a big river with a strong current and anglers should take due care when wading.

Salmon fishing

The Suir produced Ireland's record-rod caught salmon: a fish of 57lb caught way back in 1874. The most up-to-date information (2001) indicates that salmon are now so scarce and the run is so late that the river can no longer be considered a salmon fishery of any consequence. It gets a late run after the season closes and these are useful as brood fish.

THE SUIR FISHERIES

This description of the fisheries starts at the bottom of the river and, as far as is practical, they are dealt with in sequence moving upstream.

Portlaw Clodiagh River

The Portlaw Clodiagh River joins the Suir east of Portlaw. The fishing rights are owned by the Marquis of Waterford, but trout fishing is available outside the boundary of Carraghmore Estate – upstream of Lowry's Bridge and downstream of Portlaw. It is a sandstone river and has moderate stocks of trout averaging 10 inches.

Blackwater, River

The River Blackwater (not to be confused with the more famous Cork Blackwater) enters the Suir from the north a short distance upstream of Waterford City. It has good stocks of trout to 10 inches between Kilmacow and Mullinavat. Much of the river is overgrown and difficult to fish. There is some fishing available with the consent of riparian owners and inquiries should be made locally.

Lingaun River

The Lingaun River rises on the eastern slopes of Slievenamon and joins the Suir two miles downstream of Carrick-on-Suir. It holds good stocks of trout up to 10 inches. The fishing is with the permission of the riparian owners.

Tidal Water
The Tidal Water extends up to Carrick-on-Suir. Fishing is free on the tidal water downstream of Miloko and the trout are very small.

Carrick-on-Suir Angling Club
The Club has approximately a mile-and-a-half of fishing on the left bank from Duffcastle downstream to Miloko.

Information/permits
John O'Keefe, OK Cycles and Sports, New Street, Carrick-on-Suir, Co. Tipperary
Tel: 051 640626
The Tackle Shop, Bridge Street, Carrick-on-Suir, Co. Tipperary

Clonmel Salmon and Trout Anglers' Association
The association has fishing on the left bank downstream of Kilsheelan, a short stretch upstream of Sir Thomas Bridge below Clonmel and downstream of Knocklofty Bridge.

Enquiries
Mr Pierce Hallahan, Hon. Secretary, Clonmel Salmon and Trout Anglers' Association, Powerstown, Clonmel, Co. Tipperary. Tel: 052 22232
Tommy Williams, Old Spa, Clonmel, Co. Tipperary

Permits
Kavanagh's Tackle Shop, West Gate, Clonmel, Co. Tipperary

Suir Valley Fishery
The Suir Valley Fishery consists of a number of separate fisheries on the main river and tributaries. In all, there is more than 17 km (12 miles) of really excellent trout fishing, with some very big wild brown trout. These fisheries are so located as to give the best possible chance of catching a Suir salmon for the angler who wishes to try. Visitors are welcome as the fishery is managed with tourist anglers in mind. The fishing is mostly catch-and-release, but anglers may take the occasional trout for a barbecue.

The fishery includes:
1½ miles of single bank fishing, downstream of Ballydine
One mile of single bank, upstream of Ardfinnan
The Molough Abbey Fishery – approximately two miles on the left bank, opposite the River Nire confluence
The Cloghardeen Fishery (half a mile)
The Newtown Fishery – approximately 1.6 miles of double bank fishing downstream of the River Anner confluence
The Poulatrass Fishery – approximately one mile of single bank fishing downstream of Kilsheelin

Enquiries
The manager, Mr Trautner, can also arrange fishing on a number of the Suir tributaries. He speaks French and Italian.

Jean-Loup Trautner, Rathkenty, Lisronagh, Clonmel, Co. Tipperary. Tel: 052 32497, fax: 052 32498, mobile: 086 8176055, email: jltrautner@oceanfree.net, web: www. trautner-peche-Irlande.com

Clonmel and District Anglers' Association
The Association has extensive fishing on the Suir downstream of Clonmel. Enquiries for permits to fish for trout and salmon should be made to:

John Carroll, c/o Skinner & Co. Solicitors, 3 Dr. Croke Place, Clonmel, Co. Tipperary

Kilsheelan Angling Club
The Kilsheelan Angling Club has leased the trout fishing on a mile of the river on the left bank upstream of Kilsheelan.

Permits
Mr J. Moriarty, Kilsheelan,Co. Tipperary

Local tackle shop
Kavanagh Sports, West Gate, Clonmel, Co. Tipperary

Anner and Clashawley rivers
These two rivers are limestone streams that come down from Slievenamon and join the Suir just east of Clonmel. Fethard and Killusty Angling Club has reserved the fishing from Thorny Bridge upstream to Fethard town. There are moderate stocks of trout from Thorny Bridge downstream to the confluence and the fishing is available to visitors with the permission of the riparian owners – except the Anner Castle Fishery. The Clashawley has a stony bottom whereas there is a lot of erosion and shifting gravel on the Anner. In summer, the Clashawley suffers from excessive weed growth and the Anner has a problem with filamentous algae.

Permission
All fishing is restricted to members only. Application for membership to:
Mr Thomas Fogarty, Ballingarry, Thurles, Co. Tipperary. Tel: 052 54675

Clonanav Flyfishing Centre
The Clonanav Flyfishing Centre has 2.5km of prime double-bank salmon fishing downstream of Whitesford and access to other stretches on the River Suir and on the River Nire. These fisheries offer good dry-fly and nymph fishing from April to September. Up-to-date information is always available. The Centre has a lodge, tackle shop, tackle can be hired and there is a guide service and tuition and day permits available.

With the demise of the drift nets the salmon fishing has improved on the river and the fishing has really improved in late summer and autumn.

Enquiries
Andrew Ryan, APGAI-IRL; FFF, MCI, Clonanav Lodge and School, Ballymacarbry, Clonmel, Co. Waterford. Tel: 052 36141, fax: 052 36294, email: andrew@flyfishingireland.com, web: www.flyfishingireland.com. Member of the Great Fishing Houses of Ireland Group

Knocklofty House Hotel
The hotel has approximately one mile of double-bank fishing upstream of Knocklofty Bridge. The trout fishing is excellent and now there are salmon to be caught. The fishing is available to residents of the hotel.

Knocklofty House Hotel, Knocklofty, Clonmel, Co. Tipperary. Tel: 086 1260950
Web: www.knockloftyhotel.com

Nire, River
The Nire is 16 miles long and is a fast-flowing mountain river, which flows through farmland and a scenic wooded valley. It has good stocks of trout averaging about 12oz, with some to 3lb or better. The water is sparkling clear and, while the best of the fishing is from Madden's Bridge downstream, the rocky pools hold sizeable trout away up into the Comeragh Mountains – a great place to learn the skills of flyfishing

Enquiries
Andrew Ryan, APGAI-IRL; FFF, MCI, Clonanav Lodge and School, Ballymacarbry, Clonmel, Co. Waterford. Tel: 052 36141, fax: 052 36294, email: andrew@flyfishingireland.com, web: www.flyfishingireland.com. Member of the Great Fishing Houses of Ireland Group

Tar, River
The Tar is 19 miles long. It joins the Suir from the west just over a mile upstream of Newcastle Bridge. The main Tar itself, from Clogheen downstream, flows over a limestone base while its two tributaries, the **Shanbally** and the **Duag**, which flow down from Ballyporeen, drain areas of sandstone. All three rivers hold good stocks of trout averaging half-a-pound, but there are some good ones there too, to 3lb and better. The fishing is with the consent of the riparian owners. The stretch downstream of Goat's Bridge by the public road to Tar Bridge is regarded as free fishing.

Further information
Andrew Ryan, Clonanav Flyfishing Centre. Tel: 052 36141
Jean Loup Trautner, Suir Valley Fishery, Rathkenty, Lisronach, Clonmel,
Co. Tipperary. Tel: 086 8176055), web: www.traugner-peche-irlande.com

Ardfinnan Angling Club

Ardfinnan AC as some excellent trout fishing over about four miles between Ardfinnan and Newcastle. From Ardfinnan Bridge downstream to Clocully you have a big, fast-flowing, meandering river which holds good numbers of trout. At the confluence of the River Tar and upstream of Newcastle the river is shallow and holds moderate stocks of trout. The club waters start at Rochestown, nearly two miles upstream of Ardfinnan. This section of the river consists of long, shallow glides, which hold excellent stocks of trout averaging a little under a pound. The stretch upstream of the weir at Ardfinnan holds only moderate stocks and is best fished on summer evenings. In all, the Club water extends for nearly four miles on both banks from Rochestown to Cloncully, but excludes: the left bank for 550 yards upstream of Ardfinnan Weir; the stretch between the weir and Ardfinnan Bridge; and the Cloghardeen Fishery.

Permits for Ardfinnan Angling Club water

John Maher, Green View, Ardfinnan, Co. Tipperary. Tel: 052 66242

Cahir and District Anglers' Association

The Association has a lot of fishing near the town of Cahir. The club controls the fishing on the right bank from Suir Castle (upstream of New Bridge) to the Bakery Weir upstream of Cahir and downstream of the town from the Swiss Cottage to Carrigatha on the right bank and from the Swiss Cottage to Garnavilla Ford on the left bank. The character of the river varies here, as do the trout stocks.

From Suir Castle to Knockacalla the river is broad and meandering, with glides, riffles and occasional pools. It holds a very good stock of trout averaging around 12oz. From Knockacalla to Cahir, the river is deep and lazy, with limited stocks, and is best suited to evening fishing in summer. From the Swiss Cottage to Carrigatha there are fast, shallow glides and streams and the river holds an excellent stock of trout.

Season

17 March–30 September

Permits

Kevin Roe, Reiska, Cahir, Co Tipperary. Tel: 052 42729, mobile: 08764 09271
Patrick O'Donovan, The Heritage, 1 The Square, Cahir, Co. Tipperary
Tel: 052 42730

Fishing methods

Flyfishing only

Guide

Kevin Roe (see above)

Local flytyer

Ms. Alice Conba, St. Michael's Terrace, Tipperary Town. Tel: 062 52755
Email: conba@eircom.net, web: http://homepage.eircom.net/~conba

Tackle shop

Kavanagh's, West Gate, Clonmel, Co. Tipperary

Disabled anglers' facility

There are three stands downstream of the Swiss Cottage.

ARA, RIVER   R 95 33

The Rivers Ara and Aherlow (see separate entry) are two tributaries that join the Suir from the west four miles north of Cahir.

The Ara comes down from Limerick Junction and Tipperary town. It lies mainly on limestone and provides good angling from Kilshane downstream to the confluence. The river is about 10 yards wide and holds good stocks of trout to 12oz and some to 1¾lb. From Bansha upstream to Kilshane it consists of a series of riffles, glides and pools and from Bansha downstream it is a continuous deep glide with some short riffles and a few pools. The Ara can provide some excellent dry-fly fishing, but you must bring your body waders. Useful patterns include a 'black' Greenwell's Glory, Red Quill, BWO (all size 16) and Brown Sedge. John Evans (address below) can help with useful information on the quality and availability of a lot of the fishing in the south Tipperary area.

Angling information
John Evans, Lacken, Tipperary Town. Mobile: 08728 10645

Guide
Kevin Roe, Reiska, Cahir, Co. Tipperary. Tel: 052 42729, mobile: 08764 09271

AHERLOW, RIVER   R 95 29

The Aherlow is more acid than the Ara and drains off old red sandstone. It holds large numbers of small trout up to a maximum of 12oz. The fishing is with the permission of the landowners. The best fishing water is in the Galbally area and in the lower reaches downstream of Cappa Old Bridge. It is very overgrown, but nonetheless it is well worth a visit.

Season
17 March–30 September

Angling information
John Evans, Lacken, Tipperary Town. Tel: 087 2810645

Fishing methods
Flyfishing only

Guide
Kevin Roe, Reiska, Cahir, Co. Tipperary. Tel: 052 42729, mobile: 08764 09271

Local flytyer
Alice Conba, 2 St. Michael's Terrace, Tipperary Town. Tel: 062 52755
Email: conba@eircom.net, web: http://homepage.eircom.net/~conba

MULTEEN, RIVER   R 99 40

The Multeen River joins the Suir from the west near Cashel. It flows off old red sandstone onto limestone and holds a big stock of trout averaging about half-a-pound in the middle and lower reaches. The fishing is with the permission of the riparian owners and the best of it is from Dundrum House, on the north channel, and from Morpeth Bridge, on the south channel.

Cashel-Golden-Tipperary Angling Association
The Association controls extensive stretches on both banks downstream from Camus Bridge to Suir Castle and also shares the right bank with the Cahir and District Angling Club, from Suir Castle downstream to New Bridge. This stretch is nearly 8 miles long and extends from Camus Bridge, downstream past Golden to New Bridge.

The river is wide and shallow in the vicinity of Camus Bridge and holds good stocks of trout. The next section at Castlelake, two miles downstream, is a continuous deep glide and holds relatively poor trout stocks. It is best suited to evening dry-fly fishing in summer. From Mantlehill downstream through Golden and on to Athassel Abbey, the river meanders attractively with pools and glides. This is prime trout water with the exception of one deep stretch between the confluence of the Multeen River and Golden Bridge, which is best suited to evening dry-fly fishing.

From Athassel Abbey to New Bridge (nearly two miles) the river is characterized by fast-flowing shallow glides and has an excellent stock of trout from 8oz–1½lb, and some much better. This stretch has a number of weirs, downstream of which some daytime fishing may be had even in mid-summer. This stretch has a mayfly hatch and they are also to be found at Two Fords Bridge, the mouth of the Clodiagh, at Ardmayle and at Knocklofty.

Permits
Tom Cahill, The Sports Shop, Paddywell, Bank Place, Cashel, Co Tipperary. Tel: 062 63106, email: info@casale2000ltd.com, web: www.casale2000.ltd.com

Lodge/accommodation
Mary and Ed Hunt, Abbeyvale House B & B, Cashel Road, Holycross, Thurles, Co. Tipperary. Tel: 0504 43032, email: info@abbeyvalehouse.com
Web: www.abbeyvalehouse.com

Thurles-Hollycross-Ballycamus Anglers' Association
This Association has about four miles of fishing extending downstream from Holycross Abbey. It was developed by the Southern Regional Fisheries Board and now holds good trout stocks. Holycross weir diverts the water to a hydro-head race and this results in low summer flows and considerable aquatic vegetation. From Agents Flats to Twoford Bridge the river has a nice mix of glide and pool suitable for either wet- or dry-fly. It holds moderate stocks of trout to 1¾lb.

From Twoford Bridge to the confluence of the Clodiagh River is moderate fishing, but from the confluence downstream to Ballycamus Ford is excellent dry-fly water and can hold plenty of trout, though their numbers seem to fluctuate at times. This club also has a short stretch at the bottom end of the Clodiagh River, and access to fishing on the River Drish.

Flyfishing only is allowed. There is a daily bag limit of six trout and a minimum size of 10 inches.

Permits

Hayes' Hotel, Liberty Square, Thurles, Co. Tipperary. Tel: 0504 22122
Mr Jimmy Purcell, Rathconnon, Thurles, Co. Tipperary. Tel: 0504 43192
Hayes' Shop, Holycross, Co. Tipperary
Eamon O'Gorman, Publican, Bohernacrusha Cross Road, Holycross, Co. Tipperary

Guide

Pat Noonan. Tel : 087 2625742

Lodge

Mary and Ed Hunt, Abbeyvale House B & B, Cashel Road, Holycross, Thurles, Co. Tipperary. Tel: 0504 43032, email: info@abbeyvalehouse.com
Web: www.abbeyvalehouse.com

Hotel

Hayes' Hotel (see above)

Suir and Drish Anglers' Association

This Association has 7½ miles of fishing on the Suir from Rossestown Bridge downstream to Holycross village. Between Thurles and Holycross, the Suir is a big river with a good diversity of fishing water. It is highly recommended by both Fishery Board staff and local anglers. There are some very nice stretches for trout fishing, holding good stocks of fish and the water produces quite a few big trout up to 4lb.

The Association's stretch has a good mix of streamy water and slow deeps and provides some attractive fishing. The bottom is mostly gravel. The water quality is good and runs very clean, though aquatic vegetation can be a problem in summer. The river produces a good evening rise from the end of April. The mayfly hatch is good upstream of Holycross and the river is only lightly fished after the end of May. Trout stocks are very good with many fish in the 2–2½lb bracket and a good few up to 4lb. It has all the usual hatches associated with a limestone river, including mayfly and hawthorns in season, and can offer excellent fishing with upstream nymph, wet- and dry-fly. There is good access at all the bridges and full chest waders are an asset.

NB Fishing is prohibited on a short private stretch at Beakstown and in the grounds of the Ursuline convent.

Season

17 March–30 September

Permits

Pat McCormack, Hon. Secretary, Thurles, Suir & Drish Anglers' Association, Moyne Road, Thurles, Co. Tipperary

Pat Noonan, Clonmore, Templemore, Co. Tipperary. Tel: 050 431737

Hayes' Shop, Holycross, Thurles, Co. Tipperary

Seamus Butler, Saw Mill, Mill Road, Thurles, Co Tipperary

Anner Hotel, Dublin Road, Thurles, Co. Tipperary

Glasheen's, Holycross, Thurles, Co. Tipperary

Permits and accommodation

Hayes' Hotel, Liberty Square, Thurles, Co. Tipperary. Tel : 050 422122

Lodges

Mary and Ed Hunt, Abbeyvale House B & B, Cashel Road, Holycross, Thurles, Co. Tipperary. Tel: 0504 43032, email: info@abbeyvalehouse.com Web: www.abbeyvalehouse.com

Anner Hotel (see above)

Regulations

Flyfishing and catch-and-release preferred

Local flytyer

Alice Conba, 2 St. Michael's Terrace, Tipperary Town. Tel: 062 52755 Email: conba@eircom.net, web: http://homepage.eircom.net/~conba

Accommodation

There are several hotels and B&B accommodation in the vicinity

DRISH, RIVER   S 14 56

The River Drish is a rich, slow-flowing, limestone stream, which joins the Suir about a mile south of Thurles. It drains large areas of peat bog. In its lower reaches, it is a typical clean, slow-flowing, lowland limestone stream, with banks laden with lush vegetation. The trout stocks are declining. The average size is mostly 4oz–12oz. Sadly, the large Drish trout of 3lb and 4lb are but a memory. From Drish Bridge downstream, the river is usually fishable throughout the summer and can provide lovely dry-fly fishing on summer evenings. The middle reaches of the river near Athlummen and upstream become very weeded in summer.

Season

17 March–30 September

Permits

Pat Noonan, Clonmore, Templemore, Co. Tipperary. Tel: 050 431737

Hayes' Hotel, Liberty Square, Thurles, Co. Tipperary. Tel : 050 422122

Glasheen's, Holycross, Thurles, Co. Tipperary

Anner Hotel, Dublin Road, Thurles, Co. Tipperary

Hayes' Shop, Holycross, Thurles, Co. Tipperary

Seamus Butler, Saw Mill, Mill Road, Thurles, Co Tipperary

Regulations
Flyfishing and catch-and-release preferred.

Local flytyer
Alice Conba, 2 St. Michael's Terrace, Tipperary Town. Tel: 062 52755
Email: conba@eircom.net, web: http://homepage.eircom.net/~conba

Club Secretary
Patrick McCormack, Hon. Secretary, Thurles, Suir and Drish Anglers' Association, 15
Moyne Road, Thurles, Co. Tipperary. Tel: 050 423809
Email: suirdrishangling@hotmail.com

Templemore & District Anglers' Association
This Association has access to about 15 miles of wild brown trout fishing that runs
through unspoilt countryside at the headwaters of the river Suir. The river is relatively
small here and suffers from excessive weed growth in summer in certain areas. The
average size of the trout is 8–12oz, with fish to 3lb taken on the sedge in late evening
fishing during the summer. The best of the fishing is from Aughall Bridge to No. 7
bridge on Templemore-Thurles road. It has all the usual fly hatches associated with a
limestone river including a sparse mayfly hatch.

Season
1 March–30 September

Permits/membership
Ricky O'Brien, Hon. Secretary, Templemore & District Anglers' Association,
Richmond, Templemore, Co. Tipperary

Local tackle shop
Jim Hassey, Templemore Post Office, Co. Tipperary. Tel: 050 431098 (day) 050 431213
(evenings)

* CLODIAGH, RIVER   S 23 95

The Clodiagh River flows south from Borrisoleigh, Co. Tipperary and joins the Suir
from the west about three miles south of Holycross. There is some nice fishing on
the Clodiagh, with free-rising trout and a good fly life. It is under the control of the
Clodiagh Anglers' Association from its source to Milltown Castle, half a mile above
the confluence.

Enquiries
Mr T. Delaney, Hon. Secretary, Clodiagh Anglers' Association, Aughboulaghane,
Borrisoleigh, Thurles, Co. Tipperary. Tel: 050 451292

* COLLIGAN, RIVER   X 23 95
* FINISK RIVER   X02 96

The Colligan River rises in the Monavallagh Mountains of south Waterford and flows south for 15 miles into Dungarvan Bay. The upper reaches tumble through a wooded valley and the last 2 miles flow more slowly, with some lovely pools. It is strictly a spate river and is reputed to be one of the fastest-flowing rivers in Ireland. Its catchment is 40 sq. miles.

It is a brilliant little river when in condition for both salmon and seatrout, particularly the latter. The first seatrout now run in early May, and July can see large shoals enter the river. The average size is 2lb and the Colligan is said to hold seatrout to 10lb or better. In terms of the quality of its seatrout, it is very close to a Welsh sewin river, and small wonder, for Wales is only a short distance across the Celtic sea.

The seatrout can be fished on a falling spate, but the best sport is with the fly at night. Local favourites include Mallard & Red, Mallard & Claret, Silver Doctor, Teal, Blue & Silver, Butcher, Peter Ross, Black Pennell and Wake lure. The main run of salmon comes with the first spate in September.

The local club controls the fishing and has done a lot of work clearing the banks. There is about seven miles of fishing in all, but local knowledge is important.

The nearby Finisk River fishes well for brown trout with a lot of fish up to 8ozs and some bigger ones.

Season
17 March–30 September

Contact
Jason O'Riordan, Hon. Secretary, Colligan District Angling and Conservation Club, 34 Caseyville, Dungarvan, Co. Waterford. Mobile: 087 2965712
Email: joriordan@wit.ie

Club regulations
Minimum size: 12 inches
Spinning only is allowed in coloured water

Tackle shop
Baumann's Tackle Shop, 6 Mary Street, Dungarvan, Co. Waterford. Tel: 058 41395

Local flytyer
Jason O'Riordan, 34 Caseyville, Dungarvan, Co. Waterford. Mobile: 087 2965712
Email: joriordan@wit.ie

BLACKWATER, RIVER (MUNSTER OR CORK)   X 04 98

The Munster (or Cork) Blackwater rises in east Co. Kerry near the source of the Brown Flesk River and flows for 105 miles east through the counties of Cork and Waterford, to the tide at Cappoquin. Its entire catchment is more than 1,200 square miles. It has a long, narrow estuary, some 15 miles long. It dominates the southern province, draining five ranges of mountains, and in times of heavy rainfall the levels can fluctuate wildly by more than 12 feet on the gauge at Careysville. The peaty nature of the terrain in the upper reaches and of some of the tributaries gives the water a pronounced dark colour. It is indeed 'black' water. The geology of the catchment is divided roughly into old red sandstone and limestone and lower limestone shales.

The river is noted for its good runs of salmon over the years, with spring fish in February-March, grilse in June-July and a late run of salmon in September. The average size of the brown trout is rather small and it gets seatrout up to Careysville. A distinguishing feature of the Blackwater is that it probably holds more species of fish than any other Irish river. It used to be notable for its dace (now found in the Nore and Barrow) and also its roach, which were introduced to Ireland via the Blackwater in the late 1800s.

It is important for salmon anglers to note that the water condition can fall into about four different categories, graded on the amount of colour. In a flood, when the river carries a lot of suspended solids, it will be heavily-coloured and unfishable. The river is said to have 'dark water' when it has a lot of colour but no suspended solids, in which condition spinning is more likely to succeed. In slightly coloured water, fly, spinner or worm will all take fish. The Blackwater tends not to run really clear until July when some maintain that the fly or the natural shrimp (if permitted) give best results.

The river is characterised by mighty pools, lovely streams and glides. There is generally a good push of water coming through, except in very low water. Careysville (Clonulane) Weir, downstream of Fermoy, is one of the dominant features on the river. It controls the run of fish in low, cold water conditions and the fish will hold back, below the weir until there is a rise in the water. In high water, the weir is no impediment. Anglers say 'you can get a spring fish at Millstreet on opening day', meaning that there are always a few fish upstream of Fermoy early in the season.

Peak seasons for salmon
Spring Salmon: March/April
Grilse: June/July
Summer Salmon: July/August
Autumn Salmon: August/September

Season
Salmon and seatrout: 1 February–30 September
Brown trout: 15 February–30 September

Fishing methods
The Blackwater is a great multi-method salmon river. Spinning and flyfishing are allowed on all fisheries, but on some the use of worm and shrimp is prohibited. No one method is completely effective in all water conditions, though flyfishing is probably more generally effective than any other. Those who blindly place all their hopes in the natural shrimp are often disappointed and fishermen would be well advised to wait for clear water in July before fishing it (note national and local regulations).

Tube flies and Esmond Drury trebles are used for spring fishing and I have found a gold-bodied Willie Gunn tube fly especially effective. In summer, smaller flies (6–12) are more effective. Flies with a touch of yellow work well and favoured patterns include: Lemon & Grey, Silver Rat, Garry Dog, Munro Killer, Thunder & Lightning, Curry's Shrimp, Stoat's Tail, Blue Charm, Hairy Mary, Silver Stoat's Tail, McDermott's Badger and Curry's Red Shrimp.

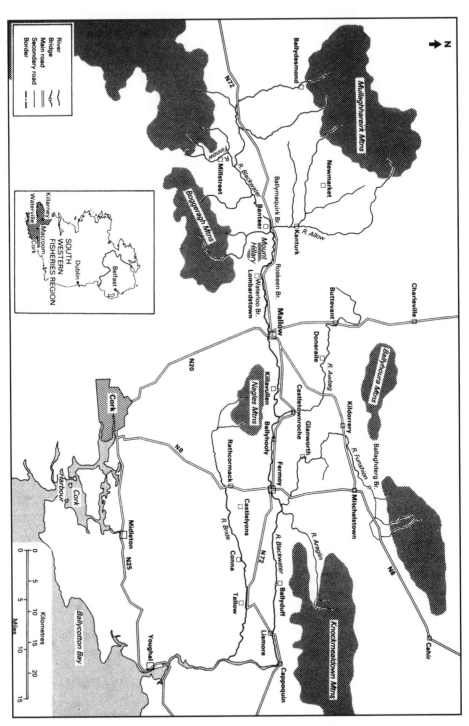

Cork Blackwater

The Blackwater is a river with a lot of streamy water, so it is not surprising to find that the spun shrimp is frequently used for summer fish. It is a method that requires the correct tackle and not a little skill.

For the spring and back end, Flying Cs (various weights) and Devons (up to 3 inches) are used. Smaller brown-and-gold Devons and Lane Minnows are favoured by some in summer.

THE BLACKWATER FISHERIES

Cappoquin Salmon & Trout Anglers' Association

The Cappoquin A.A. has some four miles of double-bank fishing on the tidal part of the river. This water holds a lot of fish particularly in August and September. It has some nice streamy water with many good holding areas. Much development work has been carried out in recent years, including instream enhancement with deflectors, stiles, a car park, etc.

The river is tidal here, so check with tide table for Cobh times and add one hour.

It is not really a spring fishery and the best of the fishing is from June onwards. The best fishing is probably in low water and the annual rod catch averages about 200 fish.

Wading is relatively safe. Have a wading stick and life jacket and beware of the rising tide.

Daily and weekly permits
Titelines Tackle Shop, Main Street, Cappoquin, Co. Waterford. Tel: 058 54152

Guides/local tackle shop
Titelines Tackle Shop (see above)
John O'Brien. Angling & Outdoor Centre, Westgate Retail Park, Tramore Road, Waterford
Gene Murphy, 26A Ballybricken, Waterford, Co. Waterford

Disabled anglers' facility
The Club now provides a boat suitable for disabled anglers.

Accommodation
Ballyrafter House Hotel, Lismore, Co. Waterford. Tel: 058 54002
Web: www.waterfordhotel.com

Fortwilliam Fishery

The Fortwilliam Fishery consists of two miles of double bank fishing plus a further two miles on the Lismore Estate. It has a good mix of pool and stream and is divided into four beats. The beats are rotated daily with three rods (max. four) per beat. Local anglers fish three evenings and on Saturdays on one beat. The river here fishes best in low water and favourite flies are shrimp patterns: Silver Stoat's Tail and Xmas Tree (sizes 6-8 in high water, 12-14 in low).

Fortwilliam rod catch 2000-2008

Year	2000	2001	2002	2003	2004	2005	2006	2007	2008
Salmon	300	294	256	183	516	337	308	303	445

During 1998 and 1999, the Fortwilliam Fishery embarked on large-scale river improvements involving major engineering works. This river work is ongoing. The river has fly pools separated by slower, deeper streams, suited to spinning. Wading is safe over a mainly level gravel bottom, except when the river is high. Waders may be preferred. Overhead casting is generally possible, but Spey casting is far preferable. Locally tied flies are readily available and are recommended. Both sinking and floating lines are required and a fast sink tip line is very useful.

September is the most prolific month for catches and the numbers build up from the end of May onwards. Single rod bookings may be available but will not be confirmed more than two weeks in advance.

Season
1 February–30 September

Permission
Paul Whelan, Fortwilliam, Glencairn, Lismore, Co. Waterford. Tel: 058 53748, mobile: 087 8292077, email: info@fortwilliamfishing.net, web: www.fortwilliamfishing.net

Tackle shops
John Murphy, Titelines Tackle Shop, Cappoquin, Co. Waterford. Tel: 058 54152

Lodge
There are two self-catering cottages on the Fortwilliam Estate, fully furnished, with private car parking.

Mocollop and Ballinaroone and Carrigane Fisheries

These are now all under one management. The former two are located 1½ miles from Ballyduff Bridge. Carrigane is two miles downstream, next to Fortwilliam. These fisheries offer the prospect of a spring fish and are all very productive summer and autumn salmon fisheries.

The annual catch is approximately 450 fish.

Bookings
Mrs Esta McCarthy, Elgin Cottage, Upper Ballyduff, Co. Waterford. Tel: 058 60255
Alfred Deppeler, Carrigane Crescent, Ballyduff Upper, Co. Waterford. Tel: 058 60278
Email: alfreddeppeler@eircom.ie, web: www.swissfishireland.com

Local guide
Alfred Deppeler (as above)

Lodge and accommodation
Mrs. Esta McCarthy (see above)

One from the Blackwater Lodge fishery

Blackwater Lodge

The lodge has sixteen beats, extending for some 40 miles from the lowest beat, 3 miles above the tide, upstream to Mallow. The lodge is located a mile west of the village of upper Ballyduff in Co. Waterford, between Lismore and Fermoy. It caters especially for angling parties and its facilities include a tackle shop, drying room and smoking and freezing facilities. All legal fishing methods are allowed. Glenda Powell, APGAI-IRL offers fly casting tuition and gillies can be arranged. The beats are rotated daily and each is about ¾ mile long. Up to four rods per beat are allowed (usually only two rods, when flyfishing).

Favourite flies

All types of shrimp flies, especially Ally's, Cascade, Bann Special, Apache and the classics such as Stoats, Silver Stoat, Silver Rat, Green Highlander and Thunder and Lightning.

Angling regulations

The Lodge doesn't allow worming until all of the kelts are safely out of the river – usually late March.

Permits

The Lodge issues permits to residents and day permits to non-resident anglers. State licences are available in the Lodge tackle shop.

Blackwater Lodge Hotel rod catch 2001–2008

Year	2001	2002	2003	2004	2005	2006	2007	2008
Salmon	773	769	553	1079	647	660	804	1025

The beats on this fishery are all single bank fishing. It has some lovely fly water, particularly Lower Kilmurray, Ballyhooly, Ballincurrig, Ballygally, Kents and the Wood Stream.

Season

1 February–30 September

Peak season

Spring salmon: March/April

Grilse: June/July

Summer salmon: July/August

Autumn salmon: August/September

Permission

Blackwater Lodge Fishery, Upper Ballyduff, Co. Waterford. Tel: 058 60235

Fax: 058 60162, email: info@ireland-salmon-fishing.net

web: www.ireland-salmon-fishing.net

Guides

Available through the Lodge

Tackle shop

At the Blackwater Lodge

Instructor

Glenda Powell APGAI-IRL, SH, DH, Blackwater Lodge (above)

Email: Glenda@ireland-salmon-fishing.net, mobile: 08723 51260

John Woodside APGAI-IRL, SH, DH, Shean Road, Ballyduff Upper, Co. Waterford

Tel: 05860414. Mobile: 0887644618

Accommodation

At the Hotel and self-catering cottages.

Kilbarry Syndicate Water

The syndicate's water consists of three beats, Upper Kilbarry, Middle Kilbarry and Kents. Beats one and three are excellent fly water while Middle Kilbarry is more suited to bait fishing. Usually, only two rods are allowed on the fly beats and in low water, the fishing is strictly fly-only.

Permission
Mr Gerry Dempsey, Mocollop, Upper Ballyduff, Co. Waterford. Tel: 058 60165
Mobile: 087 2527371

Local guide and flytyer
Doug Lock, Kilbarry Stud, Fermoy, Co. Cork. Tel: 025 32720, fax: 027 33000
Email: flyfish@eircom.net, web: www.speycast-ireland.com

Lodge/accommodation
Mrs. Esta McCarthy, Elgin Cottage, Upper Ballyduff, Co. Waterford. Tel: 058 60255

Careysville Fishery
Careysville is one of the best-known salmon fisheries in Ireland. It consists of 13/4
miles of double-bank fishing, with well-defined pools for flyfishing and spinning, at
Head, gillie's discretion. This is a magnificent fishery with good prospects of a fish
from opening day – 1 February – if water conditions are favourable. There is good
spring fishing in February and March with an excellent chance of fish on the fly when
the water drops to 3-foot on the gauge. The Cabin stream is one of the most challenging
and productive stretches of spring fish water I have ever fished and the Sand Hole must
be one of the finest grilse pools on the entire river. The maximum number of rods
allowed on the fishery is five.

There is a comfortable fishing hut (once a cricket pavilion) by the river bank in
which a hot lunch is served every day and where rods and tackle may be stored while
guests are staying.

Careysville rod catch 2001–2008

Year	2001	2002	2003	2004	2005	2006	2007	2008
Salmon	612	534	426	565	398	646	642	520

The fishing at Careysville is booked by the week: an all-inclusive package includes the
fishing and full board and accommodation in Careysville House.

Season
1 February–30 September

Bookings
Estate Office, Lismore Castle, Lismore, Co. Waterford. Tel: 058 54424, fax: 058 54896
email: lismoreestates@eircom.net or careysvillefishing@eircom.net

Local guides
Patrick Devennie, Head Gillie, Careysville House, Fermoy, Co. Cork
Two guides are in attendance Monday to Friday and a guide may also be arranged by
prior appointment at weekends.

Lodge
Careysville House, Lismore, Co. Waterford. Tel: 058 54424, fax: 058 54896
Email: lismoreestates@eircom.net. Member of the *Great Fishing Houses of Ireland
Group.*

FUNSHION, RIVER   R 80 02

The River Funshion rises in the Galtee Mountains, five miles N.N.E. of Kilbeheny on the slopes of Galteemore and flows south and west to join the River Gradoge a mile and a quarter west of Mitchelstown. From here it flows W.S.W. for almost five miles where it is joined by the River Sheep (Owenageragh River). At Glenavuddig Bridge, a mile further downstream, it begins to change direction and follows a generally south-easterly route for a further 25 miles to join the main channel of the River Blackwater 2 miles north-east of Fermoy. On this, its final stretch, the Funshion is joined by a number of minor streams and it skirts the town of Glanworth and passes just west of Kilworth.

Most of the main channel of the Funshion and much of the Cradoge pass over the floor of a limestone/lower limestone shale valley and this accounts for its alkaline nature (pH 7.2–8.4). The valleys of both rivers contain fertile agricultural land. Livestock-rearing, including the intensive rearing of pigs, is a feature of both catchments. Tillage is also important.

Mitchelstown Trout Anglers' Association controls the fishing from source to Carrigdonane Bridge – midway between Kildorrery and Glanworth. The river is easily accessible and trout stocks are good, ranging from 6oz–1½lb. Daytime fishing is best in spring; and evening fishing from mid-May. It has good hatches of olives and sedges.

Season
15 March–30 September

Permits
Dan Roche, Emoh-Ruo, Ballinwillin Inner, Mitchelstown, Co. Cork. Tel: 025 24980
Tom Lane, Sarsfield, Casey Drive, Mitchelstown, Co. Cork. Tel: 025 85258
Community Information Office, Mitchelstown, Co. Cork
David Lee, Kildorney, Co. Cork . Tel: 022 25595
Sean Dennehy, Kildorrery, Co. Cork. Tel: 022 25497

Regulations
Only thigh waders are permitted.
Worm fishing is prohibited and maggot fishing is illegal.
Minimum size: 9 inches.
Bag limit: 6 trout.

Kilworth/Glanworth Trout Anglers' Association
This Association has about seven miles of trout fishing from Moor Park to Charlie Burke's Bridge. There are a few prohibited areas on which the permit sales outlet will give information. Current stocks are small with trout of 8–12oz being the norm.

Information
Mr Gerry Keating, Chairman, Kilworth/Glanworth Trout Anglers' Association, Monadrishane, Kilworth, Co. Cork. Tel: 025 27461
Tom Whelan, Hon. Secretary, Kilworth/Glanworth Trout Anglers' Association, 11 Castle Park Avenue, Mallow, Co. Cork

Kildorrery Trout Anglers' Association

The Kildorrey Trout Anglers' Association has the fishing from Marshalstown Bridge to Moorpark. There is an excellent stock of trout and the average size is 9 inches.

Season

15 March–30 September

Permits

All anglers must have club membership, contact:
Mr G. O'Connor, Hon. Secretary, Kildorrey Trout Anglers' Association, Rockmills, Kildorrey, Co. Cork

Fermoy Salmon Anglers' Association

This association has about three miles of double bank fishing and 1¼ miles of single bank fishing which is divided into two beats for day permit holders. This is primarily a salmon fishery but no record is kept of catches. This is all mostly deep slow water extending from Fermoy Weir downstream to Clondulane Weir with a small piece of good spring fishing on the left bank below Careysville Weir. The most popular fishing methods are trolling spoons, spinning and bait fishing. It is mostly too deep for wading.

Information

Mr Tommy Butterworth, Ballyclough, Glanworth, Co. Cork

Ballyvolane Fishery

The Ballyvolane fishery consists of nearly ten miles of fishing on some of the best-known beats on the Cork Blackwater. These include two beats at Ballyhooley; Grange and the Quarry above Ballyhooley; Fallon's, at Killavullen; O'Neill's and Kilbarry, downstream of Careysville and Gaihra, at Ballyduff. Rods and waders can be hired, gillies are available and there is a small tackle shop.

Ballyvolane House is an award-winning country house. It also has three trout lakes within easy walking distance of the house. Two have rainbow trout and one has brown trout.

Ballyvolane Fishery rod catch 2004-2008

Year	2004	2005	2006	2007	2008
Salmon	98	63	54	165	86

Ballyvolane established a Fishing School in 2008 and the salmon fishing course is designed for up to four participants under the tuition of Norman Gillet, who is both a qualified instructor holding the Salmon & Trout Association National Instructors Certificate (STANIC) and a member of the Game Angling Instructors' Association (GAIA). All aspects of modern flyfishing and spinning techniques are covered but emphasis is placed on as much practical fishing as possible. The courses are spread over two days and three nights starting with dinner at Ballyvolane on the first night and finishing up after breakfast two days later.

Enquiries

Justin Green, Ballyvolane House, Castlelyons, Co. Cork. Tel: 025 36349
Fax: 025 36781, email: info@ballyvolanehouse.ie, www.ballyvolanehouse.ie

Lodge

Ballyvolane House, Castlelyons, Co. Cork. Tel: 025 36349, fax: 025 36781
Email: info@ballyvolanehouse.ie, www.ballyvolanehouse.ie

Fox's Fishery at Killavullen

Fox's is about ¾ mile long, left bank only, and is situated about a mile downstream of
Killavullen Bridge, some 10 miles west of Fermoy. It has a nice mix of streams and
pools, including the famous Poul Caum and is noted for both spring fish and grilse.
This is an excellent stretch of water. The big advantage of this fishery is that some part
of the beat is fishable at almost any height of water. It can take up to four rods, but the
proprietor only lets to single groups, so there may be only two or three rods fishing at
any one time.

Fox's Fishery rod catch 2001–2008

Year	2001	2002	2003	2004	2005	2006	2007	2008
Salmon	46	N/A	26	87	27	41	83	92

You can get a spring fish from 15 March but the main run goes through from 1 April.
Grilse appear early in May but expect to see them in increasing numbers from 1 June
and fresh autumn fish keep coming till the season closes on 30 September.

Following the drift net buy-out there was a big increase evident in stocks from July
to September in 2007 and 2008. There are signs of an improving spring run and in
2008 it was noticeable in June and early July that almost every fish caught was a fresh
10 or 12 pounder.

The fishery has a very good map of the pools as well as directions to the beat.

Bookings

Mr Dan O'Donovan, Craigside, Blackrock, Cork. Tel: 021 4358218 (evenings)

Killavullen Angling Club

The club has access to fishing near the village. The best of the trout fishing is from
April to August and salmon are also taken on the club water.

Enquiries

Mr Sean Flynn, Hon. Secretary, Killavullen Angling Club, Killavullen, Mallow,
Co. Cork.

Fox's Fishery at Killavullen: the angler is playing a salmon in 'The Clinkers'

AWBEG, RIVER

The Awbeg River is about 30 miles long and flows down from near Charleville in north Co. Cork, through Buttevant and Doneraile (where steeple chasing originated) and on through Shanballymore and Castletownroche, before joining the Blackwater downstream of Killavullen at Bridgetown Abbey. This is a lovely trout stream as anyone who has ever viewed it at Castletownroche will know. It is mainly spring-fed on limestone, with a good mix of stream and pool. Weed can be a problem in summer, especially upstream of Doneraile. It is a difficult river to flood, so the water is always clear.

Annes Grove Gardens, at Castletownroche, is a prohibited area for about one mile. The Awbeg holds an excellent stock of 9-inch trout, with bigger fish upstream of Doneraile. The relatively slow growth-rate of the Awbeg trout is ascribed to the low average water temperature. From Shanballymore, downstream to Castletownroche, the river holds very good stocks and bigger fish are caught upstream of Caramile Bridge to Buttavant. The river can be fished with wet- and dry-fly. In recent years, upstream nymph tactics and Czech nymphing has been growing in popularity, especially on the gravel runs.

Season
15 February–30 September

Tony McCarthy with a couple of fish from Poul Caum, Fox's fishery

Permission
David O'Donovan, Secretary, Shanballymore-Doneraile and Castletownroche Trout Angling Club, Shanballymore, Mallow, Co. Cork. Tel: 022 25545
Denis O'Mahony, Buttevant Trout Angling Club, Waterhouse, Knockenard, Buttevant, Co. Cork

Regulations
Fly-only
Minimum size: 9 inches
Bag limit: 6 trout

Local guide and flytyer
David O'Donovan (see above)

Tackle shops
Pat Hayes, Country Life Style, The Spa Square, Mallow, Co. Cork. Tel: 022 20121

Mallow Trout Anglers

Mallow Trout Anglers has access to about eight miles of fishing on the Blackwater. The club's fishing holds a good stock of trout to half-a-pound, with some to 2lb. An 8lb trout was caught recently by an angler spinning for salmon.

Season
1 February–30 September

Permission
Mr John Ruby, Hon. Secretary, Mallow Trout Anglers, 18 O'Sullivan Place, Mallow, Co. Cork

Tackle shop
Pat Hayes, Country Life Style, The Spa Square, Mallow, Co. Cork. Tel: 022 20121

Flytyer
Shane Kelly. Tel: 087 9808598

Longueville House Fishery

Longueville House has extensive salmon and trout fishing on the Blackwater, upstream of the town of Mallow.

Longueville House Fishery rod catch 2004–2008

Year	2004	2005	2006	2007	2008
Salmon	55	53	37	41	48

Fishing and accommodation enquiries
Longueville House, Mallow, Co. Cork. Tel: 022 47156, fax: 022 47459
Email: info@longuevillehouse.ie, web: www.longuevillehouse.ie. Member of the Great *Fishing Houses of Ireland Group*

Mallow Salmon and Trout Anglers' Association

The Mallow S&T AA has access to fishing on the river.

Information
Pat Hayes, Tackle Shop, The Spa Square, Mallow, Co. Cork. Tel: 022 20121

Lombardstown Trout Anglers' Association

Lombardstown Trout Anglers' Association has about four miles of double bank fishing on the Cork Blackwater. There are some restricted areas, which change from year to year, so up-to-date information should be sought. The river is not too big at this point. It has a natural appearance with little or no drainage-work despoilment. It has a good gradient, flowing over a stony bottom and weed growth is not a problem in summer. The water is quite clear, but holds its colour for a few days after a flood. Local anglers mostly fish wet flies. The river holds a good stock of trout to 12oz and some to a pound. March and April fishing can be very good. Access is good with more stiles provided every year.

Season
15 February–30 September

Permission and guide
Declan Noonan, Pallas, Lombardstown, Mallow, Co. Cork. Tel: 022 47285/47572

Regulations
Flyfishing only and all trout under 9 inches must be returned.

Accommodation
Longueville House, Longueville, Mallow, Co. Cork. Tel: 022 47156

Tackle shops
Pat Hayes, Tackle Shop, The Spa Square, Mallow, Co. Cork. Tel: 022 20121
John O'Sullivan, Tackle Shop, Mallow Road, Kanturk, Co. Cork. Tel: 029 50257

Ballymaquirk Fishery and Lodge
The fishery is located at Ballymaquirk Bridge between Kanturk and Banteer. It consists of 1 km on the left bank of the Blackwater and ½ km of the Allow.

The fishery is one of few which have a full-time Manager/Water Keeper. Since the arrival of Stephen's Glaves two years ago, a great amount of improvement works have been carried out. Two weirs have been resurrected, banks and old weirs have been repaired and five new pools developed. Bank clearing and river works have also been undertaken in the Allow, which now holds a good head of summer fish.

The improvement works have resulted in a dramatic increase in the number of spring fish as well as grilse being caught. It is expected that, because of the Drift Net ban, 2009 and future years will continue to show larger numbers of fish returning to the river. Certainly the number of spawning fish has increased in the last two years.

Ballymaquirk is a 3-rod, fly-only fishery. Stephen is happy to advise and will provide tutelage if requested. Catch-and-release is recommended. There is very easy access to the pools and wading is unnecessary. There is excellent brown trout fishing as well.

Rods are let on a daily or weekly basis. The lodge is not now being let. There is good guest accommodation nearby, with pubs, restaurants, golf, riding, etc. in the locality.

Flies
Ally's Shrimp, Blue Shrimp, Cascade, Comet, Silver Stoat

Booking
Stephen Glaves, Ballymaquirk Lodge, Banteer, Co. Cork. Tel: 086 4081911
Email: brianmoc@haranka.com, web: www.ballymaquirk.com

ALLOW, RIVER (AND DALLOW RIVER)

The Allow and Dallow rivers converge at Kanturk and join the Blackwater a further three miles south, a short distance downstream of Ballymaquirk Bridge. These are spate rivers, with fast runs and occasional pools. They hold fair stocks of small brown trout. The best fishing months are in spring, March to May and at the back end, in September. Recommended wet flies include Greenwell Spider, Williams Favourite, March Brown Spider, Red Spinner, Black & Silver and the Partridge series of flies.

Season
15 February – 30 September

Permission
Thomas Lofts, Hon. Secretary, Kanturk Trout Anglers' Association, Highgreenane, Kanturk, Co. Cork

Local guide and flytyer
John O'Sullivan. Tel: 029 50257

Millstreet Trout & Game Anglers
The club has about six miles of trout and salmon fishing in the vicinity of the town. It is primarily a brown trout fishery but can also produce salmon after a flood in September.

Permission
The fishing is reserved for members only, contact:
Billy O'Donoghue, Club Secretary, Millstreet Trout & Game Anglers, Drishane View, Millstreet, Co. Cork. Tel: 029 71384

Upper Blackwater Anglers' Association
The Upper Blackwater Angers' Association has about ten miles of fishing on the river on the Cork-Kerry border, in the vicinity of Ballydesmond and Rathmore. The banks in the upper two miles are boggy and the remaining eight miles are mostly pasture-land. The river here consists of fast streams and some lively flats. The trout are small, ranging from 3oz to a pound, and there can be an excellent rise on summer evenings. The best evening fishing is from mid-May to the end of July and a dry sedge can produce the occasional trout to 2lb. There are very good stocks of trout upstream of Duarigle Bridge, but there are plenty of trout all over the stretch. Access is good at the seven bridges and waders are essential. Partridge & Orange and Partridge & Yellow are two of the most effective flies on the river.

Season
15 February–30 September

Permits
Visitors must obtain associate membership of the Association from:
Benny O'Dea, 1 The Terrace, Knocknagree, Co. Cork.Tel: 064 58145
John O'Connor, Restaurant, Knocknagree,Co. Cork

Regulations
Strictly flyfishing only.

Local guides
Pat Cotter, Knocknagallane, Rathmore, Co. Cork. Tel: 064 58484

Three beautiful Blackwater fish (above and below) for Doug Lock, fishing the Kilbarry beat

Tackle shop and flytyer
John O'Sullivan, Kanturk, Co. Cork. Tel: 029 50257

ARAGLIN, RIVER

The Araglin flows southwards past the villages of Kishkeam and Cullen to join the Blackwater at Shamrock Bridge, about three miles downstream of Rathmore. It is about 15 miles long and, I reckon, must have more bends than any other river in Ireland. Furthermore, the whole area around it has some kind of carboniferous base and it doesn't at all surprise me that it holds trout of two and three pounds.

Season
15 February–30 September

Permits
Mr John J. Murphy, Hon. Secretary, Araglin Anglers' Association, Cullen, Mallow, Co. Cork

Regulations
Strictly fly-only

BRIDE, RIVER (TALLOW) also known as the NORTH BRIDE   W 99 93

The River Bride rises in the Nagle Mountains in central Co. Cork and flows easterly through Cork and Waterford before entering the Munster Blackwater well down in the tidal waters, three miles from Youghal Bay. It generally holds a good head of water, which is typical of the Blackwater tributaries. In nature, it is made up of numerous runs of fast water and glides into deep holes formed from the winter floods. A single handed 8ft–10ft fly rod, rated for an AFTM 6 line, is suitable for the whole of the Bride. This river differs from its sister rivers in its being tidal right up to Tallow Bridge. The tidal influence can have important effects on the salmon and seatrout fishing during low water. Migratory fish will often hold in the tidal reaches until rain or high water allows them to run.

Throughout the season, flyfishing for brown trout provides great sport. The trout rise freely to traditional wet-fly patterns, which is the preferred method by the locals. At low summer levels, a dry-fly can produce quite unexpected rewards. The upper and middle Bride, around Castlelyons and Conna, have excellent dry-fly waters.

The Bride has a lot of small wild brown trout of about 4oz–6oz. However, there are quite a few larger fish of around ¾lb. The trout are well-marked and hard-fighting when fished for on light tackle.

Although there are salmon in the river throughout the season, the Bride is considered to be a late river. The main runs begin with the grilse in June. All legal methods of salmon fishing are allowed: worming, spinning and shrimping are by far the most common methods used. Most of the salmon caught on the fly are usually taken by people fishing for brown trout or seatrout. Small low-water salmon flies should prove successful.

The seatrout also enter the river in late June/July. Locals reckon that the larger fish come in first. In high water, both salmon and seatrout will run through into the upper reaches. In low water, salmon and seatrout fishing is mostly confined to the lower and tidal stretches of the Tallow Club water. The standard seatrout flies all take fish: Teal, Blue & Silver; Peter Ross; Butchers (various); Royal Coachman, etc. Most patterns with some sparkle from a silver rib should prove successful.

Season
Salmon and seatrout: 1 February–30 September
Brown trout: 15 February–30 September

There are five angling clubs on the River Bride, an indication of its worth and the quality of the fishing.

Upper Bride Anglers' Association
The club has fly-only fishing at the top of the river. This water has some lovely streams and there are trout to ¾lb.

Local contacts
Mr Padraig Fitzgerald, Church Road, Glenville, Co. Cork. Tel: 021 4880398

Rathcormac Trout Anglers' Association
The Rathcormac Trout Anglers have about seven miles of fishing. Their water holds a good stock of free-rising trout, with good hatches of olives and sedges in season.

Enquiries
John Drinan, Hon. Secretary, Rathcormac Trout Anglers' Association, Moulane West, Rathcormac, Co. Cork. Tel: 087 2144838

Castlelyons Trout Anglers' Association
The association has a stretch of about a mile which provides excellent dry-fly fishing in April.

Enquiries
Pat Collins, Hon. Secretary, Castlelyons Trout Anglers' Association, 24 Hillside View, Castlelyons, Co. Cork

Conna Trout Anglers' Association
This association has about five miles of fishing with good stocks of trout to about 11 inches. April and May is best for daytime fishing and there is great evening fishing from June to August.

Enquiries
Michael Budds, Hon. Secretary, Conna Trout Anglers' Association, Copper Alley, Youghal, Co. Cork

The Ballymaquirk Fishery on the Cork Blackwater

Day permits
English's Shop, Conna, Co. Cork
The Fisherman's Rest Pub, Conna, Co. Cork

Tallow and District Angling Club
The Tallow club has about five miles of fishing, much of which is tidal. This water can produce a lot of seatrout, particularly from the deep pools near the bridge at Tallow. It also gets a fair run of salmon.

Mr Ian McEntosh, Hon. Secretary, Tallow and District Angling Club, Tallow Hill, Tallow, Co. Waterford. Tel: 050 432909

Day permits
Forde's Spar Shop, Main Street, Tallow, Co. Waterford

Tackle shop
Tight Lines, Main Street, Cappoquin, Co. Waterford

Guide
Patrick Henley, 13 New Street, Tallow, Co. Waterford. Tel: 058 56435

Accommodation
Latch Restaurant, Main Street, Tallow, Co. Waterford

9. South-Western Fisheries Region

The South-Western Fisheries Region extends from Kerry Head south and then east to Ballycotton and covers the greater part of Counties Kerry and Cork. The fisheries of the region are administered from the headquarters of the South-Western Regional Fisheries Board:

South-Western Regional Fisheries Board, Sunnyside House, Masseytown, Macroom, Co. Cork. Tel: 026 41221, fax: 026 41223, email: swrfb@swrfb.ie
Web: www.swrfb.com

In addition to its great natural beauty the region's rivers are especially rich in salmon and seatrout. Spring salmon enter some of the river systems from early January. Grilse – locally referred to as 'peal' – are plentiful and large early season seatrout are a special feature of the south-west. A few systems hold good-quality brown trout.

Note:
Rivers marked ** are – at the time of writing – closed for salmon fishing, and seatrout over 40cm must be returned.
Rivers marked * are catch-and-release for salmon, and seatrout over 40cm must be returned.

For up-to-date information on these closed and catch-and-release rivers, see:
www.cfb.ie or **www.fishinginireland.info**

Accommodation

For your hotel, lodge and bed and breakfast accommodation, see:
Failte Ireland South West, Aras Failte, Grand Parade, Cork, Co. Cork. Tel: 021 4255100
Email: corkkerryinfo@failteireland.ie, web: www.discoverireland.ie/southwest

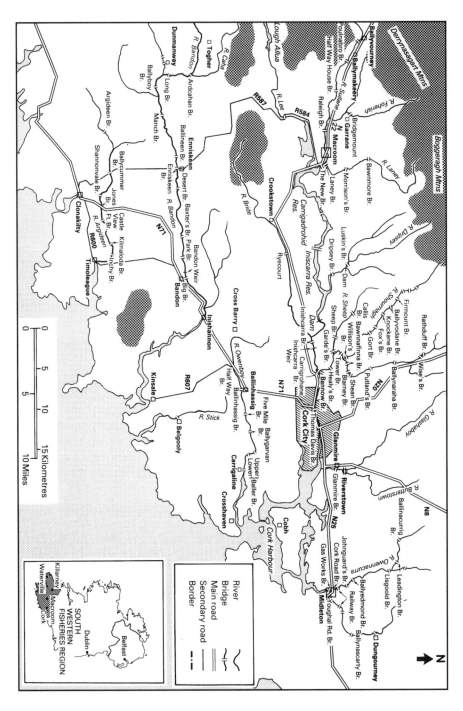

The rivers Owennacurra, Lee, Bandon and Argideen

OWENNACURRA, RIVER   W 87 74

The Owennacurra River flows for 14 miles in a southerly direction through Midleton into Cork Harbour. It drains a catchment of 66 sq. miles. Much of the land along the river is under tillage.

It is regarded primarily as a seatrout fishery. It gets a few grilse in July and August, but the numbers are so small they are not worth fishing for specifically. Strangely enough, the river gets a good run of salmon outside the season from November to January. It holds big stocks of very small brown trout.

Access is good, with the R626 Midleton–Rathcormack road running close to the bank and bridges at about one mile intervals.

A small number of big seatrout come in May, but the peak of the run is in June, July and through August and September. The seatrout fishing has improved out of all recognition in recent years: so much so, that some now consider it one of the best in the south-west region.

In low water, fishing is confined to the lower section – downstream from the Gas Works Bridge – and there is also excellent fishing upstream to the Cork Road Bridge. After a spate, it is worth fishing up as far as Ballyedmond Bridge and there are five or six good pools in the vicinity of John Guard's Bridge. The majority of the seatrout are small (12oz) and the annual catch is said to be about 1,000 fish and on the increase.

The majority of local anglers fish a fly at night. Some persist from dusk to dawn. The favourite patterns are Peter Ross, Teal Blue & Silver, Watson's Fancy and Silver Jungle Cock. Visiting anglers are welcome.

The river holds a big stock of free-taking brown trout averaging seven inches, with better fish up to 1lb. It is no longer stocked with brown trout to improve the fishing. The best of the fishing is from Cork Road Bridge up to Lisgoold Bridge – a distance of about 4 miles. After a spate, the river can be fished up to Ballincurrig Bridge. The banks are overgrown in places and there is room for a lot of development work. The best of the fishing is in late April, May and June, with evening fishing during the summer. Wet-fly and dry-fly fishing tactics both have a place and the trout can sometimes respond in a very lively fashion.

Season
Salmon: 1 February–30 September
Seatrout: 1 February–12 October
Brown trout: 15 February–12 October

Permission
Midleton and District Anglers' Association has the goodwill of the fishing. The Hon. Secretary is Ned Reck, Old Rocky Road, Midleton, Co. Cork. Up-to-date information and membership cards are available from T. H. Sports in Midleton.

Tackle shop
T. H. Sports, Main Street, Midleton, Co. Cork

ROXBORO (DUNGOURNEY), RIVER   W 90 74

The Roxboro River rises north of Dungourney and flows south and then west before entering the same estuary as the Owennacurra River. It is a small stream, about nine miles long, and the fishable stretches are about four yards wide. It flows through countryside dominated by tillage and pastureland. It holds some good brown trout and gets a small run of seatrout. About 200 seatrout are taken annually.

The seatrout fishing stretch is about half-a-mile long and is situated immediately upstream of Youghal Road Bridge as far as the distillery (Irish Distillers). The access is through the town park at a place called 'The Baby's Walk'. The banks are clear and there is room for about six anglers. The best of the fishing is usually in July and August.

The best of the brown trout fishing is from Ballynascarty up as far as Dungourney. Midway along this stretch there are some nice pools at Ballynacole. There are trout here up to a pound. It is lightly fished and said to be well worth a visit. A basket of half a dozen trout is a distinct possibility. Access is off the R627 Midleton–Dungourney road.

Season
Salmon: 1 February–30 September
Seatrout: 1 February–12 October
Brown trout: 15 February–12 October

Permission
Midleton and District Anglers' Association has the goodwill of the fishing.

Hon. Secretary, Ned Reck, Old Rocky Road, Midleton, Co. Cork. Tel: 086 0576744

Up-to-date information and membership cards are available from:
T. H. Sport, Main Street, Midleton, Co. Cork

GLASHABOY, RIVER   W 72 75

The Glashaboy River (15 miles long), with its main tributary, the Butterstown River, drains a 38 sq. mile catchment and flows through a heavily-wooded valley through the village of Glanmire into the Lee estuary. It is a spate river, noted for its huge runs of seatrout, which begin about the third week of June every year. The angling stretch is from Glanmire village up to the confluence at Riverstown, a distance of about a mile. The pools are deep and slow-moving – Poulcaum, the Rocky Hole, the Long Reach and the Barleycorn Pool. The water quality is good. The river supplies the Glashaboy Water Works, a secondary system to the Lee Reservoir, so quality is monitored on a 24-hour basis by Cork County Council. However, when pumping is in progress during low water, a noted decrease in flows seems to put the fish down.

The Glashaboy River's main attraction is the excellent runs of seatrout and its suitability for night fishing. Since the fish pass has been built, and court-appointed Water-keeper Warrants obtained with the help of the SWRFB, there has been a huge improvement in the numbers of seatrout returning. The large fish thrash about the pools after dark and give any dedicated night fly angler the enthusiasm to stay well into the small hours when the best sport is enjoyed. Fishing is concentrated in the area from the John Barleycorn Pool to Glanmire Bridge. Much work has been done in recent years to improve the angling amenity. This has been done with the help of the local Community Association and Cork County Council and under the guidance of the Fishery Board. The next phase will include angling platforms and pathways for physically challenged and wheelchair anglers. The 'in-stream work' will include strategically placed natural rock boulders to improve flows and cover and, also, a number of vortex weirs to be established below the main fish pass.

For the past two years, we have seen a return in good numbers of the very large seatrout, up to specimen size which is 6lb. It is extremely encouraging to the angler to hear these big fish are splashing about the pools at night. The river comes alive after dark in the summer months from about the second week in June. Sport begins to fade towards the end of August, but some good nights can still be had up to the end of the season. There has also been a noted increase in the amount of salmon/grilse running during the summer months but few fall victim to the fly. Popular seatrout patterns include: Silver Rail, Teal Blue & Silver, Peter Ross, White Moth, Muddler, Coachman and Medicine.

Wading is generally safe in the lower beat in Glanmire but, as with all rivers, there are some deep sections. Anglers should familiarize themselves with the river in daylight and exercise caution. It is also wise to have a companion while night fishing. The John Barleycorn Pool and the long reach has some very deep sections over 10 feet deep. The water intake area near the Pump House is excavated regularly, it is very deep and silty and is definitely not suited for wading. In general, all the river can easily be covered from the bank and this is to be recommended since it is also less likely to disturb the fish.

All night anglers are reminded not to use bright white light torches on the river. Small, red filtered pencil torches provide sufficient light for fly changing, etc., but are less likely to spook the fish or offend fellow anglers.

Access to the river bank is quite easy, with steps in the riverside wall at Glanmire; at the country park further up and at Riverstown village opposite the John Barleycorn Hotel.

The Butterstown River is a fast flowing and rocky tributary. The banks are wooded and overgrown. The pools in the lower reaches hold fish but are not fished much because of the difficult bankside conditions.

Season
Salmon: 1 February–30 September
Seatrout: 1 February–12 October

Permission
Enquire – local tackle shops

Disabled anglers' facility
A wheelchair access pathway in Riverstown Park is under construction. Phase 2 will have extended pathways to river edge and defined/designated disabled angler platforms. It is hoped that this work will have been completed in 2002.

Local tackle shops
T. W. Murray & Co. Ltd, 87 Patrick Street, Cork. Tel: 021 4271089
Cork Angling Centre, Kinsale Road Roundabout, Cork. Tel: 021 4321000

Local flytyers
Billy Creedon. Tel: 021 4502836, email: billyc2@eircom.net
Edward Lyall. Tel: 021 812847, email: eddielyall@eircom.net

Local fishing lodge/accommodation
Vienna Woods Hotel, Glanmire, Cork. Tel: 021 4821146

John Barleycorn Hotel, Riverstown, Cork. Tel: 021 44821499

LEE, RIVER   W 60 71

The River Lee rises in a wild and lovely mountainous region near Gauganebarra in west Cork and flows 56 miles due east and through the city of Cork. The Lee and its tributaries drain a catchment of 484 sq. miles. The Lee and some of the tributaries rise high in the mountains before reaching a terrain of alternating moorland and small farms. The valleys were flooded after the erection of two dams for hydroelectric power generation in 1956. The resulting elongated reservoirs stretch for approximately 16 miles and have obliterated miles of river fishing from Inniscarra Dam to Macroom and above.

The erection of the dams appears to have interfered greatly with the free passage of fish, particularly salmon, and it is alleged that while some salmon make it through the fish pass very few smolts survive to go back to sea. In order to supplement the smolt run, the Electricity Supply Board built a hatchery at Carrigadrohid and is committed to stocking 136,000 smolts annually into the river.

Salmon fishing is now confined to an eight-mile stretch of river, reaching from Inniscarra Dam to the centre of Cork City. The progeny of the generous stocking programme, together with the wild smolts ensures a very substantial run of both spring salmon and grilse and provides some of the best salmon fishing in Ireland. It is difficult to get accurate statistics for the various fisheries, but a figure well in excess of 1,000 salmon to rod-and-line is possible in good seasons. Of these, possibly a half would be spring fish. According to Fishery Board staff, the spring fishing is improving. The catch of spring fish in 2001 was one of the best ever.

The peak of the run is usually in the last two weeks in March and continues into early May. A lot of fish are caught then, even on high water. Flyfishers use tube flies dressed on brass tubes from 1½–2½ inches and fast sinking and sink tip lines, depending on the height of the water. Others spin, or fish worm, or shrimp. The grilse run peaks in mid June/early July and the river continues to fish through August and September. Small flies (sizes 8-14) and light tackle give good sport and favourite patterns are Thunder & Lightning, Blue Charm, Silver Stoats Tail, Hairy Mary and various shrimp patterns, including the Bann Special and Curry's Red shrimp.

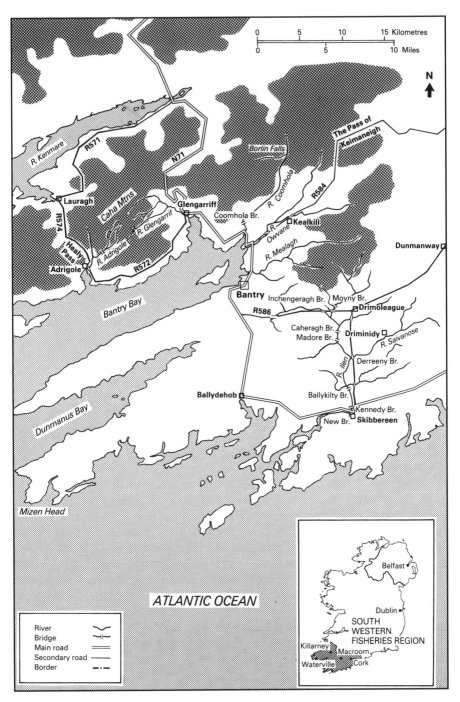

The West Cork rivers

The average weight of spring fish is 10lb and the grilse are small, averaging about 4lb. There is a nice mix of water on the various fisheries with streams, pools and flats. The local angling associations have done much to improve the waters by way of constructing weirs and groynes, deepening streams and clearing bank cover.

The fisheries are located in an environment of woodlands, pasture lands and, finally, an urban setting. The level of the water is artificially controlled and the flow depends on how many E.S.B. turbines are in operation. Local anglers actually talk in terms of 'megawatt flows': 1½MW is low flow; 4MW equates to nice fly water; 15MW is for spinning and 19MW is a 'full load'. As is the case on all rivers, the periods just before the water rises and after it drops are considered the best taking times.

Brown trout
The river holds a fair stock of beautifully marked, pink-fleshed brown trout in the three-quarters to a pound-and-a-half range. As with all rivers where salmon are the primary attraction, the trout fishing is virtually ignored. The best of the day fishing is in May and June and there is good evening fishing during the summer. Both angling associations accommodate genuine flyfishing trout anglers.

Season
Salmon: 1 February–30 September
Brown trout: 15 February–12 October

Permission
Most of the fishing is controlled by clubs and the E.S.B. There is, however, a 3-mile stretch of free fishing.

The controlling parties are:

(i) Cork Salmon Anglers' Association
Cork Salmon Anglers' Association is a limited company with 50 shareholders and it grants 30 annual permits. It also welcomes bone fide tourist anglers and salmon fishing day permits are available from:

John Buckley, Raheen House, Carrigrohane, Co. Cork. Tel 021 4872137

Day permits are also available for trout fishing, at a nominal fee, but anglers must seek permission.

The Association's fisheries are in three sections: the left bank above and below Inishcarra Bridge; the right bank below the same bridge; and up near the dam on the left bank.

This is a club fishery with no facility for outsiders with the exception of day permits and tourist anglers who are given access to an upper section of the fishery only. There is a bag limit of two fish per day.

Fishing the Sheen Falls Lodge water on the Sheen river

(ii) **Lee Salmon Anglers' Club**
The club limits membership to 70 and issues 70 annual permits. Day permits for tourists are available for fishing Monday to Friday from:

Paul Lawton, Secretary, Lee Salmon Anglers' Club. Mobile: 086 8500146
Ken Stout, Chairman, Lee Salmon Anglers' Club. Mobile: 086 8042923

(iii) **Electricity Supply Board Fishery**
The ESB Fishery is located at Inniscarra Dam and extends downstream for about half-a-mile and takes 12 rods. It is very productive, with a tally of 200 salmon in 2001. Permits are available from:

Dan O'Riordan, ESB Amenity Warden. Mobile: 087 7506605
Brown's Garage (beside Inniscarra Bridge), Inniscarra, Co. Cork

(iv) **Free fishing**
There is free fishing on a three mile stretch extending upstream from the first weir above the tide and up through the Lee Fields, for approximately three miles. Some of this water is deep and slow but, in low water conditions, the stretch between the two weirs at the bottom is one of the most productive stretches on the River Lee.

N.B. The ESB Fishery at Fitzgerald Park is closed to fishing (at the time of writing) for conservation reasons.

Tackle shops
Cork Angling Centre, Kinsale Road Roundabout, Cork. Tel: 021 4321000
T. W. Murray & Co. Ltd, 87 Patrick Street, Cork. Tel: 021 4271089
Peter Horne, Blarney, Co. Cork

MARTIN, RIVER   W 60 80

The Martin is a small brown-trout river, 11 miles long and about 15 yards across at its widest point. It rises north-north-west of Cork City and flows in a southerly direction, through Blarney, to join the River Shournagh, a tributary of the Lee. Access to the river is easy, with roads running close to the river banks. The banks are wooded and very overgrown and fishing can be difficult. It was once considered to be one of the best brown trout rivers on the Lee System but persistent overfishing has greatly reduced both the quality and quantity of the stocks. The average size of the trout is about 6oz, though some grow to about 2lb in the stretch at Blarney Bridge and again up between Wise's Bridge and Rathduff Bridge. This latter section is very overgrown. From Blarney Bridge up to Wise's Bridge has a lot of fishable water.

On the River Martin the 'Wood Bee' is fished – a local method of dapping the natural fly which, to my knowledge, is unique to this area. I am indebted to Dr D.P. Sleeman of the Department of Zoology and Animal Ecology at University College, Cork (U.C.C.) who tells me that the Wood Bee is in fact sp. polietes lardaria of the order Diptera. He also tells me that the flies are common in June and July, and on warm days they can be trapped in boxes (in woodland) using cow dung as bait. The local practice is to use these plentiful natural flies as a very effective 'dap'.

Season
Brown trout: 15 February–12 October

Permission
Free

SHOURNAGH, RIVER   W 60 74

The Shournagh rises at an altitude of 1,000 feet and rushes and tumbles for about 17 miles, passing to the west of Blarney Castle, before entering the Lee at Leemount Bridge. It holds a large stock of brown trout up to about 9 inches, with some better fish downstream, where it is joined by the River Martin. There is a nice pool below Bannow Bridge and some good water above it. The rest of this stretch, up to Healy's Bridge, is sluggish, but there is a bit of nice water below the bridge. From Healy's Bridge to the golf course is very overgrown and suitable only for spinning. However, from the golf course (on the left bank) up to Tower Bridge it is possible to flyfish. There is a piece of fly water at the confluence and the rest is spinning water. A lot of the water from Willison's Bridge up to Gort Bridge is suitable for flyfishing and all is easily accessible from the road. The section below Fox's Bridge has some decent pools but is very overgrown, although there is a nice stretch of fly water for two fields above Fox's Bridge. From Knockane Bridge to Ballyvodane Bridge is a favourite stretch, suitable for flyfishing, with nice open water and a good stock of 8–9 inch trout. It also holds a limited number of nice trout to 1½lb. The river becomes very overgrown above Ballyvodane Bridge and it is not worth the effort trying to fish any further upstream.

April, May and June are considered the best months.

Season
Brown trout: 15 February–12 October

Permission
Free

Tackle shop
Angling Supplies, Killard, Blarney, Co. Cork

OWENNAGEARAGH (OR SHEEP), RIVER   W 57 74

The Owennagearagh or Sheep River is about seven miles long and joins the River Shournagh west of Blarney. It holds a good stock of brown trout between Garde's Bridge and Ballyshoneen Bridge, but they are very small. There is a section of clear bank suitable for flyfishing upstream of Garde's Bridge and a clear section on the right bank above Sheep Bridge. The Yellow House is a well-known landmark and there is a nice piece of fishing downstream from Callis Bridge for a couple of miles. The banks are reasonably clear and it is possible to wade.

Season
Brown trout: 15 February–12 October

Permission
Free

Note
Blarney and District Trout Anglers' Association has an interest in the fishing on the Rivers Martin, Shournagh and Owennagearagh. For information, contact:
Francis O'Riordan, Hon. Secretary, Blarney and District Trout Anglers' Association, 43 Hibernian Buildings, Albert Road, Cork

N.B. While these rivers are regarded as 'free' fishing, it is well to consult riparian owners, just to make sure.

DRIPSEY, RIVER   W 49 73

The River Dripsey is 14 miles long and feeds Inniscarra Reservoir, west of Coachford. It holds a good stock of 10 inch to 13 inch brown trout. It is most suited to wet-fly fishing, with the best of the fishing being in the lower reaches. A dam a couple of miles up from the reservoir possibly prevents the migration of reservoir trout upstream, late in the season, but there is some very good dry-fly fishing in the last mile up from the lough in summer.

Season
Brown trout: 15 February–12 October

Permission
Free

SULLANE, RIVER	**W 33 73**
LANEY, RIVER	**W 36 73**
FOHERISH AND FINNOW RIVERS	**W 29 76**

It is best to deal with these four rivers together as the Macroom Fly Anglers' Association. The Fishery Board and local organisations are carrying out development work and trying to assist the trout stocks to recover after years of bad fishing practice.

The **Sullane River** and its tributaries drain the western slopes of the Derrynasaggart Mountains. The river has some lovely features and flows for 23 miles in an easterly direction, through Ballyvourney and Macroom into Carrigadrohid Reservoir. It is mainly a moorland river flowing over sandstone.

The Sullane holds a good stock of brown trout from Ballyvourney downstream, averaging just over half-a-pound, but it also gets a run of larger fish up from the reservoir and 1½lb trout are not uncommon. In 2001, a 4½lb trout was taken and several of 2lb. The good trout are generally found in localized populations. Why this should be, nobody knows. It fishes well right through the season and there can be good flyfishing there on summer evenings – which can last till midnight – through July and August.

The fishing extends upstream as far as Ballyvourney and the most popular stretches are from the New Bridge upstream to Macroom; a stretch upstream of Raleigh Bridge on the right bank; a half-mile stretch on the right bank downstream of the Half-Way House Bridge; and a stretch on the right bank upstream of Poul na Bro Bridge.

The Sullane has hatches of various olives, the iron blue, blue-winged olives, stoneflies and sedges. Popular fly patterns for wet-fly fishing include Greenwell's Spider, Greenwell's Glory (with an emerald green body), Orange Grouse, Red Spinner, small sedge patterns and all the Partridge family. The lower sections give the best fishing for the bigger fish but, upriver, the fishing can be very good as it is not as heavily fished. Wading is not difficult and chest waders are a must for the serious dry-fly fisher.

The **Laney River** is 15 miles long and joins the Sullane River three miles east of Macroom. It is a fast-flowing moorland stream and has the reputation of having trout of the highest average weight of all the Lee tributaries. The banks are very overgrown up to Morrison's Bridge, but this stretch has some good pools. From Bawnmore Bridge downstream, the banks are reasonably clear of obstructions, except for a stretch immediately above Morrison's Bridge. It is not really worth fishing above Morrison's Bridge. Dry-fly is best but some wet-fly fishing is done after a spate. The Laney is a lovely clean river and not overfished. It holds plenty of trout but they are small – the best one taken in 2001 was about 1½lb. Prime fishing is from Morrison's Bridge down to where it joins the Sullane. Chest waders would be a great asset but be careful as the bottom is very rocky and uneven. Hatches and artificial flies as for the River Sullane.

The **Foherish** and **Finnow Rivers** have their confluence about two miles before joining the River Sullane, near Macroom. They hold small trout in the upper reaches but there are some good pools and nice glides in the lower reaches. The best fishing is after a spate to wet-fly, though some very good sport can be had with the dry-fly in the late evening in June, July and August.

The Macroom Fly Anglers' Association has waters on all these four rivers.

Season
1 April–30 September

Permission
Tom Sweeney, Honorary Secretary, Macroom Fly Anglers' Association, Mary Anne's Bar, Masseytown, Macroom, Co. Cork
The Mills Inn, Ballyvourney, Co. Cork
McCarthy's Newsagent, Main Street, Macroom, Co. Cork

The Angling Association requests that anglers purchase permits as the proceeds go towards river development.

Note
On some of the upper reaches, permission of the riparian owners is required.

Regulations
Bag Limit: 4 trout
Minimum Size: 10 inches
No ground baiting
One rod per angler

Local guides
Tom Sweeney, Mary Anne' Bar, Masseytown, Macroom, Co. Cork. Tel: 026 41566
Denis Cronin, Dromree, Macroom, Co. Cork. Mobile: 086 1713909

Local tackle shop
Mary Anne's Bar, Masseytown, Macroom, Co. Cork

Local flytyers
Tom Sweeney (see above)

BRIDE (SOUTH), RIVER   W 55 70

The River Bride (South) rises in west Cork and meanders for nearly 20 miles through Crookstown, Ryecourt and Ovens, to join the River Lee upstream of Inishcarra Bridge. The upper reaches flow over sandstone and the middle and lower stretches lie on limestone. It is a very lovely and productive river and holds a really excellent stock of small fat brown trout. The average size is probably just under half-a-pound, but it can produce some better fish to as much as 1½lb. This is a lovely trout stream, with pools and riffles and meanders. It can be fished to well above Crookstown and, indeed, some of the best fishing on summer evenings is from there down to Ryecourt. The rise of trout can be spectacular. Access is mainly from the bridges. Angling pressure can be heavy at weekends, particularly in spring, but it is not usually overcrowded for the evening rise on weekdays during the summer. It has all the usual fly hatches found on a limestone river, except mayfly. The Bride gets a big run of salmon but they don't arrive till after the season closes.

Season
Brown trout: 15 February–12 October

Permission
Riparian owners. Much of it is considered free.

OWENBOY, RIVER   W 70 62

The Owenboy flows some five miles south of Cork City. It is about 14 miles long and mostly slow-flowing and sluggish. It flows eastwards through Ballinhassig and Carrigaline and empties into Cork Harbour at Crosshaven through a narrow 4½ mile long estuary. It is primarily regarded as a seatrout fishery up to Ballinhassig and produces over 500 seatrout annually. Sadly, at the time of writing, seatrout stocks are really in decline. The best of the fishing is through July, August and September.

The seatrout are fished for mainly at night and flyfishers favour the Butcher, Silver Rail and Teal, Blue & Silver. Prime fishing locations are at the Pier Hole, the estuary and the flats below John A. Wood's gravel pit, near Ballygarvan Bridge, but a lot of drainage work has been carried out here recently.

The salmon fishing is unpredictable and the run is small, with a good percentage of the summer fish being stray ESB fish from the Lee. Most of the salmon are caught on worm in the lower stretches.

The brown trout fishing has deteriorated greatly in recent years and is confined mainly to the stretch between the upper and lower Ballea bridges. Access to the fishing is at the bridges. The banks are relatively clean and easily fished.

This river was badly damaged as a fishery by an arterial drainage scheme from Cross Barry downstream to Ballinhassig, when much spawning and nursery water was lost. There is now a heavy weed growth in summer, which makes fishing nearly impossible. However, a friend of mine reported some good success with both brown trout and seatrout while fishing a Klinkhåmer (size 12) 'on the blind' at Ballygarvan.

Season
Salmon: 1 February–30 September
Seatrout: 1 February–12 October
Brown trout: 15 February–12 October

Permission
The fishing is strictly with the permission of the riparian owners.

BANDON, RIVER   W 50 55

The Bandon River rises in the Shehy Mountains in west Cork and flows for 45 miles in an easterly direction through Dunmanway, Ballineen, Enniskeane, Bandon and Innishannon. It drains an area of 235 sq. miles. The tide comes up to Innishannon and the narrow estuary stretches for 11 miles to Kinsale. The upper reaches drain mountain, bog and moorland before the river enters a rich, fertile and very scenic valley at Manch Bridge.

About eight draft nets work the estuary. Unsupervised arterial drainage works caused a lot of damage to the river from Dunmanway downstream to Manch Bridge and, more recently, serious damage has been done to the head waters reducing this fine river to virtually a spate river. It is good to see that the situation regarding agricultural and industrial pollution has improved in recent times.

The Bandon River offers a great variety of fishing and its potential is vastly under-estimated. It gets a very good run of salmon, has excellent seatrout fishing, good fly hatches and good brown trout fishing.

The salmon fishing extends all the way from Innishannon upstream to Togher Castle – depending on the season and water conditions. It is estimated that the river produces 1,000 salmon annually to rod and line. About 200 of these are spring fish taken before 1 May. Bandon Weir controls the run of spring fish. When the water is cold – February to mid-March – the majority of fish are taken below the weir. This corner of the south-west is never cold for too long, being quickly warmed by the influence of the Gulf Stream. From about mid-March the fish are usually moving steadily upstream, with the spring run peaking in April.

The grilse run occurs at the end of June and water levels can be critical for good fishing. The river weeds up badly when the water drops, though a couple of fisheries carry out weed cutting.

The river gets a very good run of big fresh fish in August and September after the nets come off, and this is again dependent on good water.

According to informed local opinion, the salmon fishing is all considered to be very good from Innishannon upstream to Desert Bridge. In low water, fishing can be excellent in the tidal pool below the bridge at Innishannon. It becomes more spread out further up the river. The fishing from Desert Bridge upstream to Enniskeane Bridge is considered fair. From Enniskeane Bridge up to the Carbry Milk Products factory (upstream of Ballineeen) the fishing is not thought of highly. From the factory up to Manch Bridge is again good salmon water. There are eight pools between Manch Bridge and Ballyboy Bridge and, of these, McCarthy's High Bank (a short distance above Manch) and the Weir Pool are best. From Ballyboy Bridge up to the Long Bridge at Dunmanway is rarely worth fishing by the salmon angler, except, perhaps, Poulamount, half-a-mile up from Ballyboy Bridge.

There are five pools worth the angler's attention between the Long Bridge and Ardcahan Bridge: Turn Hole, the Fox's Hole, the Tailor's Hole and the Tinker's Hole are all worth a try and all within a mile of the Long Bridge. The middle section of this stretch is inaccessible and useless. Poulatagart is about 400 yards downstream from Ardcahan Bridge and well worth a visit. It should be approached along the left bank.

From Ardcahan Bridge to Togher Bridge is nearly four miles of desolate moorland and bog. There are three or four pools worth fishing a short distance above Ardcahan Bridge and the best of the fishing should be approached from Togher Bridge, where Poulgorm (upstream of Togher Castle), the Turn Pool, the Punch Bowl and the Ford all deserve attention.

It should be remembered that from Togher Bridge to Manch Bridge the river has been severely damaged by drainage works and the best of the fishing is on a falling spate.

The fisheries allow all methods, except David Lamb's Kilcoleman water, which is fly-only from 1 April. Favourite spring baits are the Flying 'C', Brown & Gold, Blue & Silver and Yellow Belly Devons. The Hairy Mary is probably the most popular salmon fly, followed by Silver Wilkinson, Silver and Blue (not unlike a Teal, Blue & Silver) and Garry Dog. There is a very interesting locally devised shrimp pattern known as 'Yer Man'. A 14-foot fly rod is recommended in big water, while a single-handed rod is adequate in summer.

The river gets an excellent run of seatrout. The big run commences in early July and can last till the end of August and later. It is estimated that thousands of seatrout are taken every year on the free waters of the estuary and the fishing can be really good on the 4-mile stretch from Bandon to Innishannon. A smaller number of better-quality seatrout are taken up as far as Enniskeane. Peter Ross, Teal Blue & Silver, Bloody Butcher and Connemara Black are the most commonly-used flies.

Brown trout

The river holds an excellent stock of brown trout and a number of fisheries allow flyfishing only. The average weight is about half-a-pound and there is a 9-inch size limit (10 inches on some fisheries). The best fishing months are April, May, early June and September.

The river gets good hatches of olives, sedges, black gnats, blue-winged olives and stoneflies, in season, as well as falls of hawthorn and woodfly. Favourite wet-fly patterns are Greenwell's Glory (with bright green body) Light and Dark Olives, Snipe and Purple, Partridge and Orange, Orange Grouse, Wickham's Fancy, Hare's Ear, Black Zulu, Bracken Clock and Blue Dun.

Weed growth poses a big problem in summer.

Bandon Angling Association

The Bandon Angling Association has about eight miles of good brown trout, seatrout and salmon water. The best fish caught in 2001 were: a brown trout of 3lb; seatrout of 7¼lb and a salmon weighing 18½lb. The best months are April, May and September for salmon; May-June for seatrout and April, May and June for brown trout. The Association's fishing has hatches of large dark olives, iron blues, blue-winged olives, yellow may dun and yellow evening dun, a variety of sedges and plenty of 'black flies'. Access is excellent. The wading is safe, but bring your chest waders. There is a bag limit of 2 salmon and 4 trout (over 10 inches) per day.

Season

15 February–30 September.

A bye-law prohibits fishing below Innishannon Bridge before 17 March.

Regulations
Minimum size: 25cm (trout)
Bag limit: 4 trout

Permission
While there are a few small sections of free fishing on the Bandon, the vast majority of the fishing is under private ownership or controlled by syndicates or angling associations. Fishing is available through the following:

Bandon Angling Association, Michael J. O'Regan, Oliver Plunkett Street, Bandon, Co. Cork. Tel: 023 41674, email: bandonangling@eircom.net
Robert Smith, Moulnarougha, Ahiohill, Enniskeane, Co. Cork

Local tackle shops
Jeffersport, Pearse Street, Bandon, Co. Cork
Dan Lynch, Halfway Tackle, Halfway, Bandon, Co. Cork. Mobile: 086 3357334

Guides
Can be arranged through Bandon Angling Association

Kilcoleman Fishery
This fishery is a mile long and two-thirds of this is double bank. It has salmon, seatrout and brown trout and takes four rods. It is a fly-only fishery and small shrimp patterns work well for salmon. There is a self-catering cottage that sleeps four, to let with the fishing and an apartment that takes two persons.

Kilcoleman Fishery rod catch 2000–2008

Year	2000	2001	2002	2003	2004	2005	2006	2007	2008
Salmon	81	41	26	54	59	43	42	35	43
Seatrout	6	8	8	10	0	1	3	0	6

Season
15 February–30 September

Permission
David Lamb, Kilcoleman Park, Enniskeane, Co. Cork. Tel: 023 8847279
Email: gamefishing@eircom.net, web site: www.indigo.ie/~dlamb/

Regulations
Flyfishing only
1 salmon per day and 6 trout (over 10 inches)
Catch-and-release is encouraged

Tackle shop
Cork Angling Centre, Kinsale Road Roundabout, Cork. Tel: 021 4321000

Lodge
Kilcoleman Fishery. Email: gamefishing@eircom.net
Web: www.flyfishing-ireland.com

The Manch Fishery

The Manch Fishery consists of about two miles of double bank salmon and trout fishing. It has about 10 pools and a lot of work was carried out in recent years by the late Con Conners to develop and enhance the fishing. This fishery is now syndicated.

Ballineen and Enniskeane Anglers' Association

This association has about four miles of salmon and brown trout water and make day permits available to bona fide tourist anglers. Apply to:
Ballineen and Enniskeane Anglers' Association, Tom Fehily, Bridge Street, Ballineen, Co. Cork.

Dunmanway Salmon and Trout Anglers' Association

The association has about ten miles of river and the best fishing is in the lower section where there is some lovely water and good access. Weed growth can be a problem in summer. The trout fishing extends from Manch Bridge up to Togher Castle. One stretch on the lower river at Billy Dineen's farm is out of bounds.

Permits and information
Patrick McCarthy, Yew Tree Bar, Dunmanway, Co. Cork. Tel: 023 8855196
Pat Galvin, Derrygra, Ballineen, Co. Cork. Tel: 023 8847726
Jerry Walsh, Chapel Street, Dunmanway, Co. Cork. Tel: 023 8855194

Regulations
Fly-only for trout
Minimum size: 10 inch
Bag limit: 4 trout

Local flytyer
Patrick McCarthy Jnr., Yew Tree Bar, Dunmanway, Co. Cork. Tel: 023 8855196

CAHA RIVER   W 24 57

The Caha River is a tributary of the Bandon and joins it from the north above Ardcahan Bridge. It holds a good stock of trout up to 14oz for about three miles up from the confluence. It is best fished early in the season as weed becomes a problem later and there may also be discoloration from sand washing. This is a lovely little trout stream with about 2½ miles of fishing downstream from Poulnaberry Bridge where the water conditions are right.

Permission
Fishing on the Caha is generally considered to be free.

ARGIDEEN RIVER   W 45 45

The Argideen River (in Irish, the little silver stream) rises north west of Clonakilty and flows due east for 18 miles, draining a catchment of 56 sq. miles before entering the estuary at Timoleague. The water is beautifully clear and clean. It is tidal up to Inchy Bridge.

This is primarily a good seatrout river and it produces an occasional salmon. In fact, it is probably one of the best seatrout fisheries in Ireland when water conditions permit. The seatrout stocks have improved steadily in recent years and the average size is excellent – probably just over 2lb.

Part of the river is jointly managed by the South-Western Regional Fisheries Board and the Argideen Anglers' Association. Part of it is let by private owners and the head waters are fished with the permission of the riparian owners. There is quite good brown trout fishing, with trout to 1½lb up at Shannonvale, but the banks are overgrown.

The big seatrout arrive in late April and May and the main run occurs between the end of June and late August.

For night fishing, bright flies give best results in the estuary pools and darker flies are preferred up-river.

Season
Salmon: 15 February–30 September
Seatrout and brown trout: 15 February–12 October.

Permission
Argideen Anglers' Association, The Fishery Office, Inchy Bridge, Courtmacsherry, Co. Cork
Anthony Crestwell, Ummer Smoked Salmon, Inchy Bridge, Courtmacsherry, Co. Cork

Lisselan Estates have one mile of very good double bank fishing with the spring seatrout averaging 2½lb:
The Estate Office, Lisselan Estates, Clonakilty, Co. Cork. Tel: 023 8833249
Permission to fish the upper river may be obtained from riparian owners.

Disabled anglers' facility
There is a disabled anglers' stand situated on a good seatrout pool below Inchy Bridge.

ILEN RIVER   W 12 34

The Ilen River is a medium-sized spate river, 21 miles long, with numerous tributaries which drain an area of 117 sq. miles. It flows south and enters the tide at Skibbereen.

The spring salmon run has declined badly in recent years and those fish that come generally arrive in May. The seatrout fishing is also patchy and grilse numbers are also down. The first run of grilse coincides with the first flood in June and they continue to run through July and August. A small run of good seatrout to 5lb, with an average weight of 2lb, enters the system in April and May. The big runs of three-quarter-pound juniors arrive in July and August. Access to the river is good. It is relatively easy to worm or spin on all of the river. However, in places, overhead bushes present a problem to the flyfisher. Shrimp fishing is not permitted.

The lower part of the Ilen can become somewhat crowded in good water conditions, but there is unlimited scope upstream for those who are prepared to make the effort to walk and explore.

The Dromore Falls were removed in 1999 by the South-Western Regional Fisheries Board to facilitate fish running to spawn on the Dromore River.

Spinning and worming are the methods most commonly used for salmon and grilse. Favourite baits include bronze and copper Mepps (No 3); Devon minnows in blue-and-silver and black-and-gold, 2¼–2½ inches; blue-and-silver and copper Tobys up to 18g. Hairy Mary, Thunder & Lightning and Silver Doctor are all good salmon flies on the river.

Dark flies, like the Bibio, Teal & Black and Black Pennell are considered best for the spring seatrout fishing, In summer, bright flies are favoured, such as Butchers, Ilen Blue, Teal & Silver, Silver Rail and Peter Ross (sizes 8–14).

Season
Salmon: 1 February–30 September
Seatrout: 1 February–12 October

Permission
The ownership of the fishing rights is fragmented and generally held by the riparian owners. The River Ilen Anglers' Club now has about eight miles of the river. The club waters stretch up to Caheragh Bridge, with some exceptions, but there is fishing to be obtained with the permission of riparian owners up as far as Inchengeragh Bridge on the R5 and 6 Drimoleague–Bantry road. Day and weekly permits are available from:

Tony Kelly, Fallon's Sports Shop, North Street, Skibbereen, Co. Cork. Tel: 028 21435

Tackle shop
Fallon's Sports Shop (see above)

Disabled anglers' facility
Stand at Ballyhilty Bridge

MEALAGH, RIVER   W 1 50

The Mealagh River is located one mile north of Bantry. It is 11 miles long and drains a valley of 20 sq. miles. It gets a run of both salmon and seatrout – which is surprising, considering the seemingly impassable falls a short distance up-river. Salmon and seatrout are taken in the falls pool and there are some nice deep pools upstream, which are worth exploring after a spate. There is an improved run of grilse and seatrout above the falls and some nice brown trout fishing for a good distance upstream.

Season
Salmon: 17 March–30 September
Seatrout: 17 March–12 October

Permission
The bottom pool – below the falls – is private and the rest of the river is fished with the permission of the riparian owners.

OWVANE, RIVER   W 1 53

This little spate river is 12 miles long and drains a catchment of 31 sq. miles comprising pastureland, moorland and mountains. There are four good pools in the first mile of river above the tide, three more nice pools below Carriganass Falls, three miles up from the tide, and another good pool above the falls. Access is off the R584 leading to the Pass of Keamaneigh. A drainage scheme did great damage to the pools below Kealkill village and the river is rather featureless up to the weir near Kealkill. Both the seatrout and grilse run has declined greatly and it struggles to produce a few fish.

Season
Salmon: 17 March–30 September
Seatrout: 17 March–12 October

Permission
Riparian owners

COOMHOLA, RIVER   V 99 55

This delightful little spate river – 12 miles long and draining a catchment of 26 sq. miles – tumbles down an incredibly beautiful, rough, rugged moorland valley into the top of Bantry Bay. There are netting rights in existence in the estuary but they are not exercised. Poaching is, however, a problem that the Coomhola shares with all the other rivers in this locality.

It gets a good run of grilse with the best fishing in July, August and September and produces about 150 to the rod every season. The best fishing is after a spate. Access is good, with a road running up the valley parallel to the river, but the bankside terrain is terribly difficult. The fishing extends for five miles up to Borlin Falls, but the best of it is on the first three miles near Kilgarvan. There are about twelve pools altogether and the water is gin clear, flowing over a very light coloured river bed. The banks are difficult to walk, in parts, but this all adds to the charm. Upstream spinning gives good results on a spate.

Big seatrout are a particular feature of this river. They come in around mid-April, in sufficient numbers to warrant fishing and average 4lb. The 'juniors' run in late June and July. However, the fishing was disappointing in the 2001 season.

There is an active angling club on the river.

Season
Salmon: 17 March–30 September
Seatrout: 17 March–12 October

Permission
Teddy O'Brien, Coomhola Salmon & Seatrout Angling Association, Coomhola Bridge Shop, Bantry, Co. Cork. Tel: 027 50563

Local tackle shop
Bantry Tackle, H. Harley Feather, Fur & Field, Glengarriff Road, Bantry, Co. Cork

GLENGARRIFF, RIVER   V 92 56

The Glengarriff River is just seven miles long and drains a 16 sq.-mile catchment of scenic mountain valley which is thickly wooded with newly-planted pines and ancient oak, yew, rowan and holly. The river, though short, is characterized by nine pools – two of them huge, deep holding pools. There is Brook's Pool, Poulcaum, Poulacranna and Thompson's Pool, which is by the road side; then the Otter Pool, the Crooked Hole, the Doctor's Pool, Inchaneer and Pouleen, below the waterfall. Anglers are strongly advised not to stand on the slippery rock formation at the head of Pouleen.

The Glengarriff gets a fair run of grilse, but, I am told it can be written off as a seatrout fishery – numbers have declined drastically recently.

The salmon fishing is best after a spate and spinning and worms are the popular angling methods.

The banks are difficult to negotiate, with pine forest planted right down to the edge of the water.

A positive development is the fact that the local angling association bought out the draft net at the estuary. In spite of this, stocks are in decline!

Season
Salmon: 17 March–30 September
Seatrout and brown trout: 17 March–12 October

Permission
Glengarriff Angling Association, The Maple Leaf, Glengarriff, Co. Cork

* ADRIGOLE, RIVER   V 81 51

This small river on Bantry Bay is about six miles long and drains a catchment of 12 sq. miles, which includes several lakes. The seatrout smolts are reported to be returning prematurely, infested with sea lice. I fear that the future looks bleak. The best pools are in the vicinity of Adrigole Bridge. The road up to the Healy Pass in the Caha Mountains runs parallel to the right bank for about one mile.

Season
Salmon: 17 March–30 September
Seatrout: 17 March–12 October

Enquiries
The South Western Regional Fisheries Board, Sunnyside House, Masseytown, Macroom, Co. Cork. Tel: 026 41222

SHEEN, RIVER   V 93 70

The Sheen River is a fast flowing spate system, 14 miles long and draining a catchment of approximately 36 sq. miles. It rises in the Caha Mountains and flows northwards through a magnificent scenic valley into the head of Kenmare Bay. The water runs off very quickly after a spate and the prime fishing time can be of quite short duration. Thereafter, many of the pools become slow and sluggish. It is highly regarded as a salmon fishery.

The once prolific seatrout runs have virtually disappeared.

The Sheen gets a small run of spring salmon and fishing starts from opening day on 15 March. It gets a good run of grilse and these fish can arrive at the end of May or early in June, depending on water conditions.

Access to the river is relatively easy, with roads running parallel to the river for the first seven miles and bridges at frequent intervals. The first six miles of fishing up from the sea are regarded as the best. The water is beautifully clear, even in flood conditions.

There are approximately fourteen pools up to Dromanassig Bridge, ten pools to Drumgurteen Bridge, five pools to Bunane Bridge, five pools to Releagh Bridge and a big pool at Raw, above Releagh Bridge. The Comeen River is a tributary which comes in on the right bank a mile above Drumgurteen Bridge and it has five pools in the first mile above the confluence.

All legitimate fishing methods are allowed. Natural shrimp is used a lot in low water and worm and spinning in a spate.

There is no beat system. The fishing is reserved strictly for the guests staying at the hotel.

The river has a hydroelectric turbine down near the mouth and there can be a build-up of salmon in the pool downstream in low water.

Season
Salmon: 15 March–30 September
Seatrout and brown trout: 15 March–12 October

Permission
The Health Club, Sheen Falls Lodge, Kenmare, Co. Kerry. Tel: 064 6640003
Email: info@sheenfallslodge.ie, web: www.sheenfallslodge.ie

Regulations
All legitimate methods
Bag limit: Two fish per rod per day – subject to change

Guide
May be booked through the Lodge, Brendan Grant. Tel: 087 6979395

Local tackle shop
John O'Hare, Main Street, Kenmare, Co. Kerry. Tel: 066 41499

ROUGHTY, RIVER AND SLAHENY, RIVER   V 96 72

The **Roughty River** is medium sized, 19 miles long, and drains a catchment of 78 sq. miles. It rises in the mountains on the borders of west Cork and flows in a westerly direction through the village of Kilgarvan into the top of Kenmare Bay. The lower 7 miles flow through a fertile valley over a limestone base. It is a river beset with many problems, including poaching, land drainage and pollution. A draft net operates in the narrow estuary.

The Roughty gets a small run of spring salmon and an excellent run of grilse. No exact figures are available, but it is generally believed that the Kenmare Club's water at Ardtully produces approximately 200 salmon and grilse in a good season. The seatrout run has improved to excellence. The best of this fishing is just above the tide, at Poultadagh, and on the Slaheny, a tributary. This river has some beautiful fly water on a falling spate. The local advice is that it runs dirty for five hours after a spate, followed by five hours good fishing. Of course, the good fishing can last for several days in wet weather.

The river in its lower reaches is characterized by big slow pools. The salmon fishing, on a spate, extends all the way up to Inchee Bridge and for two miles of the Slaheny up to Shandrum School.

Access to the river is relatively easy, with roads running close to all the fishable water. However, the banks are very overgrown and this precludes flyfishing on much of the water. Spinning, worm and shrimp fishing are the most frequently practised methods. Where flyfishing is possible, Ally's Shrimp does well, as does a yellow Shrimp and a Silver Rat.

The **Slaheny River** (map ref W 01 72) is a tributary of the Roughty. Like the Roughty, it features several huge pools and is not easy to flyfish. Access is also difficult. On the other hand, it is a very productive piece of water up as far as Shandrum School. It holds a good head of seatrout in late June, July, August, September and an equally good stock of grilse. The Slaheny grilse must be a genetic strain peculiar to that one river. They are most distinctive: quite short, but very deep in the body. Local anglers refer to them as Slaheny 'bonhams' – Gaelic for 'little pigs'.

Season
Salmon: 15 March–30 September
Seatrout and brown trout: 15 March–12 October

Permission
The fishing rights are fragmented among riparian owners. There is one stretch at Ardtully Castle, four miles from Kenmare off the R569 Kilgarvan road, which is the property of Kenmare Salmon Angling Ltd and for which day permits can be obtained from:

John O'Hare, Main Street, Kenmare, Co. Kerry. Tel 064 41499

The day permits allow fishing from 09.00–19.00 on one mile of double-bank fishing. There is no Sunday fishing for visitors.

The Ring of Kerry

Kilgarvan/Roughty Angling Association

Kilgarvan/Roughty Angling Association has six miles of fishing on the Roughty and Slaheny.

Permits

Quill's Shop, Kilgarvan, Co. Kerry. Tel: 064 45300

Guide and local flytyer

Hans Venture, Kenmare, Co. Kerry. Tel: 064 41463

Tackle shop

John O'Hare, Main Street, Kenmare, Co. Kerry. Tel 064 41499

Accommodation

Tom & Mary MacDonnell, Birchwood, Kilgarvan, Co. Kerry. Tel: 064 85473
Fax: 064 85570, email: info@birchwood-kilgarvan.com
Danny & Kathleen O'Sullivan, Gortna Bowl House, Kilgarvan, Co. Kerry
Tel: 064 85979, email: neilosullivan@eircom.net

FINNIHY, RIVER   V 90 71

This is a lovely little seven mile long spate river, with a catchment of 12 sq. miles. It enters Kenmare Bay a short distance west of the town of Kenmare. It is very overgrown and unfishable except by the very determined, to whom it quietly produces a few summer grilse when the water is right and maybe a seatrout.

There are seven pools in all: the Barrack Hole, the Crow's Dip, the Falls (Killarney Road), Lee's Weir, Two-Mile-Bridge Falls, the Turnpool and Sullivan's Falls, at Rinacollee Bog.

Season

Salmon: 15 March–30 September
Seatrout and brown trout: 15 March–12 October

Permission

Keith Johnston & Associates, Pier Road, Kenmare, Co. Kerry. Tel: 064 41341
Email: kjandassociates@eircom.net

BLACKWATER (KERRY), RIVER   V 79 69

The Kerry Blackwater, which is managed by the South Western Regional Fisheries Board, enters Kenmare Bay from the north seven miles west of Kenmare. It is 10 miles long and drains a catchment of 34 sq. miles, including three loughs. It has several tributaries draining magnificent scenic mountain valleys. The river is characterized by streams and about thirty pools, including some huge holding pools.

It is divided into four beats, each having eight to ten pools, depending on water levels. It takes 22 rods in good water conditions.

The peak months are June, July and August for both seatrout and grilse. Flyfishing is widely regarded as the best method to take the grilse, seatrout and brown trout but spring fish are more likely to be caught on spinner, followed closely by fly.

The river gets a fresh run of salmon and seatrout in the first two weeks of September and after that, it starts to slow down.

The best beats for spring salmon and grilse are Beat 5, 3 and 4. These are the lower beats towards the tide. For seatrout, Beat 3 is considered the best, though Beats 1 and 2 can also be productive in spate.

The best-known pools for salmon are the Flat, the Boat Pool, the Weir, the Sports Field Pool, the Sofa and the Island Pool.

The seatrout pools are the Sally Pool, Brennan's Pool and the Racecourse Pools. I'm told that there is some great seatrout night fishing at the top of the river. Access is a bit difficult, but avid seatrout fishers should enquire about it from the manager.

The fishery has some very nice fly water on all beats. The weir at the end of the Boat Pool seldom fails to produce a salmon to the fly on a spate. When the river is in good order, all beats are good flyfishing water.

The river fishes best in a falling spate. A good height for all methods of fishing is when a level of 1.2m shows on the fishing hut gauge. The river runs quite clean during a spate and can be fished profitably right through the dropping water. The river is also worth a go in low water conditions. With a breeze on the pools, a small mini-tube fly works very well. The upstream worm also works quite well in the steamy water down river. The fishing varies up and down the river depending on prevailing conditions. The most popular flies are shrimp patterns in sizes 12 to 8. Flying Cs and Rapalas are very popular lures amongst spin fishers. No wading is necessary as all of the water can be reached easily from the bank.

The South Western Regional Fisheries Board manages the fishery and the river is open to all anglers on a day permit. However, it's important for anglers to book fishing in advance to avoid disappointment.

Kerry Blackwater rod catch 2002–2008

Year	2002	2003	2004	2005	2006	2007	2008
Salmon	92	42	124	114	154	118	71

Season
15 March–30 September

Permission
The Fishery Manager, The Kerry Blackwater Fishery, Fishery Hut, Blackwater, Killarney, Co. Kerry. Tel: 087 2241095, office: 026 41221 (South-Western Regional Fisheries Board), email: swrfb@swrfb.ie

Regulation
Bag limit: two salmon per day

Guide
Can be arranged by booking in advance with the Fishery Manager.

Lodge
The Management can advise visiting anglers on suitable accommodation.

SNEEM, RIVER / ARDSHEELANE, RIVER   V 69 66

The Sneem River and its tributary, the Ardsheelane River, drain two mountain valleys and a number of lakes. The total catchment is approximately 34 sq. miles.

The Sneem river gets a run of grilse and seatrout in July and August. The Ardsheelane is noted mainly as a seatrout river. Both are very much spate rivers – best after a flood – and there is about 2 miles of pools and fishing on each of them, some of which are overgrown and difficult to fish. Nonetheless, this is a lovely productive fishery when the water conditions are right. This is still a very good seatrout fishery with early fish running in from May.

Season
Salmon: 15 March–30 September
Seatrout: 15 March–12 October

Permission
Jean-Yves Lettanneur, Hon. Secretary, Sneem Angling Club, The Tourist Office, Sneem, Co. Kerry

* CROANSAGHT (GLANMORE), RIVER   V 77 57

This little river is barely two miles long and drains Glanmore Lough and a 16 sq. mile catchment into Kenmare Bay. It looks so insignificant that some anglers ignore it – to their cost. It used to produce about 25 spring salmon a season – from March to May – and the lake produces the same again. Sadly the seatrout were virtually wiped out due to a fish farm located about a mile out from the mouth of the river. If water conditions are not good on the river, Glanmore Lough is often worth a try. It is a mistake to ignore its potential for both seatrout and spring salmon.

Season
Salmon: 15 March–30 September
Seatrout: 15 March 12 October

Enquiries
Keith Johnston & Associates, Pier Road, Kenmare, Co. Kerry. Tel: 064 41341
Email: kjandassociates@eircom.net

* OWENSHAUGH, RIVER   V 78 62

This small river near Larragh, Kenmare, gets a run of summer salmon and seatrout. It is very overgrown and is difficult to fish. It too has been affected by the fish farm.

Season
Salmon: 15 March–30 September
Seatrout: 15 March–12 October

Enquiries
Keith Johnston & Associates, Pier Road, Kenmare, Co. Kerry. Tel: 064 41341
Email: kjandassociates@eircom.net

CLOONEE, RIVER   V 79 63

This river drains the Cloonee Lakes and gets a run of grilse. It is in private ownership
and permission to fish it is not normally available.

DAWROS, RIVER   V 89 67

This little river lies three miles south of Kenmare on the R571. It was badly damaged
by drainage works and is very overgrown. There is a small grilse run in August and it
can hold some very nice seatrout – but not many.

Season
Salmon: 15 March–30 September
Seatrout: 15 March–12 October

Permission Free

WATERVILLE RIVER   V 50 66

This is a private fishery on which rods are let occasionally. The maximum number of
rods allowed is two, the letting period is for three hours, there is a bag limit of three
salmon in summer and spinning is allowed in spring but it is flyfishing only after 1
May.

This short fishery extends for 400 yards approximately from the bridge on the N70
at Waterville to the sea. It consists of a pool, a stream, the fish traps (which are no
longer in operation), another stream and a pool – the renowned Butler's Pool.

This river drains Lough Currane and the entire Waterville system and all fish
entering these lakes and rivers must pass up the Waterville River.

The spring salmon tend to run through to the lough rather than rest in the river
and it is as a grilse fishery, from July to September that it is best known. Records are
not kept, but locally it is thought to produce at least 200 fish annually. It fishes best in
medium to high water or with a good ripple on the pools. Favourite patterns are Hairy
Mary, Silver Rat and shrimp flies.

An enormous run of seatrout passes up the river. The water upstream of the fish
traps is a noted hot spot and it can be all very good at dusk through July and August.
Useful seatrout patterns include Jungle Cock Spider, Bibio, Bloody Butcher, Silver
Doctor, Invicta and Wickham's Fancy and Hairy Mary, Badger, Silver Rat or Yellow
Shrimp, for the grilse.

Flyfishing only.

Season
Salmon and Seatrout: 17 January–30 September

Permission/lodge
The Manager, Waterville House, Waterville, Co. Kerry. Tel: 066 9474244

Gillies/guides and boat hire
The following is a list of gillies or guides who through their knowledge and experience will allow you to fully realise the wonderful fishing that is on offer throughout the Waterville catchment. All are experienced with many years of angling between them. The cost of a gillie with boat and engine on Lough Currane is generally around €100. Rates for the upper fisheries and spate rivers vary. The fishing day is generally of seven hours duration but longer days are available if required.

Boats and engines are also available for hire from the following list of approved operators. All boats are insured and are of an excellent standard. Please employ a gillie if you are unsure of the lakes as these fisheries can be dangerous for the inexperienced.

Neil O'Shea. Tel: 066 9474527, mobile: 087 9942792
Email: oshealoughcurrane@eircom.net, www.oshealoughcurrane.ie
John Murphy. Tel: 066 9475257, mobile: 086 3991074
Email: john@fishingkerry.com, web: www.fishingkerry.com
Terence Wharton. Tel: 066 9474264
Tom O'Shea. Tel: 066 9474973
Junior Scully.Tel: 066 9474270
Bob Priestly. Tel: 066 9474726
John Griffin. Tel: 066 9474370
Dominic McGillicuddy. Tel: 066 9474023, email: dominicmcgillicuddy@eircom.net
Mike Dwyer. Tel: 066 9474081
Vincent Appleby. Tel: 066 9475248, email: salmonandseatrout@eircom.net
Brod Sullivan. Tel: 066 9474249
Roger Baker. Tel: 066 9478009, email: rogerbaker@eircom.net
Web: www.cloghvoola.com
Paddy Carey. Tel: 066 9474973
Donal O'Shea. Tel: 066 9474146
Frank Donnelly. Tel: 066 9474303, email: lakelands@eircom.net
Web: www.lakelandshouse.com
Tim Moore. Tel: 066 064 40698
Michael O'Sullivan. Tel: 066 9474800/9474255
John Quinlan. Tel: 066 9474721, email: info@thatchcottageireland.co.uk
Web: www.thatchcottageireland.co.uk
Sylvester Donnelly. Tel: 066 9474327
Vincent O'Sullivan. Tel: 066 9474661

Local tackle shop
Kevin Brain, The Tackle Shop, Main Street, Waterville, Co. Kerry. Tel: 066 9474433

Lodge/accommodation
Web: www.loughcurrane.com

CUMMERAGH, RIVER   V 55 69

The Cummeragh River drains a catchment of 46 sq. miles, including ten loughs, into Lough Currane. The fishing is approximately five miles long and holds its water for several days after a spate due to the slow release of water from the upper loughs. It is managed by Waterville Fisheries Development (Web: www.loughcurrane.com)

The Cummeragh meanders through a flat moorland of blanket peat and is slow-flowing, except when in spate. There are a few nice streams on each beat which can provide good flyfishing and nice spinning conditions for several days after a spate. Thereafter, a fly can get results when a breeze puts a ripple on the pools. The pools are narrow and weed is a problem in low water.

The river holds occasional spring salmon from opening day, but it is as a grilse fishery that it excels through the summer to the end of September. Good seasons will produce 150–200 fish.

The banks are rough and difficult to negotiate in places. It is advisable to organize your fishing through the local gillies in Waterville.

This is also an excellent seatrout river from July onwards. Most of the fishing is done during the day and the seatrout come as a by-product of the salmon fishing. Small flies work best. The seatrout will take a small Shrimp Fly and Watson's Fancy and Connemara Black are especially recommended.

This is a club fishery. Day permits are also available at The Tackle Shop in Waterville.

The top two kilometres is spawning and nursery water. It is preserved by the management (Waterville Fisheries) and the fishing is not let.

Season
Salmon: 1 April–30 September
Seatrout: 1 April–30 September

Permission
Waterville Fisheries, The Tackle Shop, Waterville, Co. Kerry. Tel: 066 9474433

INNY, RIVER   V 51 71

With its tributaries, the River Inny drains a long narrow mountain valley and has a catchment of 47 sq. miles. It is very much a spate system, with the fishing confined to the spate conditions and rarely lasting more than eight hours. The locals advise taking a gillie if you are not to miss the best of it. There is about eight miles of fishing up to Cuslagh Bridge.

It is regarded mainly as a grilse fishery, with fish running from mid-June. September can be really good. It is estimated to produce 150 fish annually. Flyfishing and spinning are the usual methods and the fly can be very productive when fish are running. Useful patterns are Hairy Mary, Silver Doctor and Thunder & Lightning (sizes 6-10), single or double.

A lot of the river is flat and featureless, with short streams and long shallow pools in low water. It gets a small run of spring fish in March and April and some good seatrout in April and 'juners' from June onwards, but is not seriously regarded as a seatrout fishery. It gets a run of good fish (10lb or better) in September which is by far the best month for fishing.

The Inny is usually fished by anglers who have come to fish the Waterville lakes. If water conditions come good on the river from June to September, they will seize the opportunity of a few hours river salmon fishing and are often accompanied by their gillie from the lake.

Some beats have a good mix of stream and pool and there is some nice water for flyfishing. Favourite flies are Hairy Mary, Stoat's Tail, Claret Shrimp or any dark fly. It can run very dirty and then anglers usually spin with Flying Cs, Mepps or Tobys.

Season
Salmon: 17 January–30 September
Seatrout: 14 February–12 October

Guides
See Waterville River (page 377)

Permission
Ownership of the fishing rights is very fragmented. The fishing can be booked through any of the following:

Waterville Fisheries, The Tackle Shop, Waterville, Co. Kerry. Tel: 066 9474433

** CARHAN, RIVER   V 50 79

This little spate river enters Valentia Harbour north of Cahersiveen. It gets seatrout in June and grilse from July on a flood. It is mostly overgrown with only about three fishing locations and worm is considered the best bait. Little or no fishing takes place on this river.

Season
Salmon: 1 April–30 September
Seatrout: 1 April–30 September

** FERTA, RIVER   V 51 81

The Ferta enters the head of Valentia Harbour. It is a spate river with about 12 miles of fishing above and below Failmore Bridge. It is not worth fishing.

Season
Salmon: 1 April–30 September
Seatrout: 1 April–30 September

CARAGH RIVER   V 71 87

The Caragh River drains the southern slopes of Macgillicuddy's Reeks and half a dozen small loughs before it enters Lough Caragh. On leaving Caragh, it flows approximately two miles to the tide at Rossbehy Creek on Dingle Bay. The catchment is 66 sq. miles. This is one of the best spring salmon and seatrout rivers in the south-west and it gets quite a good run of grilse too.

The river is divided into two distinct fisheries: the Upper Caragh Fishery, situated above Caragh Lake and the Lower Caragh Fishery, which runs from Caragh Lake down to the tide.

Upper Caragh Fishery
Primarily a salmon and grilse fishery. The spring fish run from February to April and the grilse begin running at the end of May and the run peaks in July, depending on water conditions.

From the lake up to Blackstones Bridge is known as 'The Caol'. It is deep and sluggish, with the exception of Lickeen Pool, which has a stream and can be fished with a fly. The rest is fished from a boat – either spinning or trolling.

The stretch from Blackstones Bridge to the joinings at Boheeshil – a distance of four miles approximately – is divided into seven beats and has fourteen pools. The beats are rotated daily at 13.30 and there is only one rod per beat, though a child under 16 years or a wife or husband can also share the beat.

All legitimate methods are allowed except natural shrimp or prawn. An orange tube fly (orange hair and black body) is good in spring and on dropping water. The Lemon & Grey is considered the fly for the Caragh River and after it, Blue Charm and Silver Doctor, in sizes 6 and 8 single and 10 double.

Upper Caragh rod catch 2001–2008

Year	2001	2002	2003	2004	2005	2006	207	2008
Salmon	149	287	N/A	157	202	266	246	261

Season
Salmon: 17 January–30 September
N.B. The Upper Caragh does not open until about 20 February to allow stocks to build up in the river.
Seatrout: 17 January–12 October

Permission
Mike O'Shea, Fishery Manager, Lyranes Lower, Glencar, Co. Kerry. Tel: 066 9760199 Mobile: 087 2213835, email: uppeercaraghmanager@msn.com, web: www.safiex.com
Mrs. Ursula Doppler, Lyranes Lower, Glencar, Co. Kerry

Lodge/accommodation
Glencar House Hotel, Glencar , Killarney, Co. Kerry. Tel: 066 9760102, fax: 066 9760167, email: info@glencarhouse.com, web: www.glencarhouse.com. Member of the *Great Fishing Houses of Ireland Group*

Blackstones House B&B, Mrs. Breda Breene, Blackstones Bridge, Glencar, Co. Kerry. Tel: 0 9760164

Regulations
Bag limit: one spring salmon per day; three per week

Guides
The fishery has a number of resident guides who can be booked in advance with the fishing.

Lower Caragh River
The Lower Caragh Fishery is located between Killorglin and Glenbeigh on the famous Ring of Kerry. The Lower Caragh River flows beneath an ancient Coaching Bridge approximately 2km northeast of Glenbeigh. The Lower Caragh Fishery comprises part of Lough Caragh and the entire lower Caragh River. The fishery also includes commercial salmon fishing rights in the Caragh estuary. The Lower Caragh River runs clear even in high water conditions. Due to this clarity and the river's gradient between Lough Caragh and the estuary (the Lower Caragh river falls 15m over a distance of 2.8km) the river lends itself in particular to flyfishing. Atlantic salmon and seatrout run the river throughout the season which extends from 17 January to the end of September. The fishery gets a run of spring salmon, early grilse, summer grilse and summer salmon. Seatrout enter the river from late March/April onwards.

The season opens on 17 January. Spring salmon run the river from early January and the peak of the run occurs during March and April depending on water conditions. The average weight of spring salmon is about 9lb. May heralds the arrival of the early grilse which increase in numbers through June and July. On the Lower Caragh grilse average 5lb. Summer salmon also enter the river during the months of June through August averaging 12lb. The period April through July would be considered by most anglers with a knowledge of the Lower Caragh to be the best months on the fishery. Seatrout run early on the Lower Caragh and from late March/April onwards average 0.75-3lb. The heaviest seatrout taken in recent years was 11lb. A peculiar feature of these seatrout is that they tend to hold in the Lower Caragh River and do not appear to enter Lough Caragh in appreciable numbers.

The Lower Caragh River can accommodate up to seven rods (five between Caragh Lake and Caragh Bridge and two downstream of Caragh Bridge.

The fishery has entered into an agreement with the local angling club, Caragh Bridge Angling Club, and club members have access to the water at specified times throughout the angling season. The partnership approach between the fishery owners and the club has potential to benefit the fishery immensely.

Season
Salmon: 17 January–30 September
Seatrout: 17 January–12 October
Brown trout: 15 February–12 October

It is a fly-only fishery. However, during high water conditions, other methods (eg. spinning) may be allowed by management. A feature of the river is the long duration of flood events. Lough Caragh dampens the severity of floods and discharges water into the lower Caragh River in a manner which does not result in rapid changes in flow. The fishery has a full time Fishery Manager and a number of waterkeepers appointed by the state legislature.

Permission
Enquiries should be made to:

Henry Macaulay, Fishery Manager. Mobile: 086 1562828
Email: info@lowercaraghfishery.com, web: www.lowercaraghfishery.com

Further information is available at the following website: www.kerryfisheries.ie

LAUNE, RIVER   V 89 91

The River Laune (pronounced 'lawn') is a great salmon and trout river – both seatrout and brown trout. It is some 14 miles long and drains the lakes of Killarney and a catchment of some 320 sq. miles into Castlemaine Harbour at the head of Dingle Bay. There are 10 miles from the lake to the tide – the river is tidal for nearly two miles above Killorglin – and it has at least sixty named pools. The extensive loughs ensure good fishing water for lengthy periods after a flood. The river gets an excellent run of spring salmon and grilse. It is not unusual to see a spring fish on the bank by 10.00 on the opening day of the season at the top section of the Muckross Fishery.

The best early season spring fishing is at the mouth of the lake. Spring fishing on the rest of the river does not really begin till late April-early May. As the season progresses, the fish tend to slow down and populate the pools downstream. By May, good fishing extends all over the river and this is probably the best month of all for spring fish. A feature of the May fishing is the number of big fish the river produces (17lb and 18lb) and it is generally accepted that the bigger fish don't run till May.

The first grilse begin appearing in May, but the peak of the run takes place in June and salmon fishing lasts right through the summer, with September being regarded as a particularly good month for flyfishing.

All legitimate methods are allowed and some of the fisheries, particularly club waters, are heavily fished when the fish are running.

The river used to get an excellent run of seatrout, but this has declined in recent times. The Laune seatrout run early – May and June – and individual anglers could take over thirty a day, averaging about a pound-and-a-half. The night fishing could be very good but equally good during the day when conditions were right. The best of the fishing is in the tidal water above Killorglin, Poulnahalla and the Bridge stream below Beaufort Bridge.

The Laune also holds a marvellous stock of brown trout, with quite a good percentage of them ranging from ¾–1lb. It is a river with a great variety of fly life: olives, sedges, stoneflies and terrestrials, including the hawthorn. On summer evenings, the number of trout taking the blue-winged olive and its spinner has to be seen to be appreciated. They can be difficult to tempt in the clear water and the best chance is at dusk with a dry-fly and fine tippet.

This is a quite exceptional river and fishery. It has fish, it has character and it is located in one of the most beautiful parts of Ireland.

Season
Salmon: 17 January–30 September
Seatrout: 17 January–12 October
Brown trout: 15 February–12 October

Permission
The ownership of fishing rights on the River Laune is fragmented among disparate groups and private owners.

Guides
Denis Cronin, mobile: 086 1713909
John Buckley, mobile: 086 8435028

THE LAUNE FISHERIES

State-owned Fisheries
The State owns extensive fishing right extending over several miles of single and double bank fishing. Permits can be obtained from:

Fishery Board staff. Tel: 026 41221, email: swrfb@swrfb
O'Neill's Tackle Shop, Plunkett Street, Killarney, Co. Kerry. Tel: 064 31970

Beaufort House Fishery
The Beaufort House Fishery is two miles long and is a private fishery reserved for residents at Beaufort House Hotel and Cottages. The fishery has some beautiful fly water. It is worth fishing from late April, gets a good run of spring fish in May, grilse in June, July and can be very good in September.

Permission
Beaufort House Hotel, (proprietor, Donald Cameron), Beaufort Post Office, Co. Kerry. Tel: 064 44764, email: info@beaufortireland.com, web: www.beaufortireland.com

Guides
Guides can be arranged through the hotel.

Accommodation
Beaufort House Hotel and four self-catering cottages.

Mangan's Fisheries
John Mangan leases two fisheries, one is three-quarters-of-a-mile of single and double bank and the other is half-a-mile of single bank. They are normally let to angling parties. Fishing begins at the end of April. One of the fisheries has a fly-only stretch of water.

Permission

John Mangan, Ardlahas, Killorglin, Co. Kerry. Tel: 0 66 9761393
Mobile: 087 2418018, email: irbaltic@iol.ie

Regulations

One section is fly-only. No shrimp or prawn fishing.

Guides

By arrangement through Mr. Mangan

Local tackle shop

Landers Outdoor World, Mile Height, Tralee, Co. Kerry. Tel: 066 712664
Web: www.landers.leisure@oceanfree.net

Accommodation

Can be arranged, contact:
Laune Salmon Anglers' Association, Billy Downes, Hon. Secretary, Laune Salmon
Anglers' Association, 10 Pairc na Dun, Mounthawk, Co. Kerry. Tel: 066 7123950

In addition to the above-named, there are a number of short stretches let on a day
permit basis by individual riparian owners.

FLESK, RIVER   V 98 90

The River Flesk is 28 miles long and a medium-to-large spate river. It drains the west
Cork Mountains and flows in a north-westerly direction into Lough Leane at Killarney.
The lower reaches are deep, but with enough flow to carry a fly. The middle is well-
endowed with holding pools and fishing, and in the upper reaches, it is a fast-flowing
boulder-strewn stream with occasional holding pools.

Because it is not developed nor actively managed, the Flesk is not held in high
esteem. Nonetheless, it is a great little salmon river with the potential to be a real
gem.

It gets a run of spring salmon and an excellent run of grilse. The first of these fish
arrive late May or early June, depending on water. The spring run may produce as
many as thirty springers by the end of February every season. In all, there is over 12
miles of fishing. Water levels rise very quickly and drop just as fast. The angler who
knows the river or has a good guide will know which section to fish, depending on the
height of water. A feature of this river is the amount of free fishing that is available for
the angler who is prepared to enquire about it.

There is good brown trout fishing at various points from Flesk Bridge down to
the lake. The trout average half-a-pound or better and there can be some excellent
evening and night fishing in the summer months when the stocks of river trout are
augmented by a run of trout up from the lough. Once again, local knowledge is the
key to success.

Season

Salmon: 17 January–30 September
Brown trout: 15 February–12 October

Permission

Cahernane Hotel, Killarney, Co. Kerry. Tel: 064 31895

Lough Leane Anglers' Association, O'Neill's Tackle Shop, Plunkett Street, Killarney, Co. Kerry. Tel: 064 31970

There is some free fishing available with permission from riparian owners.

OWNEYKEAGH, RIVER   W 87 06

The Owneykeagh River joins the Flesk from the north, midway between Gortahoosh Bridge and Glenflesk. It is narrow and deep, with a reputation for holding good stocks of brown trout. Access is difficult, with soft undercut banks and a lot of virtually impassable marshland on either side. In other places, it is very overgrown and a great deal of bank clearance is required. It also gets a good run of grilse on falling water from late June onwards and there is a good pool at the mouth where it joins the Flesk.

Season

As for River Flesk, above.

Permission

Riparian owners/free fishing

* MAINE, RIVER   Q 90 06
* LITTLE MAINE RIVER   Q 94 06
* BROWN FLESK RIVER   Q 98 04

These three rivers are all part of the one system. The Maine is an extension of the Brown Flesk and the Little Maine is a tributary. The entire catchment is 154 sq. miles. The Maine and the Little River Maine drain flat countryside from Castleisland to Castlemaine and on into Castlemaine Harbour at the head of Dingle Bay. The Brown Flesk River is 20 miles long and is a much swifter stream as it flows westwards through Scartaglin and Farranfore.

This river system was subjected to an arterial drainage scheme in the 1950s. Consequently, many of the famous old salmon pools are no more and the banks are very high in some places. It has, however, recovered quite well and the Brown Flesk River had at least 35 holding pools before losing half a dozen to Farranfore Airport. Being a 'free fishery', it is badly maintained and completely overgrown in places. It also has problems with poaching and pollution. Despite considerable potential as a fishery for salmon (grilse), seatrout and brown trout, it has never been actively managed and has fallen into a state of dereliction.

It gets a big run of salmon and seatrout and has five draft nets operating at the mouth. One, in fact, operates above Castlemaine. It is highly regarded as a grilse (end of June) and autumn salmon river. Fish average 8lb–9lb.

It still gets a good run of big spring seatrout (2–4½lb) in April and smaller fish from July.

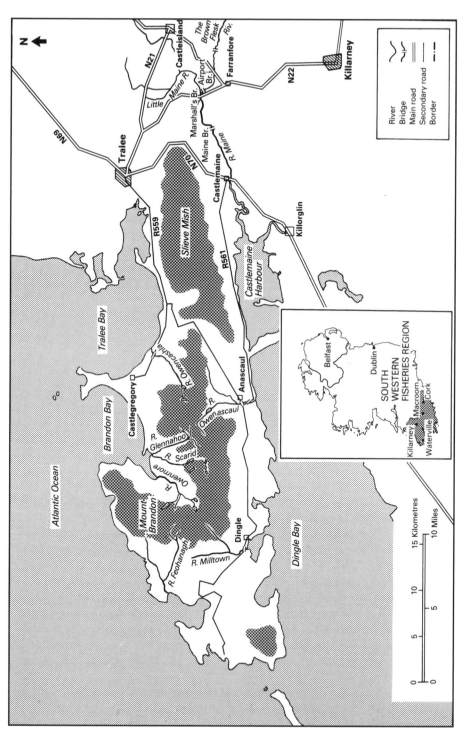

The Dingle Peninsula

The River Maine is best fished in medium-to-low water. Much of it is overgrown and it is necessary to wade. The best water is from Marshall's Bridge right down to and below Ballyfinane Bridge. It gets a great run of grilse in June and the September fishing can be really good. Favourite flies are Claret & Olive, Claret & Blue and Peter Ross, in sizes as large as 6 and 4. There is good brown trout fishing in this area. They average half-a-pound. April can be an especially good month and some very big baskets are taken here. Try a Greenwell's Glory, a Red Spinner or a Bloody Butcher in the evening.

The Little Maine is better known as a brown trout and seatrout river and the best salmon fishing is in seven or eight pools up as far as the Riverside Inn at Currans. The brown trout come 'four to the pound', with some to half-a-pound. The best of the seatrout fishing is at night. The banks are quite open and the water runs low and very clear in summer.

The Brown Flesk River is a typical spate river and can give really excellent fishing for salmon and seatrout after a spate. It produces well over 500 fish to rod and line every season and it is quite common for an angler who knows the river to take three or four salmon and up to two dozen seatrout in a day's fishing. The best of it is from the Metal Bridge down to the Airport Bridge at Currow – a stretch that has at least thirty good holding pools. A lot of it is overgrown and hard to fish. On the other hand, it is this cover that helps the fish to survive.

Season
Salmon: 17 January–30 September
Seatrout: 17 January–12 October
Brown trout: 15 February–12 October

Permission and information
John Reiddy, Maine & Brown Flesk Anglers' Association. Tel: 066 7142216

OWENMORE RIVER   Q 51 10

There are few places left in Western Europe that are as unspoiled, as natural and as unique as the little Owenmore River that flows into Brandon Bay. It is a spate river on the Dingle Peninsula, draining nine loughs and a 17 sq. mile catchment on the eastern slopes of Mount Brandon. It is surrounded by bog and mountain and is totally unspoiled.

This is a very special place with two unusual corrie lakes and Mount Brandon, where the glacial ice was 800 feet deep. At the beginning of the 21st century, it is nice to know that it is still home to the Gaelic language, the salmon and the seatrout, the woodcock and the snipe. The Owenmore has much to offer the angler who appreciates a wild and beautiful country. There are nearly five miles of fishing on the river and the estuary is unusual in that part of it is privately owned and there you can fish seatrout and bass.

The big seatrout begin to run in May and they are accompanied by both salmon and grilse. The 2008 season produced about 150 grilse and 30 salmon over 8lb and an unknown number of seatrout.

Owenmore River rod catch 2003-2008

Year	2003	2004	2005	2006	2007	2008
Spring salmon	4	-	5	6	12	5
Grilse	24	15	80	32	20	38
Seatrout	430	180	300	390	432	240

It has a series of good holding pools running high up into the valley and they can be accessed via a dirt road and a short walk across the bog. There is a boat on two of the lakes that hold salmon, seatrout and brown trout.

The salmon and grilse fishing is done by day but the seatrout are best fished at night. This is a classic spate seatrout fishery when it has water, where an angler can start fishing at dusk and continue till past midnight. It is then time for a rest and start again at 02.00 and fish till first light when the fishing can be very good. The first choice of fly for local anglers would be Bibio, Teal Blue & Silver and Connemara Black on the point. There might also be place for Black Pennell, Watson's Fancy, Claret Bumble and Butcher.

One piece of good news is that the poaching, to which the river was subjected for decades, has been firmly and effectively brought under control.

Regulations
In the interest of conservation, there is a catch-and-release regime for salmon. Seatrout may be retained.

There is a fly-only stretch above the bridge.

Season
Salmon: 1 April–30 September
Seatrout: 1 April–30 September

Permission
Frank Mansell, Fishery Manager, The Gables, Lisnagree, Camp Post Office, Tralee, Co. Kerry. Tel: 066 7139408

Lodge/Guesthouse
O'Connor's Hotel, Cloghane, Castlegregory, Co. Kerry. Tel: 066 7138113

SCARID, RIVER   Q 54 11
GLENNAHOO, RIVER   Q 54 11

These two small rivers flow into Brandon Bay and get a run of seatrout from April and grilse from June. They are worth fishing on a spate.

Season
1 March–30 September

Permission
Enquire locally

OWENCASHLA, RIVER   Q 65 11

The Owencashla flows north into Tralee Bay. It is overgrown and difficult to fish, but its appearance belies its potential, for it gets a good run of seatrout and grilse during the summer. By all accounts it is a good fishery and one that is well worth fishing on a falling spate.

Season
1 March–30 September

Permission
Enquire locally

** FEOHANAGH, RIVER   Q 41 10

The Feohanagh River is seven miles long and drains a catchment of 11 sq. miles on the western slopes of Mount Brandon into Smerwick Harbour – which is west of Dingle. It used be a really good river for seatrout and grilse from June onwards after a spate but, sadly, the nets have taken their toll and few fish now run it. However, according to reports, it held a lot of seatrout in the 2001 season. If you get one, just remember that you have taken your fish on the most westerly river in Europe.

Season
1 March–30 September

Permission
Enquire locally

** MILLTOWN, RIVER   Q 43 02

This small spate river drains southwards into Dingle Harbour, a mile west of Dingle. It gets occasional grilse and a few seatrout on the spate. It is very narrow and rocky and not much fished.

Season
Salmon: 17 March–30 September
Seatrout: 17 March–12 October

Permission
Enquire locally

** OWENASCAUL, RIVER   Q59 01

The Owenascaul River drains a number of small loughs into the northern end of Dingle Bay. It is generally regarded as free fishing and even though it may be small – six miles long, with a six sq. mile catchment – it can be well worth fishing on the spate for both grilse and particularly its seatrout. The fish usually arrive on the first flood in June and it gets some fish on every flood thereafter through the summer. It is neglected and derelict, poached and abused and someone once said of it that it was a good job that there was a lake on it for at least the fish that make it to the lake are safe. This little, out-of-the-way, Kerry river may occupy the last place in this book but, make no mistake, it deserved at least three stars out of five and rather more respect for its silvery treasure than it is getting at present.

Season
Salmon: 17 March–30 September
Seatrout: 17 March–12 October

Permission
Enquire locally

Index

D

N

O